Publications from

The Mineral Economics and Policy Program of
Resources for the Future and
The Colorado School of Mines

General Editors

Hans H. Landsberg
Resources for the Future

John E. Tilton
The Colorado School of Mines

World Metal Demand: Trends and Prospects
edited by John E. Tilton (1990)

The World Aluminum Industry in a Changing Energy Era
edited by Merton J. Peck (1988)

World Mineral Exploration: Trends and Economic Issues
edited by John E. Tilton, Roderick G. Eggert, and
Hans H. Landsberg (1988)

Metallic Mineral Exploration: An Economic Analysis
by Roderick G. Eggert (1987)

The Mining Law: A Study in Perpetual Motion
by John D. Leshy (1987)

**State Mineral Enterprises: An Investigation into Their Impact on
International Mineral Markets**
by Marian Radetzki (1985)

Material Substitution: Lessons from Tin-Using Industries
by John E. Tilton (1983)

WORLD
METAL
DEMAND

Trends and Prospects

John E. Tilton, editor

A Project of
Resources for the Future and
The Colorado School of Mines

Resources for the Future
Washington, D.C.

Printed in the United States of America

Published by Resources for the Future
1616 P Street, N.W., Washington, D.C. 20036
Books from Resources for the Future are distributed worldwide by
The Johns Hopkins University Press

1073039 7

Library of Congress Cataloging-in-Publication Data

World metal demand : trends and prospects / John E. Tilton, editor.
    p.   cm.
    "A project of Resources for the Future and the Colorado School of Mines."
    Includes bibliographical references and index.
    ISBN 0-915707-56-X (alk. paper)
    1. Metal trade. 2. Steel industry and trade. I. Tilton, John E.
II. Resources for the Future. III. Colorado School of Mines.
HD9506.A2W62   1990
382'.45669—dc20   90-8953
                                                                CIP

This book is the product of RFF's Energy and Natural Resources Division, Douglas R. Bohi, director. It was edited by Martha S. Cooley and designed by Brigitte Coulton. The index was prepared by Julie Phillips. The cover was designed by Gehle Design Associates.

∞ The paper in this book meets the guidelines for permanence and durability of the Committee on Production Guidelines for Book Longevity of the Council on Library Resources.

Contributors

Istvan Dobozi

Visiting Professor, Mineral Economics Department, Colorado School of Mines, Golden, Colorado; Director, Centre for Development Research, Institute for World Economy, Budapest, Hungary

Roderick G. Eggert

Associate Professor, Mineral Economics Department, Colorado School of Mines, Golden, Colorado

Carmine Nappi

Professor of Mineral Economics and Industrial Organization, École des Hautes Études Commerciales, Montreal, Quebec

Marian Radetzki

Visiting Professor, Mineral Economics Department, Colorado School of Mines, Golden, Colorado; President, SNS Energy, a research institute for international energy markets, Stockholm, Sweden

John E. Tilton

Coulter Professor and Head, Mineral Economics Department, Colorado School of Mines, Golden, Colorado; University Fellow of Resources for the Future

Contents

Figures

Tables

Statistical Appendix Tables

OECD

Australia	Greece	Norway
Austria	Iceland	Portugal
Belgium	Ireland	Spain
Canada	Italy	Sweden
Denmark	Japan	Switzerland
Federal Republic of	Luxembourg	Turkey
Germany	The Netherlands	United Kingdom
Finland	New Zealand	United States
France		

EEC-9

Belgium–Luxembourg	Ireland
Denmark	Italy
Federal Republic of	The Netherlands
Germany	United Kingdom
France	
Greece	

Developing (Less Developed) Countries

All countries except those listed under OECD and Centrally Planned Economies.

Centrally Planned Economies

Albania	North Korea
Bulgaria	North Vietnam
China	Poland
Cuba	Romania
Czechoslovakia	USSR
German Democratic Republic	Other countries in Eastern Europe
Hungary	and Eastern Asia

CMEA-6

CMEA-6	CMEA-7
Bulgaria	Bulgaria
Czechoslovakia	Czechoslovakia
German Democratic Republic	German Democratic Republic
Hungary	Hungary
Poland	Poland
Romania	Romania
	USSR

Note: OECD = Organisation for Economic Co-operation and Development; EEC = European Economic Community; CMEA = Council for Mutual Economic Assistance.

Foreword

Allegedly there is a Chinese curse that goes somewhat like this: "May you live in interesting times!" Whether or not apocryphal, it seems to fit the metal industries. Steep increases and equally steep declines in consumption, production, prices, and profits are the norm rather than the exception. Nor is this a phenomenon of recent vintage. What is recent, however, is that, in contrast to earlier ups and downs, the industry this time around has been slow to move "up" from the lastest "down" that began sometime in the 1970s. So slow in fact that it has driven producers to make a thorough assessment of their operations in an attempt to make them lean and profitable, rather than wait for what might or might not be the next upswing. As a result, the corporate balance sheets at the beginning of the century's last decade have improved, as prices have rebounded and sales increased.

To the student of trends, the interesting question and demanding task, then, are to distinguish persistent underlying forces from temporary glitches. This kind of investigation does not necessarily make for absorbing reading. Inevitably, authors are driven to protracted comparisons between percentages, rates of change, by commodity, by country, by time period, and so on.

Fortunately, the book has something for everybody. Theoreticians will attentively study the discussion of the merits and deficiencies of the "intensity of use" technique and the relative importance of changes in macroeconomic variables. Those interested in specific metals will find all the details they want relevant to those commodities. For readers whose mind-set is toward differences in behavior between types of economies, the contrast between fully mature market economies, developing countries, and centrally planned economies (a dying breed?) provides ample occasion for confirming or questioning conventional wisdom. Finally, industry analysts and students of technological change will pay special attention to the two case studies: automobiles and containers.

Looked at as a whole, the book should offer a welcome respite from the preoccupation with seemingly pressing problems of national significance, such as the role of the so-called strategic and critical materials, or the anticipated early depletion of this or that mineral. By focusing on the longer run and the underlying determinants of demand, the study provides, or, I should say more cautiously, attempts to provide, a more measured pace of assessment.

The book makes its appearance at a point in history that may well signal the beginning of a novel era and point of view. The European Community's drawing together in 1992; the turn toward market economies in Eastern Europe and, at a slower pace, in the Soviet Union; the prospect of a nonviolent transition in South Africa toward an increasingly tolerable political regime—all of these factors are bound to affect the mineral industries on a worldwide basis. Some old issues will fade, some new ones will arise. This study makes its appearance in what retrospectively might well appear as a welcome pause during which to draw up a balance sheet of where we have been, are, and might be going. Resources for the Future has been a happy partner with the Colorado School of Mines in this research venture.

Hans H. Landsberg
Senior Fellow Emeritus
Energy and Natural
Resources Division
May 1990   Resources for the Future

Preface

Mineral economists and other scholars conducting research on the metal industries during the 1950s, 1960s, and even most of the 1970s concentrated largely on supply issues—the likelihood of resource depletion, investment needs for new capacity, the prospects for cartels. This focus reflected the prevailing preoccupation of public officials and others with the availability of mineral resources.

Rapid economic growth in Western Europe, the Soviet Union, and Japan called for a tremendous expansion of the world's mining industry over the short run, while the possibility of an explosion in metal demand in the less developed countries over the more distant future hovered in the background. These needs raised concerns about the long-run adequacy of the resource base, and about the security of mineral supplies as the industrialized countries became increasingly dependent on the growing output of South Africa, China, the Soviet Union, and the developing countries. Demand, aside from the fact it was possibly expanding too rapidly, was not a pressing issue.

This focus shifted in the 1980s, as the break in the growth of metal demand that first appeared in the industrialized countries around the mid-1970s was reinforced by similar slowdowns in the developing and centrally planned countries in the late 1970s. What originally was thought to be just another temporary downturn associated with the business cycle in the developed countries not only persisted in those countries but spread to much of the rest of the world.

Meanwhile, the captains of the traditional mining companies, relying on their own past experience, the counsel of their forecasters and advisers, and the prevailing wisdom of the scholarly community, continued to expand capacity in anticipation of the market recovery that had to be just around the corner. Moreover, this rosy view of the future was contagious. Oil companies and new state enterprises rushed to enter the mining industry and to expand their share of metal markets.

Thus, as time passed and demand failed to recover, the consequences were catastrophic. Surplus capacity depressed metal prices for over a decade, creating serious hardships for producing firms, for their employees and suppliers, and for those countries dependent on metal exports for government revenues and foreign exchange. Public policy analysts and in turn the research community began to focus on the problems of the metal industries, which inevitably led to greater interest in metal demand.

This book is a product of the revival of interest in metal demand. It was initially motivated by several vexing questions: How could so many informed and experienced people have been so wrong about trends in metal demand? To what extent did academics, consultants, and other outside specialists aggravate and prolong the crisis by lending support and comfort to corporate officials in the process of making serious mistakes? Is the community of outside experts and specialists so inbred that decision makers can no longer obtain independent verification of the advice flowing from their own staffs? How can such costly mistakes be prevented in the future?

In seeking answers to these questions, our interest was soon drawn to the causes for changes in the long-term trends of metal demand growth, not just in the industrialized countries but in the rest of the world as well. The scope of the inquiry then expanded as the sharp differences in metal use among countries and country groups became apparent, crying out for explanation.

Many individuals provided valuable assistance over the course of the study. From the early planning to the writing of the foreword, Hans H. Landsberg, co-director of the Mineral Economics and Policy Program of Resources for the Future and the Colorado School of Mines, has been as actively involved in the project as the authors. He has read and commented extensively on successive drafts of each chapter—for which he has not only earned our gratitude but probably also deserves a Purple Heart. Phillip C. F. Crowson— author of an extensive chapter in the 1988 volume *World Mineral Exploration: Trends and Economic Issues,* which also emanated from the Mineral Economics and Policy Program—though not so involved on a day-to-day basis, provided the initial encouragement for undertaking the study and, at several critical junctures, constructive suggestions for strengthening the nature of the analysis. While it is not possible to identify all of the other individuals who kindly contributed information or suggestions, the authors and I would like to acknowledge the particularly helpful comments of Frederick R. Demler, Tapani Erling, David Humphreys, Richard T. Newcomb, and Merton J. Peck.

The final volume, it should also be noted, benefited greatly from the careful work of copyeditor Martha S. Cooley and project editor Dorothy Sawicki, and from the management of the book's design and production by Brigitte Coulton.

The necessary financial support for this project was kindly provided by RTZ Limited, the World Bank, the Coulter Foundation, the Exxon Foundation, and Resources for the Future. We are also grateful to Outokumpu Oy, which hosted a conference in Helsinki at which an international group of experts reviewed and critiqued an earlier version of this study.

John E. Tilton
Coulter Professor and Head
Mineral Economics Department
Colorado School of Mines

Golden, Colorado
May 1990

WORLD
METAL
DEMAND

Trends and Prospects

1

Introduction

JOHN E. TILTON

The world economy, battered first by the Great Depression and then by World War II, lay largely in ruin in the mid-1940s. The pent-up demand for new homes, roads, factories, tractors, schools, telephones, automobiles, and other goods was so great that for a quarter of a century it would help fuel rapid economic growth, particularly in Europe, the Soviet Union, and Japan, whose economies had suffered the most.

For steel, aluminum, and other metals, the result was a boom in world consumption that lasted until the early 1970s. To be sure, growth rates varied among metals. Aluminum consumption grew nearly 10 percent a year over the 1950–1973 period, whereas tin consumption expanded at a rate of somewhat less than 3 percent annually. In addition, as metal consumption is highly sensitive to cyclical trends in the general economy, these long-run growth rates were periodically punctuated by short-run contractions, the result of downturns in the business cycle.

Such setbacks, however, were widely recognized as temporary. Positive and stable long-run growth rates were considered a durable if not permanent feature of metal markets. Quick or radical changes seemed unlikely. Indeed, this conviction gave rise to some concern in the early 1970s, as expressed in the widely read *Limits to Growth* (Meadows and coauthors, 1972) and other studies, over the adequacy of the earth's resource base for sustaining growth in the consumption of metals and other natural resources into the twenty-first century and beyond. And, ironically, at just about the time these studies were appearing, a substantial decline in the long-run growth of metal consumption was taking place. This change is highlighted in figure 1-1, which compares actual consumption with consumption as it would have been after 1973 had

1

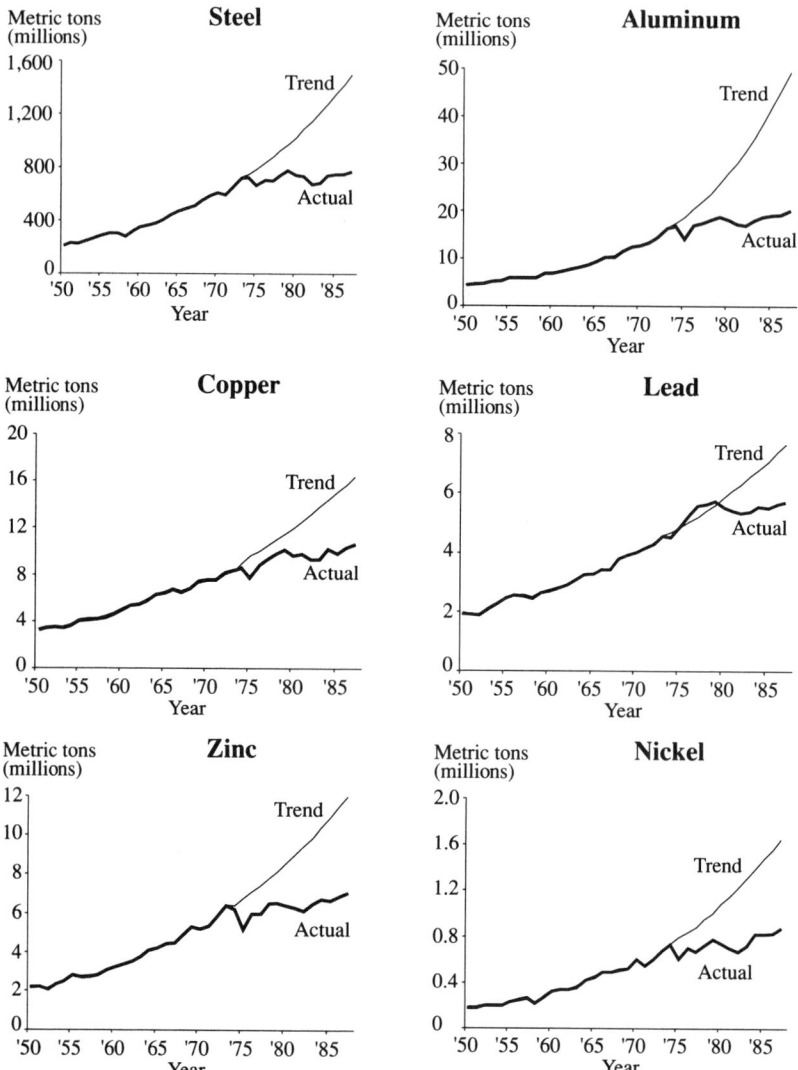

Figure 1-1. World consumption of selected metals: actual and projected trends, 1950–1987.

Notes: The projected trend indicates the consumption that would have occurred during the 1974–1987 period if consumption had continued to grow at the average annual rate that prevailed during the 1950–1973 period.

Consumption generally refers to refined metal and excludes the direct use of scrap. Steel consumption figures are for crude steel and include both primary and secondary metal. Aluminum consumption figures are for primary refined metal only. Nickel consumption figures include the nickel consumed in nickel salts and other chemicals.

Source: Statistical appendix in this volume.

the growth in metal consumption continued at pre-1973 rates. By the end of the 1980s the gap between the projected trend and actual consumption was substantial; for aluminum the gap between the two even exceeded actual consumption.

At first this break was presumed to be just another cyclical downturn. Prevailing opinion envisioned metal demand bouncing back once the economy recovered, and consumption once again proceeding on its long-run growth trajectory. To some extent, as figure 1-1 shows, the very sharp decline in 1975 was temporary. Yet recovery, when it came, failed to recapture even the old growth rates, let alone the old growth trajectory. As the years passed, failing to vindicate the prevailing view, that view slowly changed. It is now generally agreed that something more permanent, more structural, than just another cyclical downturn occurred.

The resulting decline in long-run rates of growth in metal consumption produced some important consequences. Concern over the possibility that resource depletion might produce metal shortages evaporated. Public policy instead became preoccupied with the problems of struggling mineral producers.

Perhaps more serious was the combination of miscalculations—the failure to anticipate the break in long-run demand growth followed by the belief that the slowdown was temporary—which caused investment in new mines and processing facilities to continue at a pace far beyond what was needed to accommodate the new reality. The result, as is well known, was a huge surplus of unneeded capacity that depressed metal prices for more than a decade. Indeed, it is not yet entirely clear whether the recent recovery of many metal prices that began about 1987 reflects the elimination of this surplus.

Another consequence of the decline in long-run metal growth rates is that the planning process has been greatly complicated. Mineral producers can no longer make investment decisions based on the assumption that world metal demand will expand over the long term along a known and fairly stable growth path.

What explains the break in long-run metal growth trends? Since consumption is determined by both supply and demand, it could conceivably have been the result of supply constraints. This possibility, however, seems highly unlikely. Supply constraints normally produce higher real prices, but metal prices except during the last three years have generally been depressed since 1973. Moreover, it is hard to identify significant supply bottlenecks, especially when so many metal industries were for so long awash in idle capacity. The available evidence points instead to a decline in the growth of world demand.

The critical role that demand apparently has played, first in shaping the brisk rates of growth in metal consumption during the 1950s and 1960s and then in bringing about their subsequent decline during the 1970s, raises a number of questions. One of the more intriguing is why the growth in metal consumption slowed in the early 1970s. Part of the explanation certainly lies with the decline in world economic growth that occurred at that time, but is this the sole explanation? Or have changing trends in intensity of use—the tons of metal consumed per million dollars of real gross domestic product (GDP)—also been important? If so, what has caused these trends in intensity of use to change? The shift toward a postindustrial society and the growth of the service sector in the United States and other developed countries? New resource-saving technologies? The substitution of plastics, composites, ceramics, and other advanced materials for the more traditional metals? The growing importance of computers and other high-technology goods within the manufacturing sector?

A second set of questions might focus on the implications of the slowdown. Does it mean, as Larson, Ross, and Williams (1986) have suggested, that the "Era of Materials" is over, or, as Drucker (1986) has argued, that primary products are now uncoupled from the industrial economy? Is the historical link between economic growth and metal demand now severed, permitting development to proceed independent of the availability of metal supplies?

A third set of questions might be posed with regard to the similarities and differences in the nature of metal demand among countries and country groups. Why, for example, is demand growing very rapidly in some developing countries, such as South Korea, but not in others? Does the faster growth of metal consumption in the developing countries as a group mean that within the foreseeable future they will replace the more mature industrial states as the major market for metal producers? Why is the intensity of metal use in the Soviet Union and other centrally planned economies so much higher than in industrialized countries? Why does the United States, often accused of being profligate in its use of resources, have such low intensities of use compared to those of Japan and the Federal Republic of Germany? Where such differences exist among countries, why do they arise? Is the level of economic development, as reflected by per capita income, a critical consideration, as is often suggested? Is the nature of trade important? Do countries with a comparative advantage in material-intensive goods tend to have high intensities of use? Does central planning foster extravagant metal use?

The chapters that follow attempt to provide insights and answers to questions such as those just posed in the belief that better understanding of past trends in metal demand and of the forces shaping these trends is prerequisite to improving our ability to anticipate future changes in the course of metal consumption. Such understanding is, thus, necessary to prevent serious and prolonged imbalances between our capacity to mine and process metals on the one hand and demand on the other. As recent history has so clearly demonstrated, such imbalances are costly and disruptive, not just for metal-producing firms but for their host governments and for consumers as well.

The analysis is selective rather than comprehensive. To avoid the tedium and excessive detail involved in examining the demand for all metals in all countries, the focus is on the major metals—namely, steel, aluminum, copper, lead, zinc, and nickel. For purposes of the analysis, the world is divided into three country groups: (1) the Organisation for Economic Cooperation and Development (OECD) countries,[1] (2) the less developed (also referred to as developing) countries, and (3) the centrally planned countries. Within each of these groups the spotlight is on the major consuming countries: on the United States, Japan, the United Kingdom, France, the Federal Republic of Germany, and the European Economic Community (EEC) as a whole for the industrialized OECD countries; on Brazil, India, and South Korea for the less developed countries; and on the Soviet Union and other East European states for the centrally planned countries. This choice can, of course, be challenged. One might, for example, question the omission of China, in light of the dramatic economic developments occurring in that country. Yet together, the selected countries consumed between 70 and 85 percent of the world's steel, aluminum, copper, lead, zinc, and nickel during the 1980s and even greater shares in earlier years. As a result, these are the countries that have shaped trends in world metal consumption.

The period from 1960 to 1987 receives the most attention in this book, largely because of the ready availability of data, although at times the 1950s are examined as well. It would, of course, be interesting to go back much further, prior to World War II and even World War I. Many believe that the growth in world metal demand since 1973 has been unusually slow. This perception, however, is largely derived from a comparison with growth rates during the 1950s and 1960s, which, for reasons noted earlier, were unusually brisk. Although a longer time horizon would help put the postwar experience in perspective, it would also greatly complicate the analysis. Obtaining comparable data for the period before World War II is particularly difficult, in part because different sources have to be used and in part because the boundaries of Germany and certain other states have changed.

AN OVERVIEW OF WORLD METAL DEMAND

A brief overview of world metal demand will help provide the setting for the investigations of the chapters that follow. As shown in figure 1-2, the OECD countries are the biggest consumers of all the major metals. Consumption has, however, been growing faster in the centrally planned and the less developed countries, thereby slowly reducing the dominance of the OECD countries. Indeed, the centrally planned countries have almost overtaken the

---

[1]The OECD member states include all the developed countries other than the Republic of South Africa and those with central planning. For a list of the countries, see page xviii in this volume.

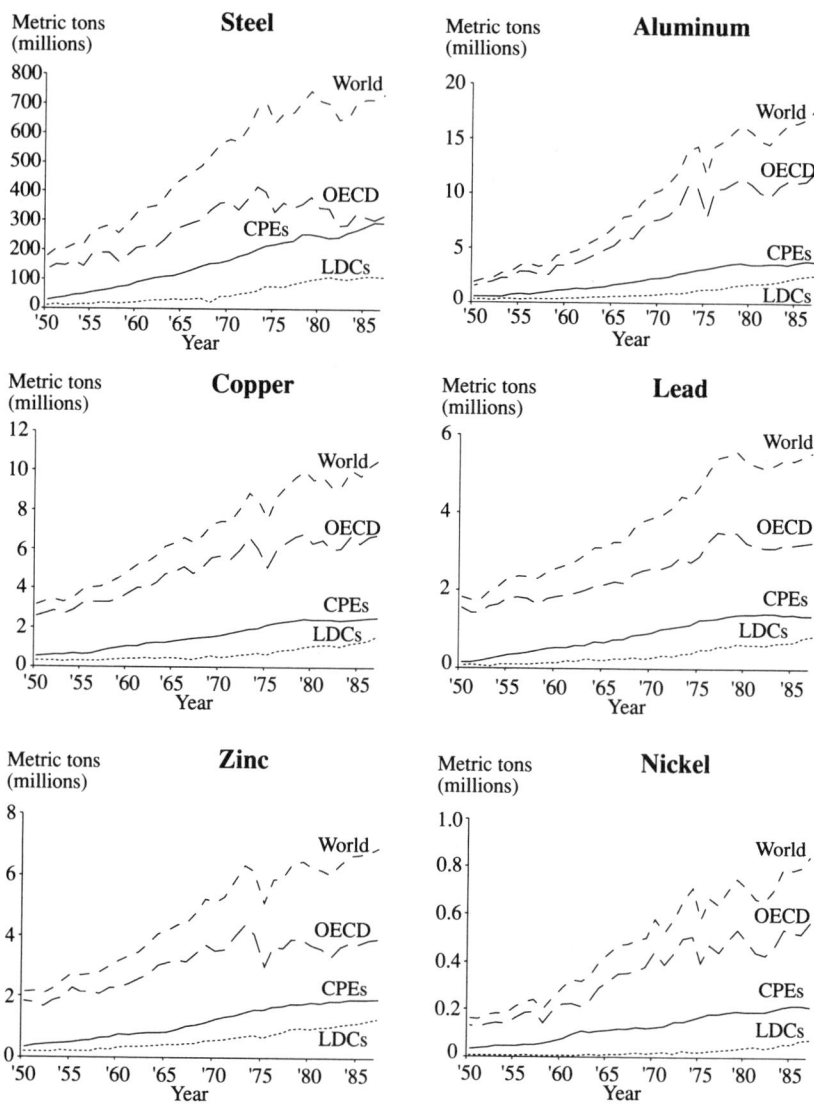

Figure 1-2. Consumption of steel, aluminum, copper, lead, zinc, and nickel by the world, the OECD countries, the less developed countries (LDCs), and the centrally planned economies (CPEs), 1950–1987.

Source: Statistical appendix in this volume.

Table 1-1. Growth in Metal Consumption for the World, the OECD Countries, the Less Developed Countries, and the Centrally Planned Economies over Three Periods: 1960–1973, 1973–1979, and 1979–1987

(average annual percentage change)

Area or group and period	Steel	Aluminum	Copper	Lead	Zinc	Nickel
World						
1960–1973	5.8	9.6	4.8	4.2	5.6	6.4
1973–1979	1.2	2.7	2.0	4.0	0.4	2.2
1979–1987	−0.2	1.1	0.7	0.0	0.9	1.5
OECD countries						
1960–1973	5.3	9.7	4.6	3.5	5.3	6.6
1973–1979	−1.4	1.3	0.6	3.2	−1.8	1.1
1979–1987	−2.2	0.5	−0.1	−0.8	0.0	0.8
Less developed countries						
1960–1973	8.3	13.8	5.7	7.0	6.5	21.7
1973–1979	8.0	12.9	9.9	9.7	7.4	7.9
1979–1987	1.3	6.3	6.4	3.3	4.0	11.8
Centrally planned economies						
1960–1973	6.1	8.1	5.4	5.5	6.2	5.2
1973–1979	3.7	4.5	4.2	3.8	3.1	4.7
1979–1987	2.5	0.7	0.5	0.0	1.8	1.7

Source: Statistical appendix in this volume.

latter in the use of steel. These findings suggest that although the OECD countries have largely determined trends in world metal demand in the past, the centrally planned and less developed countries will play an increasingly important role in shaping future trends.

In this regard, figure 1-2 indicates that the OECD countries were primarily responsible for the break in long-run metal demand in the early 1970s, both because their growth rates experienced the most pronounced downward shift at that time and because their large share of the world market accentuated the impact of the changes in their growth rates.

Further support for this conclusion is provided by table 1-1, which shows that, with the exception of lead, growth in metal demand dropped sharply in the OECD countries after 1973. For the less developed countries, the break came later. Their metal demand growth experienced little decline in the early and middle 1970s but then fell substantially around 1979. For the centrally planned economies, metal demand growth also fell, but in what appears to be two steps: first, a decline around 1973 that was more modest than the decline in the OECD countries but more pronounced than that in the less developed countries, and then a further decline around 1979. The slowdown in growth of metal demand around 1979 in the centrally planned and less developed countries reinforced the earlier break emanating largely from the OECD countries.

This delayed response on the part of the developing and the centrally planned countries, explored more fully in chapters 4 and 5, respectively, reflects differences in trends in GDP and intensity of metal use. As table 1-2 shows, the sharp decline in the growth of these two determinants of metal consumption around 1973 in the OECD countries also occurred in the less developed countries, though some six years later. In the centrally planned countries the slowdown in GDP growth took place about 1973, accounting for most of the first downward step in metal demand growth, whereas the break in trends for intensity of use occurred largely around the end of the decade and accounted for the second downward step.

Other differences in intensity of use among country groups are highlighted in figure 1-3. Perhaps most striking is the high intensity of metal use in the centrally planned countries, particularly in recent years. In the case of steel, where this tendency is most pronounced, metal consumption per million dollars of GDP is more than double that of the OECD countries.

Also of interest is the persistent tendency since the late 1960s for intensity of use to rise in the less developed countries, in contrast to recent trends in the OECD and centrally planned countries. As a result, the huge differences in intensity of use between the less developed countries and the OECD countries in the early 1960s were largely gone by the mid-1980s.

ORGANIZATION OF THIS BOOK

Research on metal demand inevitably encounters a number of data and conceptual problems that confront the analyst with various methodological issues. Marian Radetzki and I examine these issues in chapter 2, along with the intensity of use technique, which is used in later chapters. Readers with little interest in these somewhat technical concerns may simply want to skim chapter 2 or proceed directly to chapter 3.

Chapters 3 through 5 explore metal consumption trends in the OECD countries, the developing countries, and the centrally planned countries, respectively. These chapters in a sense are parallel studies, forming part of the larger integrated effort to understand better the changing nature of metal demand throughout the world. Each of the three chapters is also an independent study with its own organization, focus, and approach, as each has its own author with particular concerns and approaches. Moreover, the quantity and quality of information and data available for the three groups of countries differ considerably, and each group of countries raises its own set of interesting questions.

In chapter 3, for example, I concentrate on the reasons why the growth of metal consumption stalled in the OECD countries in the early 1970s, and explore the changing nature of the relationship between metal demand and overall economic growth in these countries. The chapter also tries to explain

Table 1-2. Growth in GDP and Intensity of Use for the World, the OECD Countries, the Less Developed Countries, and the Centrally Planned Economies over Three Periods: 1960–1973, 1973–1979, and 1979–1987
(average annual percentage change)

Area or group and period	GDP	Intensity of use					
		Steel	Aluminum	Copper	Lead	Zinc	Nickel
World							
1960–1973	5.2	0.6	4.2	−0.3	−0.9	0.4	1.2
1973–1979	3.2	−1.9	−0.5	−1.1	0.7	−2.7	−0.9
1979–1987	2.7	−2.7	−1.4	−1.8	−2.5	−1.6	−1.0
OECD countries							
1960–1973	5.0	0.3	4.5	−0.4	−1.5	0.3	1.5
1973–1979	2.7	−4.0	−1.2	−2.1	0.5	−4.4	−1.5
1979–1987	2.4	−4.4	−1.9	−2.3	−3.0	−2.3	−1.4
Less developed countries							
1960–1973	6.7	1.7	6.9	−0.8	0.5	−0.1	14.2
1973–1979	5.1	2.6	7.2	4.4	4.3	2.0	2.5
1979–1987	2.8	−1.3	3.6	3.7	0.7	1.4	9.0
Centrally planned economies							
1960–1973	4.8	1.3	3.1	0.6	0.7	1.4	0.4
1973–1979	3.2	0.5	1.3	0.9	0.5	−0.2	1.5
1979–1987	3.4	−1.5	−2.8	−3.0	−3.3	−2.0	−2.1

Source: Statistical appendix in this volume.

why intensity of metal use is so much higher in Japan and the Federal Republic of Germany than in the United States, France, and the United Kingdom—an inquiry that ranges over the nature of the manufacturing trade, the purchasing power of GDP, the proclivity to invest, and the propensity for metal recycling.

Chapter 4, by Marian Radetzki, focuses on the positive growth in the intensity of metal use in the developing countries, which in recent years has run counter to trends in the rest of the world. The study also highlights, and attempts to explain, the surprisingly large discrepancies among the developing countries in intensities of use. The search for a cause leads ultimately to the nature of public policies, including differences in the trade and industrialization policies that governments pursue as part of their overall strategies for fostering economic development. In seeking answers to these questions, chapter 4 draws heavily on case studies of India, Brazil, and South Korea.

Much of chapter 5, by Istvan Dobozi, is devoted to testing the hypothesis that the nature of the economic system in the Soviet Union and other centrally planned countries is largely responsible for their unusually high intensities of metal use. It also explores why intensities of use in the centrally planned countries, although still quite high, have nevertheless been declining in recent

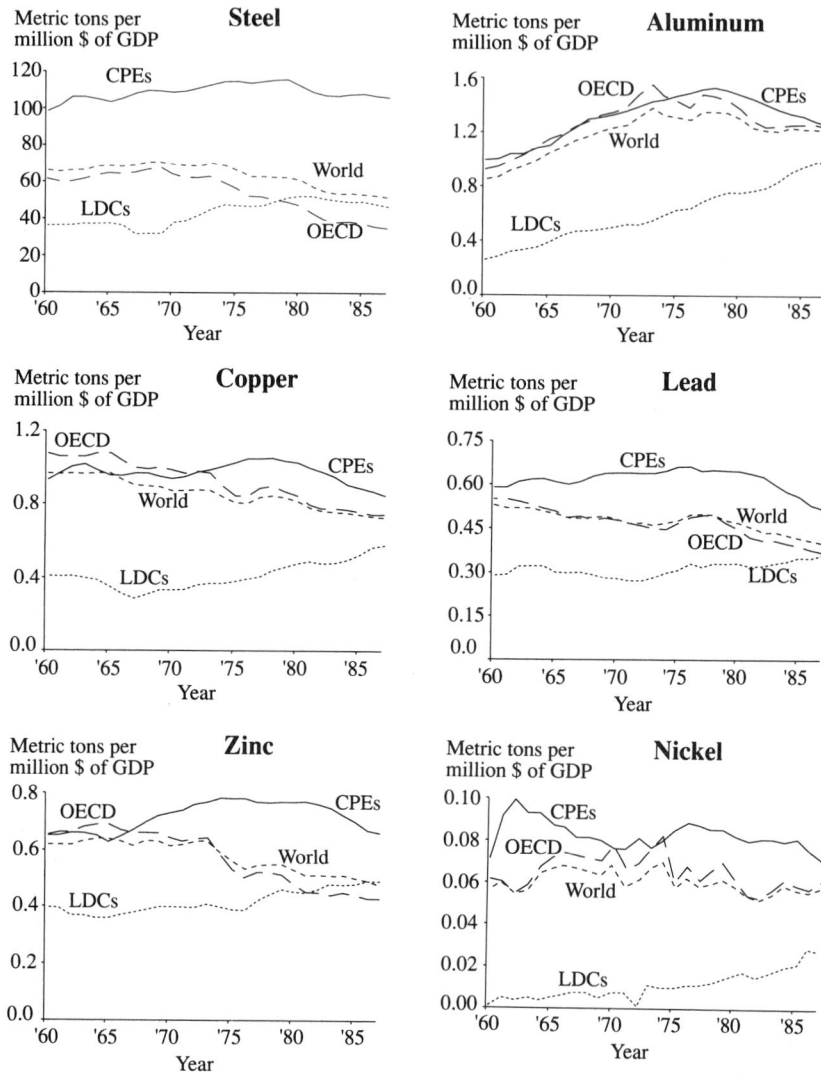

Figure 1-3. Intensity of use of steel, aluminum, copper, lead, zinc, and nickel by the world, the OECD countries, the less developed countries (LDCs), and the centrally planned economies (CPEs), 1960–1987.

Source: Statistical appendix in this volume.

years, contributing in the process to the stagnation in their metal consumption noted earlier. In reviewing the possible reasons, the author rejects two explanations: first, that the centrally planned countries have moved into a post-industrial era, and second, that their adoption of material-saving new technology has accelerated in recent years. In analyzing these issues the chapter specifies and estimates several econometric models, an approach not used in other chapters.

Chapters 6 and 7 are likewise independent studies—specifically, case studies of material use in the automobile and packaging industries, which contribute to the overall study as well. Through their in-depth investigations into the use of metals in two specific end uses, they provide insights into the evolving nature of metal demand, particularly in the industrialized states, both concentrating on the OECD countries. In chapter 6, for example, Roderick G. Eggert highlights the continuing vitality of steel in the automobile market as new technologies enhance corrosion resistance, reduce weight, and in other ways improve the quality of steel and thereby help maintain the attractiveness of this metal despite growing competition from other materials. And, in an interesting contrast, author Carmine Nappi illustrates in chapter 7, with its penetrating examination of the beer and soft drink container markets, the tremendous change and diversity in material use that technology can produce.

In the last chapter, I draw on the findings of the intervening chapters in an attempt to provide some answers to the questions raised above. In particular, why did world metal demand growth stall in the early 1970s, and why do some countries and some groups of countries have such high intensities of metal use? Chapter 8 then considers the outlook for world metal demand, assessing where the metal markets of the future will be, as well as the future pace of growth in metal demand and the important factors likely to govern this growth.

REFERENCES

Drucker, Peter F. 1986. "The Changed World Economy," *Foreign Affairs* vol. 64, no. 4 (Spring) pp. 768–791.

Larson, Eric D., Marc H. Ross, and Robert H. Williams. 1986. "Beyond the Era of Materials," *Scientific American* vol. 254, no. 6 (June) pp. 34–41.

Meadows, Donella H., Dennis L. Meadows, Jørgen Randers, and William W. Behrens III. 1972. *The Limits to Growth* (New York, Universe Books).

2

Conceptual and Methodological Issues

MARIAN RADETZKI and JOHN E. TILTON

A variety of conceptual and methodological issues as well as data problems are encountered in analyzing metal demand. How these difficulties are handled in a particular analysis can significantly affect the results and conclusions of that analysis. This chapter explores these issues and describes how they are treated in this volume. The first section concentrates on measures of metal demand, and the second focuses on indicators of macroeconomic activity. The third section describes the intensity of use (IU) technique, the approach used in this study. The technique is compared in the fourth section with the IU hypothesis and then, in the fifth section, with other approaches used to analyze metal demand.

MEASURES OF METAL DEMAND

The *demand function* identifies the significant variables determining the demand for a particular good, such as the commodity's price, the price of close substitutes, and the level of overall economic activity, and specifies the nature of the relationship between these variables and the amount of the good demanded. The *demand curve*, which is derived from the demand function, shows how the demand for the good varies with its own price, assuming all other variables affecting demand remain at some prescribed level.

The *quantity demanded* is determined by the point at which the demand curve intersects an analogously derived supply curve. In contrast to demand functions and demand curves, which are theoretical constructs, the quantity demanded is an observable entity.

The quantity demanded can decline over time for either of two reasons. First, there may be a leftward shift in the supply curve (that is, at any given price, less of the good will be offered). This shift may be caused by higher wage rates, producer collusion, or other factors. The quantity demanded will now be determined by a point further to the left on the same demand curve; in this case price is normally higher than before the shift.

Second, there may be a leftward shift in the demand curve (that is, at any given price, less of the good will be demanded). This shift may be caused by a decline in the general economy, the introduction of new, material-saving technology, or other factors. The quantity demanded will now be determined by the point of intersection between the old (unchanged) supply curve and the new demand curve, to the left of the original intersection. In this case price is normally lower than before the shift.

As chapter 1 points out, there is little to suggest, in the case of metals, that the break in long-run growth of the quantity demanded in the early 1970s was caused by supply problems, or leftward shifts in the supply curve. Real metal prices for the most part declined after 1973. In addition, many metal producers reported substantial reductions in production costs, especially during the 1980s, which suggests that the world supply curves for many metals have actually shifted to the right. For these reasons, changes in demand trends that slowed the rightward movement of the demand curve after 1973 appear principally responsible for the break in growth.

Metal demand, it should be noted, can be measured and analyzed at different stages of use. In the case of copper, for example, as figure 2-1 illustrates, there is demand on the part of (1) smelters and refiners for copper in concentrates, (2) smelters and refiners for copper in scrap, (3) fabricators for copper in the form of refined metal, (4) fabricators for copper in the scrap they use directly in making ingot and mill products, (5) fabricators for copper in both refined metal and scrap, (6) manufacturers for copper in fabricated and semifabricated products, and (7) consumers for copper in the final goods they purchase.

This study focuses on demand for finished but unwrought metal (that is, metal in primary shapes, such as cathodes or bars, which is at the first stage of processing). For instance, the use of refined copper (flow 3 in figure 2-1) is examined, not the use of copper contained in concentrates, in semifabricated or fabricated products, or in final goods. For the other metals, attention is similarly focused on the demand for crude steel, unwrought aluminum, refined lead, refined zinc, nickel metal in various primary shapes, as well as ferronickel and nickel oxides and sinters.

The treatment of secondary metal, which is produced from the recycling of scrap, differs from metal to metal. Crude steel encompasses all secondary metal except that produced from home scrap (that is, scrap generated and used by the same metal plant). Data on the latter, which is generated and directly recycled by steel-producing firms, are generally not available. The

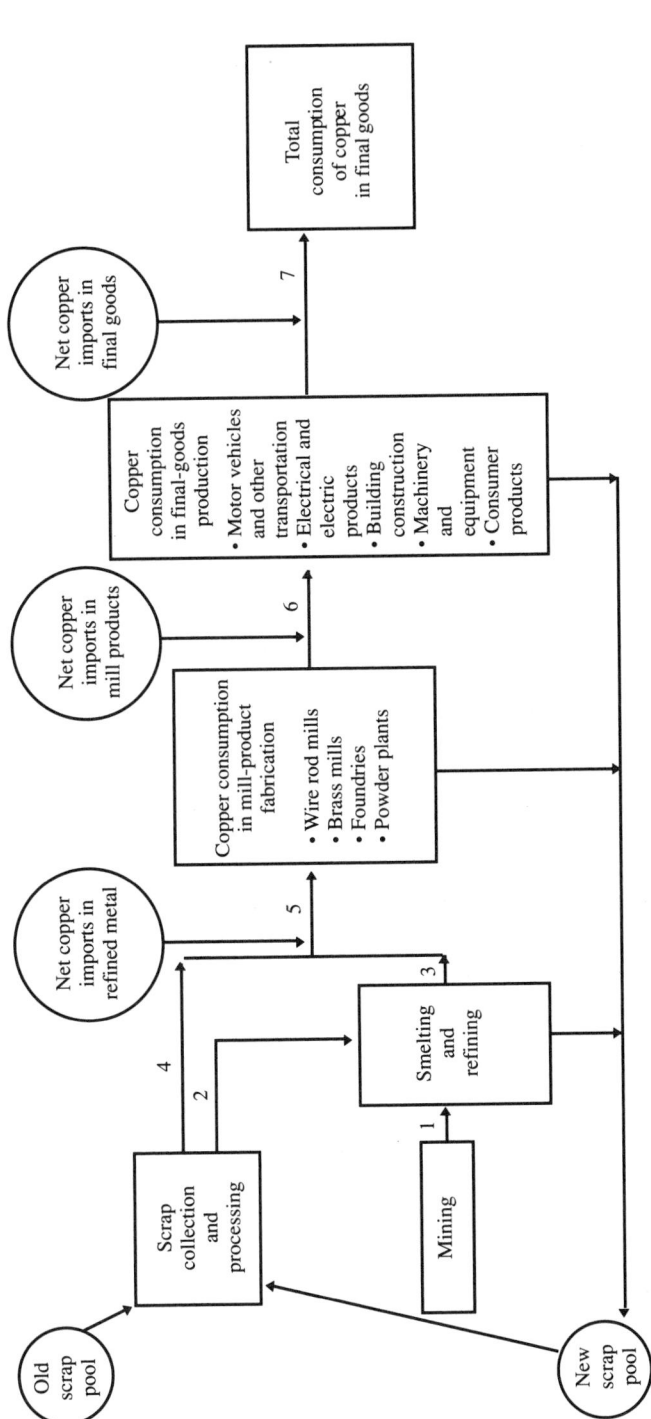

Figure 2-1. Copper consumption at various stages of use.
Source: Roger S. Hutchison and John E. Tilton, "Is the Intensity of Copper Use Still Declining in the United States?" *Natural Resources Forum* vol.11, no. 4 (1987) pp. 325–334, figure 2. Adapted, with permission.
Note: Flows at the points indicated reflect copper demand on the part of (1) smelters and refiners for copper in concentrates, (2) smelters and refiners for copper in scrap, (3) fabricators for copper in the form of refined metal, (4) fabricators for copper in the scrap they use directly in making ingot and mill products, (5) fabricators for copper in both refined metal and scrap, (6) manufacturers for copper in fabricated and semifabricated products, and (7) consumers for copper in the final goods they purchase.

15

figures for lead also include secondary consumption, whereas those for aluminum, nickel, and zinc cover only primary metal. The figures for copper include the scrap used to produce refined metal but exclude the scrap used directly by ingot makers, brass mills, and other fabricators (flow 4 in figure 2-1). The figures for tin include the consumption of secondary metal for some but not all countries.

Another characteristic of the measures of metal demand used in this study should be noted. Quantity demanded has two components. The first is the quantity demanded for use, or *consumption*, during the current period. For metals this is the amount of unwrought metal used by fabricators for transformation into fabricated products, alloys, and chemical compounds. The second is the quantity demanded for changes in inventory. Although demand for consumption must be zero or positive, the demand for inventory additions can be negative.

The available data are intended to represent only the quantity demanded for consumption. The annual *Metal Statistics* and the other statistical publications from which these data are obtained define a country's consumption as domestic production of the unwrought metal plus imports, minus both exports and net additions to domestic inventories. To the extent that inventory movements are recorded correctly and completely, these consumption figures are identical to the current use of unwrought metal by fabricators.

To recapitulate, the measures of metal demand used in this volume reflect the *reported consumption*,[1] measured in tons of unwrought metal at the first stage of processing. The figures cover the consumption of secondary metal completely or almost completely for steel and lead; partially for copper and tin; and not at all for aluminum, nickel, and zinc. To the extent that the data permit, the figures are adjusted for changes in inventories and so reflect demand for consumption during the current period. Metal demand is so defined and measured because there is no alternative for which consistent statistical series exist for numerous countries and extended periods of time. In this volume these figures are referred to, somewhat loosely, as either demand or consumption.

Limitations of the Data

Use of reported consumption raises both data problems and conceptual issues. Looking first at the data problems, one finds that in addition to lapses

---

[1]Although this term is sometimes used to distinguish estimates of consumption obtained by direct surveys of consumers, from *apparent consumption* estimated indirectly from production, trade, and inventory data, that is not the case here. Our data reflect apparent consumption, and we use the term *reported consumption* to emphasize the fact that our data are those published, and hence available.

in coverage for particular periods or countries, the available time series suffer from problems of reliability. As noted, reported consumption is derived from data on production, trade, and inventory changes. Because the centrally planned countries publish only very incomplete statistics on metal consumption and trade, the figures for these countries are often no more than qualified guesses by specialists. The same is also true for many of the less developed countries, even though an increasing number of these countries publish reasonably good statistics on metal production and trade.

The data problems are greatest with regard to inventory changes. No inventory figures at all are released by the centrally planned countries, and only fragmentary information is available for a few less developed countries. For these two country groups, therefore, the reported consumption figures are largely equal to the total quantity demanded—that is, the sum of the quantities demanded for both consumption and changes in inventories.

The reporting of inventory movements is somewhat better in the countries of the Organisation for Economic Cooperation and Development (OECD). In particular, reliable data are available on inventories held on the major metal exchanges and by metal producers. Nonetheless, the data on stocks held by fabricators and traders are very incomplete.

Unfortunately, not a great deal is known about unreported metal inventories and the extent to which movements in these inventories alter short- and long-run trends in metal demand. The limited available information is examined in chapter 3.

Conceptual Questions

The selection of metal demand measures largely on the basis of data availability raises an important question: To what extent does reported consumption conform to the data one would ideally like to have? In this regard, four conceptual issues or questions are of particular interest. Does it matter (1) at which stage of use demand is measured? (2) Whether demand is measured in terms of tons, value, or some other indicator? (3) How the demand for secondary metal is treated? (4) Whether net additions to inventories are fully excluded?

Stage of Use   Since the reported metal consumption figures reflect the use of metals in fabrication, they include the metal contained in domestic mine output as well as in net imports of ores, concentrates, and unwrought metal. They do not take into account, however, *indirect metal trade*, which includes the metal contained in imports and exports of semifabricated products and final goods.

At the global level, because world exports of semifabricated and final goods equal world imports, reported consumption closely approximates ultimate *metal absorption*, or the demand for metal embodied in final consumer and producer goods. Thus, only small differences would be expected as a result of the lag between the consumption of a metal in fabricated products and its consumption in final goods as long as the period over which consumption is measured is not too short.

At the level of individual countries, however, metal absorption will be higher than reported consumption when the metal contained in the imports of semifabricated and final goods exceeds the metal contained in the exports of these commodities, and metal absorption will be lower when the reverse is the case. Not only will these two measures of metal demand differ at a particular point in time, but they are also likely to proceed over time along different growth paths. Metal absorption may evolve along a reasonably smooth path, whereas reported consumption will jump from zero at the point at which the first metal-fabricating plant in the country goes into operation and will advance subsequently in discrete jumps as additional fabricating facilities are brought on line.

Data from which metal absorption can be derived are unfortunately seldom available. Even in countries with highly developed statistical services, data on the metal content of the final goods being exported and imported are rarely obtainable. The limited evidence available (examined in subsequent chapters) suggests that the difference between reported consumption and metal absorption can be substantial.

Thus, the level of and trends in metal demand and, in turn, intensity of use, for individual countries and groups of countries depend on the stage of use at which demand is measured. As Humphreys (1987, p. 336) has stated,

> the point at which consumption is measured will dictate the outcome of IU (intensity of use) analysis. The directions of change may be the same . . . but the rates of change may diverge. On the other hand it is at least theoretically possible that the trends in IU under the various definitions of consumption could actually move in different directions, for example, the IU of unwrought metal declining but that of metal-bearing products rising.

Although the point raised by Humphreys is important, discrepancies between reported consumption and metal absorption are not necessarily of great significance. In the first place the appropriate stage of use at which to measure demand varies with the purpose of the analysis and is not always the ultimate stage of metal absorption. If, for example, Caribbean bauxite producers wish to assess long-run trends in North American demand for aluminum contained in bauxite, then demand on the part of U.S. and Canadian alumina refiners,[2] rather than on the part of the consumers of final goods, is the most appropriate to measure. In this case the figure on reported

---

[2]Alumina, which is aluminum oxide, is an intermediate product in the process through which bauxite is converted into aluminum metal.

consumption of unwrought aluminum is deficient not because it fails to include the aluminum in net imports of semifabricated and finished products, but because it includes net imports of aluminum in alumina and unwrought aluminum. Alternatively, if, say, Pechiney or Alcan wishes to assess trends in the French market for unwrought aluminum, then the reported consumption figures are the most appropriate, and even sizable discrepancies between these figures and those for aluminum absorption are irrelevant. The common perception that metal absorption is always the most appropriate measure of demand apparently stems from the fact that demand at earlier stages of use is derived from the demand for metal in finished products. Although this is true, as we have seen, a one-to-one relationship between metal absorption and demand at earlier stages of use does not necessarily exist for individual countries with open economies.

Moreover, even where metal absorption or demand at some other stage of use than that reflected by reported consumption is the most appropriate to measure, an analysis of reported consumption can still provide useful insights. In this situation relevant metal-containing imports and exports can be treated as one of the independent variables affecting metal demand. Their effect can thus be assessed, providing some indication of the discrepancy between reported consumption and demand at the appropriate stage of use. Roberts (1987) provides an interesting example of this possibility.

One final point, though obvious, is worth noting. Discrepancies between reported consumption and demand at the most appropriate stage of use are not a problem only for analyses based on the intensity of metal use, but they also affect all investigations of demand that rely on metal consumption data.

Measurement in Terms of Tons, Value, and Quality   This volume follows the common practice of measuring metal demand in physical units, specifically, metric tons. However, this procedure has been questioned on the grounds that it ignores changes over time in the quality and value of metals. Considine (1987, pp. 350–351), for example, contends that

> while this practice may be useful for very specific end-uses, it can be very misleading for aggregate metal consumption analysis. Metals have different physical properties and serve a variety of functions. . . . Simple tonnage measures of aggregate metal consumption do not capture these quality differentials. . . . [A] ton of carbon sheet steel does not provide the same amount of metal services as a ton of stainless steel.

Considine proceeds to develop an index of U.S. consumption for sheet and strip-steel products that weights the percentage changes of twelve particular types of these products by the share of total revenues that each produces. He then calculates the percentage difference between this index and a comparable index based on aggregate tonnage over the 1970–1985 period. Because the tonnage index is more than 9 percent higher than the weighted index at the beginning of this period and almost 8 percent lower at the end, he concludes that the use of tons significantly overestimates the decline in steel consumption.

Humphreys (1987, p. 339) raises the same concern:

> A major weakness of much IU (intensity of use) analysis is that it focuses exclusively on tonnage considerations. There is nothing in the equation about changes in quality or value. This is unsatisfactory from the point of view of the economist since value is a far better measure of economic importance than quantity. It is also unsatisfactory as an indicator of the problems of the mining industry since what motivates the industry is making money, not simply shipping tons of metal.

Humphreys goes on to suggest that the value of metal consumption may have grown much more rapidly in recent years than has the tonnage of metal consumption. In support of this possibility, he provides evidence showing that (a) the metals with the fastest consumption growth over the 1963–1983 period tend also to be those with the highest per unit values; (b) the quality and purity of steel, zinc, and other traditional metals are rising; and (c) many fabricated products are moving toward greater sophistication and value added. The latter fact, he notes, does not affect the value of unwrought metal consumption but does enhance the value of demand at subsequent stages of use.

The easiest argument to make in response to these reservations and in defense of using tons to measure metal consumption, as both Considine and Humphreys recognize, is the practical one of data availability. Assembling quality-adjusted consumption figures across a wide spectrum of countries and years simply is not feasible. Even the use of value as a proxy for quality (along the lines of Considine's weighted consumption index) is not practical on a broad scale. It is not an accident that his analysis applies only to a subsector of the steel industry in one country. Moreover, this problem is not peculiar to analyses of intensity of use; it confronts all studies of demand using metal consumption data. Indeed, the quality issue affects a broad range of economic analyses. (It is generally acknowledged, for example, that the rising costs of medical care are overstated because they fail to take account of improvements in medical services.)

The validity of concerns about changes in quality, moreover, depends on the ultimate purpose of analyzing metal demand—an issue examined earlier. For iron ore producers the shift toward higher-quality and higher-value steel products may help explain why the demand for their output has stagnated in recent years, but it does not alter that fact. At the other extreme, interest may focus on the demand for the functions that metals perform, as Considine suggests. The number of two-way voice conversations, for example, that can be carried over a single twisted pair of copper wires increased from one to fourteen with the introduction in the early 1960s of multiplexing. Although it may seem paradoxical, one might say that in this end use the consumption of copper increased in terms of the service provided, even though the new technology may have caused the number of tons or the value of the copper used in telecommunications to decline.

However, trying to construct measures that reflect the consumption of the functions or attributes provided by metals, aside from a few specific end uses, is probably not very promising. The problems are just too complex. In most applications, metals provide a variety of attributes—strength, appearance, corrosion resistance, heat conductivity, and so on. Determining the appropriate tradeoffs and weights to assign to these attributes is very difficult, in part because they are not the same for all users.

The case for using value to capture quality changes also has problems. The price of metal and hence the value of its consumption may rise over time even though quality remains unchanged. No one would argue, for example, that the sharp rise in the world price of crude oil during the 1970s reflected improvements in quality. In addition to such market manipulations, metal prices can increase simply because wages and capital costs are rising. In contrast, as the example of multiplexing indicates, new technology can enhance quality without increasing the value of metal production.

In short, even leaving aside the practical consideration of data availability, a superior alternative to measuring consumption in tons or some similar physical unit may not exist. It is nonetheless clear that quality improvements allow consumers to do more with less. Therefore, if consumption is measured in tons, quality improvements should be considered as one of the factors contributing to the slower growth in metal demand in recent years.

Secondary Metal Demand   Secondary metal is produced from the recycling of new and old scrap. New scrap is generated in the process of manufacturing consumer and producer goods; it includes the skeletons of the aluminum sheet remaining after beverage-can tops have been punched out, the turning from metal lathes, and other such products. Old scrap, in contrast, results when consumer and producer goods come to the end of their economic lives.

As noted earlier, secondary metal is included in the reported consumption figures for steel and lead but not for aluminum, nickel, or zinc, and only partially for copper and tin. In the case of copper, scrap used directly (for example, by ingot makers and brass mills) is not counted, whereas scrap used to produce refined copper is counted.

These differences in the treatment of secondary metal raise several questions. Which approach is the most appropriate? How serious are the problems when the appropriate approach is not the one reflected in our measures of metal demand? How can these problems best be dealt with?

As has been the case for the other conceptual issues examined, the answer to the first question—concerning the most appropriate approach—depends on the ultimate purpose of the analysis. As Hutchison and Tilton (1987, pp. 326–327) have pointed out in the case of copper:

If the goal is to assess the amount of copper contained in new final goods over a particular period, the inclusion of refined copper produced from new scrap involves double counting (assuming that the scrap is generated and recycled during the same period). This material is counted when it is first used, resulting in new scrap, and then again when it is recycled. As a result, including production from new scrap tends to overestimate copper consumption.

This is not the case for refined copper produced from old scrap since this material was first consumed several years earlier, and its recycling and re-use during the current year constitutes a net addition to supply. Moreover, even if the first use, scrapping and recycling all occurred during the same year, as could be the case with some of the aluminium used in beverage cans, this material would be absorbed twice during the same year in final goods, and so counting it both times is appropriate.

The exclusion of new scrap and the inclusion of old scrap, it should be noted, apply to the scrap used to make refined or unwrought metal (which our measures of copper demand take into account) and to the scrap used directly by ingot makers, brass mills, and others as a substitute for unwrought metal (which our measures of copper demand ignore).

If, however, the principal aim of the analysis is to assess the demand for primary metal at earlier stages of use—for example, for bauxite on the part of alumina refineries or for alumina on the part of aluminum smelters—then the appropriate measure of metal demand should entirely exclude the consumption of secondary metal. The rapid growth in the recycling of used beverage cans may help explain why the demand for bauxite and alumina on the U.S. market has not expanded more rapidly in recent years, but it does not distort the reported consumption figures for bauxite and alumina, or cause these figures to underestimate demand growth at these earlier stages of use.

Finally, if the principal purpose of the analysis is to assess aluminum demand on the part of fabricators, then all secondary metal, including that produced from new as well as old scrap, should be considered part of demand. The scrap material that fabricators generate is as much a part of demand at this stage of use as the metal embodied in fabricated and final goods.

Thus, the treatment of secondary metal demand may be appropriate or inappropriate, depending on the aim of the analysis and the nature of the questions being asked. Moreover, where the treatment is inappropriate, the distortions introduced can be substantial.

In such situations we would ideally like to modify our measures of metal demand. Although this is not possible to do in a comprehensive manner, covering all countries and extended periods of time, considerable data do exist on secondary production for particular countries and periods. Moreover, the countries for which such information is available are generally the larger and more important secondary producers and consumers. We can, for example, obtain information on aluminum recycling in the United States and, as shown in chapter 3, adjust that country's reported consumption for the tremendous increase in recycling (particularly of used beverage cans) that has taken place over the last decade. In this way the distortions introduced by the inappropriate treatment of secondary metal consumption can in some instances be eliminated. Where this is not possible, they can often at least be assessed.

Changes in Inventories   As pointed out earlier, reported consumption figures reflect the amount of metal consumed or used during the current period to the extent that they exclude net additions to inventories of unwrought metal. Unfortunately, however, inventory data are not available for most of the less developed countries and the centrally planned countries and are incomplete even for the OECD countries. Moreover, comprehensive data are even harder to find on the stock of metal contained in inventories of fabricated and finished products.

As a result, metal absorption, or the actual metal demand of final consumers, tends to exceed reported consumption when such unreported inventories are declining, whereas the opposite is true when unreported inventories are growing. This distortion, however, does not arise at earlier stages of use. A buildup of the stock of aluminum, for example, in inventories of fabricated or finished products, or even in ingot inventories, contributes to an increase in the current consumption of aluminum in bauxite and alumina. Indeed, in analyzing demand at these stages of use, it is inappropriate to exclude inventory changes downstream in the production process.

Fortunately, swings in metal inventories pose a less serious problem over the long run than over the business cycle or short run. Indeed, if inventories as a percentage of current consumption remain largely unchanged over the long run, any distortions introduced by unreported inventories will be small. It is possible, however, for the level of inventories to decline, relative to current consumption, over the long run in response to improved inventory control procedures, higher interest rates, or other factors. Conversely, the level of inventories relative to consumption could rise. This might occur, for example, if dependence on more insecure foreign sources of supply were growing.

In such cases inventory changes cause a divergence between reported consumption and actual demand trends. Where evidence of such changes exists, an effort to assess their nature and the magnitude of the bias they introduce in the reported consumption figures is necessary.

INDICATORS OF MACROECONOMIC ACTIVITY

The macroeconomic data used in the chapters that follow, along with the reported metal consumption data discussed in the previous section, are given in this volume's statistical appendix. The source of the figures on gross domestic product (GDP), gross domestic investment (GDI), manufacturing, and services for the world as a whole, for three groups of countries, and for several individual countries is largely the World Bank, although as noted in the statistical appendix, macroeconomic data for some of the centrally planned countries are from other sources.

Despite the best efforts of the World Bank and other international organizations, several problems inhibit the compilation of systematic and uniform international macroeconomic data. The first concerns the centrally planned countries, whose national accounts are governed by principles different from those used by market-economy countries. Converting these accounts so that they are reasonably comparable is not easy.

The second problem is that the national accounts data for many of the less developed countries rest on very fragile foundations. In many cases the figures constitute no more than informed judgments.

The third problem arises in converting the data from current units of the local currency to constant 1980 U.S. dollars. Two different procedures can be used to accomplish this task. The first, which the World Bank and this volume use, converts the original data into constant 1980 units of the local currency using the home country's GDP deflator, and then converts the resulting series to constant 1980 dollars using the average 1980 exchange rate between the local currency and the U.S. dollar. The second procedure converts the original data into current U.S. dollars using the average exchange rate for each year, and then deflates the resulting series using the U.S. GDP deflator to obtain the data in constant 1980 dollars. The advantage of the first procedure is that it minimizes the distortions introduced by the often sharp swings in exchange rates from year to year. To the extent, however, that the 1980 exchange rates are not representative of the appropriate rates, the first procedure can also introduce distortions, although in this case they will be maintained over the entire 1960–1985 period.

Just what the appropriate exchange rate should be is an intriguing question. One possible response is that rate or set of rates which produce equilibrium in the balance of trade—or, alternatively, the balance of payments minus involuntary capital flows—of the countries in question. In the analyses that follow, however, the macroeconomic data are used to assess the effect of the level and composition of economic activity on the demand for metal. Studies performed for the World Bank (Kravis, Heston, and Summers, 1978, 1982) and others (Organisation for Economic Cooperation and Development, 1985) indicate that a dollar of income can purchase more (including metal-containing products) in some countries than others. Although ideally the macroeconomic data should be adjusted for such differences in purchasing power, in practice the necessary data are available for only selected countries and periods. With the information available, chapter 3 assesses the extent to which the use of prevailing 1980 exchange rates appears to distort the results.

INTENSITY OF USE TECHNIQUE

In analyzing long-run trends in metal demand, the chapters that follow rely primarily on the intensity of use (IU) technique, so named because it first separates the influence of intensity of metal use on demand from the influence of GDP, and then concentrates on identifying the factors determining IU.

The rationale behind this approach, as discussed in Tilton (1988), rests on the proposition that the use of a metal depends on (1) the amount directly and indirectly consumed per unit of output of each final good produced by the economy, and (2) the output of each final good. Mathematically, this relationship is an identity that can be expressed as follows:

$$D_t = \sum_{i=1}^{n_t} a_{it} P_{it} \tag{1}$$

where D_t indicates the consumption (demand) of the metal, P_i the output in physical units of the ith final good, a_i the amount of the metal consumed directly and indirectly in the ith good, and n_t the number of final goods produced throughout the economy, all in year t.

Defining the ratio of the output of the ith good (P_{it}) to national income (Y_t) in year t as

$$b_{it} = P_{it}/Y_t \tag{2}$$

and substituting for P_{it} in equation (1) gives

$$D_t = Y_t \sum_{i=1}^{n_t} a_{it} b_{it} \tag{3}$$

This identity indicates that changes in metal demand over time are the result of three causal factors—the overall level of national income (Y_t), the material composition of products (a_{it}), and the product composition of income (b_{it}). The latter reflects shifts in the mix of goods being produced by the economy, while the material composition of products reflects changes in the mix of materials used to produce individual goods.

If intensity of use (IU_t) is defined in the normal manner as the ratio of metal use (D_t) to national income (Y_t), from equation (3) it is clear that intensity of use is simply a function of the product composition of income and the material composition of products. Specifically,

$$IU_t = D_t/Y_t = \sum_{i=1}^{n_t} a_{it} b_{it} \tag{4}$$

and

$$D_t = IU_t\, Y_t \qquad (5)$$

The first step in the IU technique involves assessing and, to the extent possible, separating the influence on metal demand of changes in IU and in GDP. The second step involves considering the reasons for the changes in GDP. Explaining why rates of economic growth differ among countries and vary over time is, of course, a specialty of its own in the field of macroeconomics and mostly beyond the scope of our analyses. Nonetheless, drawing on this literature we may gain some insights into the important factors causing economic growth to vary among countries over time.

The third step in the IU technique involves focusing on the two factors that in the first instance cause IU to change—the product composition of income and the material composition of products. The fourth step then attempts to explain changes in the product composition of income. This step is concerned with intersectoral shifts in the economy, such as the growth of the service sector, and with intrasectoral shifts, such as the growth of computers and other high-technology products in the manufacturing sector. It also examines the effect of imports and exports on the product composition of income. In a similar fashion the final step attempts to explain changes in the material composition of products. During this stage of the analysis, the role of new technology and material substitution—and how these variables are in turn influenced by metal and other material prices—is examined.

Although the first of these five steps is relatively easy to perform, assessing the influence on IU of the product composition of income and the material composition of products, along with the important factors causing these two determinants to change over time, is much more difficult. Consequently, as the analysis proceeds through these five steps, it tends to become less rigorous and quantitative and more qualitative in nature.

It is worth noting that intensity of use is the inverse of metal productivity. When IU is falling, metal productivity and efficiency are rising, and vice versa. This suggests that the intensity of metal use, like aggregate measures of labor or capital productivity, is itself of some intrinsic economic interest, and hence more than simply the mathematical result of dividing one variable by another. In addition, it makes clear that declining IU, though often lamented by metal producers and others, may not be bad. Indeed, from the point of view of resource efficiency it is often desirable.

THE IU HYPOTHESIS AND THE IU TECHNIQUE

Despite the similarity in names, the *intensity of use technique* should not be confused with the *intensity of use hypothesis*, which the International Iron

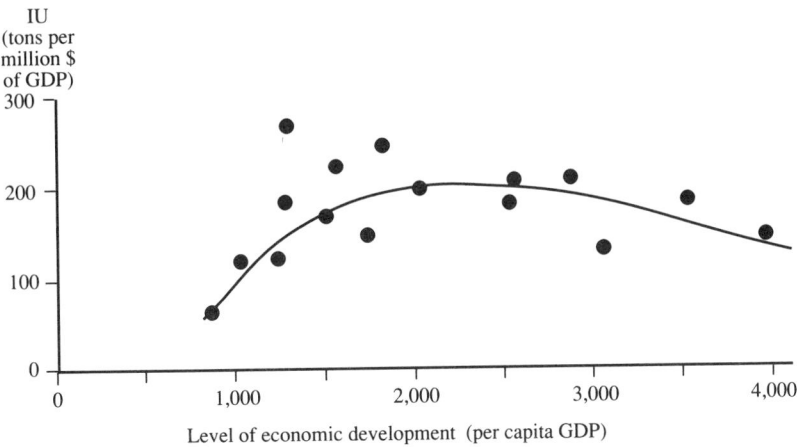

Figure 2-2. Relationship between intensity of steel use and per capita income in the United States, 1888–1967.
Source: Organisation for Economic Cooperation and Development, *Forecasting Steel Consumption* (Paris, OECD, 1974), p. 58. Redrawn with permission.
Notes: GDP is measured in constant 1963 dollars; points shown are five-year averages, through which a free-hand curve has been drawn.

and Steel Institute (1972), Malenbaum (1973, 1975, 1978), and others have used to make long-run forecasts of metal demand. The latter postulates that the intensity of metal use is a function of the level of economic development as reflected by a country's per capita income (GDP_t/Pop_t). The exact nature or specification of this relationship, which equation (6) expresses in its general form, is determined empirically, and generally varies among countries and materials. Its general shape, however, is presumed to follow an inverted U-shaped curve, such as that shown in figure 2-2 for the intensity of steel use in the United States.

$$IU_t = f(GDP_t/Pop_t) \qquad (6)$$

The standard rationale for this hypothesized behavior is rooted in changes in metal requirements over the development cycle. At the early stages of economic growth when per capita income levels are low, material requirements are also low, for such economies are based largely on unmechanized agriculture. As industrialization occurs, manufacturing, construction, and other material-intensive activities expand. As development continues, however, the need for houses, factories, roads, automobiles, and machinery gradually is satisfied, and consumer demand shifts increasingly toward services. The service sector, it is argued, is less material-intensive than the manufacturing and construction sectors, so this shift in consumer demand leads first to a slowing and eventually to a reversal in the upward rise in intensity of metal use as per capita income advances.

The big advantage of the IU hypothesis is its simplicity. As a comparison of equations (4) and (6) indicates, it offers an easily obtainable proxy—per capita income—for the combined effects on IU of the material composition of products and the product composition of income. Consequently, it allows the analyst to avoid the cost and difficulties associated with traditional forecasting procedures involving in-depth analyses of the principal end uses of a material and the likely effects on past and future consumption trends of new technology, changing tastes, and other factors. All that is required are projections of GDP and population, which are readily available for most countries, and historical data on material consumption, GDP, and population with which to estimate the relationship between intensity of use and per capita income.

The IU hypothesis does, however, suffer from some shortcomings. Probably the most serious is the implicit assumption that the relationship between IU and per capita income is stable. As noted earlier, intersectoral shifts, first from agriculture to manufacturing and construction and then eventually to services, are presumed to link IU with economic development. Material substitution, new technology, and other factors, however, may also influence IU. While the proponents of the IU hypothesis are well aware of this possibility, they offer no rationale for assuming that the influence of these variables varies over time or among countries in a systematic manner with per capita income. This is not surprising, for such a rationale is difficult to construct.

New technology and material substitution generally are discrete events that occur at irregular intervals. Their number, speed of adoption, and ultimate impact on metal use in specific applications vary greatly in response to a variety of factors, including the opportunities they provide for reducing costs and expanding markets. Neither new technology nor material substitution, however, appears to depend primarily on changes in per capita income.

As a result, and as Tilton (1983) and, more recently, Radetzki (1987) point out, the inverted U-shaped IU curve reflecting the relationship between IU and per capita income is likely to shift over time in response to changes in technology, material substitution, and other factors that are not closely correlated with per capita income. In light of the tendency of new technology to be resource saving, these factors will normally shift the true IU curve downward over time, as illustrated by the curves C_1, C_2, . . . C_5 in figure 2-3. This need not always be the case, however. Both material substitution and new technology can push the IU curve upward. The development of the aluminum beverage can, for example, increased the intensity of aluminum use in the United States.

Such shifts pose a dilemma for the analyst. The observable data used to determine the estimated IU curve, shown as the heavy black curve in figure

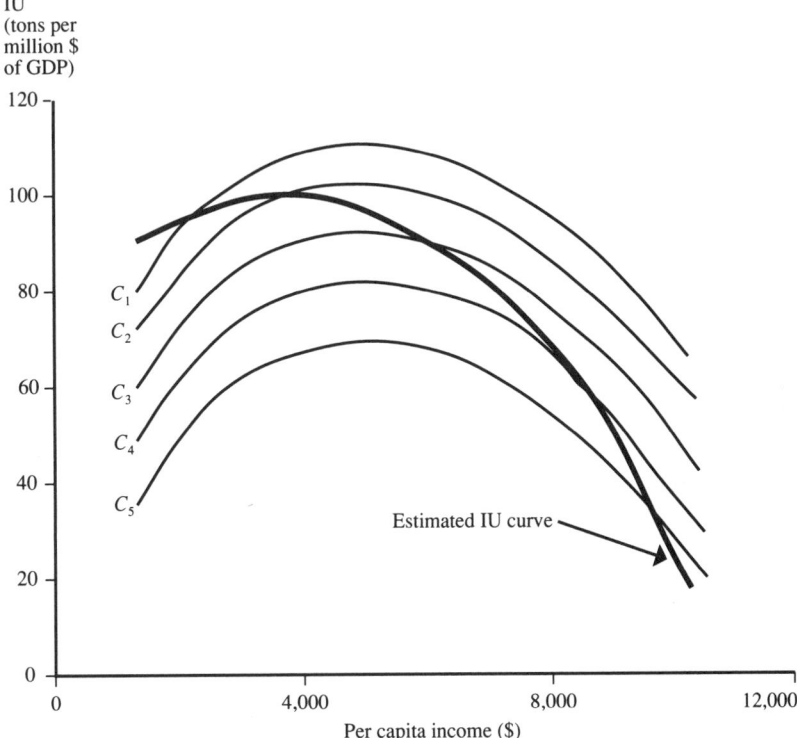

IU
(tons per
million $
of GDP)

Figure 2-3. Relationship between true intensity of use (IU) curves ($C_1, C_2 \ldots C_5$) and estimated IU curve.

2-3, are actually from different IU curves. The estimated curve, as a result, is a hybrid—a collection of points on different true curves—and may provide a poor approximation for any of them.

The viability of the IU hypothesis as a forecasting technique could be salvaged if the net influence of those factors affecting IU which are not closely correlated with per capita income were small compared to the influence of those factors closely correlated with per capita income. In this case shifts in the true IU curve would be minor compared to movements along the curve in response to changes in per capita income. This, however, requires that changes in the product composition of income resulting largely from intersectoral shifts in the economy are the principal determinant of the intensity of metal use, and that changes in the material composition of products caused by new technology and material substitution are of much less consequence. Unfortunately, the evidence presented in subsequent chapters and elsewhere indicates that the roles of technological change and material substitution are often quite significant and too important to ignore in analyzing long-run trends in metal demand.

Another possibility for saving the IU hypothesis is to assume that the aggregate effect of new technology and other factors causing the IU curve to shift will continue to evolve in the future as in the past. When true, the estimated IU curve captures both the effect of changes in those determinants of IU correlated with per capita income (the movement along the true IU curve) and the effect of changes in other determinants (the shift in the true IU curve), and it can provide reasonably good forecasts. Unfortunately, however, this approach guarantees poor performance at precisely those points at which accurate forecasts are most needed, that is, when significant breaks with the past are occurring.

For our purposes, however, what is important is to distinguish between the IU technique and the IU hypothesis. The former, used in subsequent chapters, does not make the assumption that per capita income can serve as a reliable proxy for all important variables determining the intensity of metal use. It thus avoids the problems that this assumption creates for the IU hypothesis.

OTHER APPROACHES TO THE ANALYSIS OF METAL DEMAND

Of the other approaches that economists use to analyze metal demand, probably the most common entails the specification and estimation of demand functions. For example, the world demand for copper is typically assumed to be a function of the price of copper, the price of close substitute materials such as aluminum, and GDP or some other activity variable (such as industrial production) as well (Fisher, Cootner, and Baily, 1972; Bozdogan and Hartman, 1979). This relationship is then estimated, usually by econometric techniques.

This procedure can produce useful and interesting results; however, accounting in a realistic manner for the effects of technological change is often difficult. Properly specifying the relationship between demand and its determinants, particularly the appropriate lag structure to use for the price variables, can also be troublesome. In addition, the relationship itself may change over time in ways that make it difficult or impossible to estimate.

A second approach, employed somewhat less frequently, involves the specification and estimation of production functions (or the corresponding cost functions). Used primarily to analyze material substitution, this approach can focus on individual metal applications, such as the study by Valdes (1987) on the use of copper and aluminum in the insulated cable market. More often, however, attention is devoted to entire industries, economic sectors, or even the economy as a whole. These studies, which Kopp and Smith (1980), Slade (1981), and Field and Berndt (1981) have reviewed, generally treat minerals as a single factor of production and assess the extent to which they substitute for or complement labor, capital, and other aggregate factor inputs. Their findings vary greatly, depending on how the production function is specified, how technological change is accounted for, and how other considerations are resolved.

A third approach, used by Leontief and coauthors (1983), Myers (1986), and others, involves the use of input–output analysis. Where input–output tables are sufficiently disaggregated to identify individual metals, they indicate metal flows to intermediate and final uses. Where they exist in comparable format at periodic intervals over an extended period of time, they also show how the pattern of metal use is evolving. Changes in input–output coefficients indicate changes in the amount of metal consumed per constant dollar of output for each end-using industry. If the end-using industries are narrowly defined and if the mix of products within these industries remains relatively stable, shifts in input–output coefficients largely reflect changes in the material composition of products and in turn the influence on metal demand of new technology and material substitution. The major limitations of the input–output approach are the lack of tables for recent years (because of the time they require to compile), compatibility among tables for different countries, and the lack of tables over extended periods of time for many countries.

Each of these approaches has its own strengths and shortcomings as well as a set of applications for which it is particularly useful. In this sense all three approaches as well as the IU technique are complementary and can help provide insights that extend our understanding of long-run trends in metal demand.

The advantage of the IU technique lies in its initial appraisal of the relative importance of GDP and IU in explaining demand trends and then, in turn, in its appraisal of the relative importance of the material composition of products and the product composition of income in explaining IU trends. This advantage allows the analysis to concentrate on those variables of greatest significance. If, for example, long-run trends in metal demand are largely shaped by changes in GDP growth, a better understanding of these trends primarily requires greater knowledge of the determinants of macroeconomic growth.

It is important to stress, however, that GDP, the material composition of products, and the product composition of income are not the final determinants of metal demand. Ultimately, metal demand is determined by consumer tastes, production technology, material prices, and government policies, including monetary and fiscal policies. A full understanding of metal demand trends thus requires looking behind GDP, the material composition of products, and the product composition of income to the factors that cause these variables—and, in the process, metal demand—to change over time. The later steps in the IU technique are intended to do just that, although doing so in a rigorous manner is often difficult, and many analyses have stopped short of these steps.

In such cases, as Considine (1987) and others have pointed out, the IU technique is mechanistic and devoid of economic theory. Indeed, as equations (1) through (5) indicate, the relationships among metal demand, GDP, IU, the material composition of products, and the product composition of income are based on a series of identities, and hence are tautological. This does not detract, however, from the potential usefulness of such analyses, as some have suggested. If, for example, the material composition of products is found to have little or no effect on metal demand, it would be difficult to argue that material prices are an important ultimate determinant of metal demand, for in this situation changes in either GDP or the product composition of income or both would be driving demand, and neither is likely to be influenced greatly by material prices.

Indeed, similar concerns have been raised about the comparative studies of economic growth carried out by Denison (1967, 1985) and others. However, as Maddison (1987, p. 651) states in his recent review of this important field of economic research,

> growth accounting . . . cannot provide a full causal story. It deals with "proximate" rather than "ultimate" causality and registers the facts about growth components; it does not explain the elements of policy or circumstance, national or international, that underlie them, but it does identify which facts need more ultimate explanation. This kind of exercise forces one to merge and match data in a way that provides valuable cross-checks on the consistency and plausibility of the basic growth indicators both for individual countries and across countries.

The IU technique need not be completely mechanistic or devoid of theory, nor need it ignore the ultimate determinants of metal demand. The later steps in this technique look behind trends in GDP, the material composition of products, and the product composition of income in an attempt to identify and assess original causal forces. These steps can draw as heavily on the existing body of economic theory as any of the other approaches described in this section.

REFERENCES

Bozdogan, Kirkor, and Raymond S. Hartman. 1979. "U.S. Demand for Copper: An Introduction to Theoretical and Econometric Analysis," in Raymond F. Mikesell, *The World Copper Industry* (Baltimore, Md., The Johns Hopkins University Press for Resources for the Future), pp. 131–163.

Considine, Timothy J. 1987. "Understanding Trends in Metal Demand," *Materials and Society* vol. 11, no. 3, pp. 349–370.

Denison, Edward F. 1967. *Why Growth Rates Differ* (Washington, D.C., Brookings Institution).

_____. 1985. *Trends in American Economic Growth 1920–1982* (Washington, D.C., Brookings Institution).

Field, Barry C., and Ernst R. Berndt. 1981. "An Introductory Review of Research on the Economics of Natural Resource Substitution," in Ernst R. Berndt and Barry C. Field, eds., *Modeling and Measuring Natural Resource Substitution* (Cambridge, Mass., MIT Press) pp. 1–14.

Fisher, Franklin M., P. H. Cootner, and M. N. Baily. 1972. "An Econometric Model of the World Copper Industry," *Bell Journal of Economics and Management Science* vol. 3, no. 2 (Autumn) pp. 568–609.

Humphreys, David. 1987. "Perspectives on Intensity of Use," *Materials and Society* vol. 11, no. 3, pp. 333–347.

Hutchison, Roger S., and John E. Tilton. 1987. "Is the Intensity of Copper Use Still Declining in the United States?" *Natural Resources Forum* vol. 11, no. 4, pp. 325–334.

International Iron and Steel Institute. 1972. *Projection 85: World Steel Demand* (Brussels, IISI).

Kopp, Raymond J., and V. Kerry Smith. 1980. "Measuring Factor Substitution with Neoclassical Models: An Experimental Evaluation," *Bell Journal of Economics and Management Science* vol. 11, no. 2 (Autumn) pp. 631–655.

Kravis, Irving B., Alan Heston, and Robert Summers. 1978. *International Comparisons of Real Product and Purchasing Power* (Baltimore, Md., The Johns Hopkins University Press for the World Bank).

_____. 1982. *World Product and Income: International Comparisons of Real Gross Product* (Baltimore, Md., The Johns Hopkins University Press for the World Bank).

Leontief, Wassily, James C. M. Koo, Sylvia Nasar, and Ira Sohn. 1983. *The Future of Nonfuel Minerals in the U.S. and World Economy* (Lexington, Mass., Lexington Books).

Maddison, Angus. 1987. "Growth and Slowdown in Advanced Capitalist Economies: Techniques of Quantitative Assessment," *Journal of Economic Literature* vol. 25, no. 2 (June) pp. 649–698.

Malenbaum, Wilfred. 1973. *Material Requirements in the United States and Abroad in the Year 2000*. Research project prepared for the National Commission on Materials Policy (Philadelphia, University of Pennsylvania).

_____. 1975. "Law of Demand for Minerals," *Proceedings of the Council of Economics*, 104th Annual Meeting of the American Institute of Mining, Metallurgical and Petroleum Engineers (New York, AIME) pp. 146–155.

_____. 1978. *World Demand for Raw Materials in 1985 and 2000* (New York, McGraw-Hill).

Metallgesellschaft Aktiengesellschaft. Annual. *Metal Statistics* (Frankfurt am Main, Metallgesellschaft AG).

Myers, John G. 1986. "Testing for Structural Change in Metals Use," *Materials and Society* vol. 10, no. 3, pp. 271–283.

Organisation for Economic Cooperation and Development. 1974. *Forecasting Steel Consumption* (Paris, OECD).

_____. 1985. *Purchasing Power Parities and Real Expenditures in the OECD* (Paris, OECD).

Radetzki, Marian. 1987. "The Intensity of Use Hypothesis: Theory Versus Fact," *CIPEC Quarterly Review* (January–March) pp. 21–32.

Roberts, Mark C. 1987. "The Consumption of Metals and International Trade," *Materials and Society* vol. 11, no. 3, pp. 391–406.

Slade, Margaret E. 1981. "Recent Advances in Econometric Estimation of Materials Substitution," *Resources Policy* vol. 7, no. 2 (June) pp. 103–109.

Tilton, John E. 1983. "La Previsione Della Domanda Di Minerali E Metalli Attraverso L'Impiego Della Tecnica Di Intensita D'Uso" (Forecasting Mineral and Metal Demand with the Intensity of Use Technique), *Materie Prime* no. 2, pp. 111–115.

———. 1988. "Mineral Investment in Developing Countries in the Wake of Slower Growth in World Metal Demand," in G. Jaenicke and coeditors, *International Mining Investment: Legal and Economic Perspectives* (Deventer, The Netherlands, Kluwer).

Valdes, Raymundo M. 1987. "Substitution in the Insulated Cable Market: A Study of Copper-Aluminum Materials Substitution," *Materials and Society* vol. 11, no. 3, pp. 259–277.

3

The OECD Countries:
Demand Trend Setters

JOHN E. TILTON

The twenty-four member states of the Organisation for Economic Cooperation and Development (OECD) together account for some two-thirds of the
world's entire output of goods and services. They include the major industrialized powers and all the developed states, other than the Republic of South
Africa, outside the centrally planned countries. (See the list of OECD countries on p. xviii.) In recent years they have consumed almost one-half of the
world's steel output and well over one-half of its aluminum, copper, lead,
zinc, and nickel output. Over most of the postwar period, their dominance
of world metal markets has been even more pronounced. The OECD countries, as chapter 1 points out, are also largely responsible for the break in the
long-run growth of world metal demand in the early 1970s.

This chapter examines metal demand in the OECD countries. In particular,
it attempts to find the answers to two questions. First, why did growth of
metal demand in the OECD countries decline in the early 1970s, dragging
world demand in tow? Second, why do such large differences in metal
consumption exist among the major OECD countries? This question sparks
several others. Can these differences be attributed primarily to differences in
the overall economies of these countries, or does the intensity of metal use
vary among countries as well? In this regard, is the intensity of metal use,
like the intensity of energy use, high in the United States compared to other
developed countries? In light of the importance of the OECD countries,
answers to these questions are prerequisites to understanding long-run trends
in world metal demand.

The focus of this study is on six metals—steel, aluminum, copper, lead,
zinc, and nickel—and the evolution of the demand for them over the last

several decades. Within the OECD the emphasis is on the United States, Japan, and the European Economic Community (EEC),[1] which together account for about 85 percent of the total goods and services produced in the OECD and a similarly large share of OECD metal consumption. Within the EEC the three largest metal consumers—France, the Federal Republic of Germany, and the United Kingdom—receive the most attention.

The analysis in this chapter uses the intensity of use (IU) technique and follows closely the five steps described in chapter 2. The first section examines metal consumption patterns in the OECD countries and assesses the relative importance of gross domestic product (GDP) and IU in shaping these patterns. The second section looks behind the GDP trends and tries to identify their determinants. The third section concentrates on IU patterns and the importance of changes in the material composition of products and the product composition of income (that is, the mix of goods and services produced by the economy) in affecting IU patterns; the fourth and fifth sections explore the forces causing these changes. The final section presents some conclusions regarding discrepancies in IU levels among the major OECD countries as well as various factors affecting the slowdown in growth of metal demand in these countries.

METAL CONSUMPTION PATTERNS IN THE OECD COUNTRIES

The consumption of steel, aluminum, copper, lead, zinc, and nickel over the 1950–1987 period is shown in figure 3-1 for the United States, Japan, the EEC, and the OECD as a whole, and in figure 3-2 for the United Kingdom, France, and the Federal Republic of Germany. In recent years metal consumption in the EEC has roughly equaled that in the United States. The two exceptions are aluminum, whose consumption is still much greater in the United States, and zinc, whose consumption is now considerably greater in the EEC. In the early postwar period Japan consumed far less of all the metals than did the United States or the EEC, but during the 1960s and early 1970s Japan's consumption grew very rapidly, thereby substantially narrowing this gap.

Significant changes have occurred within the EEC as well. The largest consumer in the early 1950s was the United Kingdom. Over the decades that followed, however, its growth was among the lowest of the industrialized countries, and by the 1980s both France and especially the Federal Republic of Germany were more important metal markets.

Figures 3-1 and 3-2 also indicate that for certain countries the slowdown in the growth of demand for some metals occurred prior to 1973 (or at least

[1] Although the number of EEC member countries has grown over time, to maintain comparability the EEC is defined throughout this study as including Belgium–Luxembourg, Denmark, the Federal Republic of Germany, France, Greece, Ireland, Italy, The Netherlands, and the United Kingdom.

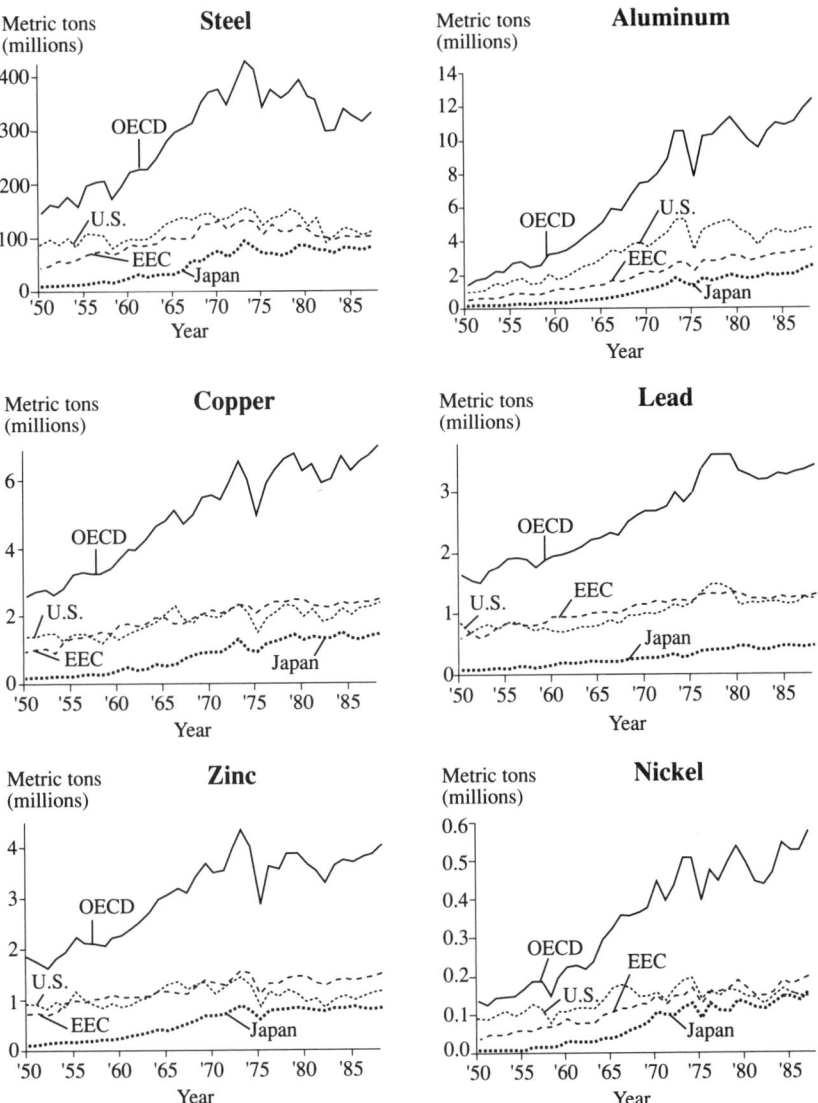

Figure 3-1. Steel, aluminum, copper, lead, zinc, and nickel consumption for the United States, Japan, EEC, and OECD, 1950–1987.

Source: Statistical appendix in this volume and the sources cited therein.

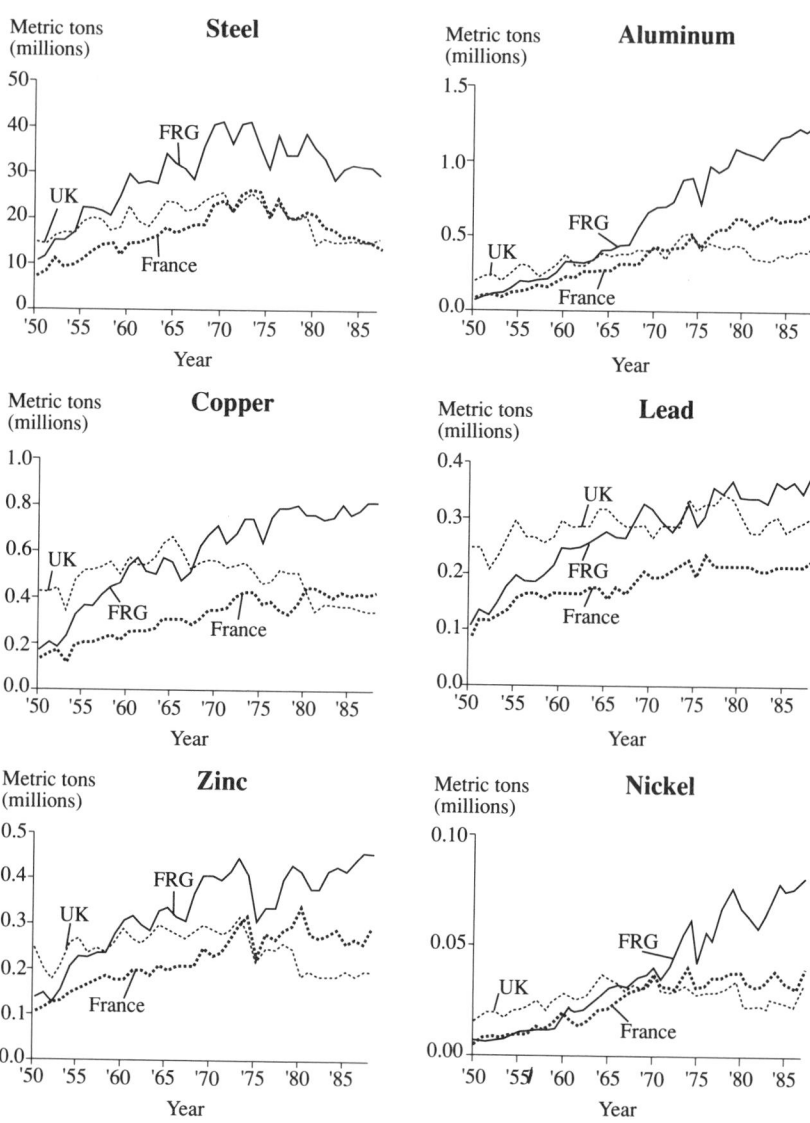

Figure 3-2. Steel, aluminum, copper, lead, zinc, and nickel consumption for the United Kingdom (UK), France, and the Federal Republic of Germany (FRG), 1950–1987.

Source: Statistical appendix in this volume and the sources cited therein.

started before this date) and took place over an extended period of time. In the United States, for example, the rise in steel and copper consumption appears to have stalled in the mid-1960s. In the EEC the break in steel consumption occurred around 1970, and the date of the break for copper is far from clear.

Nonetheless, 1973 represents the most pronounced turning point for the OECD as a whole and for most countries and metals. For this reason, and to maintain consistency, table 3-1 (like most of the tables in this chapter) uses 1973 to divide the years 1960 through 1987. In addition to the average annual growth rates of actual metal consumption over the 1960–1973 and 1973–1987 periods (and the declines in growth rates between the two periods), this table also shows, in its fourth and fifth columns, the extent to which the declines can be attributed to changes in GDP and IU trends.

The recorded figures highlight the magnitude and pervasiveness of the consumption slowdown. With the exception of lead in the United Kingdom, all the metals examined experienced a significant decline in the growth of demand in every major OECD market. The decline was most severe for aluminum, which enjoyed the most rapid growth during the 1960–1973 period. Its growth within the OECD, which averaged nearly 10 percent annually before 1973, fell to less than 1 percent after 1973. However, its consumption did continue to expand, in contrast to that of steel and zinc, which actually declined. In contrast, lead, the metal that grew most slowly during the 1960–1973 period, continued to expand and appears to have suffered the smallest drop in growth.

Among countries, the decline in growth of demand was most severe in Japan, where metal markets had been expanding the fastest. In the United Kingdom and the United States, however, the growth of demand not only declined but turned negative, as consumption for nearly all the metals examined actually fell after 1973.

For the OECD as a whole, both IU and GDP trends contributed to the slowdown in long-run metal demand growth. Of the two, IU was the most important, particularly for aluminum and steel. Only for copper and lead did slower GDP growth account for over one-half of the decline in consumption growth.

For the United States and Japan the findings are similar. In these countries both IU and GDP caused the slowdown; the former generally had the greater effect. In the EEC, GDP rather than IU exerted the greatest influence, and for three metals it alone caused the decline in consumption.

The dominant role of GDP in the EEC can be explained in part by the greater decline in economic growth that these countries experienced after 1973. As table 3-2 indicates, their GDP growth fell by 2.7 percentage points. By comparison, the decline was only 1.5 points in the United States. Yet this is not the full explanation, as GDP growth dropped by 6.0 points in Japan and still IU, not GDP, was largely responsible for the slowdown in Japan's growth of metal demand.

Table 3-1. Growth of Metal Consumption in the OECD, United States, Japan, EEC, United Kingdom, France, and Federal Republic of Germany, 1960–1973 and 1973–1987, and Percentage Change in Metal Growth Due to GDP and Intensity of Use (IU)

(percent)

Area or country and metal	Average annual consumption growth			Change in consumption growth due to GDP[a]	Change in consumption growth due to IU[a]
	1960–1973	1973–1987	Difference		
OECD					
Steel	5.3	−1.9	−7.2	35	65
Aluminum	9.7	0.8	−8.9	29	71
Copper	4.6	0.2	−4.4	59	41
Lead	3.5	0.9	−2.6	96	4
Zinc	5.3	−0.8	−6.1	42	58
Nickel	6.6	1.0	−5.6	46	54
United States					
Steel	4.0	−2.7	−6.7	24	76
Aluminum	9.6	−0.8	−10.4	16	84
Copper	4.7	−0.3	−5.0	32	68
Lead	4.1	0.7	−3.4	53	47
Zinc	4.3	−1.8	−6.1	26	74
Nickel	4.9	−1.8	−6.7	24	76
Japan					
Steel	12.2	−1.0	−13.2	45	55
Aluminum	20.0	1.8	−18.3	34	66
Copper	11.2	0.5	−10.7	56	44
Lead	7.9	2.5	−5.4	100[b]	0[b]
Zinc	13.9	−0.8	−14.7	42	58
Nickel	15.4	2.2	−13.2	47	53
EEC					
Steel	3.6	−2.1	−5.7	49	51
Aluminum	6.9	1.9	−5.0	56	44
Copper	2.3	0.3	−2.0	100[b]	0[b]
Lead	2.1	0.5	−1.6	100[b]	0[b]
Zinc	3.4	−0.7	−4.0	67	33
Nickel	4.7	2.1	−2.6	100[b]	0[b]
United Kingdom					
Steel	1.0	−3.6	−4.6	35	65
Aluminum	2.4	−1.7	−4.1	38	62
Copper	−0.3	−3.5	−3.3	48	52
Lead	−0.1	0.1	0.3	0[c]	100[c]
Zinc	0.8	−3.4	−4.2	37	63
Nickel	1.0	0.4	−0.6	100[b]	0[b]

40

Table 3-1 (continued)

Area or country and metal	Average annual consumption growth			Change in consumption growth due to GDP[a]	Change in consumption growth due to IU[a]
	1960-1973	1973-1987	Difference		
France					
Steel	4.8	−3.7	−8.6	41	59
Aluminum	5.9	2.3	−3.7	95	5
Copper	4.3	−0.2	−4.5	78	22
Lead	2.2	−0.2	−2.4	100[b]	0[b]
Zinc	4.1	−1.1	−5.2	66	34
Nickel	3.3	2.1	−1.2	100[b]	0[b]
Federal Republic of Germany					
Steel	2.6	−2.3	−4.9	53	47
Aluminum	8.0	2.4	−5.7	47	53
Copper	2.7	0.7	−2.0	100[b]	0[b]
Lead	1.6	1.2	−0.4	100[b]	0[b]
Zinc	3.1	0.2	−2.9	92	8
Nickel	6.9	2.9	−4.0	67	33

Source: Statistical appendix in this volume.

[a]The change in metal consumption growth due to GDP was estimated by calculating the portion of the change in metal consumption growth that would have occurred had only GDP growth changed (assuming IU continued to change over the 1973–1987 period as during the 1960–1973 period). Similarly, the percentage change in metal consumption due to IU was estimated by the portion of the change in metal consumption that would have occurred had only the rate of growth (or decline) in IU changed (assuming GDP continued to change over the 1973–1987 period as during the 1960–1973 period). Because the product, not the sum, of IU and GDP determines consumption, as shown in equation (5) of chapter 2 in this volume, some of the change in metal consumption growth may be due to the multiplicative effect of changes in both of these variables. Such effects, which generally are small, are attributed to IU and GDP in proportion to their direct effects on metal consumption growth, so that the percentage changes in metal consumption growth shown for GDP and IU sum to 100.

[b]Where the percentage change in metal consumption growth due to GDP equals 100, IU trends would have increased metal demand growth during the 1973–1987 period compared with the 1960–1973 period, had their stimulating effect not been offset by slower GDP growth.

[c]The percentage change in metal consumption growth due to IU equals 100 in the case of lead in the United Kingdom because rising IU trends more than offset the effect of slower GDP growth, thereby causing an increase in the growth of lead consumption.

Table 3-2 also shows the change in IU. For the OECD as a whole, intensity of metal use generally rose over the 1960–1973 period. The amount of aluminum consumed per million dollars of real GDP, for example, grew an average 4.5 percent a year. For the other metals the increase was more modest. Nonetheless, except for copper and lead, IU was rising; after 1973, however, it fell for all six metals. The decline for steel, an average 4.2 percent a year, was particularly great, but even the smallest decline (the average 1.5 percent for nickel and lead) was far from negligible. The rise and subsequent fall in IU levels accounts for the dominant role played by this variable in the decline of growth in metal demand after 1973.

Table 3-2. Growth of GDP and Intensity of Use (IU) in the OECD, United States, Japan, EEC, United Kingdom, France, and Federal Republic of Germany, 1960–1973 and 1973–1987
(average annual percentage growth)

Area or country and period	GDP	IU					
		Steel	Aluminum	Copper	Lead	Zinc	Nickel
OECD							
1960–1973	5.0	0.3	4.5	−0.4	−1.5	0.3	1.5
1973–1987	2.5	−4.2	−1.6	−2.2	−1.5	−3.2	−1.5
United States							
1960–1973	4.0	−0.1	5.3	0.6	0.0	0.2	0.8
1973–1987	2.5	−5.1	−3.2	−2.7	−1.8	−4.2	−4.2
Japan							
1960–1973	9.7	2.4	9.5	1.4	−1.6	3.9	5.3
1973–1987	3.7	−4.6	−1.9	−3.1	−1.2	−4.4	−1.5
EEC							
1960–1973	4.6	−1.0	2.2	−2.2	−2.4	−1.2	0.1
1973–1987	1.9	−3.9	0.0	−1.5	−1.4	−2.5	0.2
United Kingdom							
1960–1973	3.1	−2.1	−0.7	−3.3	−3.1	−2.3	−2.1
1973–1987	1.6	−5.1	−3.2	−5.0	−1.4	−4.9	−1.2
France							
1960–1973	5.6	−0.7	0.4	−1.2	−3.2	−1.4	−2.1
1973–1987	2.1	−5.7	0.2	−2.2	−2.3	−3.2	0.0
Federal Republic of Germany							
1960–1973	4.5	−1.8	3.4	−1.8	−2.8	−1.4	2.3
1973–1987	1.9	−4.1	0.5	−1.2	−0.7	−1.6	1.0

Source: Statistical appendix in this volume.

In the United States and Japan the situation parallels that for the OECD as a whole; IU generally rose before 1973 and fell thereafter. Again the EEC deviates from the prevailing pattern. This group of countries already experienced falling IU levels in the 1960–1973 period for steel, copper, lead, and zinc, and the rise recorded for nickel was negligible. After 1973 the growth in IU declined for aluminum and became more negative for steel and zinc. For nickel, however, there was little change; and for copper and lead the rate of decline actually slowed. Here too lies part of the explanation for the dominant role of GDP in affecting EEC metal consumption trends.

These differences suggest that 1973 may not represent as pronounced a turning point for IU as for metal consumption and GDP. Figures 3-3 and 3-4, which show trends in the three-year averages of IU for the OECD, its

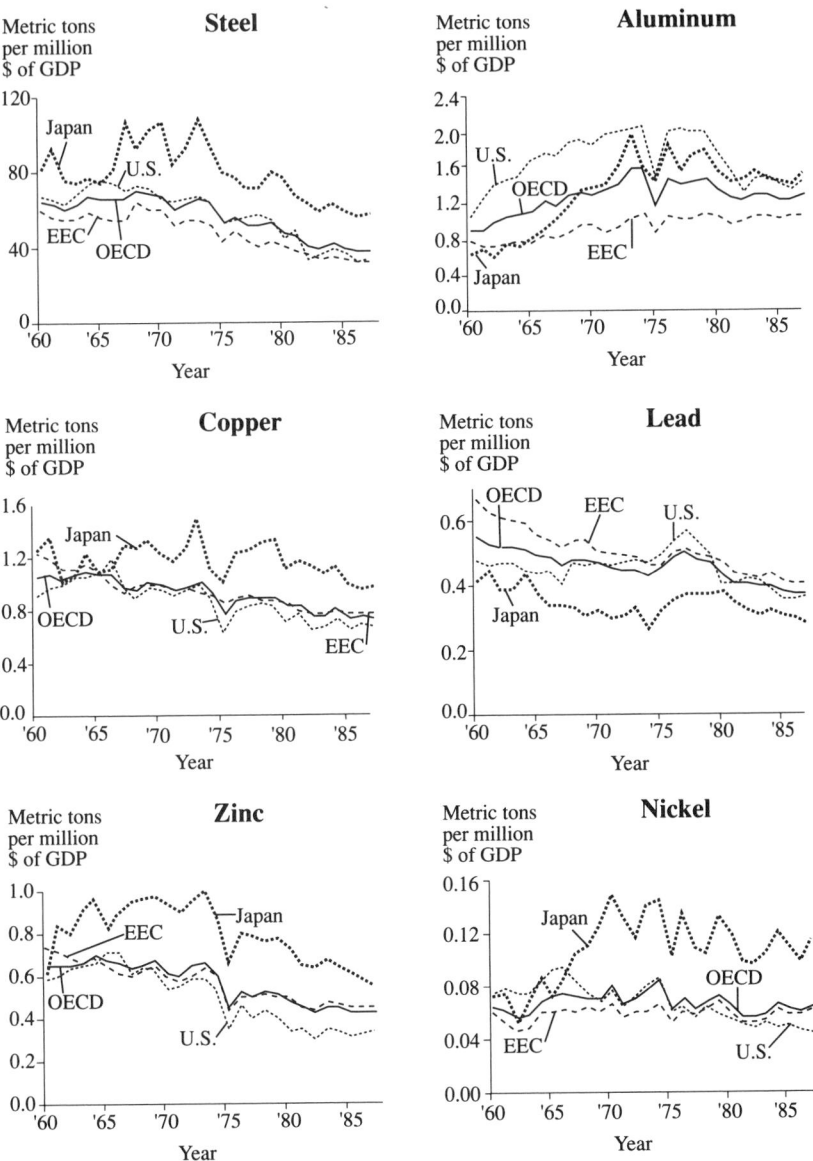

Figure 3-3. Intensity of use of steel, aluminum, copper, lead, zinc, and nickel for the United States, Japan, EEC, and OECD, 1960–1987.

Source: Statistical appendix in this volume and the sources cited therein.

43

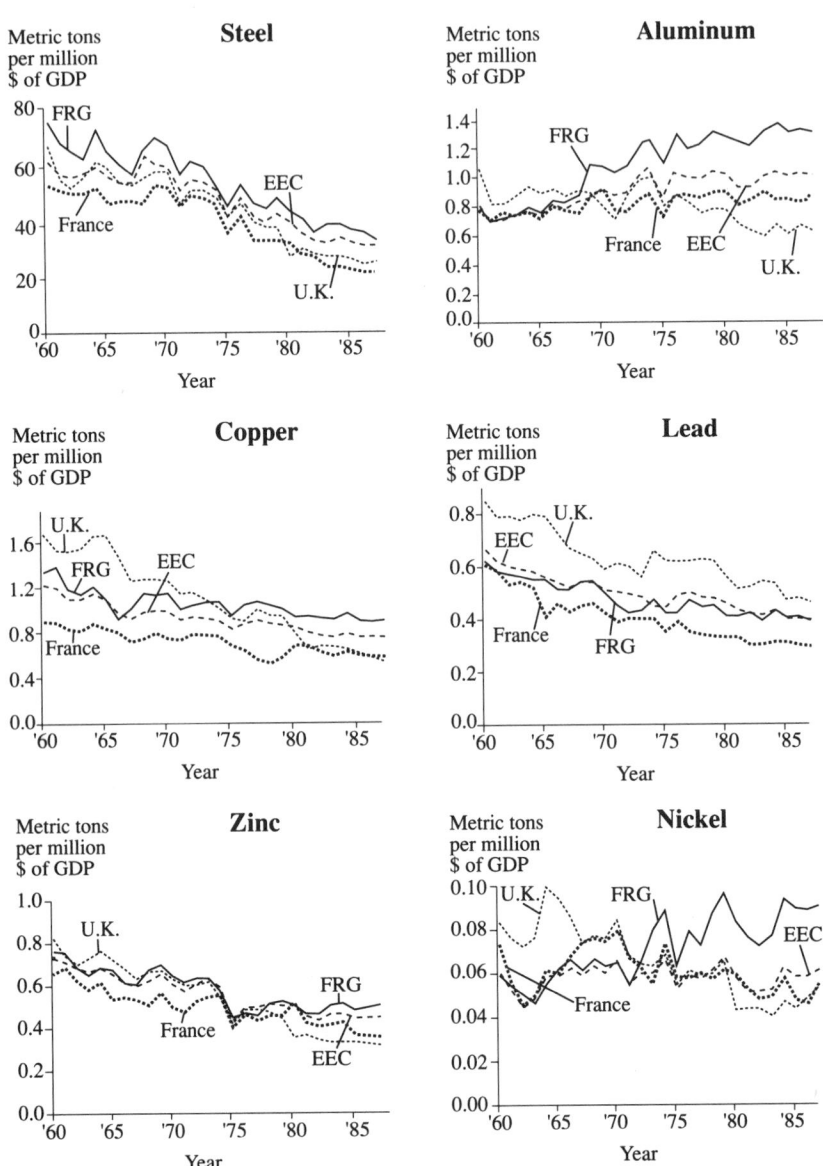

Figure 3-4. Intensity of use of steel, aluminum, copper, lead, zinc, and nickel for the EEC, United Kingdom (UK), France, and the Federal Republic of Germany (FRG), 1960–1987.

Source: Statistical appendix in this volume and the sources cited therein.

major member states, and the EEC, indicate that this is indeed the case. The IU of steel has been declining in the United States and the United Kingdom since the mid-1960s and in France and the Federal Republic of Germany since the late 1960s. The intensity of copper and lead use appears on the decline throughout the entire 1960–1987 period. Indeed, 1973 marks a clear turning point in IU trends only for aluminum in the United States and Japan and for steel in Japan. Apparently the decline in the growth of metal demand around 1973 was largely the result of the break at that time in GDP growth, even though IU trends accounted for over one-half of the slowdown in demand growth between the 1973–1987 period and the 1960–1973 period.

ACCOUNTING FOR ECONOMIC GROWTH

The explanation of economic growth is a major field of inquiry in its own right, and beyond the scope of the studies in this volume. Nonetheless, in light of the importance of economic growth for long-run metal demand, it is important at least to examine the existing literature and its findings concerning the significant determinants of economic growth.

Fortunately Maddison (1987) surveys and extends the literature on economic growth in a way that is particularly useful for our purposes. Specifically, Maddison's article examines GDP growth over three periods—1912 to 1950, 1950 to 1973, and 1973 to 1984—for the United States, Japan, the United Kingdom, France, the Federal Republic of Germany, and The Netherlands. The results for all but The Netherlands are summarized in table 3-3.

The first row of the table gives the average annual rate of GDP growth for each of the five countries of particular interest to our inquiry. The figures indicate that economic growth between 1950 and 1973 was abnormally rapid and that, contrary to popular perception, growth since 1973 has not been unusually sluggish at least when compared with the 1913–1950 period. Indeed, in recent years economic growth in France, Germany, and Japan, although down sharply from the unusual 1950–1973 period, is still considerably higher than the rate of growth over most of the first half of the century.

Table 3-3 also shows the contribution to economic growth of the following factors:

1. Labor input, which reflects the contribution of changes in (a) man-hours worked, (b) labor quality as measured by educational level and the proportion of women in the work force, and (c) underemployment or labor hoarding.

2. Capital input, which indicates the percentage of GDP growth caused by changes in (a) the quantity of capital, (b) the quality of capital as indicated by its average age, and (c) the abnormal slack in the use of physical capital in Japan and Germany in 1950 prior to those nations' full recovery from World War II.

Table 3-3. Sources of GDP Growth for the United States, Japan, United Kingdom, France, and Federal Republic of Germany, 1913–1950, 1950–1973, and 1973–1984

(average annual percentage-point contribution to growth rate, except where otherwise indicated)

	United States			Japan			United Kingdom			France			Germany		
	1913–1950	1950–1973	1973–1984	1913–1950	1950–1973	1973–1984	1913–1950	1950–1973	1973–1984	1913–1950	1950–1973	1973–1984	1913–1950[a]	1950–1973	1973–1984
Average annual rate of GDP growth	2.78	3.72	2.32	2.24	9.37	3.78	1.29	3.02	1.06	1.06	5.13	2.18	1.30	5.92	1.68
Labor input	0.60	1.14	1.31	0.41	2.51	0.59	0.12	-0.02	-0.73	-0.31	0.36	-0.38	0.20	0.47	-0.83
Capital input	0.99	1.53	1.28	0.99	3.46	2.55	0.79	1.51	1.15	0.76	1.66	1.63	0.58	2.41	1.38
Catch-up effect	0.00	0.00	0.00	0.00	1.02	0.44	0.00	0.14	0.29	0.00	0.52	0.49	0.00	0.68	0.40
Structural shifts	0.29	0.12	-0.07	0.62	1.22	0.21	-0.04	0.10	-0.26	0.09	0.46	-0.12	0.20	0.36	0.05
Other considerations	0.09	0.12	-0.19	0.09	0.52	-0.06	0.04	0.23	0.12	0.04	0.32	-0.03	0.00	0.37	-0.01
Growth explained	1.97	2.91	2.33	2.11	8.73	3.74	0.91	1.96	0.57	0.58	3.32	1.59	0.98	4.29	0.99
Growth unexplained	0.81	0.81	-0.01	0.13	0.64	0.04	0.38	1.06	0.49	0.48	1.81	0.59	0.32	1.63	0.69
Percentage of total growth explained	71	78	100	94	93	99	71	65	54	55	65	73	75	72	59

Source: Calculated from Angus Maddison, "Growth and Slowdown in Advanced Capitalist Economies: Techniques of Quantitative Assessment," *Journal of Economic Literature* vol. 25 (June 1987) pp. 649–698, table 20.

[a] For the 1913–1950 period, the figures for Germany presumably cover both the Federal Republic of Germany and the German Democratic Republic.

3. The catch-up effect, which captures the benefits that countries other than the United States enjoyed from their relative technological backwardness and their resulting opportunities to follow the lead of the United States.

4. Structural shifts, which measure the contribution of the movement of employment from agriculture to industry and, more recently, from both agriculture and industry to services.

5. Other considerations, which include (a) the beneficial effects of the growth in foreign trade and economies of scale, (b) the stimulating effects of North Sea oil and gas development for the British economy, and (c) the adverse consequences of crime and governmental regulation as well as higher energy prices during the 1970s.

These five variables, as the bottom rows in table 3-3 indicate, together account for or explain from 54 to 100 percent of GDP growth. Although for some countries this leaves a significant portion to be explained by unidentified causes, table 3-3 provides some useful clues regarding the important factors affecting the patterns and trends in GDP growth.

Looking first at the booming 1950-1973 period and at Japan, whose economy expanded during this period at an average annual rate of over 9 percent, one finds four sets of factors largely responsible for this incredible growth: (1) an increase in the quantity and quality of labor input; (2) an increase in the quantity and quality of capital input; (3) the benefits associated with the structural effect of moving workers from agriculture to the industrial and service sectors; and (4) the opportunities associated with catching up and learning from more advanced countries.

The rapid economic growth in France and the Federal Republic of Germany, which averaged between 5 and 6 percent annually during the 1950–1973 period, was more modest than in Japan, primarily for two reasons. First, the tremendous surge in labor input that accounted for over one-quarter of Japanese economic growth was much smaller, in part because the opportunities for reducing underemployment or labor hoarding were far more modest in the Federal Republic of Germany and nonexistent in France. In addition, the quality of the labor force improved more in Japan as the average number of years of formal education increased by 2.1 years between 1950 and 1973, compared with 1.4 years for France and 0.8 years in the Federal Republic of Germany (Maddison, 1987, p. 688). Of even greater importance was the lack of growth in man-hours worked in these countries, in sharp contrast with Japan. In Japan employment grew rapidly and the hours worked annually per employee declined modestly; in France and the Federal Republic of Germany, growth in employment was slower and offset by a substantial reduction in hours worked per employee.

The second reason for slower economic growth in these two countries is simply that the other three sets of variables responsible for the boom in the Japanese economy—growth in capital input, the structural effect of moving workers from agriculture to other sectors, and the catch-up effect—were less stimulating. In particular, Japan invested much more heavily in capital during this period.

The economies of the United States and the United Kingdom, expanding at an average annual rate of between 3 and 4 percent during the 1950–1973 period, experienced the slowest growth among those of the five countries examined. With the highest per capita income and the most advanced economy in 1950, the United States was not in a position to benefit from the catch-up effect. The United Kingdom similarly received little stimulation from this source, as its economy also was relatively industrialized and advanced.

Another important factor explaining the slower growth of these two countries is the modest contribution of structural shifts. In 1950 only 13 percent of the work force in the United States and 5 percent in the United Kingdom remained in agriculture, compared with about 25 percent in France and the Federal Republic of Germany and nearly 50 percent in Japan (Maddison, 1987, p. 689). Thus, the opportunities for expanding GDP by moving workers from agriculture to industry and services were far more limited.

Finally, table 3-3 highlights an interesting difference between the United States and the United Kingdom. In the United States as in Japan, a substantial part of overall economic growth was due to growth in labor input. In the United Kingdom as in the two other European countries, this was not the case. Again, this is in part because U.S. employment grew more rapidly and in part because the hours worked per employee declined more slowly.

The decline in economic growth around 1973 affected all five countries. Japan was particularly hard hit as its economy had been expanding the fastest. The same factors that accounted for the prior rapid growth explain this slowdown. First, the rise in labor input tapered off in Japan as labor hoarding increased, employment grew more slowly, and hours worked per employee declined more rapidly. In the three European countries labor input actually declined, exerting a major drag on economic growth. Only in the United States did growth in labor input accelerate after 1973 as employment rose sufficiently to offset the greater decline in hours worked per employee.

Second, the growth in the quantity and quality of capital also declined as investment fell and the average age of the capital stock rose. Except for the United States, however, this development had a smaller negative effect on economic growth than did changes in the quantity and quality of labor.

Third, after 1973, opportunities were far more limited for moving workers from agriculture to sectors with higher labor productivity. Less than 15 percent of the work force remained in agriculture in any of these countries. Moreover, labor productivity had grown rapidly in agriculture, thus reducing the benefits of such sectoral transfers. In addition to these developments, labor in all five countries was increasingly moving into the service sector, where labor productivity rose very slowly during the 1973–1984 period. The net result was that structural shifts ceased to be a major force for growth after 1973 and even slowed growth in France, the United Kingdom, and the United States.

Finally, as the technology and per capita income gaps between the United States and the other countries narrowed, opportunities to follow the technological paths pioneered by the United States declined. As a consequence, the catch-up effect became a weaker engine for economic growth after 1973, particularly in Japan.

In addition to slowing the pace of economic growth, these developments also produced a convergence in growth rates among the five countries. Although the Japanese economy expanded the fastest over the 1973–1984 period and the economy of the United Kingdom the slowest, growth rates varied over a narrower range, from over 1 percent to not quite 4 percent. The differences that remained were largely the result of faster expansion in labor input in Japan and especially the United States, and in the greater investment in capital in Japan. Structural shifts and the catch-up effect, though much less powerful, also still fostered growth more in some countries than in others.

These findings are helpful in understanding the slowdown in GDP growth after 1973 as well as differences among the major OECD countries during the entire postwar period. However, as chapter 2 points out, the growth-accounting literature on which these findings are based identifies and analyzes the immediate or direct causes rather than the ultimate causes of GDP growth. The literature does not tell us, for example, why the average number of hours worked per employee has fallen so much more quickly in Europe than in Japan or the United States. Is there a greater craving for leisure time in Europe and for material goods in the United States and Japan? Perhaps. But differences in preferences may not be the issue at all; it may be that cultural or institutional constraints prevent one group or another from realizing an optimal mix of leisure and goods. Similarly, explaining faster growth in Japan in part on the basis of greater investment in capital only raises the question of why Japan invested more, hence is only the first step in a full explanation that would include, among other considerations, the role of monetary and fiscal policies.

It is for such reasons that higher prices of energy globally during the 1970s play a minor role in explaining the 1973 slowdown in OECD growth in Maddison's work (and in the growth-accounting literature in general), in contrast to many other analyses. The energy effect (reported in table 3-3 under "Other considerations") takes account only of the direct effects of higher energy prices. The indirect effects, however, probably are of far greater significance. In particular, the macroeconomic policies that the major industrialized countries pursued to offset the inflationary and balance-of-trade effects of sharply higher oil prices undoubtedly are an important causal factor for slower economic growth in the post-1973 period. The effects of these policies, however, are reflected in the slowdown in the growth of capital and in the rise in unemployment and underemployment that reduce labor input.

PATTERNS IN INTENSITY OF USE

GDP is one determinant of metal demand; intensity of use is the other. Like GDP, IU reflects the net effect of various forces. This section looks behind the patterns of IU shown in figures 3-3 and 3-4 and table 3-2 in an attempt to identify and assess these forces. It examines, first, differences in currency purchasing power, inventory behavior, the consumption of secondary metal, and indirect metal trade, which, as chapter 2 indicates, can pose conceptual difficulties in the measurement of IU. The section then considers the influence on IU of its two basic determinants, the material composition of products and the product composition of income.

Currency Purchasing Power

Because the aggregate purchasing power of an economy so greatly affects metal demand, it is helpful to abstract from or control for this variable when assessing the influence of other determinants. This is why intensity of metal use is a useful measure. By indicating metal consumption per constant (1980) U.S. dollar of GDP, IU controls for differences in the purchasing power of countries to the extent these differences are reflected by GDP.

Ideally, as a result, we would prefer to convert GDP data expressed in constant (1980) units of domestic currency into a common currency—in our case, constant (1980) U.S. dollars—using exchange rates that reflect parity in the purchasing power of the domestic currencies and the dollar. If, for example, five French francs in 1980 could buy a representative basket of goods and services that cost one dollar in the United States, then the purchasing power exchange rate between these two currencies would be 5 to 1. It is this rate that should be used to convert French GDP data expressed in 1980 francs into 1980 dollars.

Unfortunately, purchasing power exchange rates are difficult and costly to estimate, and only in recent years have such rates been estimated reliably. Moreover, estimates are available only for certain countries. Consequently, the GDP figures reported in the statistical appendix and used throughout this volume are converted to constant (1980) dollars using market exchange rates. These exchange rates indicate the prices at which currencies are actually bought and sold. They are influenced by central bank policies, the expectations of speculators, and all the other factors determining the overall supply and demand for currencies. Market exchange rates can fluctuate considerably over time and often deviate significantly from purchasing power parity exchange rates.

Table 3-4. Purchasing Power Parity and Market Exchange Rates for the United States, Japan, United Kingdom, France, and Federal Republic of Germany, 1980

| Country | Exchange rates (in national currency units per U.S. $) | | Difference between purchasing power parity and market exchange rates (percentage) |
	Purchasing power parity	Market	
United States	1.00	1.00	0.0
Japan	240	227	5.7
United Kingdom	0.487	0.430	13.3
France	5.24	4.23	23.9
Federal Republic of Germany	2.37	1.82	30.2

Source: Reprinted, with permission, from Michael Ward, *Purchasing Power Parities and Real Expenditures in the OECD* (Paris, OECD, 1985, table 1).

This raises the possibility that the exchange rates used in calculating GDP in constant (1980) dollars, an average of the market rates over the year 1980, do not closely reflect purchasing power parity exchange rates. In this case some of the reported differences among countries in intensity of metal use would simply reflect the fact that the GDP figures overestimate the purchasing power of some countries and underestimate that of others.

Although purchasing power parity exchange rates for 1980 are not available for all OECD countries, they do exist for the United States, Japan, the United Kingdom, France, and the Federal Republic of Germany. These rates, shown in table 3-4 along with market exchange rates for the same year and the percentage differences between the two, indicate that the dollar was substantially undervalued in 1980 in terms of its purchasing power. For the same amount of money converted at the prevailing market exchange rate, one could buy in the United States nearly 6 percent more than in Japan, over 13 percent more than in the United Kingdom, nearly 24 percent more than in France, and an amazing 30 percent more than in the Federal Republic of Germany.

To take account of these differences, we should reduce the GDP figures and increase the figures for intensity of metal use for Japan, the United Kingdom, France, and the Federal Republic by the percentages just cited. Surprisingly, doing so accentuates the more interesting intercountry differences identified earlier. The relatively low intensity of metal use in the United States, for example, becomes more pronounced. Within the EEC the high IU in the Federal Republic of Germany in recent years becomes even larger vis-à-vis that of the United Kingdom.

Adjusting for discrepancies between market and purchasing power parity exchange rates does not, it should be noted, affect trends over time in IU, such as those reported in table 3-2. Such adjustments simply shift intensity of use up or down by the same percent for all years. (This is because, as chapter 2 points out, GDP data in constant 1980 U.S. dollars are derived by using the 1980 exchange rate between the domestic currency and the U.S. dollar to convert GDP data expressed in constant 1980 units of the domestic currency.)

Inventory Behavior

Inventories of metal-containing products are held all along the production pipeline. In the case of aluminum, for example, there are stocks of bauxite, alumina, aluminum ingot, fabricated products, and final investment and consumer goods, all of which contain aluminum. IU figures, it will be recalled, reflect apparent metal consumption, determined by adding refined metal imports to domestic production and then subtracting from this total any exports and net additions to reported refined metal inventories. Consequently, the IU figures shown in table 3-2 and in figures 3-3 and 3-4 do not take into account unreported changes in refined metal inventories or changes in the metal contained in inventories of fabricated and finished goods. This raises the possibility that some of the observed trends and patterns in IU within the OECD are simply the result of inventory adjustments.

Very little information on unreported or invisible stocks, as they are sometimes called, is available precisely because they go unreported. Generally, inventory behavior is thought to have a much greater effect on short-run fluctuations in metal consumption and IU than on long-run trends. If, for example, the level of invisible stocks fell from the equivalent of six to four months of annual consumption within a year, reported IU would decline by over 15 percent, even if IU at the final stage of consumption remained unchanged. If the same decline in invisible stocks occurred over a ten-year period, however, reported IU would underestimate the average annual change in IU at the final stage of consumption by less than 2 percent.

Nevertheless, changes in inventory behavior may help explain some of the long-run trends in IU described earlier. Improved inventory control measures facilitated by the widespread introduction of computers, along with high interest rates, have provided fabricators and final goods producers with both the means and the incentives to reduce their inventories relative to consumption. It is also possible that unreported stocks in 1973, a pivotal year for our analysis, were unusual, as 1973 was a boom year for the economies of the OECD countries. Metal inventories tend to fluctuate greatly over the business cycle. The available data on reported metal stocks generally indicate that inventories decline during the upswing in the cycle and rise during the downswing, as Grubb (1981), for example, has shown for copper. Just the opposite, however, may be the case for unreported or invisible stocks, and it is the behavior of these stocks that is relevant for our purposes. Within the metal industries it is widely thought that consumers and speculators scramble to build up their holdings when final demand is rising, in anticipation of higher prices and possible shortages, and then draw down their stocks when final demand and prices are falling.

Radetzki (1977), in the one known study that estimates movements in invisible stocks over time, provides some empirical support for this speculation. Focusing on copper, he assumes that consumption at the final-goods stage of use depends on industrial production. Radetzki uses regression analysis to estimate this relationship for the OECD as a whole and for several of the more important OECD countries. With a few exceptions the results indicate that a 1 percent increase in industrial production creates slightly less than a 1 percent increase in copper consumption at the final stage of use (specifically, between 0.63 and 0.96 percent). These results are then used to estimate copper consumption at the final stage of use for the years from 1955 to 1975 for the OECD and several member countries. Radetzki assumes that differences between these figures and reported consumption, which measures demand on the part of copper fabricators, reflect changes in invisible copper stocks.

Using his findings for the years 1960 and 1973, we can assess the extent to which our estimates of copper IU are altered by taking into account changes in invisible stocks. The results, shown in table 3-5, raise the IU of copper in 1960 in the United States and lower it in Japan and the Federal Republic of Germany, bringing these three countries closer together for that year. The results also suggest that the IU of copper in the United States was actually falling rather than rising during the 1960–1973 period, whereas in Japan IU was rising faster than the reported consumption figures indicate. In the period after 1973, it appears that IU was falling more slowly in both countries than the reported figures indicated.

It is important, however, to stress the tentative nature of these findings. As Radetzki (1977, p. 12) points out, his simple two-variable regression "causes the emerging error term [i.e., the difference between his estimates of consumption and the reported figures] to catch not only the invisible stock movement, but also a variety of other influences not considered in the regression. It should be clear, therefore, that the error term will not provide any precise measure, but only a rough approximation of the invisible stock change." In addition, his findings pertain only to copper. As a result, we are left wishing that more information on invisible stock movements were available. Such movements may significantly alter the patterns and trends of IU derived from available reported consumption, but there is as yet little hard evidence to indicate that this in fact is the case.

Consumption of Secondary Metal

Another variable that may affect IU is consumption of secondary metal. As chapter 2 points out, to reflect IU at the final stage of use, that is, on the part of the consumers of final goods, consumption should include secondary

Table 3-5. Intensity of Use (IU) of Copper, Including and Excluding Estimated Changes in Invisible Stocks, for the United States, Japan, United Kingdom, France, Federal Republic of Germany, and OECD, 1960, 1973, and 1987

Area or country	IU level (tons per million 1980 U.S.$)			IU growth (average annual percentage)	
	1960	1973	1987	1960–1973	1973–1987[a]
United States					
Excluding invisible stocks	0.89	0.96	0.66	0.59	−2.69
Including invisible stocks	0.99	0.89	N.A.	−0.86	−2.13
Japan					
Excluding invisible stocks	1.23	1.47	0.94	1.37	−3.13
Including invisible stocks	1.02	1.31	N.A.	1.92	−2.43
United Kingdom					
Excluding invisible stocks	1.65	1.07	0.52	−3.28	−4.99
Including invisible stocks[b]	N.A.	1.05	N.A.	−3.40	−4.87
France					
Excluding invisible stocks	0.89	0.76	0.55	−1.23	−2.20
Including invisible stocks	0.85	0.72	N.A.	−1.24	−1.89
Federal Republic of Germany					
Excluding invisible stocks	1.32	1.04	0.88	−1.77	−1.17
Including invisible stocks	1.18	1.02	N.A.	−1.10	−1.00
OECD					
Excluding invisible stocks	1.04	0.99	0.72	−0.41	−2.21
Including invisible stocks	1.03	0.93	N.A.	−0.75	−1.84

Notes: Estimates of changes in invisible stocks are from Marian Radetzki, "Fluctuations in Invisible Stocks: A Problem for Copper Market Forecasting," World Bank Commodity Paper no. 27 (Washington, D.C., World Bank, 1977). See text of this chapter for an explanation of how these changes were estimated.
N.A. = not available.
Sources: Statistical appendix in this volume and Radetzki (1977).
[a]Since no estimates of changes in invisible stocks are available for 1987, changes for that year were assumed to be zero in calculating the growth rates of IU including invisible stocks over the 1973–1987 period.
[b]Since the procedure used to estimate changes in invisible stocks in other countries performed poorly in the case of the United Kingdom, Radetzki used an alternative approach for that country. No estimates were provided for 1960, so the growth of IU including invisible stocks during the 1960–1973 period for the United Kingdom assumes that no change in invisible stocks occurred in that country in 1960.

metal produced from old, not new, scrap. Old scrap used directly as well as that passing through the refining process should be considered.

Unfortunately, for none of the metals examined is secondary consumption so treated. For steel, as chapter 2 notes, consumption encompasses all secondary metal except home scrap (a portion of new scrap) and so tends to overestimate the IU at the final stage of consumption. Data for the United States (U.S. Bureau of Mines, 1989, p. 84) suggest that the removal of all new scrap would show a reduced IU of steel in recent years of roughly 15 percent.

For copper the available consumption data include refined metal produced from both new and old scrap and exclude all secondary metal produced directly from scrap. In the United States, where again the desired data are available, secondary production from the direct use of old scrap historically has exceeded the production of refined copper from new scrap. As a consequence the reported figures tend to understate the IU of copper at the final stage of consumption. This underestimation was about 17 percent in 1960, 5 percent in 1973, and 12 percent in 1984 (Hutchison and Tilton, 1987).

The reported figures also understate IU on the part of final consumers for aluminum, nickel, and zinc, as the consumption data for these metals exclude all secondary production; just the opposite is true for lead. For aluminum, secondary production data over several years are available for the United States, Japan, the United Kingdom, France, and the Federal Republic of Germany, allowing us to assess how the IU of aluminum use for these countries is altered.

The results, shown in table 3-6, indicate that secondary consumption substantially increases the IU level of aluminum, in many instances by 30 percent or more. The relative rankings of individual countries, however, are not altered. Intensity of aluminum use in the United States, Japan, and the Federal Republic of Germany in recent years is high relative to the other two countries whether or not secondary consumption is taken into account. However, some of the decline in the growth of IU of primary aluminum in these three countries since 1973 can be attributed to the rising IU of secondary aluminum.

Because the secondary figures shown in table 3-6 include aluminum produced from new as well as old scrap, the total figures do not reflect IU at the final stage of consumption. IU at this stage of consumption, it will be recalled, includes only secondary metal produced from old scrap, data for which unfortunately are not available for many countries. IU at the final stage of consumption consequently lies somewhere between the primary and total figures shown in this table. In the United States about one-half of the secondary aluminum produced in recent years has been made from new scrap (U.S. Bureau of Mines, 1989, p. 12). In earlier years, however, new scrap was of greater relative importance. Assuming that the same holds true for other countries, the figures shown in table 3-6 for primary aluminum more closely approximate IU at the final stage of consumption than do those for total aluminum.

Indirect Metal Trade

Another source of distortion between the available figures and IU at the final stage of consumption is indirect metal trade. Reported consumption takes into account net imports of refined or unwrought metal but not imports or exports of metal contained in fabricated and finished goods. As a result the IU levels of countries such as the United States and the United Kingdom, which import a significant portion of their automobiles and other metal-intensive final goods, may be understated; the opposite may be the case for countries such as Japan and the Federal Republic of Germany, which on balance export such products.

Table 3-6. Intensity of Use (IU) of Aluminum for Primary and Secondary Metal Consumption for the United States, Japan, United Kingdom, France, and Federal Republic of Germany, 1960, 1973, and 1987

Country	IU level (tons per million 1980 U.S.$)			IU growth (average annual percentage)	
	1960	1973	1987	1960–1973	1973–1987
United States					
Primary	1.12	2.20	1.39	5.3	−3.2
Secondary	0.30	0.50	0.62	4.0	1.5
Total	1.42	2.70	2.01	5.1	−2.1
Japan					
Primary	0.61	1.97	1.50	9.5	−1.9
Secondary	0.21	0.45	0.58	6.0	1.9
Total	0.82	2.42	2.09	8.7	−1.0
United Kingdom					
Primary	1.06	0.97	0.61	−0.7	−3.2
Secondary	0.37	0.39	0.13	0.4	−7.6
Total	1.43	1.36	0.74	−0.4	−4.2
France					
Primary	0.80	0.83	0.85	0.4	0.2
Secondary	0.10	0.25	0.28	7.3	0.9
Total	0.90	1.08	1.14	1.5	0.3
Federal Republic of Germany					
Primary	0.80	1.23	1.31	3.4	0.5
Secondary	0.29	0.41	0.57	2.7	2.4
Total	1.09	1.64	1.88	3.2	1.0

Sources: Statistical appendix in this volume and *Metal Statistics* (Frankfurt am Main, Metallgesellschaft Aktiengesellschaft, various years).

Estimating the metal contained in indirect trade is both difficult and laborious. In what is perhaps a unique set of studies in this area, the International Iron and Steel Institute (1982, 1985) has assessed indirect steel trade for a number of countries for selected years between 1962 and 1982. The procedure employed by the Institute involves multiplying the volume of exports or imports for particular commodities, obtained from national trade statistics and measured in tons, by a coefficient reflecting the portion of each commodity's total weight accounted for by the steel consumed in its manufacture, including the scrap generated. Individual coefficients for a wide variety of steel-containing products were estimated by a group of experts.

Table 3-7, which is based on the Institute's analyses, shows how the level and growth of the IU of steel is altered when indirect steel trade is taken into account. For the United States, including indirect steel trade makes very little difference. This is somewhat surprising, as this country is a major importer of automobiles and other metal-intensive goods and a major exporter of agricultural products and high-technology goods whose production requires relatively less metal input. Apparently, however, the steel contained in the automobiles and other products coming from abroad is roughly equal to that

Table 3-7. Intensity of Use (IU) of Steel, Including and Excluding Indirect Steel Trade, for the United States, Japan, EEC, United Kingdom, France, and Federal Republic of Germany, 1962, 1973, and 1982

	IU level (tons per million 1980 U.S.$)			IU growth (average annual percentage)	
Area or country	1962	1973	1982	1962–1973	1973–1982
United States					
Excluding indirect trade	63.2	67.1	32.2	0.54	−7.81
Including indirect trade	62.8	68.3	32.9	0.78	−7.79
Japan					
Excluding indirect trade	76.8	107.1	61.1	3.06	−6.05
Including indirect trade	72.8	95.6	48.4	2.50	−7.28
EEC					
Excluding indirect trade	54.3	52.9	32.6	−0.23	−5.23
Including indirect trade	49.2	48.1	27.3	−0.21	−6.08
United Kingdom					
Excluding indirect trade	50.1	49.6	26.9	−0.10	−6.57
Including indirect trade	40.0	42.8	24.9	0.62	−5.84
France					
Excluding indirect trade	49.2	46.8	25.7	−0.45	−6.47
Including indirect trade	46.6	43.8	23.7	−0.57	−6.58
Federal Republic of Germany					
Excluding indirect trade	63.9	58.0	34.4	−0.88	−5.63
Including indirect trade	55.9	48.7	24.6	−1.26	−7.29

Note: IU including indirect steel trade is estimated on the basis of information found in the sources.

Sources: Statistical appendix in this volume; International Iron and Steel Institute, Indirect Trade in Steel—1962 to 1979 (Brussels, IISI, 1982); ibid., Indirect Trade in Steel, 1982 (Brussels, IISI, 1985).

contained in machinery and other exports destined for less developed countries and other foreign states.

For Japan, however, the story is quite different. Taking into account indirect steel trade greatly reduces that country's intensity of steel use. Indeed, close to one-half of the substantial difference in recent years between the intensity of steel use in Japan and the United States can be attributed to Japan's exports of steel-intensive products. Adjusting for indirect steel trade also reduces the growth in Japanese IU of steel over the 1962–1973 period and accelerates its decline after 1973, again moving these figures closer to those for the United States.

For the EEC, indirect steel trade also causes important changes. The IU level declines, somewhat more modestly in recent years than in Japan but still appreciably. These changes, however, widen the gap between the IU of steel in the EEC, on the one hand, and in the United States and Japan, on the other.

The work of the International Iron and Steel Institute, it should be noted, does suffer from the fact that the coefficients reflecting the ratio of the steel content to total weight of traded goods have not been updated since 1962, in part to maintain consistency over time. It also would be helpful to have similar studies for other metals. Nonetheless, the figures in table 3-7 indicate that indirect metal trade can be a very important determinant of IU. Indeed, along with differences in the purchasing power of currencies, it is probably the most important of the variables so far considered.

Basic Determinants of Patterns in Intensity of Use

So far we have examined only idiosyncrasies of the reported data that introduce distortions between IU levels at the fabrication stage and at the final stage of consumption. At the final stage, as noted in chapter 2, the trends and patterns in IU are shaped by two basic determinants, the material composition of products and the product composition of income.

In the 1970s the International Iron and Steel Institute (1972), Malenbaum (1973, 1975, 1978), and others emphasized changes in the product composition of income resulting from intersectoral shifts in the economy as the principal cause of changes in IU. At early stages of economic development, they argued, countries increase their IU as growth occurs and per capita income rises. Growth involves the freeing of resources from agriculture for the construction of industrial plants, homes, roads, automobiles, and other material-intensive products. Eventually, however, as per capita income continues to rise, demand shifts toward services, which are less material-intensive, and this sector expands at the expense of the construction and manufacturing sectors. This is the basic rationale for the inverted U-shaped behavioral relationship that these investigators maintained exists between intensity of metal use and per capita income. Moreover, as noted in chapter 2, this is the critical assumption of the IU hypothesis they introduced and used for long-run forecasts of metal consumption.

By the mid-1980s Roberts (1985, 1986), Myers (1986), Auty (1985), Tilton (1986), and others were challenging this view, arguing instead that changes in the material composition of products—the result of material substitution and technological change—were the primary driving force behind changes in IU. In examining copper consumption in the United States, for example, Roberts (1985) found that the adverse effect on IU of the rise in the service sector was more than offset by the simultaneous rise in the metal-intensive durable goods sector. The IU of copper, he concluded, is falling as a result of the replacement of copper by other materials and the introduction of new copper-saving technology.

The product composition of income could still be important, however, as a result of intrasectoral shifts in the economy. Castro (1986), for example, suggests that the rising share of value added in the manufacturing sector accounted for by computers, instruments, and other high-technology products whose use of metals and other traditional materials per dollar of value added is low, contributed to the decline in the IU of tin after 1973.

In addition, Roberts (1988), using a variant of the IU technique described in chapter 2 to analyze world metal consumption, concludes that the product composition of income was primarily responsible for the changes in IU trends that contributed to the break in metal demand growth in the mid-1970s. Aluminum was the only exception he found among the metals considered in this volume. On the basis of this finding and his earlier work (Roberts, 1985, 1986), he suggests that the material composition of products may be largely responsible for long-run trends in IU, whereas the product composition of income accounts for most of the deviations around the long-run trends.

To resolve this issue, we would like to know how the output of individual products relative to GDP and how the material inputs used in the manufacture of these products have evolved over time (that is, we would like to know how the a_{it}'s and the b_{it}'s in equation (4) of chapter 2 have changed). This information could be obtained for some products, but it is not feasible to do so for all the goods produced by the economy. An alternative and more manageable approach is to examine the important factors causing the material composition of products to evolve over time or to vary among countries. If these factors themselves display considerable change over time and variation among countries, and if the resulting effects are reinforcing, then the material composition of products is presumably an important determinant of IU. A comparable inquiry into the forces governing the product composition of income similarly permits an assessment of the importance of this variable.

MATERIAL COMPOSITION OF PRODUCTS

The mix of materials used to produce specific goods evolves over time in response to new resource-saving technology and material substitution. Similarly, discrepancies among countries in the material composition of products can be attributed to differences in the pace with which they adopt resource-saving technology and carry out material substitution. This section first examines the influence of these two determinants on the material composition of products and then considers the extent to which they in turn are influenced by material prices, technology, and other considerations.

Resource-Saving Technology and Material Substitution

Resource-saving technology and material substitution have produced substantial shifts in the material composition of products, with important implications for the intensity of metal use, according to input–output studies. Myers (1986), for example, using input–output tables for the United States for the years 1972 and 1977, finds substantial shifts in the proportion of each dollar of final demand that many metal-using industries spend directly and indirectly on steel, aluminum, copper, lead, and zinc. For example, expenditures on steel by the motor vehicle industry fell from 14.9 to 12.6 cents per dollar of final demand, a 16 percent drop in only five years. Expenditures by the metal can industry on steel declined from 44.5 to 37.3 cents per dollar, again a 16 percent drop. Although shifts in the mix of goods produced by these industries may account for some of the change in input–output coefficients occurring over time, most of the change presumably is the result of material substitution and resource-saving technology.

Support for this conclusion is provided by a variety of case studies of material use in specific applications. The packaging industry, which Nappi analyzes in some detail in chapter 7 in this volume, provides a particularly striking illustration of the importance of material substitution and resource-saving technology. As table 7-3 in that chapter indicates, the amount of aluminum required to produce a typical 12-ounce beverage can fell by over 15 percent between 1964 and 1973 and has fallen by nearly an additional 20 percent since 1973 as a result of the introduction of thinner aluminum sheet and other aluminum-saving innovations. This dramatic and adverse development for the use of aluminum, however, has been offset by the growing substitution of aluminum for tinplate and glass in the production of beer and soft drink containers. The aluminum beverage can, first introduced in 1963, is now used to ship 63 percent of the beer and 31 percent of the soft drinks sold in the United States (see tables 7-3 and 7-4). As a result, a substantial shift in the material composition of beverage containers in favor of aluminum has taken place in the United States.

Although beverage containers are but one of many end uses for aluminum, this substitution has significantly altered the overall demand for this metal in the United States. In 1960, prior to the introduction of the aluminum beverage can, the intensity of aluminum use was 1.12 tons per million (1980) dollars of GDP. It reached 2.20 tons in 1973 before falling back to 1.39 tons by 1987. However, as table 3-8 shows, without the replacement of tinplate and glass by aluminum in beverage containers, the IU of aluminum use would have reached only 2.10 tons in 1973 and would then have fallen much more sharply, to 1.01 tons by 1987.

Chapter 7 also indicates that the penetration of the aluminum can in the beverage container market has generally proceeded more slowly outside the United States. As noted earlier, it has captured 63 percent of the beer container market and 31 percent of the soft drink container market in that country. The corresponding figures are 15 and 9 percent in Japan and about 3 and 8 percent in Western Europe (see tables 7-6 and 7-10). As a result, aluminum producers outside the United States have been far less successful in offsetting the adverse effects of new aluminum-saving innovations in the manufacture of beverage cans and in stimulating the intensity of aluminum use.

Table 3-8. Intensity of Use (IU) of Aluminum, Including and Excluding Aluminum in Beverage Cans, for the United States, Japan, United Kingdom, France, and Federal Republic of Germany, 1960, 1973, and 1987

Country	IU level (tons per million 1980 U.S.$)[a]			IU growth (average annual percentage)	
	1960	1973	1987	1960–1973	1973–1987
United States					
Including beverage cans	1.12	2.20	1.39	5.31	−3.19
Excluding beverage cans	1.12	2.10	1.01	4.95	−4.22
Japan					
Including beverage cans	0.61	1.97	1.50	9.45	−1.90
Excluding beverage cans[b]	0.61	1.95	1.47	9.39	−1.66
United Kingdom					
Including beverage cans	1.06	0.97	0.61	−0.67	−3.20
Excluding beverage cans[b]	1.06	0.97	0.56	−0.67	−3.21
France					
Including beverage cans	0.80	0.83	0.85	0.35	0.17
Excluding beverage cans[b]	0.80	0.83	0.85	0.35	0.14
Federal Republic of Germany					
Including beverage cans	0.80	1.23	1.31	3.37	0.47
Excluding beverage cans[b]	0.80	1.23	1.30	3.37	0.34

Sources: Statistical appendix and chapter 7, tables 7-3 through 7-6 and discussion thereof, in this volume.

[a]IU figures are for primary metal only.

[b]The aluminum contained in beverage cans for Japan, the United Kingdom, France, and the Federal Republic of Germany for 1973 and 1987 was estimated on the basis of information contained in the sources for this table.

These differences in the pace with which material substitution in beverage containers has taken place help explain an anomaly noted earlier—namely, the relatively high IU of aluminum in the United States compared with other countries, in contrast to the IU of steel, copper, nickel, lead, and zinc. As table 3-8 indicates, had aluminum not penetrated the beverage container market so much faster and more extensively in the United States, that country's intensity of aluminum use in 1987 would have been much lower than that of Japan or the Federal Republic of Germany and considerably closer to the levels for France and the United Kingdom.

The use of metals within Europe for roofing, gutters, and drainpipes provides another interesting example of intercountry differences in material substitution. The metal of preference is zinc in France and the northern part of the Federal Republic of Germany, lead in the United Kingdom, and copper in the southern part of the Federal Republic of Germany and Italy. According to the Commodity Research Unit (1985, pp. 21–22), the United Kingdom consumed 83,000 tons of lead sheet in 1984, some 70 percent of which was used for the cladding and roofing of buildings. By comparison, the Commodity Research Unit estimates the consumption of lead sheet at only 12,300 tons in the United States; 16,000 tons in Japan; 11,600 tons in France; and

Table 3-9. Intensity of Use (IU) of Copper, Lead, and Zinc in the United States, Japan, United Kingdom, France, and Federal Republic of Germany, 1987

Country	IU level (tons per million 1980 U.S.$)		
	Copper	Lead	Zinc
United States	0.66	0.37	0.32
Japan	0.94	0.28	0.53
United Kingdom	0.52	0.46	0.30
France	0.55	0.29	0.34
Federal Republic of Germany	0.88	0.38	0.50

Source: Statistical appendix in this volume.

37,000 tons in the Federal Republic of Germany. These figures suggest that some 20 percent of total lead consumption in the United Kingdom goes into roofing, which helps explain why that country has the highest intensity of lead use among the countries shown in table 3-9. Similarly, the preference for zinc roofing in France and for zinc and copper roofing in the Federal Republic of Germany helps explain their relatively high intensities of use for these metals.

Many other case studies of material use in specific industries, including studies of the automobile industry (see chapter 6 in this volume), the pipe industry (Gill, 1983), the solder industry (Canavan, 1983), and the telecommunications industry (Key and Schlabach, 1986), provide additional evidence of the important role that resource-saving technology and material substitution play in shaping the material composition of products and, in turn, the intensity of metal use. In general, the importance of these two activities is not in dispute.

Material Prices and Technology

Somewhat greater controversy and confusion surround our understanding of the role of material prices and other determinants of material substitution and resource-saving technology. In most economic analyses a commodity's own price and those of close substitutes play a central role in determining its demand. Prices are almost always included in the specification of demand functions, and the widely used demand curve focuses exclusively on the relationship between the demand for a good and its own price. The theory of the firm and the theory of consumer behavior also highlight the role of price.

The conceptual framework provided by the IU technique, as chapter 2 points out, allows material prices to play the pivotal role in the formation of demand envisaged by economic theory and the traditional demand function. They must do so, however, by influencing the material composition of products, as their influence on GDP and the product composition of income is negligible. A rise in the price of copper, for example, may induce the substitution of alternative materials for copper or encourage research and development of new copper-saving technologies, but it is not likely to alter GDP growth or even the number of new housing starts.

Confusion and controversy arise not because the IU technique is ill-equipped to analyze the role of prices but rather because the empirical evidence shows no simple, direct, and central role for prices. Table 3-10, for example, compares growth trends in real metal prices and IU over the 1960–1973 period and the 1973–1987 period. A strong link between the two, indicating that IU rises more rapidly (or falls more slowly) when real prices are declining (and vice versa), is difficult to discern. Such a link is apparent only for those metals—namely, steel, aluminum, and lead—whose real prices rose more rapidly or declined more slowly after 1973. For the other three metals, a switch from rising to declining real prices is associated with declining growth in IU.

Moreover, as table 3-10 indicates, there are substantial differences among OECD countries in growth rates of IU that are difficult to explain in terms of prices, as prices have largely followed similar trends in all the OECD countries. Although tariff and other trade barriers do exist among these countries, they generally do not give rise to major differences in metal prices. To build up Japan's domestic aluminum smelting industry during the 1960s and early 1970s, for example, the Japanese government provided protection for domestic producers that kept the Japanese price of aluminum ingot 10 to 15 percent above the prevailing world price (Goto, 1988). Such differences, however, are quite modest compared to those found in India and other developing countries, as chapter 4 (in this volume) discusses. Moreover, if the level of protection and the resulting differences in prices among countries remain relatively constant over time, growth rates in real prices are unaffected by such differences.

The data shown in table 3-10 and our analysis of them suffer, it should be recognized, from several shortcomings. Some prices are producer prices and may not reflect the true transaction costs. Prices in 1973 were unusually high for many metals, so using this year to divide the 1960–1987 period tends to bias the growth in prices upward before 1973 and downward after 1973. As noted, prices may also vary somewhat among countries.

Moreover, economic theory does not claim that a commodity's own price is the only variable determining its demand. Perhaps if we controlled for other important determinants and particularly for the prices of close substitutes, a simple, direct link between IU and metal demand, on the one hand, and real metal prices, on the other, would be clearer.

Yet, further reflection upon the way in which prices actually affect metal demand suggests that this is highly improbable. One advantage of the IU technique is that it forces us to move beyond the traditional theory of the firm where neat, continuous demand curves for factor inputs such as metals

Table 3-10. Growth of Real Metal Prices and Intensity of Use (IU) in the OECD, United States, Japan, EEC, United Kingdom, France, and Federal Republic of Germany, 1960–1973 and 1973–1987

(average annual percentage change)

Metal	1960–1973	1973–1987
Steel		
Price	−0.41	0.94
Intensity of use		
OECD	0.34	−4.22
United States	−0.09	−5.07
Japan	2.35	−4.55
EEC	−0.97	−3.87
United Kingdom	−2.08	−5.05
France	−0.70	−5.71
Federal Republic of Germany	−1.82	−4.12
Aluminum		
Price	−3.38	2.24
Intensity of use		
OECD	4.53	−1.59
United States	5.31	−3.19
Japan	9.45	−1.90
EEC	2.16	0.02
United Kingdom	−0.67	−3.20
France	0.35	0.17
Federal Republic of Germany	3.37	0.47
Copper		
Price	1.08	−3.82
Intensity of use		
OECD	−0.41	−2.21
United States	0.59	−2.69
Japan	1.37	−3.13
EEC	−2.15	−1.52
United Kingdom	−3.28	−4.99
France	−1.23	−2.20
Federal Republic of Germany	−1.77	−1.17
Nickel		
Price	2.00	−0.91
Intensity of use		
OECD	1.51	−1.45
United States	0.77	−4.19
Japan	5.26	−1.49
EEC	0.08	−0.20
United Kingdom	−2.08	−1.18
France	−2.14	−0.04
Federal Republic of Germany	2.27	0.95

Table 3-10 (continued)

Metal	1960–1973	1973–1987
Lead		
Price	−1.22	−0.52
Intensity of use		
OECD	−1.45	−1.56
United States	0.04	−1.75
Japan	−1.61	−1.18
EEC	−2.39	−1.39
United Kingdom	−3.13	−1.39
France	−3.20	−2.25
Federal Republic of Germany	−2.81	−0.72
Zinc		
Price	−0.01	−1.12
Intensity of use		
OECD	0.26	−3.20
United States	0.20	−4.20
Japan	3.85	−4.36
EEC	−1.15	−2.47
United Kingdom	−2.26	−4.88
France	−1.38	−3.16
Federal Republic of Germany	−1.41	−1.63

Notes: Steel prices are average annual *Iron Age* composite prices; aluminum prices are average U.K. producer prices for 99.5 percent ingot; copper prices are London Metal Exchange cash quotes for electrolytic copper in the form of wirebars; nickel prices are average U.K. producer prices for refined nickel; and zinc prices are LME cash quotes for standard zinc, minimum 99.8 percent. Lead prices are average U.S. producer, common grade. All prices were converted into constant (1980) dollars.

Sources: Statistical appendix in this volume; *Metal Statistics* (Frankfurt am Main, Metallgesellschaft Aktiengesellschaft, various issues); U.S. Bureau of Mines, *Mineral Facts and Problems, 1975* (Washington, D.C., U.S. Government Printing Office, 1976); U.S. Bureau of Mines, *Mineral Facts and Problems, 1980* (Washington, D.C., U.S. Government Printing Office, 1981); U.S. Bureau of Mines, *Mineral Commodity Summaries* (Washington, D.C., U.S. Government Printing Office, various years).

are derived on the basis of stable and continuous production isoquants. The technique highlights the fact that prices affect metal demand by altering the material composition of products, either by causing the substitution of one material for another or by inducing resource-saving technology.

In the case of material substitution, three different situations can be distinguished. In the first, the replacement of one material for another can be accomplished quickly with little or no cost for new capital, worker retraining, or lost production time. In building new homes, for example, contractors can switch back and forth easily and quickly among wood, aluminum, and plastic siding to take advantage of changes in their relative prices.

In the second situation the necessary technology for material substitution exists, but the changeover does involve considerable transition costs. The automobile radiator, produced largely from brass in Japan and the United States, for example, could be made out of aluminum. Indeed, as chapter 6 points out, this is the case in Europe. This substitution, however, would entail considerable cost, not only because the equipment now used to produce brass radiators would have to be scrapped but also because workers would have to be retrained, including thousands involved in radiator maintenance and repair.

In the third situation the changing of material prices encourages research and development and eventually the introduction of new technologies that permit material substitutions that previously were not possible. The surge in cobalt prices in the late 1970s caused by market disruptions following the invasion of the Shaba province of Zaire, for example, stimulated the search for substitutes in the production of magnets and other end uses. Although these efforts took time to produce results, by the early 1980s the use of alternative metals was significantly undermining the demand for cobalt in magnet production and many other traditional end uses.

Although we still have much to learn about the nature of material substitution, and in particular about the effects of changing prices on this activity, the available in-depth case studies of material substitution, such as those by Canavan (1983), Demler (1980), and Gill (1983), reveal that the material substitution made possible by new technology—that is, the third type of material substitution—is the most prevalent and has the greatest effect on long-run metal demand. Thus, material prices may largely affect metal demand indirectly via their influence on the direction of research and development and the course of new technology.

Moreover, even in the first two situations where price does have a direct effect, a simple monotonic relationship between price, on the one hand, and IU and metal demand, on the other, seems unlikely. We would rather expect that changes in price would have little effect over a given range but that once a certain threshold was breached, making substitution attractive and covering any changeover costs, an entire end use would be lost; this would have possibly severe effects on total demand.

In the case of resource-saving technology, prices clearly can affect metal demand only indirectly via their influence on innovative activity. Here, as with the third type of material substitution, the effect on metal demand of a change in material prices is both uncertain and highly variable, depending on the outcome of the induced research and development effort, and occurs only after a time lag that also is highly variable.

The foregoing discussion suggests that the relationship between metal prices and demand is highly complex in these respects:

1. The effect of a price change on demand is not likely to be uniform over time or even between similar situations at the same time, as much of this effect is likely to be realized through induced technological change. The uncertainty associated with the generation and commercialization of new technology is well known.

2. For the same reasons, the lag or gestation period between a change in

price and its effect on metal demand is uncertain and likely to vary greatly from one situation to another.

3. The relationship between prices and demand probably is not continuous but rather punctuated by jumps or breaks at particularly important threshold levels of price.

4. The relationship may not be reversible; that is, the decline in demand caused by resource-saving new technology induced by higher prices cannot usually be recaptured when prices return to their original levels.

5. The level of a metal's price may be as important as, or more important than, changes in that level in encouraging new resource-saving technologies or new material-substitution technologies.

6. In many metal applications different vintages of production equipment are used—some new, others old, each embodying the most appropriate technology of its day, which in turn reflects the resource-saving and material-substitution opportunities and the material prices then prevailing. In such situations, current metal demand depends on current and past metal prices, each weighted by that portion of existing production capacity currently in use which they influenced.

These complexities do not diminish the importance of material prices on the formation of metal demand. They do, however, suggest that we should not be surprised when empirical efforts fail to demonstrate a simple, direct, and central role for prices. Indeed, they caution us to question theories that postulate such a relationship and empirical studies that claim to demonstrate its existence. The role of prices in the formation of metal demand is important, but it is also complicated and poorly understood.

Our knowledge of material substitution and resource-saving technology also suggests the likelihood that technological change actually plays a more direct and central role in the determination of IU and metal demand than do prices. More attention, it would seem, needs to be focused on this important activity in our efforts to analyze long-run metal demand.

Finally, the case studies of material consumption in end-using industries (such as those in chapters 6 and 7) identify a host of other variables that influence IU and metal demand, including demographics, changing consumer tastes, and a plethora of government policies and regulations. The effects of such variables also need to be taken into account if trends and patterns in the material composition of products are to be understood.

PRODUCT COMPOSITION OF INCOME

The product composition of income, which is the mix of goods and services consumed by the economy, can change over time as a result of either shifts among economic sectors, such as the rise of the service sector, or shifts within sectors, such as the growth of computers and other high-technology goods within the manufacturing sector. Similarly, both intersectoral and intrasectoral differences can cause the product composition of income to vary among countries.

Intersectoral Trends and Patterns

The prevailing view of the 1970s, as pointed out earlier, focused on sectoral shifts as the primary cause of intercountry differences and intertemporal trends in the intensity of metal use. In particular, as per capita income rose, shifting preferences were thought to cause the agricultural sector to decline and the manufacturing and construction sectors to rise relative to the total economy, and then eventually were thought to cause the latter sectors to stagnate as the service sector expanded. By the mid-1980s, however, this view was being called into question and the importance of sectoral shifts discounted, largely on the basis of the U.S. experience.

A more encompassing look at the OECD as a whole and at other important OECD countries, however, suggests that it may be premature to dismiss the influence of sectoral shifts on the intensity of metal use. From what has preceded, we know several facts:

1. The intensity of metal use in general is high in Japan and the Federal Republic of Germany and low in the United States and the United Kingdom. The major exception is aluminum, whose IU is relatively high in the United States largely as a result of the widespread use of aluminum for beverage containers.

2. The growth in IU slowed after 1973 for all the metals examined and actually declined in many instances.

3. The use of metals is concentrated in four major areas: capital equipment, construction, consumer durables, and transportation (particularly the automobile industry). Again, aluminum is something of an anomaly in this respect, in light of its extensive use in the packaging industry. Yet even in the United States, transportation, mechanical and electrical engineering, building and construction, and household goods account for about two-thirds of the domestic consumption of aluminum (Metallgesellschaft Aktiengesellschaft, various years). As a result, gross domestic investment and manufacturing presumably have a greater intensity of metal use per dollar of value added than does the service sector or GDP in general—an expectation that input–output analyses such as that of Roberts (1985) tend to support.

In light of these considerations, a simple test of the prevailing view of the 1970s is possible. If the sectoral composition of the economy is an important determinant of the product composition of income and in turn of the intensity of metal use, then gross domestic investment and manufacturing should

Table 3-11. Gross Domestic Investment and the Manufacturing and Services Sectors as a Percentage of GDP for the OECD, United States, Japan, EEC, United Kingdom, France, and Federal Republic of Germany, 1960, 1973, and 1986

Sector and area or country	Percentage of GDP			Growth (average annual percentage)	
	1960	1973	1986	1960–1973	1973–1986
Gross domestic investment					
OECD	22	26	22	1.29	−1.29
United States	19	22	18	0.91	−1.60
Japan	24	38	32	3.81	−1.28
EEC	23	25	21	0.61	−1.22
United Kingdom	19	22	19	1.34	−1.33
France	23	27	21	1.31	−1.84
Federal Republic of Germany	28	26	20	−0.49	−1.83
Manufacturing					
OECD	21	27	23	1.87	−1.00
United States	23	26	23	0.89	−1.06
Japan	22	32	34	3.13	0.38
EEC	24	28	25	1.15	−0.92
United Kingdom	28	28	22	−0.08	−1.76
France	23	30	22	1.99	−2.23
Federal Republic of Germany	37	41	32	0.68	−1.93
Services					
OECD	39	46	55	1.23	1.43
United States	48	51	65	0.53	1.83
Japan	43	48	53	0.88	0.72
EEC	40	45	57	0.84	1.88
United Kingdom	50	54	49	0.60	−0.71
France	39	41	67	0.28	3.88
Federal Republic of Germany	38	38	60	−0.01	3.68

Sources: Statistical appendix in this volume.

account for a smaller portion of total GDP (and services a larger portion) in the United States and the United Kingdom than in Japan and the Federal Republic of Germany. This would help explain the lower IU in the first two countries. We would also expect the growth of gross domestic investment (GDI) and manufacturing relative to total GDP prior to 1973 to exceed their growth after 1973, and for the opposite to be the case for the service sector. In contrast, if the sectoral composition of the economy is unimportant, there is no reason to expect either of these developments.

As table 3-11 indicates, both expectations for the most part are confirmed by the data. The United States and the United Kingdom do devote a relatively low portion of their GDP to GDI and manufacturing and a relatively high portion to services. In the case of the United Kingdom, the declining contribution of manufacturing is in part the result of rising North Sea oil production, which by itself reduced the relative importance of the manufacturing sector. In addition, oil exports made it harder for British manufacturers to compete by raising the value of the pound relative to other currencies.

It is also clear that the growth in the share of GDP accounted for by GDI and manufacturing has slowed for the OECD as a whole and for all its major members since 1973. Indeed, with few exceptions the share of GDP devoted to these activities has actually declined. Simultaneously, the portion of GDP devoted to services generally has continued to expand since 1973, in a number of countries at an accelerated pace.

The large manufacturing sector in Japan and the Federal Republic of Germany reflects to some extent, of course, the propensity of these countries to export automobiles and other metal-intensive manufactured goods to the rest of the world, as discussed earlier. If these indirect metal exports could be accounted for, the relatively high intensities of use in these countries would be more modest, as presumably would be the share of their GDP devoted to manufacturing. Similarly, the size of the service sector in the United States and the United Kingdom may reflect exports as well as domestic preferences. Nevertheless, these findings raise a flag of caution, warning us not to discount the mix of economic sectors in our effort to understand long-run metal demand, as was the tendency in the mid-1980s.

Intrasectoral Trends and Patterns

A second reason for suspecting that the product composition of income is an important determinant of long-run metal demand is the shifting mix of goods within individual sectors and, in particular, within the manufacturing sector. Attention in this regard has focused on the rise of high-technology products, primarily in the United States where data are most readily available.

Castro (1988), for example, estimates that ten high-technology industries increased their share of total manufacturing output in the United States from 8 to 21 percent between 1963 and 1982. Table 3-12, which is from Castro's study, identifies the ten industries and shows the extent of their growth over time.

In a somewhat similar endeavor, Lawrence (1984) calculates the value-added shares of the U.S. manufacturing sector for four groups of products—high technology, capital intensive, labor intensive, and resource intensive—for several years between 1960 and 1980. His results, presented in table 3-13, show the share of high-technology products rising from 27 to 38 percent between 1960 and 1980, with more than one-half of this increase after 1973. Although about one-fifth of this growth can be ascribed to an increase in foreign trade, most reflects a rise in domestic demand for high-technology items. Lawrence includes some twenty industries in the high-

Table 3-12. U.S. Production of Ten High-Technology Industries and Their Share of Total Manufacturing, 1963, 1972, and 1982

Industry	Value of production (billion 1980 U.S. $)			Growth of production (average annual percentage)	
	1963	1972	1982	1963–1972	1972–1982
Electronic computing equipment (3573)[a]	6,874	11,515	31,565	5.90	10.61
Telephone and telegraph apparatus (3661)	4,355	8,052	11,499	7.07	3.63
Radio and TV communication equipment (3662)	17,926	16,264	28,358	−1.08	5.72
Semiconductors and related devices (3674)	1,726	4,812	10,671	12.07	8.29
Electronic connectors (3578)	N.A.	859	2,202	N.A.	9.87
Electronic components (3679)	N.A.	5,445	12,364	N.A.	8.55
X-ray, electrotherapeutic, and electromedical apparatus (3693)	361	790	3,666	9.09	16.59
Optical instruments and lenses (3832)	492	947	3,225	7.55	13.04
Surgical and medical equipment (3841)	713	1,712	3,506	10.22	7.43
Guided missiles and space vehicles (3761)	N.A.	7,338	8,773	N.A.	1.80
Total of above industries	32,447	57,734	115,829	6.61[b]	7.21
All manufacturing[c]	7.7	11.0	20.8		

Note: N.A. = not available.
Source: Sergio Zica de Castro, "Changing Trends in World Metal Demand: The Case of Tin," *Natural Resources Forum* vol. 12, no. 2 (May 1988) table 3. Used with permission.
[a]Figures in parentheses are Standard Industrial Codes.
[b]Because data for three industries are not available for 1963, this figure overestimates the actual growth rate for all ten industries.
[c]This row indicates the percentage of all manufacturing accounted for by the total of the ten industries (seven in 1963).

technology part of the manufacturing sector, which explains why his figures are higher than those reported by Castro.

If the intensity of use of traditional metals per dollar of value added is less for high-technology products than for automobiles, home appliances, and other manufactured products, which seems reasonable, the rising importance of high-technology goods should be causing the intensity of metal use within the manufacturing sector to fall and in the process should be contributing to a decline in IU for the U.S. economy as a whole. It is also plausible that the

Table 3-13. Share of Value Added of U.S. Manufacturing for High-Technology and Other Types of Manufacturing Industries, 1960, 1973, and 1980

Industry type[a]	Share of manufacturing (percentage)			Growth in share (average annual percentage)	
	1960	1973	1980	1960–1973	1973–1980
High technology	27	32	38	1.32	2.49
Capital intensive	32	32	27	0.00	−2.40
Labor intensive	13	13	12	0.00	−1.14
Resource intensive	28	23	23	−1.50	0.00

Source: Reprinted, with permission, from Robert Z. Lawrence, Can America Compete? (Washington, D.C., Brookings Institution, 1984), table 4-6.

[a]High-technology industries include engines and turbines, farm and garden machinery, construction and mining machinery, materials-handling machinery and equipment, metal-working machinery and equipment, special machinery, general industrial machinery, office computing and accounting machines, service industry machines, radio and TV equipment, aircraft and parts, scientific instruments, optical equipment, drugs and cleaning preparations, chemicals and selected chemical products, plastics and synthetics, miscellaneous machinery, electrical and industrial equipment, lighting equipment, and electrical components and accessories. Examples of capital-intensive industries are household appliances, motor vehicles and equipment, and metal containers. Examples of labor-intensive industries are apparel, footwear, and household furniture. Examples of resource-intensive industries are food and kindred products, lumber and wood products, and stone and clay. For a full list of industries in the capital-intensive, labor-intensive, and resource-intensive subsectors of manufacturing, along with the SIC codes included with each industry, see appendices A-1 and A-2 of Robert Z. Lawrence, Can America Compete? (Washington, D.C., Brookings Institution, 1984).

penetration of high-technology products has occurred earlier and proceeded more quickly in the United States and the United Kingdom than in the OECD nations in general, which would help explain the relatively low intensities of metal use found in these two countries. In exploring this possibility, however, it would be useful to have more information on the growth of high-technology products outside the United States.

CONCLUSIONS

As stated at the outset, this chapter seeks to explain two features of long-run OECD metal demand with important global consequences. The first is the general slowdown and in some instances even stagnation in growth that overcame metal demand in the early 1970s after nearly three decades of brisk and persistent expansion. The second feature is differences among OECD countries in metal consumption, particularly differences that economic size does not explain—such as the low intensities of metal use found in recent years in the United States and the United Kingdom and the high intensities in Japan and the Federal Republic of Germany.

Our analytical journey, a series of forays focusing on various determinants of metal demand, has encountered many important forces shaping long-run metal demand. No single factor alone is dominant. Among the more important causes of the sizable differences in IU levels among the major OECD countries are the following:

1. Differences in trade. The United States and the United Kingdom apparently enjoy a comparative advantage in the production of services and high-technology products. The United Kingdom, in addition, is an important exporter of oil. Japan and the Federal Republic of Germany, by comparison, are more successful in exporting automobiles and other more metal-intensive products.

2. Differences in currency purchasing power. Adjusting for these differences actually accentuates discrepancies among countries. IU in the United States remains generally low, whereas the high intensities of use in Japan and the Federal Republic of Germany become even larger.

3. Differences in the rate and direction of material substitution. The rapid and widespread use of aluminum in beer and soft drink cans in the United States, for example, explains much of the relatively high intensity of aluminum use in that country. Similarly, a preference for lead in roofing helps account for the unusually high IU of lead in the United Kingdom.

4. Differences in the amount of manufacturing devoted to the production of high-technology products. Comparative advantage and trade to some extent influence the product mix of the manufacturing sectors of OECD countries, but domestic preferences are also important. The substantial production of computers in the United States, for example, has occurred primarily in response to domestic demand. Because the demand for high-technology products tends to rise with affluence, this finding suggests that IU is after all linked to per capita income. (The weakness of the IU hypothesis, as chapter 2 suggests, is not that it focuses on the wrong variable but that it focuses on one variable only.)

5. Differences in the proportion of GDP devoted to services. In the United States and the United Kingdom, the provision of services accounts for a larger share of GDP than in other OECD countries. As with high-technology goods, the demand for services may rise with affluence, providing another link between IU and per capita income. However, the relatively large service sectors in the United States and the United Kingdom may simply reflect smaller construction and capital equipment industries relative to GDP than in other OECD countries whose economies are expanding faster. Some support for this explanation is provided by the fact that the ratio of services to GDP in the Federal Republic of Germany, France, and Japan remains lower than in the United Kingdom, even though per capita income in these countries is now higher.

6. Differences in the amount of income saved and invested. Over the postwar period Japan and the Federal Republic of Germany have channeled a relatively high share of their GDP into gross domestic investment, in part because World War II so severely damaged their economies. Because high saving and investment foster economic development and rising per capita income, the importance of this variable suggests that IU may vary not only with changes in the level of per capita income but also with the rate of change in per capita income. Developed countries with relatively high and rapidly rising living standards may consume as much metal per million dollars of income as do developed countries with lower and more stationary living standards.

Other variables may also contribute to the differences in intensity of metal use found among the OECD countries. Differences in the speed with which countries adopt new resource-saving technologies could be important, although the technological sophistication of the developed countries tends to ensure rapid adoption of new innovations throughout the OECD once their cost-effectiveness is demonstrated. Similarly, differences in metal prices may be significant, although again metal prices do not vary greatly within the OECD.

As with intercountry differences in metal use, the pervasive slowdown in growth of metal demand in all important OECD markets also turns out to be complicated to explain and involves many causal factors. At the most basic level the break in consumption trends in the early 1970s is the result of both declines in economic growth and in IU trends, with the latter apparently of slightly greater import. The slowdown and in many instances reversal of IU growth are the result of important changes in both the material composition of products and the product composition of income, which in turn reflect the combined effects of material substitution, resource-saving technology, an expanding service sector, and the rise of high-technology products within manufacturing.

OECD economic growth over the 1950–1973 period was unusually high as the major industrialized countries greatly increased the quantity and quality of their labor and capital inputs and exploited opportunities to move workers from agriculture to industry and to adopt the more advanced technologies in use, primarily in the United States. Recent economic growth rates, although considered abnormally low by many, are really more typical of the entire twentieth century.

REFERENCES

Auty, Richard. 1985. "Materials Intensity of GDP: Research Issues on the Measurement and Explanation of Change," *Resources Policy* vol. 11, no. 4, pp. 275–283.

Canavan, Patrick D. 1983. "The Determinants of Intensity-of-Use: A Case Study of Tin Solder End Uses," Ph.D. dissertation, Pennsylvania State University.

Castro, Sergio Zica de. 1988. "Changing Trends in World Metal Demand: The Case of Tin," *Natural Resources Forum* vol. 12, no. 2 (May).

Commodities Research Unit. 1985. *The Marketing of Metals (Part II: Case Histories)* (London, Commodities Research Unit Ltd.).

Demler, Frederick R. 1980. "The Nature of Tin Substitution in the Beverage Container Industries," Ph.D. dissertation, Pennsylvania State University.

Gill, Derek G. 1983. "Tin Chemical Stabilizers and the Pipe Industry," pp. 76–112 in John E. Tilton, ed., *Material Substitution: Lessons from Tin-Using Industries* (Washington, D.C., Resources for the Future).

Goto, Akira. 1988. "Japan: A Sunset Industry," pp. 90–120 in Merton J. Peck, ed., *The World Aluminum Industry in a Changing Energy Era* (Washington, D.C., Resources for the Future).

Grubb, Timothy J. 1981. "Metal Inventories, Speculation, and Stability in the U.S. Copper Industry," *Materials and Society* vol. 5, no. 3, pp. 267–288.

Hutchison, Roger S., and John E. Tilton. 1987. "Is the Intensity of Copper Use Still Declining in the United States?" *Natural Resources Forum* vol. 11, no. 4, pp. 325–334.

International Iron and Steel Institute. 1972. *Projection 85: World Steel Demand* (Brussels, IISI).

_____. 1982. *Indirect Trade in Steel—1962 to 1979* (Brussels, IISI).

_____. 1985. *Indirect Trade in Steel, 1982* (Brussels, IISI).

Key, P. L., and T. D. Schlabach. 1986. "Metals Demand in Telecommunications," *Materials and Society* vol. 10, no. 3, pp. 433–451.

Lawrence, Robert Z. 1984. *Can America Compete?* (Washington, D.C., Brookings Institution).

Maddison, Angus. 1987. "Growth and Slowdown in Advanced Capitalist Economies: Techniques of Quantitative Assessment," *Journal of Economic Literature* vol. 25 (June) pp. 649–698.

Malenbaum, Wilfred. 1973. *Material Requirements in the United States and Abroad in the Year 2000.* Research project prepared for the National Commission on Materials Policy (Philadelphia, University of Pennsylvania).

_____. 1975. "Law of Demand for Minerals," *Proceedings of the Council of Economics*, 104th Annual Meeting of the American Institute of Mining, Metallurgical and Petroleum Engineers (New York, AIME) pp. 146–155.

_____. 1978. *World Demand for Raw Materials in 1985 and 2000* (New York, McGraw-Hill).

Metallgesellschaft Aktiengesellschaft. Annual. *Metal Statistics* (Frankfurt am Main, Metallgesellschaft Aktiengesellschaft).

Myers, John G. 1986. "Testing for Structural Change in Metals Use," *Materials and Society* vol. 10, no. 3, pp. 271–283.

Radetzki, Marian. 1977. "Fluctuations in Invisible Stocks: A Problem for Copper Market Forecasting," World Bank Commodity Paper no. 27 (Washington, D.C., World Bank).

Roberts, Mark C. 1985. "Theory and Practice of the Intensity of Use Method of Mineral Consumption Forecasting" (Ph.D. dissertation, University of Arizona).

_____. 1986. "An Aggregate Model of Long Term Mineral Requirements," *Materials and Society* vol. 10, no. 3, pp. 303–328.

_____. 1988. "What Caused the Slack Demand for Metals After 1974?" *Resources Policy* vol. 14, no. 4, pp. 231–246.

Tilton, John E. 1986. "Beyond Intensity of Use," *Materials and Society* vol. 10, no. 3, pp. 245–250.

U.S. Bureau of Mines. 1989. *Mineral Commodity Summaries 1989* (Washington, D.C., U.S. Government Printing Office).

———. 1976. *Mineral Facts and Problems, 1975* (Washington, D.C., U.S. Government Printing Office).

———. 1981. *Mineral Facts and Problems, 1980* (Washington, D.C., U.S. Government Printing Office).

Ward, Michael. 1985. *Purchasing Power Parities and Real Expenditures in the OECD* (Paris, Organisation for Economic Co-operation and Development).

4

Developing Countries: The New Growth Markets

MARIAN RADETZKI

The worldwide interest in metal consumption by the developing countries is of very recent origin. Both the unavailability of data and the relative unimportance of the Third World as a metal consumer explained the earlier neglect. After 1973, however, metal demand in the industrialized market economies stagnated, and the growing consumption in the developing countries began to assume much greater significance. Changes in the metal requirements of the Third World have constituted virtually the only recent expansionary element in global demand, providing some hope for the world's depressed metal-producing industries. The interest in the developing nations' metal consumption has also been heightened by the realization that in recent times this group of countries has come to account for sizable shares of global demand in major metal markets. Between 1973 and 1987, the developing countries' share of world consumption rose from 5.1 to 13.5 percent for aluminum, from 5.7 to 13.8 percent for copper, from 8.5 to 15.3 percent for lead, from 2.7 to 8.2 percent for nickel, from 9.0 to 15.0 percent for steel, and from 9.1 to 17.4 percent for zinc (see the statistical appendix to this volume).

Although the interest in metal consumption in the developing countries has been awakened, there is very little known in detail about how consumption has grown or about the determinants of that process. The purpose of this chapter is to scrutinize actual demand trends, to shed light on the determinants of those trends, and so to provide better understanding of likely future developments.

The hypotheses for explaining trends in metal consumption and, in particular, trends in intensity of use (IU), to be explored in this chapter are the following:

• IU rises with gross domestic product (GDP) per capita in low-income countries as a result of sectoral shifts toward more metal-intensive activities; a saturation level for IU is reached in middle-income countries; and IU declines with rising GDP per capita in richer countries as services and high-technology manufacturing with limited metal inputs assume an increasingly important role in the economy.

• Materials-saving technological progress tends to reduce IU over time at each level of GDP per capita.

• IU levels in individual developing countries are affected significantly by the nature and thrust of economic policies; those policies result in rising and elevated IU levels in nations where high investment ratios are maintained, the growth of manufacturing industries is emphasized, and exports of metal-containing manufactures are promoted.

The first section of this chapter presents and analyzes the actual consumption trends for the developing world. The second section provides more detailed analyses of the developments in metal consumption in Brazil and India, and of the underlying determinants of those developments, ending with a short note on South Korea. The third section summarizes the chapter's findings and conclusions and comments on the outlook for future trends in metal consumption in the developing countries.

ACTUAL METAL CONSUMPTION TRENDS IN THE DEVELOPING COUNTRIES

Aggregates for the Country Group

The statistical appendix in this volume provides the details of metal consumption and intensity of use trends for selected metals in the developing countries over the period under scrutiny in this study. In line with the procedure followed in chapter 3, tables 4-1 and 4-2 divide these data into three subperiods—1960–1973, 1973–1979, and 1979–1987—to illuminate any important shifts in the trends.

Several noteworthy observations emerge. For all the metals examined, positive consumption growth was recorded throughout the entire period, interrupted by only brief spells of stagnation or decline. In contrast to the other groups of countries studied—the OECD (Organisation for Economic Cooperation and Development) countries and the centrally planned economies—the developing country group did not experience a slowdown in the

Table 4-1. Annual Average Growth of Metal Consumption in the Developing Countries, 1960–1973, 1973–1979, and 1979–1987
(percent)

Period	Aluminum	Copper	Lead	Nickel	Steel	Zinc
1960–1973	13.8	5.7	7.0	21.7	8.3	6.5
1973–1979	12.9	9.9	9.7	7.9	8.0	7.4
1979–1987	7.9	8.0	3.8	18.0	1.4	4.6

Source: Statistical appendix in this volume.

Table 4-2. Annual Average Growth of GDP and Intensity of Use (IU) in the Developing Countries, 1960–1973, 1973–1979, and 1979–1987
(percent)

Period	GDP	IU					
		Aluminum	Copper	Lead	Nickel	Steel	Zinc
1960–1973	6.7	6.7	−1.0	0.3	14.0	1.5	−0.2
1973–1979	5.1	7.3	4.5	4.4	2.6	2.8	2.1
1979–1987	2.8	4.1	4.3	0.8	12.4	−1.2	1.4

Source: Statistical appendix in this volume.

growth of metal demand around 1973. Instead, a clear-cut deceleration occurred only at the end of the 1970s.

The GDP-based intensities of use for the developing countries generally indicate a trend increase over the period surveyed, but in several cases the trends are highly unstable. Among the metals studied, aluminum exhibits the steadiest trend. Steel has a stagnant IU level until 1967, after which the level rises along an uneven and decelerating path. Nickel, somewhat like steel, experiences a very slow increase in IU until 1970, but a brisk rise beginning in the mid-1970s. The intensities of use of copper and lead begin with substantial declines followed by significant increases after turnarounds in 1967 and 1972, respectively. A gentle negative IU trend for zinc until 1973 becomes very positive in the subsequent period.

Table 4-2 does not reveal a general slowdown in IU trends after 1973, the year when the growth of world metal demand declined sharply. As with metal consumption, the deceleration in IU occurred only at the end of the decade.

The analyses of the preceding chapter note that the slowdown in metal consumption trends in the industrial market economies after 1973 was caused by a combination of declining economic growth and falling intensities of use. The present investigation of the developing countries results in a different picture. Table 4-3 reveals that the intensities of use exerted an upward push on metal consumption trends in both the 1973–1979 period and the

Table 4-3. Differences Between Actual and Trend Values of Metal Consumption in the Developing Countries, 1979 and 1987
(percent of actual consumption in each year)

Year and metal	Total difference[a]	Difference due to change in: GDP growth[b]	IU[c]
1979			
Aluminum	−5.0	−39.1	34.1
Copper	21.1	−1.7	22.8
Lead	14.1	−8.0	22.1
Nickel	−106.0	−119.7	13.7
Steel	−1.3	−15.7	14.4
Zinc	5.0	−6.4	11.4
1987			
Aluminum	−42.2	−101.1	58.9
Copper	39.4	−11.3	50.7
Lead	−13.4	−31.5	31.5
Nickel	−144.2	−216.6	72.4
Steel	−59.4	−67.2	7.8
Zinc	−2.2	−27.4	25.2

Source: Tables 4-1 and 4-2 in this chapter.

[a]*Total difference* is defined as the difference between the actual recorded metal consumption (*MC*) and the trend value that would have been attained if the 1960–1973 trend had continued until the year shown (*MC₁*).

[b]*Difference due to change in GDP growth* is defined as the difference between the trend value of metal consumption that would have been attained if consumption after 1973 had grown at the same rate as GDP (*MC₂*), on the one hand, and the trend value that would have been attained if the 1960–1973 trend had continued until the year shown (*MC₁*), on the other.

[c]*Difference due to change in IU* is defined as the difference between the actual recorded metal consumption (*MC*) and the trend value that would have been attained if consumption after 1973 had grown at the same rate as GDP (*MC₂*).

longer 1973–1987 period. All recorded slowdowns in metal consumption were due entirely to declines in the growth rate of GDP.

These findings prompt a further important question: Why have the intensities of use in the developing countries continued to increase (with the exception of steel), while they all developed negatively in the OECD countries, at least after the early 1970s? To explain these IU declines, the preceding chapter points to intersectoral shifts and materials-saving technological progress in the economies of the OECD countries. Is it possible to establish the effect of these factors on the developing countries and thereby explain the difference in IU trends between the two groups?

Some evidence of the effect of technological change is reviewed later in this section. First, however, we will explore whether the differential IU trends in the developing and the OECD countries can be explained by differences in the sectoral changes within the respective economies.

Table 4-4 compares the levels and growth rates of intensity of use in the developing and the industrialized, OECD countries. Given the instability of

Table 4-4. Levels of and Changes in GDP-Based Intensity of Use (IU) in the Developing and OECD Countries, 1960–1962 and 1984–1986

	Aluminum	Copper	Lead	Nickel	Steel	Zinc
IU level[a] in developing countries: average for—						
1960–1962	0.27	0.39	0.28	0.004	36.71	0.40
1984–1986	0.92	0.51	0.33	0.025	48.67	0.47
IU level[a] in OECD countries: average for—						
1960–1962	0.92	1.05	0.53	0.060	60.85	0.65
1984–1986	1.25	0.74	0.38	0.061	37.10	0.43
Ratio between 1984–1986 level and 1960–1962 level						
Developing countries	3.41	1.31	1.18	6.25	1.33	1.18
OECD countries	1.36	0.70	0.72	1.02	0.61	0.66

Source: Statistical appendix in this volume.
[a]In tons of metal consumed per million dollars of GDP.

the time series, the significance of compound growth rates would inevitably be unsatisfactory, especially if the entire time span under investigation were to be considered. Table 4-4 avoids this problem and yet gives a feel for the change in the intensities by showing the ratio between the three-year averages over an extended span of time.

Given the data already considered, the table should not present any surprises. As it shows, the GDP-based intensities of use have risen in the developing countries for all the metals studied. In the case of the "old" metals (copper, lead, steel, and zinc), the increase for the twenty-four-year period is moderate, between 18 and 33 percent. For the "new" metals (aluminum and nickel), however, the increase in IU amounts to hundreds of percent. This experience is at sharp variance with the developments in the industrialized market economies. For the "old" metals, this group of nations recorded IU declines of around 30 percent. Only for aluminum was an increasing IU recorded; even the "new" metal nickel, which had the fastest rate of growth in consumption in the developing countries, exhibits a stagnant IU trend in the industrialized economies.

In the early 1960s the intensities of use in the developing countries were in all cases very much lower than in the industrialized countries. In the 1980s the differences had shrunk considerably, and in the case of steel and zinc, the developing countries recorded higher IU values than those of the OECD countries.

A large-scale macroeconomic shift occurred in the developing countries during the period surveyed. Between the 1960–1962 and 1983–1985 periods (see table 4-5), the share of gross domestic investment (GDI) in GDP increased from 18.5 to 28.7 percent (data on investments in developing countries for later years were not available at the time of finalization of this

Table 4-5. Levels of and Changes in GDI-Based Intensity of Use (IU) in the Developing and OECD Countries, 1960–1962 and 1983–1985

	Aluminum	Copper	Lead	Nickel	Steel	Zinc
IU level[a] in developing countries: average for—						
1960–1962	1.46	2.11	1.51	0.022	198.4	2.16
1983–1985	3.09	1.67	1.12	0.074	170.2	1.64
IU level[a] in OECD countries: average for—						
1960–1962	4.21	4.75	2.40	0.271	275.3	2.94
1983–1985	6.02	3.52	1.83	0.287	178.8	2.05
Ratio between 1983–1985 level and 1960–1962 level						
Developing countries	2.12	0.79	0.74	3.36	0.86	0.76
OECD countries	1.43	0.74	0.76	1.06	0.65	0.70

Source: Statistical appendix in this volume.
[a]In tons of metal consumed per million dollars of GDI.

chapter). This increase is relevant for the present investigation, since a very large proportion of metal usage occurs in investment-related activities. It is also important to note that this shift occurred only in the developing countries; in the industrialized market economies, the share of GDI actually declined from 22.1 to 21.1 percent in the periods studied.

In contrast to the GDP-based IU levels in the developing countries, which all rose from the early 1960s to the mid-1980s, those levels based on GDI increased only for aluminum and nickel and declined for the other four metals (see table 4-5). In this light the macroeconomic shift emerges as a crucial explanatory factor behind the rise in the GDP-based intensities of use. If this interpretation holds true, then continued increases in the GDP-based IUs will occur only if the share of GDI continues to expand. Such expansion cannot be taken for granted, since the GDI-share is already very high in a cross-country or historical comparison.

Table 4-5 corresponds to table 4-4 but uses GDI-based instead of GDP-based IU figures. The noteworthy finding emerging from this table is that the industrialized and the developing countries experienced a similar rate of decline in the IUs for copper, lead, and zinc, and that, in the case of steel, the decline was marginally smaller in the developing countries. This finding reinforces our earlier interpretation: namely, that rising GDP-based IUs in developing countries were predominantly due to increasing GDI shares. Measured per unit of GDI, consumption of a majority of base metals declined in the industrialized and the developing countries more or less in parallel.

With this interpretation, we must still explain the large difference between the two groups of countries in IU levels and trends for aluminum and nickel. One could see this difference as a result of the technological progress that has permitted rapid proliferation of novel uses of these "new" metals. Because these technological developments have been centered heavily in the industrialized countries, there may have arisen a dissemination lag, explaining why IUs in the developing economies are so much lower. These countries' attempt to catch up could also explain their rapid increases in IU.

Data for Individual Countries

Thus far the analysis has focused on time trends in the intensity of use for the developing countries in aggregate. For further insights, we must turn to individual country statistics. Because several countries are considered, the following analysis focuses on only one metal—copper—to limit the amount of data presented and to keep the account tractable.

Table 4-6 compares the IU of copper with per capita GDP in eleven low-income countries (with the exception of Argentina in 1975, all the countries have per capita GDPs below $5,000) and in three mature industrialized economies. The countries included in this sample have all recorded significant copper consumption over an extended period. They are listed in ascending order of their 1984 per capita GDP, and are compared at four different points in time: 1965, 1975, 1980, and 1984.

The exceptionally high IU figure in table 4-6 for Chile in 1965 must be a statistical aberration, due perhaps to the temporary operation of an export-oriented copper-fabrication facility.

Two general observations can be made, based on this table. First, there is a very wide spread in the IU, both among the countries and over time, with no apparent correlation between the per capita GDP level and the IU. Second, there are very large discrepancies among the countries in terms of IU trends over time. The figures for India, Brazil, Chile, Portugal, and Mexico, among the low-income countries, do not reveal a rising IU trend at all. This contrasts with the extreme IU increases recorded by South Korea.

The regular patterns in IU developments hypothesized earlier are not confirmed by table 4-6. We now consider whether better accord between the hypothesis and the developments experienced by the countries under study can be obtained by explicitly allowing for (a) purchasing power parities instead of official exchange rates in the determination of GDP and per capita GDP; (b) the nature of the development strategies pursued by individual countries and their effects on IU; and (c) the effects of indirect trade. We also try to verify (d) the effects of materials-saving technology over time.

GDP Values Based on Purchasing Power Parity   The wide spread of IU levels and the lack of a correlation between the IUs and the per capita GDPs could be a result of the fact that conversions at official exchange rates distort the values for GDP and per capita GDP. To check this, table 4-7 compares

Table 4-6. Copper: GDP-Based Intensity of Use (IU) and Per Capita GDP in Selected Countries, 1965, 1975, 1980, and 1984
(IU in tons of metal consumed per million dollars of GDP; per capita GDP in constant 1980 dollars)

Country[a]	1965		1975		1980		1984	
	IU	Per capita GDP	IU	Per capita GDP	IU	Per capita GDP	IU	Per capita GDP
India	0.66	193	0.25	223	0.48	240	0.43	264
Philippines	N.A.	476	0.11	620	0.09	690	0.33	680
Turkey	0.26	807	0.40	1,238	0.59	1,470	0.80	1,415
Brazil	0.41	897	0.86	1,664	0.99	2,050	0.75	1,894
South Korea	0.12	602	0.64	1,232	1.35	1,520	2.26	2,069
Chile	4.27	2,006	1.40	1,883	1.56	2,150	1.34	2,235
Portugal	0.83	1,245	0.71	2,028	0.75	2,370	0.76	2,480
Mexico	0.54	1,525	0.52	2,244	0.73	2,090	0.44	2,619
South Africa	0.78	2,132	0.97	2,683	1.14	2,300	1.01	2,621
Yugoslavia	2.07	1,464	2.08	2,383	2.19	2,620	2.12	3,040
Argentina	0.34	4,411	0.31	5,370	0.34	2,390	0.31	4,779
Japan	1.11	3,904	1.00	7,378	1.09	9,890	1.10	10,360
United States	0.98	8,633	0.63	10,190	0.72	11,360	0.74	12,172
Sweden	1.14	10,804	0.81	14,223	0.85	13,520	0.88	15,798

Sources: Copper consumption data: *Metal Statistics* (Frankfurt am Main, Metallgesellschaft Aktiengesellschaft, various years); per capita GDP: World Bank files.
[a] Arranged in ascending order of 1984 per capita GDP.

Table 4-7. Copper's GDP-Based Intensity of Use (IU) and Per Capita GDP in 1980 in Selected Developing Countries: A Comparison of Figures Derived by Conventional GDP Measurement and Measurement of GDP Based on Purchasing Power Parity (PPP)

Country	Conventional approach		PPP-based approach	
	IU	Per capita GDP	IU	Per capita GDP
India	0.48	240	0.25	470
Philippines	0.09	690	0.04	1,660
South Korea	1.35	1,520	0.81	2,510
Brazil	0.99	2,050	0.58	3,490
Chile	1.56	2,150	1.01	3,330
Portugal	0.75	2,370	0.46	3,820
Argentina	0.34	2,390	0.24	4,680
Yugoslavia	2.19	2,620	1.74	3,300

Sources: Copper consumption data: *Metal Statistics* (Frankfurt am Main, Metallgesellschaft Aktiengesellschaft, annual); per capita GDP data: World Bank files; PPP calculations: World Bank, *World Development Report 1987* (Washington, D.C., 1987) p. 270. The latter source does not provide data for the rest of the low-income countries included in table 4-6 of this chapter.

the conventionally derived figures for IU and GDP per capita for 1980 in eight of the low-income countries; these figures were obtained using purchasing power parities (PPPs) (see chapter 2 for a discussion of PPPs). The PPP approach does not help narrow the intercountry variations in IU, nor help improve the correlation between the IUs and per capita GDPs.

Development Strategies and IU   Throughout the period surveyed in table 4-6 (i.e., 1965 through 1984), Yugoslavia records exceptionally high IU levels for copper. The same is true of South Korea in the 1980s. The Philippines and Argentina, in contrast, persistently exhibit very low IU levels. Table 4-8, which compares GDP-based IU in 1980 not only for copper but for all the major metals, shows that the high and low ranks of the

Table 4-8. GDP-Based Intensity of Use (IU) for Major Metals in Yugoslavia, South Korea, Argentina, and the Philippines: Rank Among Fourteen Sample Countries, 1980

Country	Copper	Aluminum	Lead	Nickel	Zinc	Steel
Yugoslavia	1	1[a]	1[a]	8[b]	2	1
South Korea	2	6[a]	4[a]	4[b]	1	2
Argentina	13	13[a]	10[a]	12[b]	14	14
Philippines	14	12[a]	11[a]	N.A.	9	11

Sources: Macroeconomic data: World Bank files; metal consumption data; *Metal Statistics* (Frankfurt am Main, Metallgesellschaft Aktiengesellschaft, annual).
[a]Out of thirteen observations.
[b]Out of twelve observations.

Table 4-9. Development Strategy and GDP-Based Intensity of Use (IU) of Copper in Eleven Developing Countries, 1980

Size and industrial orientation of economy	Trade policy orientation:		
	Inward	Neutral	Outward
	Country, IU	Country, IU	Country, IU
Large, primary	Argentina, 0.34 Mexico, 0.63	Brazil, 0.99 Philippines, 0.09 Turkey, 0.59	
Large, manufacturing	India, 0.48		South Korea, 1.35 South Africa, 1.14 Yugoslavia, 2.19
Small, primary	Chile, 1.56		
Small, manufacturing	Portugal, 0.75		

Source: M. Syrquin and H. Chenery, "Patterns of Development 1950 to 1983," World Bank Discussion Paper no. 41 (Washington, D.C., World Bank, 1989), and table 4-6 in this chapter.

four countries persist across most metals. This suggests that the levels of IU for copper in these countries have been conditioned by the choices of general development strategies that emphasize high and low levels of metal consumption, respectively.

In a series of publications, Syrquin and Chenery (1989) designed a classification typology for the development strategies pursued by the developing countries. Their development strategy matrix distinguishes between the domestic dimension, with primary and manufacturing industry orientation, and the foreign trade dimension, with inward- and outward-looking policies as the major choices of policy. Syrquin and Chenery also distinguish between large and small economies on the premise that the size of the economy determines the range of feasible options for industrial and foreign trade policy. The eleven low-income countries in table 4-6 are classified in table 4-9 in accordance with this typology in order to see if it can explain some of the variations in their IU of copper.

The Syrquin–Chenery typology does provide some perspective on the sample of low-income countries under consideration. The sample is biased in that nine of the eleven countries belong to the large-economy category. This is the result of the major criterion for inclusion in the sample: only countries with significant copper consumption over a long period of time were selected; significant copper consumption is not common in small developing countries. However, the typology does point to some relationships between development strategies and IU levels. It suggests that high IU levels are more common in large-economy countries with a manufacturing-oriented industrial thrust and with an outward orientation in trade policy. It also suggests that relatively low IU levels are more common in large-economy countries with a primary production orientation and inward-looking trade policies.

The Effects of Indirect Trade   As noted in chapters 2 and 3 in this volume, indirect trade in metals can distort the levels and trends in metal consumption and IU. Such distortions are likely to be especially important in unindustrialized and newly industrializing countries. The conventional definition of metal consumption is that it equals the metal usage for fabrication. Until fabricating facilities have been established in a country, metals will be absorbed through the imports of metal-containing semimanufactures and finished products, but reported consumption will be zero.

One can hypothesize that consumption and IU will experience discrete jumps and that their trend growth rate may be rapid as successive metal-fabricating units are established and as their output replaces earlier imports. In countries with inward-oriented trade policies (e.g., Argentina and India), increases in consumption and IU can be expected to decelerate sharply when domestic fabrication has replaced most of the earlier imports. In countries with outward-oriented trade policies, however (e.g., South Korea and Yugoslavia), the rise in consumption and IU may continue at fast rates as a result of increasing net exports of metal-fabricated semimanufactures and metal-containing finished products.

Unfortunately, little is known about total metal absorption in the developing countries, and hence about the difference between absorption, on the one hand, and reported consumption, on the other. Data are seldom available on trade in fabricated-metal products and on the metal content of manufactured trade. An exception is the work of the International Iron and Steel Institute (IISI) on indirect trade in steel (see chapter 3). The IISI studies are less useful for the present purposes, however; their focus is on the OECD economies, and the developing countries are afforded very little specific attention. Another, more relevant exception to the paucity of data is the study by Hwang (1989) on steel in South Korea. Hwang concludes that indirect imports and exports of steel in the 1980–1986 period added an average of 24 percent to South Korea's IU level for steel. He also finds that the effect of indirect trade on this IU level was negative, on average, in the 1970s.

One set of data can illuminate at least part of the distinction between absorption and reported consumption for several countries, namely, the data on the trade volume in fabricated products of copper and copper-alloy, as reported by the International Wrought Copper Council (annual). Table 4-10 presents a summary of these data for eleven industrializing economies from 1967, which is as far back as they are available.[1] A serious deficiency of these data is that the exports of fabricated products from Argentina, Brazil,

---

[1]Net imports of fabricated copper-alloy products have been recorded at 65 percent of gross weight to account for their noncopper content. In private communication in 1986, Mark Loveitt, statistician of the International Wrought Copper Council, suggested that this figure is a fair representation of the copper content in such products.

Table 4-10. Imports of Fabricated Copper and Copper-Alloy Products, by Eleven Developing Countries, in Percent of Reported Copper Consumption, 1967 to 1987

(percent)

Year	Argentina	Brazil	Chile	India	Mexico	Philippines	Portugal	South Africa	South Korea	Turkey	Yugoslavia
1967	1.1	1.0	0.8	12.0	1.1	214.2	65.9	−7.6	7.2	3.6	−20.5
1968	3.6	0.9	0.6	3.2	0.8	463.9	73.1	−18.2	6.1	4.2	−21.3
1969	2.0	1.6	0.9	4.4	0.8	42.1	65.0	−3.6	7.2	2.3	−22.6
1970	3.7	4.9	0.4	3.6	0.7	48.5	50.1	−6.0	9.8	2.2	−22.9
1971	2.4	1.1	0.3	5.2	1.7	79.2	61.4	−0.8	13.3	2.2	−31.1
1972	1.7	0.8	0.3	6.5	0.7	74.3	46.5	−28.2	8.2	8.8	−6.3
1973	1.8	1.0	0.2	6.6	3.1	28.9	48.0	−22.2	6.9	47.1	−33.6
1974	0.8	1.2	0.5	4.5	2.4	67.2	71.9	4.4	10.0	66.7	−19.4
1975	0.8	0.8	0.2	7.6	1.5	97.1	31.3	4.7	8.7	28.0	−1.8
1976	0.7	0.5	0.1	3.4	2.9	39.7	39.7	4.9	12.6	24.8	−20.2
1977	1.0	0.4	0.3	4.4	4.5	55.8	40.1	3.2	10.5	20.7	−18.2
1978	1.6	0.6	0.3	4.1	4.6	77.5	59.1	3.0	18.4	9.2	2.5
1979	0.9	1.6	0.8	12.4	6.3	157.4	92.6	6.1	15.0	9.2	−11.7
1980	1.6	0.6	0.6	25.6	9.7	148.8	73.4	4.8	7.7	12.7	−18.1
1981	1.3	0.8	1.4	31.7	11.9	156.5	79.7	9.2	−1.5	22.8	−7.5
1982	0.6	0.4	0.3	22.7	12.1	251.8	95.5	7.7	−7.5	18.2	−10.0
1983	1.8	1.0	0.3	16.6	13.5	158.4	55.3	3.6	−8.5	21.8	−8.9
1984	1.4	0.4	0.5	22.6	9.9	15.8	39.3	4.6	−10.3	20.1	−8.9
1985	0.7	0.6	0.8	22.0	10.1	30.6	70.0	0.6	8.3	9.2	−6.2
1986	1.5	0.7	0.8	12.1	12.8	20.4	38.9	−2.1	−7.2	14.6	−19.0
1987	1.3	1.3	1.5	14.2	13.3	24.3	9.9	1.7	7.6	24.7	−24.8

Notes: Fabricated copper-alloy products are recorded at 65 percent of actual weight. Figures for Argentina, Brazil, Chile, India, Mexico, the Philippines, and Turkey are gross imports; other figures are net imports.

Sources: International Wrought Copper Council, World Trade in Copper and Copper Alloy Semimanufactures (London, International Wrought Copper Council, annual); Metal Statistics (Frankfurt am Main, Metallgesellschaft Aktiengesellschaft, various years).

Chile, India, Mexico, the Philippines, and Turkey are very incompletely recorded over time; hence, the figures given for these countries are gross imports. This creates a serious bias, since some of these countries (e.g., Brazil; see the next section) are known to have generated sizable indirect exports of copper during the period under scrutiny.

The addition of the fabricated-products trade to reported consumption does not smooth the IU trends or even out the intercountry levels. Also, the plausible hypothesis that developing countries pass through a stage of import substitution during which their fabricating industries are established and the ratio of fabricated-product imports over reported consumption is sharply curtailed, although not contradicted by some of the country series, does not find any general support from the data.

It must be emphasized again that the figures in table 4-10 are extremely incomplete. Apart from disregarding fabricated-product exports in many countries, they also do not take into account trade in metal-containing manufactures. Hence, any conclusions based on this material are subject to great uncertainty.

The Effects of Materials-Saving Technologies There is little direct evidence of the effects over time of materials-saving technologies on metal consumption and IU in the developing countries. One exception, again, is the study by Hwang (1989) of steel in South Korea. Hwang employs input–output analysis to track the shifts in the coefficients of total steel input per unit of output in major steel-using industries over time. His analysis reveals that the coefficients declined in sixteen of the eighteen industries studied between 1973 and 1983. The unweighted average rate of decline in the sixteen industries was more than 40 percent. Although some of this decline could be due to altered output composition within each industry, a large portion is ascribed to materials-saving technological change.

If it were possible to control for variables such as per capita GDP and sectoral shifts in a larger sample of countries, then a finding that IU is falling over time could be seen as evidence of materials saving, either through substitution away from the metal studied or through the adoption of new technologies requiring a lesser quantity of metal input per unit of output. The data needed to control for sectoral shifts are hard to acquire; nevertheless, figures 4-1 and 4-2 have been constructed to explore whether, in fact, a decline in IU over time can be established at different levels of per capita GDP. In figure 4-1 the IU of copper in 1961 for twenty-five rich and poor countries is plotted against their per capita GDPs (in constant 1980 U.S. dollars). In figure 4-2 the exercise is repeated using 1984 data and a sample expanded to thirty-three countries.

The figures do suggest some suppression in IUs over the twenty-three-year period under investigation. (The method for establishing the suppression was suggested by Istvan Dobozi.) In 1961, 68 percent of the countries included

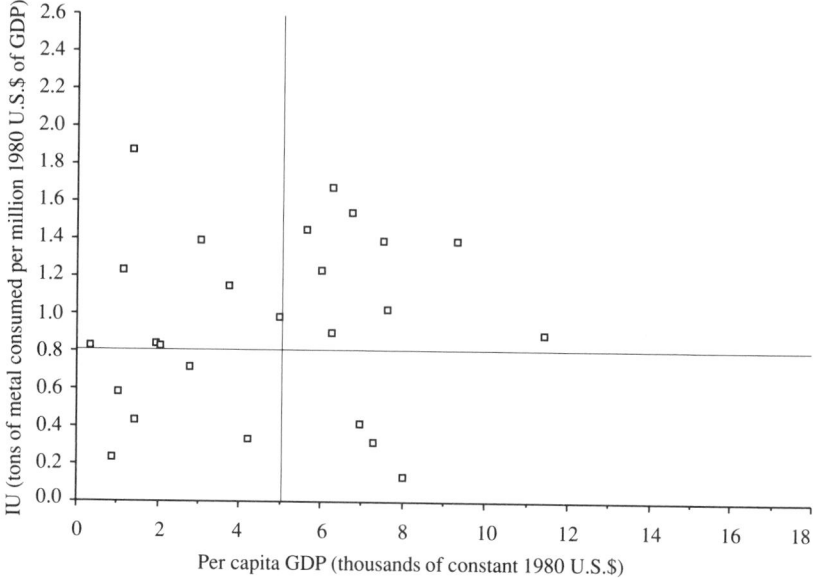

Figure 4-1. GDP-based intensity of use (IU) of copper at different levels of per capita GDP in twenty-five rich and poor countries, 1961.

Sources: GDP and per capita GDP figures from World Bank files; metal consumption figures from *Metal Statistics* (Frankfurt am Main, Metallgesellschaft Aktiengesellschaft, annual).

in the sample had IU levels above 0.8, but in 1984 the proportion had declined to 36 percent. Even though full control for per capita GDP is not practicable in view of the small sample size, it can be noted that the decline was evenly spread between the richer and poorer countries. In 1961, 75 percent of the countries with levels of per capita GDP above $5,000 (in constant 1980 U.S. dollars) had IU levels of 0.8 or higher; in 1984 the proportion had fallen to 41 percent. In countries with levels of per capita GDP below $5,000, the decline was from 61 to 31 percent.

The foregoing exercise is too imprecise to permit a quantification of the effect of materials savings through substitution and new technologies on a ceteris paribus assumption. The results do suggest, however, that the spread of savings in copper use was as pervasive in the poor countries as in the rich ones included in the sample investigated. The downward shift in IU levels in the poor countries is especially noteworthy, given that the large-scale sectoral shifts toward manufacturing and rising domestic investments in such countries should have acted as a counterbalance to the reduced IUs for copper because of substitution and materials-saving technologies.

The downward shift in the IU for the poor countries included in the sample is not in conflict with the rising IUs for the developing countries in aggregate.

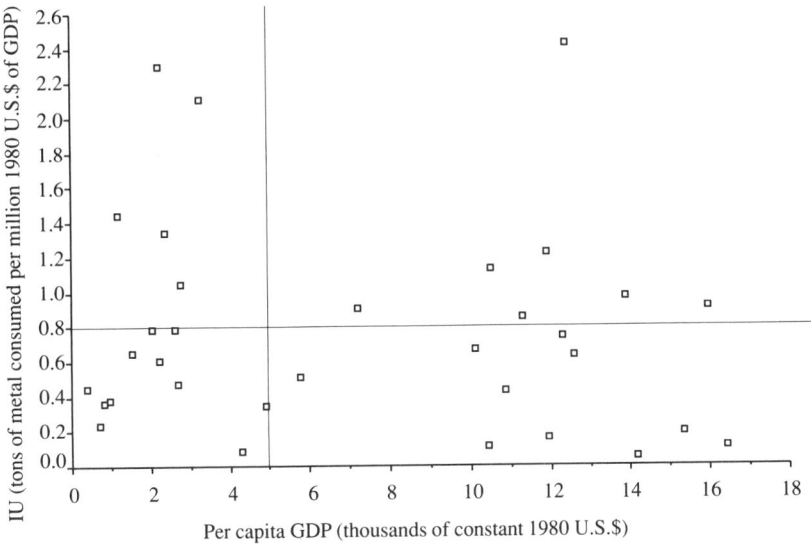

Figure 4-2. GDP-based intensity of use (IU) of copper at different levels of per capita GDP in thirty-three rich and poor countries, 1984.
Sources: GDP and per capita GDP figures from World Bank files; metal consumption figures from *Metal Statistics* (Frankfurt am Main, Metallgesellschaft Aktiengesellschaft, annual).

The aggregate probably contains many countries (not included in the present sample) whose IU levels were zero in the initial year but then rose to a positive number during the period under study, thereby contributing to a positive aggregate trend.

DETERMINANTS OF METAL CONSUMPTION IN BRAZIL, INDIA, AND SOUTH KOREA

Brazil and India were chosen for special investigation for several reasons. These two countries are important metal consumers; with few exceptions, each has accounted for 10 percent or more of the aggregate consumption in the developing countries during the 1980s. Both countries undertake sizable domestic production of most of the metals and have gone through large-scale, diversified industrialization processes. The similarities between them—the large size of each economy, the ensuing relative inward orientation of trade policy, and the assertive and powerful public involvements in all aspects of the economy—might have suggested that one of them be compared with another country exhibiting a different set of characteristics. The ultimate choice was determined by the author's need to visit the two countries for other purposes, and thus having the opportunity to carry out detailed interviews with members of industry, government, and academia for the present study.

South Korea was added to the countries to receive special scrutiny because of the remarkable growth of metal consumption and the extremely high levels of IU for some metals recorded by its economy in the latter part of the period under investigation. The South Korean development strategy differs distinctly from that pursued by Brazil and India in its relative openness and great emphasis on the promotion of manufactured exports. The author did not undertake a visit to South Korea; the account is based only on published material and hence is less penetrating and much briefer than that for the other two countries.

In table 4-11 the metal consumption of the three countries is detailed and compared with the developing countries aggregate. Table 4-12 provides the per capita GDP and GDP-based IU for Brazil, India, and South Korea for three separate years. Figures 4-3 through 4-8 track the progress of intensities of use in the three countries for each metal throughout the period under scrutiny.

Comparisons of the IU levels and trends in these three countries with the developing countries' aggregates reveal several peculiarities. The first is the marked downward adjustment in trend in Brazil's GDP-based IU for copper and steel in 1974 and for aluminum in 1975. No correspondingly large shifts in trend can be noted for India and South Korea or for the developing countries' aggregate in these years. The second peculiarity with regard to Brazil consists in the sharp and relatively short-run fluctuations in the country's GDP-based IUs for all metals but especially for copper and zinc (see figures 4-3 through 4-8). For several of the metals, the amplitude of these fluctuations increased in the latter part of the period studied.

A notable peculiarity in the Indian data, given that country's low per capita GDP, is the exceptionally high IU levels for all the metals early in the period under investigation (see table 4-12). Another is the completely stagnant IU trend in all metals except nickel since the early 1970s. A third peculiarity is India's comparatively low IU for copper in the 1980s and the very high IU simultaneously recorded for aluminum.

Table 4-11. Metal Consumption in Brazil, India, and South Korea, 1987
(thousands of tons)

	Aluminum	Copper	Lead	Nickel	Steel[a]	Zinc
Brazil	430	259	93	15	14,480	177
India	326	115	68	19	14,780	130
South Korea	208	259	112	5	11,200	179
Developing countries: aggregate	2,367	1,435	859	69	109,000	1,192
Three countries as a percentage of aggregate	41	44	32	57	37	41

[a]1986 figures.

Table 4-12. Per Capita GDP and GDP-Based Intensity of Use (IU) in Brazil, India, and South Korea: 1965, 1975, and 1986
(IU in tons of metal consumed per million dollars of GDP; per capita GDP in constant 1980 dollars)

	Per capita GDP	IU					
Year and country		Aluminum	Copper	Lead	Nickel	Steel	Zinc
1965							
Brazil	897	0.68	0.41	0.23	0.01	41.5	0.42
India	192	0.76	0.68	0.40	0.00	80.2	0.74
South Korea	602	0.01	0.12	0.13	0.00	24.2	0.53
Developing countries:							
aggregate	634	0.36	0.36	0.28	0.01	37.4	0.35
1975							
Brazil	1,664	1.16	0.86	0.28	0.02	62.5	0.46
India	223	1.06	0.32	0.26	0.02	62.3	0.60
South Korea	1,232	0.59	0.64	0.24	0.01	71.8	0.55
Developing countries:							
aggregate	941	0.61	0.34	0.31	0.01	48.1	0.36
1986							
Brazil	2,186	1.44	0.87	0.30	0.05	49.1	0.51
India	284	1.40	0.50	0.36	0.07	66.5	0.61
South Korea	2,440	1.96	2.61	0.88	0.07	111.4	1.52
Developing countries:							
aggregate	950	0.95	0.53	0.35	0.03	46.9	0.47

Sources: Data on per capita GDP from World Bank files; all other data from the statistical appendix in this volume.

In South Korea the very low IU levels in the 1960s and the extremely high ones in the 1980s emerge as the major peculiarity. The differential performance among metals is also noteworthy: in aluminum and nickel, South Korea's IU levels in 1986 are high, but not remarkably so. For copper, lead, steel, and zinc, in contrast, the levels are truly exceptional in an international comparison.

The ensuing investigations of the three countries attempt to explain these and other special features of their metal consumption.

Metal Consumption in Brazil

Macroeconomic Policy and Performance The decade from the mid-1960s to the mid-1970s is frequently referred to as "the Brazilian miracle." Economic progress in Brazil during this period was very fast in all respects. In the mid-1960s the incoming military administration launched a vast investment program, predominantly in the public sector, involving large-scale construction (for example, of power stations, airports, and roads), the

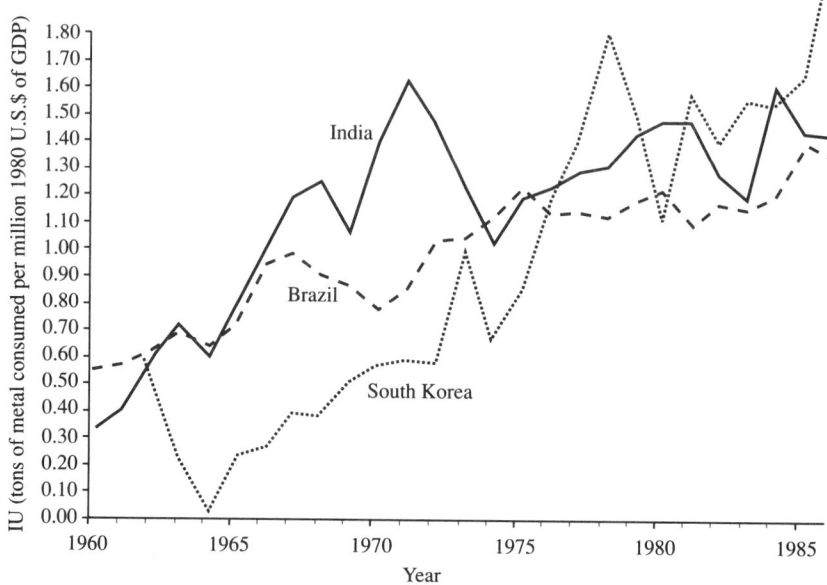

Figure 4-3. GDP-based intensity of use (IU) of aluminum in Brazil, India, and South Korea, 1960–1986.

Source: Statistical appendix in this volume.

establishment of a telecommunications system, and expansion of the mining and the steel industries; all of these ventures were important absorbers of metal.

Although total GDP and per capita GDP continued to grow at high rates until 1980, a significant change in the macroeconomic environment occurred in the middle of the 1970s. Many of the large public-sector investment programs launched in the preceding decade had been completed. Furthermore, the rise in international petroleum prices led to increasing balance-of-payments constraints, which in turn caused a variety of internal economic disruptions.[2] The share of gross domestic investments in GDP, which had risen from 20 percent in 1965 to a peak of 26 percent in 1975, declined to 22 percent by 1980. There was also a change in the relative growth of investments among industrial sectors. Investment activities in metallurgy, machinery, electrical and transport equipment, and chemicals account for a very large proportion of total metal use. The share of these sectors in total industrial investments rose briskly from 50.7 percent in 1969

---

[2]Interviews with Renato Simplicio of the Ministry of Mines and Energy, Brasilia; Joseph Young, editor of *Revistas Minerios,* São Paolo; and Eduardo Camara of Remetalica, Rio de Janeiro, all of which took place in March 1987.

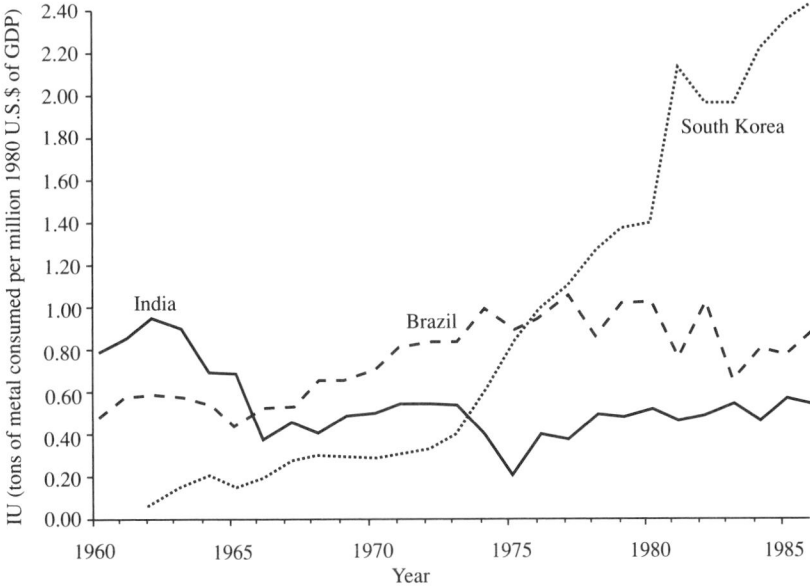

Figure 4-4. GDP-based intensity of use (IU) of copper in Brazil, India, and South Korea, 1960–1986.
Source: Statistical appendix in this volume.

to 67.8 percent in 1975 but stagnated in subsequent years, reaching 66.7 percent in 1979 (World Bank, 1983, p. 170).

In the 1980s the macroeconomic policies of Brazil were shaped strongly by the international debt crisis. In consequence of very restrictive policy measures, the per capita GDP declined from its 1980 peak. The investment ratio continued to fall, reaching 15 percent in 1985 as both public and private investments were curtailed under the impact of the financial crisis. Periods of severe, policy-induced depression alternated with bursts of economic expansion, depending on the fluctuating availability of foreign exchange. The tendency toward a "stop-go" pattern that emerged in the latter half of the 1970s was accentuated in the 1980s (World Bank, 1983, pp. 45–47).

These macroeconomic circumstances provide a reasonable explanation for the turnaround in the trend of Brazil's GDP-based IU levels for aluminum, copper, and steel in the mid-1970s. The peak in the gross domestic investment ratio, along with the coincident arrest in the growth of the share of metal-intensive investments, helps explain the shift in trend of the GDP-based IU levels. Indeed, when the GDI-based levels for the three metals are plotted, no kink in the mid-1970s can be detected. Similarly, the tendency toward "stop-go" policies in the latter part of the period provides at least a partial explanation for the increasing short-run variations in the IU figures.

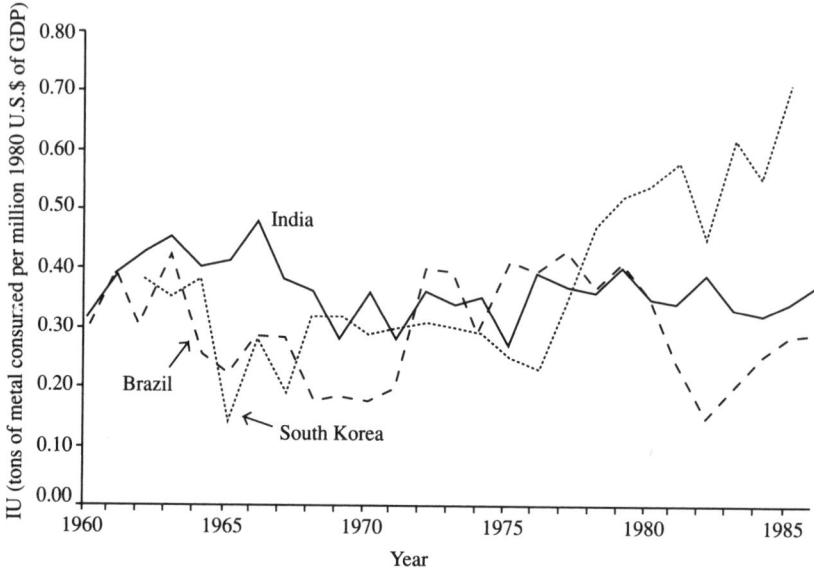

Figure 4-5. GDP-based intensity of use (IU) of lead in Brazil, India, and South Korea, 1960–1986.

Source: Statistical appendix in this volume.

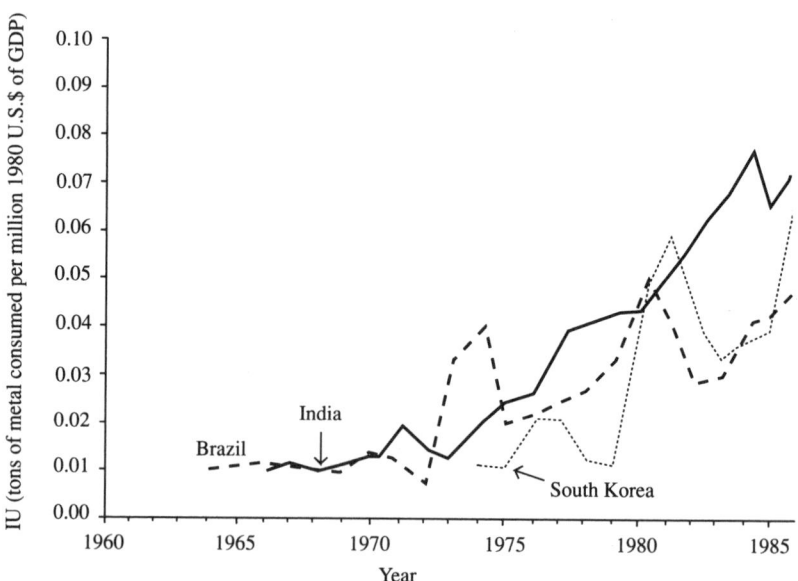

Figure 4-6. GDP-based intensity of use (IU) of nickel in Brazil, India, and South Korea, 1960–1986.

Source: Statistical appendix in this volume.

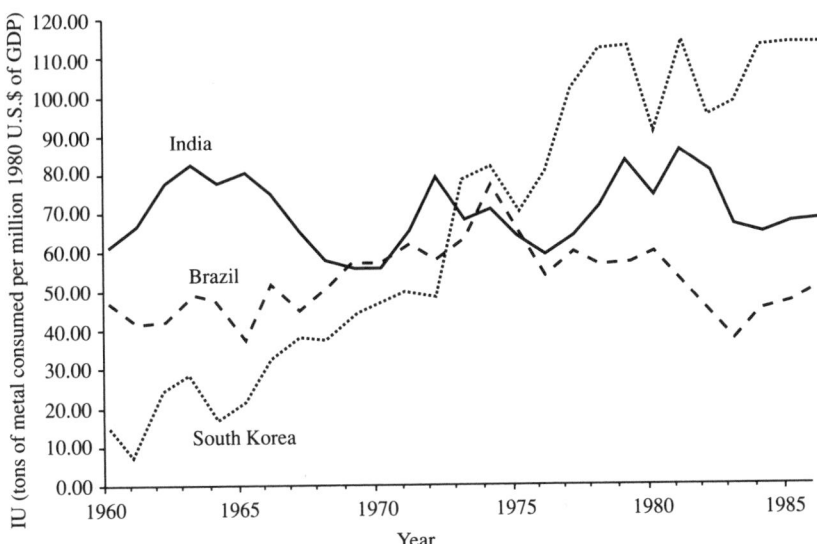

Figure 4-7. GDP-based intensity of use (IU) of steel in Brazil, India, and South Korea, 1960–1986.

Source: Statistical appendix in this volume.

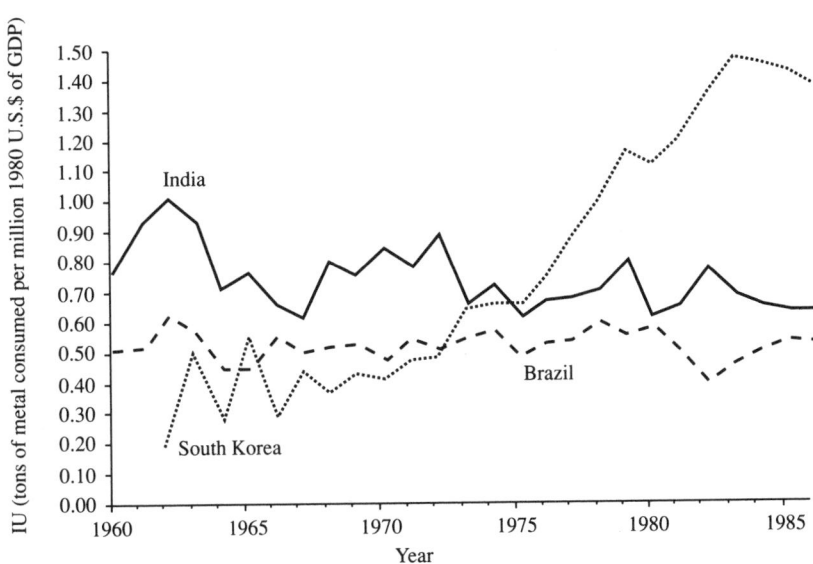

Figure 4-8. GDP-based intensity of use (IU) of zinc in Brazil, India, and South Korea, 1960–1986.

Source: Statistical appendix in this volume.

Table 4-13. Major Nonferrous Metals in Brazil in Selected Years, 1965–1987: Production Minus Consumption, in Percent of Consumption
(percent)

Metal	1965	1970	1975	1980	1985	1987
Aluminum (primary)	−42	−33	−44	−12	50	96
Copper (refined)	−90	−74	−81	−84	−38	−32
Lead	−46	−7	−16	−7	0	−10
Nickel	38	66	−43	−73	15	−8
Zinc	−100	−84	−62	−42	−16	−22

Source: Metal Statistics (Frankfurt am Main, Metallgesellschaft Aktiengesellschaft, various years).

In contrast to the GDI ratio, the share of manufacturing value added in GDP rose slowly from 22 percent in the mid-1960s to about 25 percent in the mid-1970s, stagnated at this level until the early 1980s, and then rose to over 30 percent in 1984 and 1985. Thus, the share of manufacturing value added shows little relationship to the GDP-based IU. The investment activity provides a much better explanation for metal consumption and IU developments in Brazil than does the performance of the manufacturing sector.

Trade Policies and Performance Brazil's foreign trade has long been tightly controlled by the government. For metals and metal products, imports and exports have been regulated with the help of licenses. Although import duties for metals and fabricated-metal products have not been very high, the policy has been to grant import licenses only when domestic production is deemed insufficient to satisfy demand.[3] Forceful efforts have been undertaken to replace imports with domestic production, at the stages of both metal-ingot and fabricated-metal products.

Table 4-13 presents an overview of Brazil's increasing reliance on domestic production of major nonferrous metals. Over the twenty-three-year period, the reduction in dependence on imports has been very substantial despite a sizable expansion of consumption. Large-scale expansion of domestic capacity made Brazil self-sufficient in aluminum and nickel in the early 1980s. In lead the self-sufficiency in 1985 is somewhat illusory, since it partly reflects reduced consumption during the financial crisis. Self-sufficiency in steel was attained in the late 1970s, and in the 1980s, steel, like aluminum, was exported on a large scale. In 1985, 7 million tons of steel, about one-third of domestic output, was exported (CONSIDER, 1986).

At the end of the period studied, the satisfaction of domestic needs continued to depend heavily on imports only in the case of copper and zinc. It is noteworthy that these are precisely the two metals that exhibit the sharpest short-run variations in consumption and IU since the mid-1970s.

---

[3]Interview with Alexandre Balinski of CONSIDER, Brasilia, March 1987.

The import-licensing procedure is the likely explanation for this short-run instability.

Until the mid-1970s requirements regarding metal imports were satisfied reasonably smoothly. With the accentuated foreign-exchange constraint in the subsequent period and the tendency toward stop–go macroeconomic policies, the granting of import licenses became more erratic, and the required imports were not always permitted on time. These problems were aggravated during the 1980s.[4] The metal users' response has been to import in excess of their needs at times when licenses are granted more freely. One can hypothesize that the periods of especially severe import restrictions have coincided with a generally restrictive environment for economic policy. In these periods the inventories built up through earlier excessive imports have been depleted, and since most of these inventory variations have remained unrecorded, they presumably have contributed to the short-run destabilization of reported consumption.[5]

The buildup of unreported stocks during years of economic growth and the depletion of such stocks during recessions are known to occur even in the absence of import regulations (Radetzki, 1977) and are likely to have affected the consumption trends for other metals, too. However, Brazil's greater dependence on copper and zinc imports has probably amplified the unreported inventory fluctuations for those two metals.

In conclusion, therefore, the especially strong short-run instability in Brazil's copper and zinc consumption and IU levels since the latter half of the 1970s is seen to depend on a combination of increasingly destabilizing stop–go macroeconomic policies and strong fluctuations in unreported stocks.

What IU trends would emerge in Brazil if trade in fabricated-metal products and metal-containing manufactures were added to reported consumption in order to obtain a measure of overall metal absorption? Available data provide only partial and limited insights to this question. The data on fabricated-copper imports into several developing countries since the late 1960s (presented in the preceding section) demonstrate that in the case of Brazil, these trade flows remained very small both in absolute quantities and as a share of consumption. Therefore, those flows did not affect the reported trend for copper consumption in any important way.

However, the macroeconomic crisis of the 1980s, which severely reduced the domestic requirements of fabricated-metal products, prompted strong efforts by Brazilian metal fabricators to sell in foreign markets.[6] The government assisted these efforts with a variety of fiscal incentives.[7] In conse-

---

[4]Interviews with Joseph Young, editor of *Revistas Minerios,* and Chester Lopinski, director of development for Eluma, São Paulo, both in March 1987.

[5]Interview with Chester Lopinski, director of development of Eluma, São Paulo, March 1987.

[6]Interview with Reinaldo Bock, sales manager of Eluma, São Paolo, March 1987.

[7]Interview with Adolpho Recusani of CEBRACO, March 1987.

quence, the exports of fabricated-aluminum products rose from a negative number in 1980 to a range of from 30,000 to 45,000 tons per year in the 1983–1985 period, whereas for copper, the net export figure increased from less than 3,000 tons per year in the 1978–1980 period to more than 10,000 tons in 1981 and 1982; 16,000 in 1983; 35,000 in 1984; and 20,000 in 1985. At their peaks these exports corresponded to substantially more than 10 percent of the reported consumption of aluminum and copper. These figures indicate that domestic absorption of the two metals became significantly more depressed in the 1980s than is indicated by the figures of reported consumption or IU.

It would be interesting also to quantify the metal content in manufactured trade. Although the data needed for this purpose are hard to obtain, one indication of the direction of the effect is the actual development of Brazilian exports and imports of machinery (electrical and nonelectrical) and transport equipment. These two categories probably capture most of the metals contained in finished-goods trade. Measured in constant 1980 dollars, Brazil's trade deficit in these two categories increased from $0.7 billion in 1965 to $4.8 billion in 1974. By 1980 the deficit had shrunk to $1.0 billion, and in 1983 the country recorded a surplus of $0.5 billion in this trade. (Trade figures are from World Bank [1983] and from the 1985, 1986, and 1987 issues of the World Bank's "Brazil, Country Economic Memorandum." Constant dollars were obtained by using the World Bank's Manufactured Unit Values Index published by the Commodity Studies and Projection Division.)

If the trade figures just quoted are indicative of the quantity of metals contained in traded manufactures, they suggest that domestic metal absorption in Brazil rose faster than the reported consumption series between 1965 and 1974 and that this rate of absorption rose less or fell more than reported consumption in subsequent years.

Although difficult to quantify, it is evident that trade in metal-containing semimanufactures and manufactures reinforces the shifts in the mid-1970s in GDP-based IU trends for aluminum, copper, and steel. It is even possible that a trend shift emerges in GDI-based IU levels when these trade figures are taken into account.

Metal Pricing Policies   Like foreign trade, the prices of metal ingot and fabricated-metal products in Brazil are heavily regulated by the government. As noted, imports of metal ingot are subject to a licensing procedure, and licenses are granted only when domestic production is inadequate to satisfy demand. When imported metals supplement domestic supplies, acceptance of a quota of the latter is usually a precondition for obtaining an import license. In this way the government ensures that no imports are allowed until all domestic supplies have been absorbed.[8]

---

[8]Interview with Alexandre Balinski of CONSIDER, Brasilia, March 1987.

As a rule, the prices of imported metals are not regulated. Import duties are not very high. In the case of refined copper, for instance, transport, port tax, and duty add approximately 30 percent to the international price.[9]

The overall guideline used by the government in establishing the prices for domestically produced metals is that the price should provide coverage for the domestic cost of production. However, lower prices are sometimes decreed when this cost is very high.

When Brazilian production is internationally competitive, the domestic price level will be quite similar to the international one. This is true for steel and aluminum. In the case of steel (heavy plate), the average 1982–1985 Brazilian price was 7 percent higher than the German export price.[10] For aluminum the relatively stable domestic price has been intermittently below and above the London Metal Exchange (LME) quotation, with the average for the same period some 10 percent above the LME price.[11]

For copper and lead, the situation is very different. Because of the high domestic costs of production, average Brazilian lead prices in 1982–1985 were twice as high as prices listed on the LME.[12] Domestic Brazilian price series for more extended periods of time are hard to reconstruct; however, the indications are that the lead price has been kept much above the LME level since at least the mid-1970s. The comparatively high price of this metal for Brazilian users might be at least a partial explanation of this country's very low IU for lead in the 1980s compared to that of other individual developing nations or to the average for all developing countries.

In the case of copper, Caraiba Metais, a very high cost integrated project, went into production in 1982. Since then the Brazilian price has exceeded the LME price by 55 percent[13]—that is, it is substantially above the price of imported material, which dominated Brazilian supply in earlier years. Even the high price charged since 1982 has been barely enough to cover the operating costs of Caraiba Metais. Capital costs have had to be provided for through government subsidies.[14]

Specific mention should be made of the very high level of copper consumption in 1982, which caused a record IU level. This peak is directly related to Caraiba Metais. Users of copper imported record quantities in that year. They greatly expanded their invisible inventories in anticipation of the higher domestic price required to cover Caraiba's costs and of the need to

---

[9]Interviews with Chester Lopinski, director of development at Eluma, and Adolpho Recusani of CEBRACO, both of which took place in São Paolo, March 1987.

[10]The Brazilian price was given by personnel at USIMINAS in Belo Horizonte, March 1987; the German price is from the World Bank (1986).

[11]Interview with Everaldo Santos of the Brazilian Aluminum Association (ABAL), São Paolo, March 1987.

[12]Information from Alexandre Balinski of CONSIDER, Brasilia, March 1987.

[13]Information from Alexandre Balinski of CONSIDER, Brasilia, March 1987.

[14]Interview with Reinaldo Bock, sales manager at Eluma, São Paolo, March 1987.

accept highly priced deliveries of domestic copper after the startup of this venture.

The longer-run implications of the establishment of high-cost copper production in Brazil, and the ensuing rise in relative copper prices, will be a dampening of the copper consumption trend and a reduction in this metal's IU, much as has happened with lead. A high relative price for copper and a low relative price for aluminum and steel will lead to more substitution in favor of the latter materials than would otherwise have occurred. The price disadvantage of copper and the substitution away from this metal will be enhanced if the government proceeds with its plans to develop the large copper deposit at Salobo; that project, too, appears to entail very high costs by any international comparison.[15]

The domestic price regulation also gives rise to a variety of other problems. For instance, at times when the Brazilian aluminum price is below international levels, supply scarcities tend to develop in the domestic market, since exports are more profitable to the producers (according to information provided in 1987 by the Brazilian Aluminum Association). In the 1980s the regulation of metal prices was employed as an instrument for stemming inflation. Because the permitted prices did not provide cost coverage, private producers of zinc on occasion refused to supply (according to information received in 1987 from the Brazilian Lead and Zinc Information Center).

Metal Consumption in India

Macroeconomic Performance and Sectoral Thrust   India is a much poorer country than Brazil. In the 1980s its per capita GDP was less than 15 percent of that for Brazil. In view of India's much greater population, the two nations' total gross domestic products are quite similar in size; in recent years India's GDP was some 20 percent less than Brazil's. For a country at its level of economic development, India has a very large and highly diversified industrial sector. In the 1980s its manufacturing value added was almost one-half that of Brazil's.

India's economic growth performance has been far inferior to Brazil's. From 1960 to 1986 its per capita GDP increased by 55 percent; in Brazil, per capita GDP rose by more than 150 percent. During this entire twenty-seven-year period, three phases in India's economic performance can be identified. From 1960 to 1964 and from 1974 to 1986, per capita GDP experienced a reasonably high and steady expansion. Between 1964 and

---

[15]Interviews with Leons Kovisars of Met Research Corporation, Washington, D.C., March 1986; and with Julio Senna, director of investment management at Eluma, São Paulo, March 1987.

1974, however, almost no growth in per capita GDP was recorded. In contrast to Brazil, India has experienced a relatively steady development of its gross domestic investments. The ratio of GDI to GDP rose from some 20 percent in the first half of the period surveyed to about 23 percent in the second half. The share of manufacturing value added in GDP increased very slowly, from 13 percent in the early 1960s to about 15 percent in the 1980s. During the 1980s India's economic performance remained unaffected by the international financial crisis.

The government has played a very important role in India's economy ever since the country's independence. A very large proportion of gross domestic investments has been in the public sector. In the 1980s the government owned two-thirds of the country's industrial assets (*The Economist*, January 31, 1987). The government's dispositions, as encoded in the country's five-year plans, have thus had a heavy influence on the direction of the economy.

India's early development plans were modeled on the Soviet experience, focusing on quantitative goals, and with a strong emphasis on heavy industry and infrastructure. From the mid-1960s the emphasis shifted as a result of severe agricultural failures and the ensuing need to import increasing quantities of food. Thus, between 1960 and 1965, public investment in three metal-intensive sectors (manufacturing; railways; and electricity, gas, and water) expanded annually by 6.6, 12.5, and 23.7 percent, respectively. In the following ten years the expansion figures were reduced to 1.7, -7.7, and 4.2 percent, respectively (Ahluwalia, 1985). Although this decline was partly due to the general economic stagnation in the country from the mid-1960s, it reflects an important shift of emphasis in development strategy in favor of agriculture. The emergent current-account deficits prompted a somewhat greater role for the market and for prices in the country's macroeconomic policies.

The nature and thrust of the Indian government's development efforts provide some explanation of the metal-intensity levels and developments. Thus, the very high Indian IUs by international standards in the early 1960s (see table 4-12) are certainly due to the emphasis on heavy industry and infrastructure in India's early plans. The strength of this emphasis was unique among the non-Socialist developing countries. The high IU levels could also reflect the raw-material waste typical of Soviet-type centrally planned regimes where prices play a subordinate role (see chapter 5 in this volume, and Winiecki, 1986).

The decline of IU for copper, lead, and zinc in the mid-1960s and subsequent stagnation in IU trends for all metals except nickel can be seen as adjustments to a more diversified development effort and to the greater role of markets and prices in more recent Indian development plans. India's involvements in wars during the period surveyed are also relevant, because war and accompanying armaments efforts are bound to increase metal consumption and IU.[16] In 1962 India fought a war with China, in 1965 with Pakistan, and in 1971 again with Pakistan for the liberation of what became Bangladesh. All three wars were of relatively short duration, and all left a visible imprint in the GDP-based IU values.

Direct Intervention in Patterns of Metal Consumption   Ever since the mid-1960s India has been suffering from a perennial foreign-exchange constraint that has prompted the government to encourage the use of metals in which India is relatively self-sufficient for those which are imported.

For a long time domestic output has accounted for a very high proportion of India's consumption of aluminum and steel. In copper, lead, and zinc, in constrast, one-half or more of the amount consumed has come from abroad. As a consequence, the consumption of aluminum and steel has been encouraged by the authorities, whereas that of copper, lead, and zinc has not. Encouragement and discouragement have taken a variety of forms; for instance, the government can command the publicly owned industries to substitute one metal for another, and it can issue decrees to be followed by all economic agents. The latter occurred in the mid-1960s, when the government decreed that only aluminum wire should be used in electricity transmission and housewiring; the decree was repealed in the 1970s on technological grounds.[17] The decree helps explain the substantial rise in IU of aluminum and the decline in IU of copper in the mid-1960s. At a more general level the demotion of copper, lead, and zinc use by the public authorities has certainly contributed to the stagnant IU trends for these metals from the late 1960s onward.

Relative Metal Prices   The Indian government has intervened heavily in the process of price determination for metals. Domestic producer prices have been set by the authorities in consideration of the costs of production. Import duties have been kept at levels that provide protection for domestic output. Small amounts of metals have been traded in unregulated markets in the major Indian cities, but the prices have been heavily influenced by the levels of producer price.

India's relative self-sufficiency in aluminum and steel and its dependence on imports of the other major metals reflects to some extent the country's comparative advantage as a metal producer. The costs of domestic production of aluminum and steel have exceeded the international costs of a much smaller margin than have the costs of producing copper, lead, and zinc.

The imposition of quite substantial duties on even the "favored" metals

---

[16]Interview with Dr. B. K. Ganguly of Ganguly and Associates, Bombay, December 1986.

[17]Interview with B. Binani, President of Indian Non-ferrous Metals Manufacturers' Association, Bombay, January 1987.

Table 4-14. Ratios Between Indian and International Prices of Major Nonferrous Metals, 1972 to 1985

Year	Aluminum	Copper	Lead	Nickel	Zinc
1972	N.A.	1.73	2.25	1.95	2.07
1973	N.A.	1.27	1.98	1.73	1.56
1974	N.A.	1.45	2.10	1.23	1.89
1975	2.28	2.68	2.64	1.66	2.42
1976	1.48	2.29	1.96	1.53	2.52
1977	1.57	2.42	1.60	1.70	2.77
1978	1.74	2.47	1.78	1.64	2.49
1979	1.24	2.11	1.46	1.29	2.26
1980	1.31	2.13	2.12	1.73	2.30
1981	N.A.	2.16	1.91	1.72	2.15
1982	1.99	2.30	2.37	1.96	2.65
1983	1.48	2.56	2.43	1.88	2.63
1984	1.66	2.70	2.28	1.96	2.68
1985	1.81	2.70	2.57	2.11	2.87

Note: Indian prices are Bombay market quotations, as reported by *Metals and Minerals Review, Annual* (Bombay), 1979 through 1986. International prices are London Metal Exchange cash quotations (aluminum and nickel prices prior to 1979 are free-market quotations as reported by *Metal Statistics* [Frankfurt am Main, Metallgesellschaft Aktiengesellschaft, various years]). N.A. = not available.

has produced very high Indian prices for metals in relation both to international prices and to the prices of other goods and services in India. Given the cost structure of Indian metal production, especially high duties were required for copper, lead, and zinc to ensure the survival of the uncompetitive domestic industries that produce these metals. The divergence between Indian and international prices for these three metals therefore has been particularly high. Copper in India, for instance, sold for about 2.5 times the world market price in the early 1980s. Interestingly, the Indian price for nickel, another imported metal, has been somewhat less distorted, as there is no domestic industry to protect (*Metals and Minerals Review Annual*, 1986).

The ratios of Indian to international prices of major nonferrous metals, presented in table 4-14, indicate generally increasing discrepancies between the two since the early 1970s. Although no figures are available for earlier years, it is likely that the discrepancies between Indian and international metal prices became significant only in the early 1960s as a result of the emergent foreign-exchange constraint and the need to protect the expanding domestic production of metal.

The high prices of metals in India have undoubtedly affected metal consumption. Economic logic suggests that the increasing divergence between domestic and international metal prices must have suppressed India's metal demand in general, and that the suppression has been especially strong in the case of copper, lead, and zinc. Domestic metal price policies thus provide a further explanation for the stagnant or falling IU trends for most of the metals under scrutiny.

In view of the role of domestic costs of production in determining domestic metal prices, it is important to explore the reasons for the elevated cost levels in Indian metal-producing industries. India has a relatively rich resource base in bauxite and iron ore but not in the other metals studied. Several of its copper, lead, and zinc firms were set up with the explicit objective of reducing imports even though it was clear that they would not be competitive internationally. Capital equipment is generally much more expensive in India than internationally. The reason is the same as that for the high metal prices: to protect high-cost domestic producers. Power, of which metal producers are intensive users, is predominantly supplied by public units and is priced at levels that are internationally very high (*Mining Journal*, July 10, 1987).

Depressed levels of capacity utilization in the metal-producing industries, which are the result of strikes, delays in deliveries of capital equipment, unavailability of spare parts and other inputs, and persistent power cuts, add significantly to the cost of Indian metal production. For instance, capacity utilization in aluminum was 61 percent in 1983 and 1984, 76 percent in 1984 and 1985, and 72 percent in 1985 and 1986. For steel the corresponding figures were 70, 72, and 83 percent in the three years (*Metals and Minerals Review Annual*, 1984, 1985, 1986). The inadequacy of power supply has long been an especially difficult bottleneck for Indian industry. The costs of power shortages in the mid-1970s have been estimated at an average of about 2 percent of GDP—most of this representing lost output in the industrial sector (World Bank, 1987, p. 65). These difficulties have remained in the 1980s and have hit the energy-intensive metal-producing industries with special severity (World Bank, 1987, p. 65; see also *Mining Journal*, July 10, 1987).

A major proportion of the metal-producing enterprises is publicly owned, and the units are clearly overstaffed. This may provide a social benefit, but it raises the cost of production. For instance, Hindustan Copper, with a total output of 30,000 to 40,000 tons of refined metal in the 1980s, employed 27,000 workers in 1985 (Hindustan Copper, 1985). In Zambia's copper sector, labor productivity was seven times higher; in the United States it was twenty-five times higher (*Metal Statistics;* U.S. Bureau of Mines, 1985; Radetzki, 1985). Labor costs are not particularly low in India if low labor productivity is taken into account. Labor problems resulting in production cuts are common. Saving foreign exchange and generating employment appear to be the primary objectives of India's copper industry. The cost of attaining these objectives contributes strongly to the high cost of India's copper output.

Trade in Metals and Metal Products   Metals have not been exported on a large scale. Fabricated-metal products are sold in export markets, but the sales do not constitute a large proportion of Indian metal consumption, and it is hard to obtain a record that quantifies these sales. Imports of both metal ingot and fabricated-metal products require import licenses that are granted only when the applicant can prove to the licensing agency both need and domestic unavailability of the specific product. State trading organizations predominate in the import trade.

Physical-Supply Constraints   Inadequate supply has constituted a recurrent constraint on Indian metal demand.[18] The government's planning machinery is responsible for ensuring an adequate supply of metal. Overall import needs are determined by the central bureaucracy on the basis of assessments of demand and domestic output. Given the rigidities in import planning, inadequacies regularly arise when domestic output falls below anticipation. Inadequacies also arise when the planning organs permit too small quantities of imports either because they misjudge the level of demand or because the scarcity of foreign exchange puts a limit on metal imports.

Periodic inadequacies on the supply side are likely to suppress the levels and trends of consumption and IU. If, off and on, metal supply is not physically available to satisfy the quantity demanded, one can presume that the ensuing frustration will turn Indian society toward activities that depend less on metals. In this way, supply constraints provide yet another explanation for the failure of Indian metal IU to rise.

Metal Consumption in South Korea

The outstanding feature of the South Korean economy is its extraordinarily fast growth. Between 1960 and 1986 the country's per capita GDP increased almost fivefold, more than twice as much as that of Brazil. Very few other countries have recorded rates of economic growth during the past two and a half decades that can match South Korea's. In 1986, South Korea's per capita GDP exceeded Brazil's by about 10 percent. Its total GDP was one-third as large as that of Brazil.

Metal consumption in South Korea began late; except for steel, there is no record of quantities consumed prior to 1962, and reported consumption in the following years was quite small. Significant amounts were consumed only from the late 1960s onward, but even then they were very low in comparison with consumption levels in Brazil and India. In 1968, South Korea consumed 0.8 million tons of steel. In Brazil and India, steel consumption in that year was 4.5 and 5.9 million tons, respectively.

---

[18]Interviews with P. R. Latey, director general of Technical Development of the Government of India, and with I. Z. Bhatty, director general of the National Council of Applied Economic Research, both in Delhi, January 1987.

From the late 1960s onward, however, South Korea's metal consumption has expanded rapidly, reaching levels comparable to those of Brazil and India in the mid-1980s (see table 4-11). South Korean intensities of use were quite low in the 1960s but then rose rapidly and by the 1970s exceeded those of Brazil and India for most metals. In the mid-1980s they attained a level that was very high internationally.

The growth and sectoral shifts experienced by the South Korean economy, along with indirect metal trade, provide a reasonable explanation for its trends in metal consumption and IU. In the 1960s, South Korea was essentially an agricultural economy; only at the end of the decade did the country initiate its "modern economic growth."

The direction of South Korea's development efforts has favored high metal consumption. The share of manufacturing in GDP rose from 9 percent in 1960 to 34 percent in 1986 (Hwang, 1989). Within the manufacturing sector there was a policy-induced shift toward heavy industry from the mid-1970s onward. As a result, the share of heavy industry in GDP increased from 3 percent in 1961 to about 18 percent in 1983 (Bank of Korea, 1984).

South Korea's remarkable economic growth has been made possible by an equally remarkable increase in gross domestic investment. Accounting for less than 10 percent of GDP in the early 1960s, GDI rose rapidly to some 25 percent of GDP by 1970. Since the latter half of the 1970s GDI has been maintained at above 30 percent of GDP—a very high level by international standards. By comparison Brazilian GDI peaked in 1975 at 26 percent of GDP and declined to between 15 and 20 percent in the 1980s. In India, GDI has remained at about 23 percent of GDP since the mid-1970s.

As a result of South Korea's investment performance, its recent GDI-based IU levels, while still impressive, appear less formidable than those based on GDP. In the mid-1980s the GDI-based IU for steel in South Korea was at about the same level as in Brazil and India. It was slightly higher for lead and zinc and somewhat lower for aluminum and nickel. Only in the case of copper did GDI-based IU in South Korea remain far above the Brazilian and Indian levels.

Indirect metal trade has also had a strong effect on metal consumption in South Korea. Total foreign trade has experienced an impressive growth. The share of exports in GDP expanded from 2 percent in 1960 to 23 percent in 1973 and 43 percent in 1986; that of imports, from 10 to 29 and 39 percent in the corresponding years (Hwang, 1989). Until the late 1970s, South Korea's development thrust had an import-substitution orientation, and its new industries enjoyed heavy protection. After domestic needs had been satisfied, however, the development strategy shifted toward export promotion, and in the 1980s South Korea generated rapidly expanding exports of metal-intensive manufactures such as ships, vehicles, and heavy machinery. The share of heavy industry in total exports rose from 20 percent in the early 1970s to above 50 percent in 1983 (Bank of Korea, 1984). The country's construction industry, too, became increasingly export oriented; its labor and service exports were supplemented by metal-containing physical inputs. The indirect trade in metal generated by the South Korean economy after domestic needs had been satisfied provides part of the explanation for the high IU levels recorded by South Korea in the 1980s. In the case of steel, estimates suggest that indirect trade reduced IU in the early 1970s by more than 10 percent (indirect metal imports were greater than exports). By the late 1970s indirect steel trade had attained balance, but in the 1984–1986 period, net exports of metal contained in semimanufactures and finished products added almost one-third to the IU of steel (Hwang, 1989).

Although the sectoral shifts, high level of investment, and indirect metal exports added to South Korea's IU, growth and economic change also involved rapid technological transformation with a metal-saving bias. Hwang's (1989) study on steel use by industry is helpful here. It indicates, for instance, that between 1973 and 1983 the use of steel per unit of output declined by 71 percent in power-generating machinery, 62 percent in nonresidential construction, and 57 percent in both metal-working machinery and public works. Apparently, the sectoral shifts, high investment levels, and indirect exports completely overwhelmed the metal-saving bias of technological change demonstrated by these figures.

An unresolved puzzle is why copper stands out among the metals in terms of IU levels, and why aluminum and nickel record more modest intensity values in comparison with those in other countries (see table 4-12). One possibility is that the greater use of aluminum in consumer goods has suppressed its consumption in the heavily investment-oriented South Korean economy. The modest consumption of nickel recorded for South Korea may be explained by the country's heavy reliance on imports of scrap (Vukmanovic, 1986), including ferrous scrap, whose nickel content is not counted in the statistics for metal consumption.

Macroeconomic and sectoral developments suggest that the fast increases in the country's IU levels may not continue. The GDI ratio has remained stagnant since the late 1970s, and this may be a sign that it will not rise much more from its present level, which is high by international standards. And although the country may continue to expand its exports, indirect metal exports are unlikely to grow at the rates of past years, given the recent redirection of industrial policy toward less metal-intensive, high-tech activities such as electronics, computers, and bioengineering (Bank of Korea, 1984).

CONCLUSIONS

The data for the developing countries as a group support the hypothesis that metal consumption and IU rise with per capita income in low-income nations. Metal consumption in the Third World has continued to expand over the entire period examined, although the rate of growth did decline about 1979. This slowdown was due entirely to a sharp deterioration in macroeconomic performance.

In contrast to the OECD countries, the developing countries as a group generally exhibit rising IU levels throughout the period under investigation. Closer scrutiny reveals that the difference between the two groups is primarily due to their investment performance. The share of GDI in gross domestic product rose substantially in the developing countries during the period under study, while stagnating in the industrialized market economies. Indeed, when IU is measured on the basis of GDI, the rising trend in the developing countries remains only for aluminum and nickel, the "new metals." For the other metals the IU trend declined in striking parallel with developments in the industrialized market economies.

Although it is difficult to verify the hypothesis that materials-saving technology tends to reduce IU over time at each level of GDP per capita, cross-country data for a sample of developing countries with recorded copper consumption over more than two decades do suggest some decline in IU over time. The effect of materials-saving technology is also clearly apparent from a more detailed set of data for South Korea in the case of steel.

Comparisons of IU across eleven low-income countries, and in each of these countries over time, yield a large variability in IU values and convey no coherent pattern or clear relationships with macroeconomic variables. The situation is not greatly improved by using purchasing power parities in place of official exchange rates in determining GDP, or by taking account of indirect metal trade—although it must be admitted that the data used to measure such trade are incomplete and of weak quality. This situation is thus consistent with the third hypothesis put forth at the beginning of this chapter—namely, that national policies pursued by individual countries are important determinants of intensity of metal use. The absence of coherent intercountry patterns could reflect the fact that such policies have a stronger effect on IU than do the level and change of per capita GDP or materials-saving technological progress. Indeed, some pattern in the IU figures does emerge when the eleven countries are classified according to the development strategies they pursue. IUs tend to be higher in countries where the manufacturing sector is emphasized and international trade is promoted, and lower in countries where the primary production sector is favored and trade is restricted.

The importance of national policies for metal consumption and IU levels emerges even more clearly in the detailed studies of Brazil, India, and South Korea. The rapid rise of metal IU in Brazil between 1965 and 1975, the ensuing stagnation in the late 1970s, and the decline in the 1980s are all closely related to that country's macroeconomic policies. The years 1965 through 1975 have been called the decade of the "Brazilian miracle," with very high investments made in metal-intensive heavy infrastructure. This emphasis ended in the late 1970s. The negative current account effect of higher petroleum prices was an added constraint on Brazil's economy in those years. The debt crisis of the 1980s has resulted in a declining investment ratio and highly unstable and, on average, very slow economic growth, both of which have depressed the intensity of metal use.

India's high IU levels in the early 1960s are explained by the strong emphasis on heavy industry and metal-intensive infrastructure in the country's early development plans. Subsequent declines in IU were caused by a shift in development strategy toward agriculture as well as by microeconomic and trade policies that kept metal prices very high.

Because of perennial foreign exchange constraints, the governments of both Brazil and India have pursued trade and pricing policies that promote the consumption of metals in which these countries are self-sufficient, and discourage the use of imported metals. Such policies, too, have left an imprint on IU levels.

In South Korea the emphasis on heavy industry, the very high investment ratios, and the promotion of metal-containing manufactured exports over the past two decades explain the impressive increase and currently high level of that country's metal intensities of use.

In summary, then, our studies of the three individual countries all highlight the importance of domestic policies in determining metal consumption and IU trends. The nature of macroeconomic policy plays a crucial role in this respect. So does the level and content of gross domestic investments, and the sectoral thrust of development efforts. Trade policy related to metals, as well as direct government intervention in the operation of metal-producing or metal-consuming industries, is important in some developing countries. Supply constraints caused by public policy and price regulation have also discouraged the use of metals in some of these countries.

The consumption of metals in the developing countries as a group is likely to continue to expand, assuming, as seems likely, that GDP will grow sufficiently to permit per capita income to rise. It is a more open question whether the GDP-based intensities of use will continue to increase. Such an increase appears to be contingent on rising investment ratios, and it is by no means certain that this will occur. These ratios are already quite high both in historical terms and compared to other countries.

The variations among developing countries in terms of past development performance, current conditions, and prospects are great. Hence, it is impossible to explain or forecast metal consumption and IU trends in individual countries on the basis of the overall performance of the developing countries.

Detailed analyses similar to those for Brazil and India presented earlier are needed to illuminate past performance and to clarify future consumption trends in individual countries. Our investigations point to the multitude of factors that have to be taken into account. Although such analyses may throw interesting light on the relationships that hold in the country under investigation, the results ordinarily have limited applicability to other countries. Generalizations will be of little value, in view of the considerable variation, even in countries at similar levels of per capita GDP, in the factors that shape metal consumption and in their importance.

REFERENCES

Ahluwalia, I. J. 1985. *Industrial Growth in India* (Delhi, Oxford University Press).

Bank of Korea. 1984. "Industry in Korea" (Seoul, Bank of Korea).

CONSIDER. 1986. *Statistical Yearbook* (Brasilia, CONSIDER).

Hindustan Copper. 1985. *Annual Report* (Calcutta, Hindustan Copper).

Hwang, Lee H. 1989. "Intensity of Steel Use in the Less Developed Countries: The Case of Korea" (Ph.D. dissertation, Colorado School of Mines).

International Wrought Copper Council. *World Trade in Copper and Copper Alloy Semimanufactures* (London, International Wrought Copper Council, published annually).

Metals and Minerals Review Annual. 1979 through 1986 (Bombay).

Radetzki, M. 1977. "Fluctuations in Invisible Stocks: A Problem for Copper Market Forecasting," World Bank Commodity Paper no. 27 (Washington, D.C., World Bank).

_____. 1985. *State Mineral Enterprises: An Investigation into Their Impact on International Mineral Markets* (Washington, D.C., Resources for the Future).

Syrquin, M., and H. Chenery. 1989. "Patterns of Development 1950 to 1983," World Bank Discussion Paper no. 41 (Washington, D.C., World Bank).

U.S. Bureau of Mines. 1985. *Mineral Facts and Problems, 1985* (Washington, D.C., U.S. Government Printing Office).

Vukmanovic, Z. 1986. "South Korea, a Fast Growing Economy, and Even Faster Growing Copper Consumption," *CIPEC Quarterly Review* (October–December).

Winiecki, J. 1986. "The Overgrown Industrial Sector in the STEs; Evidence, Explanations, Consequences," *Comparative Economic Studies* vol. 28.

World Bank. 1983. *Brazil, Industrial Policies and Manufactured Exports* (Washington, D.C.).

_____. 1986. *Commodity Trade and Price Trends* (Washington, D.C.).

_____. 1987. *World Development Report 1987* (Washington, D.C.).

5

The Centrally Planned Economies: Extravagant Consumers

ISTVAN DOBOZI

After a long period of strong and steady growth, the metal consumption of the European socialist countries belonging to the Council for Mutual Economic Assistance (CMEA) fell considerably in the mid-1970s. After 1979, consumption completely stagnated for many metals. This chapter investigates the fundamental forces underlying this unforeseen discontinuity in demand growth.

The first section of the chapter focuses on the slowdown in general economic activity of the CMEA countries and the evolution of their intensity of metal use. Because the decline in intensity of use (IU) is an important force behind the pronounced downward shift in growth of metal demand, particularly since the late 1970s, the second section attempts to identify the major forces underlying the marked decrease in intensity of metal use. In this context several important questions arise. Are the CMEA countries moving to a postindustrial economy with a deemphasis on highly metal-absorbing sectors? Or, rather, are intrasectoral shifts in the product composition of income at play? Has technological progress accelerated, causing shifts in the material composition of income and an increase in "metal productivity"? Has the improvement of materials management through administrative and economic measures been a factor in the decline of IU?

Despite the apparent recent peaking of IU, the CMEA countries' metal use per unit of gross domestic product (GDP) continues to be excessively high by international standards, indicating a "material efficiency gap" vis-à-vis the Western market economies. Indeed this feature seems to be the most distinctive aspect of the metal consumption patterns of the developed socialist economies. Is this condition of "profligate" use of materials system-related—that is, caused by the incentive pattern associated with central planning—as many analysts suggest? The third section of this chapter applies econometric techniques to assess the importance of systemic characteristics such as central planning on levels of steel and aluminum consumption. This section offers some explanation for the system-related causes of overconsumption under central planning.

The results throughout reflect a discrepancy between the large number of questions raised and the smaller number of firm, empirically substantiated answers. It is not easy to delineate precisely the various forces that drive shifts in metal consumption trends, especially in the IU paths. IU reflects many heterogeneous forces whose measurement is often difficult or impossible. Moreover, this investigation was particularly plagued by the unavailability of data at sufficiently low levels of disaggregation; thus, proxies are used more frequently than is ideal.

The quality of data on metal consumption and gross domestic product in the CMEA countries presents a further difficulty for the analysis. Because most of the CMEA countries do not publish complete statistics on GDP and metal consumption, production, and trade, the data for these countries represent more or less qualified guesses by experts. However, breaks in the growth of consumption by the CMEA nations appear so pronounced that it becomes clear that shifts in the underlying trends dominate the possible statistical distortions.

This chapter focuses only on the developed centrally planned economies, specifically those within the CMEA. China, other Asian centrally planned economies, and Cuba are not considered here, for several reasons. First, the developed European CMEA countries account for about 80 percent of the total metal consumption of all centrally planned economies. Second, the large discrepancies in the level of economic development and the pattern of GDP between the developed and developing centrally planned economies would create an excessively heterogeneous group of countries. Finally, there are even more severe problems with the availability and quality of data for the developing centrally planned economies.

For analytical reasons we employ two different groupings of CMEA countries: the CMEA-7 comprises Bulgaria, Czechoslovakia, the German Democratic Republic (East Germany), Hungary, Poland, Romania, and the USSR; and the CMEA-6 includes all of the former but the USSR. This separation is justified by the disproportionately large weight of the USSR in the seven-country aggregate, which may potentially bias conclusions in the context of the smaller CMEA countries.

Consumption figures refer to the apparent (or reported) consumption of the commodity, derived as domestic production of unwrought metal plus imports, minus exports. Because of the lack of data, changes in the level of national inventories of the commodity are ignored. IU measures tons of metal consumed per million dollars of GDP in constant 1980 dollars. To

Table 5-1. Growth in Metal Consumption in the CMEA-7, CMEA-6, and USSR: Average Annual Rate of Change, 1960–1973, 1973–1979, and 1979–1987

(percent)

Group or country and period	Steel	Aluminum	Copper	Zinc	Nickel	Lead	Tin
CMEA-7							
1960–1973	5.6	7.7	4.8[a]	6.1	5.2[b]	5.3	3.9[c]
1973–1979	3.0	3.8	4.2	3.4	5.2	3.7	1.8
1979–1987	0.5	−0.5	−0.3	0.0	0.9	−0.3	1.1
CMEA-6							
1960–1973	5.6	10.3	6.2[a]	5.2	N.A.	6.0	5.5[c]
1973–1979	3.7	3.5	5.1	2.5	8.1	2.3	−3.3
1979–1987	−1.3	−0.6	0.3	−0.3	1.6	−0.7	−1.3
USSR							
1960–1973	5.6	5.7	4.1	6.5	N.A.	5.0	2.4[c]
1973–1979	2.7	3.9	3.6	3.6	4.5	4.5	3.9
1979–1987	1.2	−0.4	−0.7	0.1	0.8	−0.1	2.4

Note: N.A. = not available.

Sources: Steel consumption data from International Iron and Steel Institute, *Steel Statistical Yearbook* (Brussels, IISI, various issues); consumption data for other metals from *Metal Statistics* (Frankfurt am Main, Metallgesellschaft Aktiengesellschaft, various years).

[a]From 1965 to 1973
[b]Including China.
[c]From 1963 to 1973.

track consumption trends, one would ideally be interested in total metal absorption by the economy. The latter also reflects indirect metal trade, that is, the metal contained in imports and exports of semifabricated and final goods. As data on the metal content of manufactured goods are not available, indirect metal trade is not covered here. It is worth mentioning that for the countries in the Organisation for Economic Co-operation and Development (OECD), there is limited empirical evidence suggesting that the difference between apparent consumption and metal absorption can be substantial (see chapter 3 in this volume). (For steel in the Western countries, see Keeling [1982, pp. 10–11]; for copper in the United States, see Hutchison and Tilton [1987, pp. 325–334]).

LONG-RUN CONSUMPTION TRENDS IN CMEA

The CMEA countries' consumption of metals grew briskly for many years, unaffected even by the ups and downs of the international business cycle. However, as table 5-1 and figure 5-1 show, this growth in consumption slowed in the mid-1970s and completely stalled for most metals after 1979. An especially sharp break occurred in the CMEA-6 after 1979, with the rate

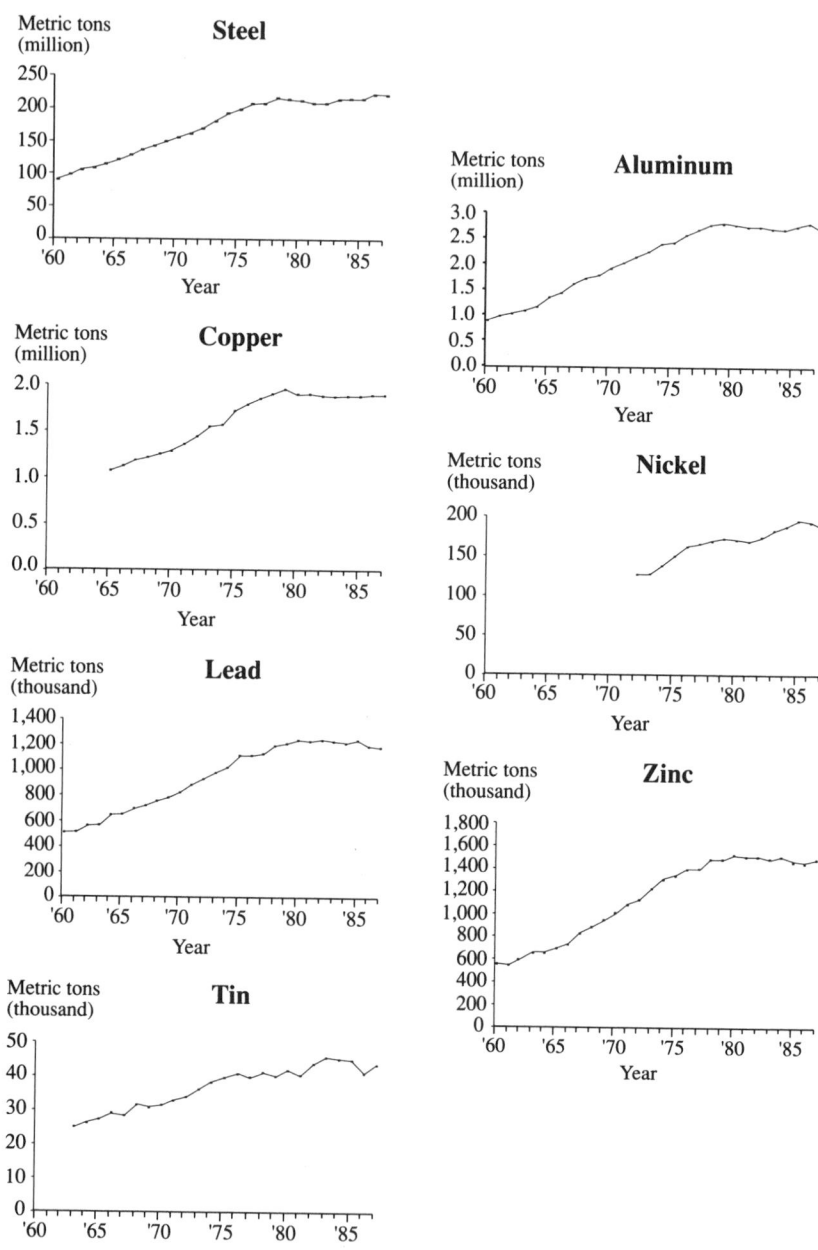

Figure 5-1. Consumption of selected metals in the CMEA-7, 1960–1987.

Note: Data earlier than those shown are not available for copper, nickel, and tin.

Source: Statistical appendix in this volume.

of growth becoming negative for all metals except copper and nickel. This striking departure from historical trends follows the same pattern observable in the OECD countries with about a half-decade lag.

What are the underlying causes of this remarkable and unexpected discontinuity in demand growth? Our approach to this question starts with conventional demand analysis. Specifically, the following double-logarithmic demand equation is estimated for the individual CMEA countries and the two CMEA country groups:

$$Y_t = a \ Q_t^b \ P_{own(t-1)}^c \ P_{oil(t-1)}^d \ e^{u_t}$$

where

Y_t = total metal consumption in thousands of tons in year t

Q_t = total GDP in year t in millions of constant 1980 dollars

$P_{own(t-1)}$ = metal's world market price in constant 1980 dollars, lagged one year

$P_{oil(t-1)}$ = world price of oil in constant 1980 dollars, lagged one year

a = constant

b = income elasticity

c = price elasticity of metal demand

d = elasticity of metal demand with respect to world price of oil

u_t = error in year t

This demand model posits a link between total metal consumption and total GDP, thus treating the demand for metal as a derived demand generated by aggregate demand for GDP. The demand for metal is assumed to be influenced by the world real price of metal. It is reasonable to assume that consumers are limited in their ability to respond immediately to a price change. Therefore, the metal price variable is entered into the model with a one-year lag. Although intra-CMEA mineral prices may deviate from world market prices, the latter (in most cases, from a London Metal Exchange quotation[1]) were chosen as explanatory variables, as most countries rely on non-CMEA imports to satisfy some of their metal import needs, and thus the marginal cost is the world market price. The oil price, which is also lagged one year, is introduced to control for the negative effects of higher oil prices on overall investment activity, which in turn generates a considerable part of the demand for most metals. Furthermore, the world oil price can be taken as a proxy for the foreign-exchange variable, as oil price increases strain the balance of payments and thus tend to reduce the oil-importing

---

[1]The copper, zinc, lead, and tin prices are based on official quotations of the London Metal Exchange. The aluminum price is based on the British price, and the nickel price is based on the Western European free market price. The oil price is that of the Arabian Light posted price.

CMEA countries' capability to import metals, particularly from extra-CMEA sources. The oil price variable also captures a public policy effect resulting from the emphasis on material savings to support the higher-priority conservation of energy, including oil. Although the CMEA-6 countries import most of their oil, the USSR is a major exporter. As a result, the negative effect of higher oil prices is expected to be more pronounced for the CMEA-6.

The results of the estimation are given in table 5-2. As expected, there is a strong relationship between the level of metal consumption and the total GDP. For the CMEA-6 the activity elasticity is greater than unity for all metals under investigation. Interestingly, Soviet metal consumption seems to be less strongly determined by the level of overall economic activity. Price generally does not show up as a significant determinant of metal use in the CMEA countries. This is not to suggest that price is irrelevant, but only that price variations in the period under review probably had a relatively small effect on demand compared with other variables—in particular the volume of GDP, the dominant variable. This makes sense when one considers the derived nature of demand for metals, the relatively small weight of the cost of primary metals in the price of final products, and the limited scope for price-induced substitution between different materials in the short term, especially when shifts in relative prices are not pronounced. Certainly, the price rigidity, an observed systemic feature of centrally planned economies, also has been a contributing factor. In this context it is worth mentioning that even in the industrial Western economies, price generally does not have a very measurable effect on the demand for many metals (see Jack Faucett Associates, 1986, pp. 12–22).

There is more evidence, however, that metal consumption in the CMEA-6 is somewhat sensitive to movements in oil prices. The oil price elasticity of metal demand is found to be a significant determinant, although with relatively small parameter value, for aluminum, tin, lead, and nickel. For instance, a 10 percent rise in oil price (other things being equal) reduces demand for aluminum by 1.7 percent. For the CMEA-7 the oil price generally does not show up as a significant factor in determining consumption, which probably reflects the large weight of the oil-exporting USSR in the CMEA-7 aggregate. In the Soviet case the effect of higher oil prices on metal demand appears to be positive for a number of metals. These results suggest that the rapidly increasing oil price, and particularly the marked slowdown in economic growth, contributed to the lagging growth in metal demand in the CMEA countries.

The growth of GDP dropped sharply in the CMEA countries after the first oil shock, and a further decline ensued as an aftermath of the second oil shock. As table 5-3 shows, in the CMEA-7 the rate of GDP growth dropped from 4.7 percent in the 1960–1973 period to 2.9 percent in the 1973–1979 period and then to 2.4 percent in the 1979–1987 period. The break in economic growth was particularly sharp in the oil-importing CMEA-6, fall-

Table 5-2. Elasticity Parameter Values of CMEA Metal Consumption, 1960–1984

Metal and country or group	GDP	Own price	Oil price
Aluminum			
Bulgaria	4.167*	−0.025	−0.210*
Czechoslovakia	4.050*	0.219	−0.210*
East Germany	1.879*	0.106	−0.128*
Hungary	3.010*	−0.458**	−0.047
Poland	1.796*	0.455	−0.160*
Romania	2.477*	−0.091	−0.012
USSR	1.314*	0.245	−0.068*
CMEA-6	2.397*	0.122	−0.166*
CMEA-7	1.533*	0.199	−0.082*
Copper			
Bulgaria	1.790*	−0.037	−0.073**
Czechoslovakia	1.324*	0.072	0.038
East Germany	0.924*	0.017	0.017
Poland	1.467*	−0.140*	0.075
Romania	2.975*	0.110	0.191**
USSR	0.769*	−0.020	0.018
CMEA-6	1.424*	−0.043	0.009
CMEA-7	0.875*	−0.043	0.018
Tin			
Bulgaria	2.352*	0.000	−0.337*
Czechoslovakia	1.152*	−0.084	−0.117**
East Germany	0.878*	0.391	−0.044
Hungary	0.893*	−0.122	0.037
Poland	1.377*	−0.042	−0.276*
Romania	0.950*	−0.250	−0.198*
USSR	0.543*	0.012	0.129
CMEA-6	1.110*	−0.071	−0.142*
CMEA-7	0.741*	−0.020	0.021
Zinc			
Bulgaria	2.797*	−0.254*	−0.002
Czechoslovakia	0.809*	0.120	0.074
East Germany	0.800*	0.002	0.020
Hungary	2.019*	0.134	−0.056**
Poland	0.585*	−0.005	−0.008
Romania	1.999*	0.038	0.133
USSR	1.496*	0.023	−0.044**
CMEA-6	1.062*	−0.007	0.018
CMEA-7	1.371*	0.009	−0.026
Lead			
Bulgaria	1.989*	0.013	−0.093*
Czechoslovakia	0.458*	0.131	0.042

(Continued)

119

Table 5-2 (continued)

Metal and country or group	GDP	Own price	Oil price
Lead (continued)			
East Germany	0.567*	0.153	0.037
Hungary	0.400*	0.054	−0.051
Poland	0.759*	−0.006	−0.044**
Romania	1.786*	−0.072	−0.186*
USSR	1.022*	0.030	0.061
CMEA-6	1.087*	0.059	−0.032*
CMEA-7	1.011*	0.041	0.032
Nickel			
Bulgaria	4.118*	0.215	0.078
East Germany	2.842*	0.540	−0.179**
Hungary	0.964**	−0.319*	0.160
Poland	2.878*	0.189	0.012
Romania	3.298*	1.164	−0.148**
USSR	0.794*	−0.116	−0.056
CMEA-6	3.251*	0.467	−0.097**
CMEA-7	1.366*	0.056	−0.016

*Statistically significant at the 5 percent level.
**Statistically significant at the 10 percent level.

ing from 4.4 percent to 3.0 percent and 1.9 percent in the two subsequent periods. Even in the USSR, a very considerable drop occurred between 1960–1973 and 1979–1987.[2]

Although lagging economic growth certainly shows up as an important factor underlying the break in historical demand expansion, table 5-3 and figure 5-2 highlight the importance of other demand-reducing forces as well. In the 1973–1979 period, the slowdown in economic growth worked in tandem with IU trends to decelerate the growth in CMEA-7 consumption of steel, aluminum, and zinc, whereas for copper, lead, and nickel, rising IU exerted a countervailing influence. In the 1979–1987 period, an identical pattern can be observed for all commodities: a further slowdown in GDP

---

[2]The marked slowdown in the economic growth of the CMEA-6 coincides with the two oil shocks, but some of the forces underlying the decline are unrelated to those shocks, basically reflecting the systemic and policy-related difficulties of the transition from an "extensive" pattern of growth to an "intensive" one. This is the case particularly for the USSR, which was a beneficiary of soaring oil prices yet could not avoid a major deterioration in macroeconomic performance. In most of the CMEA-6, emergency adjustment measures in connection with external financial imbalances, which took the form of slashed domestic absorption through steep investment cutbacks, have contributed greatly to the precipitous drop in overall economic activity since the early 1980s. In the case of Poland, the second-largest CMEA economy after the USSR, a protracted political crisis has been superimposed on this situation. For a discussion of the causes of the recent economic slowdown in the CMEA countries, see, among others, Marer (1986), Schroeder (1985), and van Brabant (1987).

Table 5-3. Changes in GDP and Intensity of Use (IU) in the CMEA Countries: Average Annual Rate of Change, 1960–1973, 1973–1979, and 1979–1987

(percent)

Group or country and period	GDP	Steel	Aluminum	Copper	Zinc	Lead	Nickel	Tin
				Intensity of use				
CMEA-7								
1960–1973	4.7	0.8	2.8	0.1[a]	1.3	0.5	0.4[b]	−1.3[c]
1973–1979	2.9	0.0	0.8	1.0	0.4	0.7	2.2	−0.8
1979–1987	2.4	−2.0	−2.7	−2.8	−2.4	−2.7	−1.5	−1.4
CMEA-6								
1960–1973	4.4	1.1	5.3	1.8[a]	0.7	1.4	N.A.	1.0[c]
1973–1979	3.0	0.6	0.4	1.9	1.1	−0.8	4.7	−4.0
1979–1987	1.9	−3.1	−2.5	−1.7	−2.2	−2.7	−0.3	−3.2
USSR								
1960–1973	4.8	0.6	1.7	0.1	1.5	0.0	N.A.	−3.2[c]
1973–1979	2.9	−0.3	1.0	0.6	0.0	1.5	1.5	1.0
1979–1987	2.6	−1.8	−3.0	−3.1	−2.5	−2.7	−1.9	0.1

Note: N.A. = not available.

[a] From 1965 to 1973.

[b] Including China.

[c] From 1963 to 1973.

Sources: **GDP data sources: For CMEA-6 (1965–1982):** Thad P. Alton, "East European GNP's: Origins of Product, Final Uses, Rates of Growth, and International Comparisons," in U.S. Congress, Joint Economic Committee, *East European Economies: Slow Growth in the 1980s* vol. 1: *Economic Performance and Policy* (Washington, D.C., U.S. Government Printing Office, 1985). **For CMEA-6 (1983–1984):** Thad P. Alton and coauthors, Occasional Paper nos. 85–89 of the Research Project on National Income in East Central Europe (New York, L. W. International Financial Research, 1985). **For Hungary, Poland, Bulgaria (1960–1964), and East Germany (1960, 1963–1964):** World Bank, *World Bank Data Tape: National Accounts, Prices, Exchange Rates and Population for the Period 1960–84* (Washington, D.C., IBRD, 1986). **For Czechoslovakia (1960–1961) and Romania (1960–1961):** derived using net material product indices in United Nations, *Yearbook of National Account Statistics 1970* vols. 1 and 2 (New York, United Nations, 1972). **For East Germany (1961):** estimated using official net material product index in Staatsverlag der Deutsche Democratische Republik, *Statistiche Jahrbuch der Deutsche Democratische Republik 1975* (Statistical Yearbook of the German Democratic Republic 1975) (Berlin, 1975). **For Czechoslovakia (1962–1964), East Germany (1962), Romania (1962–1964):** Jack Faucett Associates, *Changes in Worldwide Demand for Metal Minerals* (Bethesda, Md., Jack Faucett Associates, 1986). **For USSR (1979–1982):** Daniel Bond and Lawrence R. Klein, "Impact of Changes in the Global Environment on the Soviet and East European Economies," in U.S. Congress, Joint Economic Committee, *East European Economies: Slow Growth in the 1980s* vol. 1: *Economic Performance and Policy* (Washington, D.C., U.S. Government Printing Office, 1985). **For USSR (1960–1978):** derived from indices in U.S. Congress, Joint Economic Committee, *USSR: Measures of Economic Growth and Development, 1950–80* (Washington, D.C., U.S. Government Printing Office, 1982). **For USSR (1983–1984):** derived from indices in Jack Faucett Associates, *Changes in Worldwide Demand for Metal Minerals* (Bethesda, Md., Jack Faucett Associates, 1986). **For USSR and CMEA-6 (1985–1987):** derived using net material product indices in Economic Commission for Europe, *Economic Survey of Europe in 1986–1987* (New York, United Nations, 1987) and United Nations, *Economic Bulletin for Europe* vol. 40 (New York, United Nations, 1988).

Steel consumption data: International Iron and Steel Institute, *Steel Statistical Yearbook* (Brussels, IISI, various years).

Consumption data for other metals: *Metal Statistics* (Frankfurt am Main, Metallgesellschaft Aktiengesellschaft, various years).

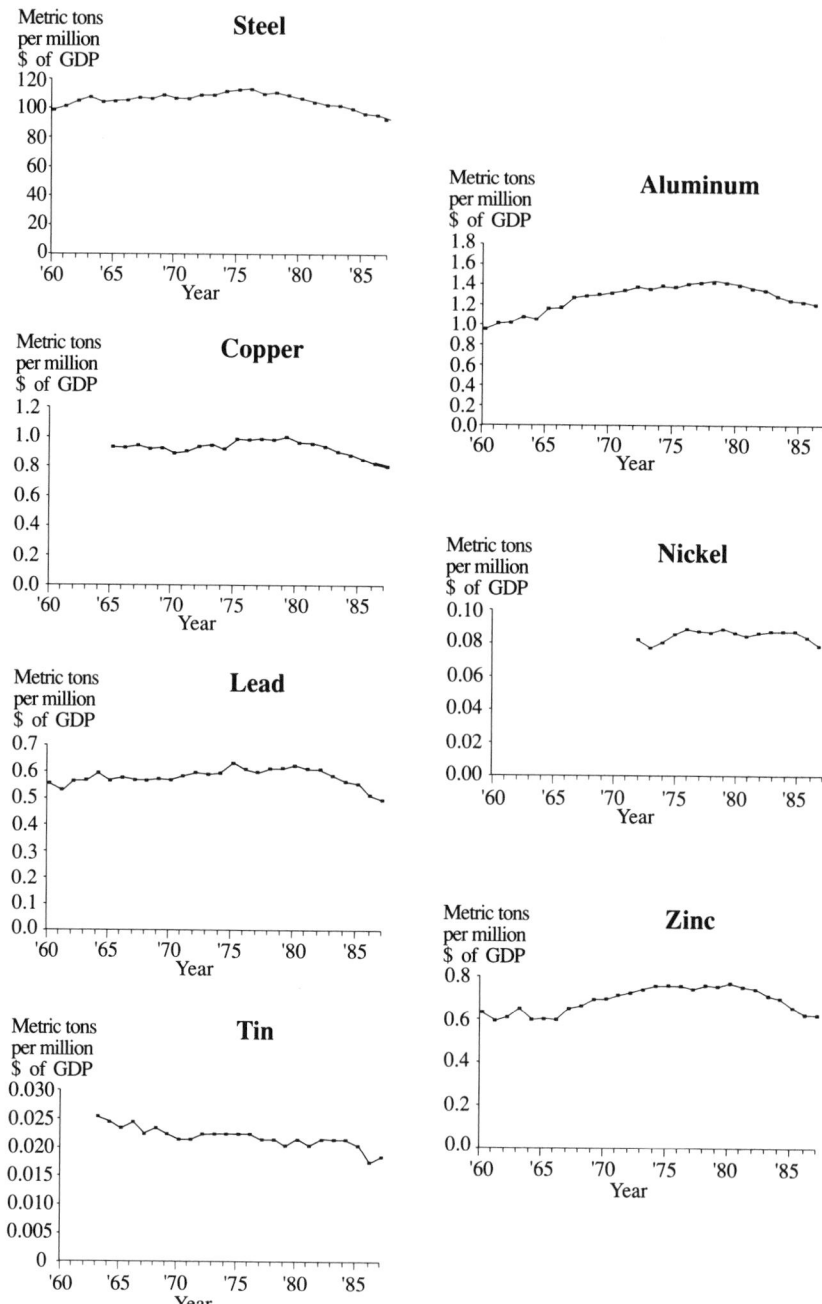

Figure 5-2. Intensity of metal use in the CMEA-7, 1960–1987.

Note: Data earlier than those shown are not available for copper, nickel, and tin.

Source: Statistical appendix in this volume.

122

Table 5-4. Determinants of Shortfall in Metal Consumption, 1973–1987

(percent)

Metal	Total shortfall[a]	Shortfall due to slowdown in GDP[b]	Shortfall due to change in IU[c]	Joint effects[d]
Steel	43.9	25.5 (58.1)	18.4 (41.9)	0.0 (0.0)
Aluminum	57.5	21.6 (37.6)	34.6 (60.2)	1.3 (2.2)
Copper[e]	36.2	16.0 (44.2)	12.4 (34.3)	7.8 (21.5)
Zinc	46.8	21.3 (45.5)	22.4 (47.9)	3.1 (6.6)
Lead	41.1	22.5 (54.7)	16.5 (40.2)	2.1 (5.1)
Nickel[f]	28.0	7.7 (27.5)	3.3 (11.8)	17.0 (60.7)
Tin	29.1	6.5 (22.3)	0.2 (0.7)	22.4 (77.0)

Note: Figures in parentheses show the relative importance of each determinant as a percentage of total shortfall.

[a]Total shortfall is the percentage difference between the projected level of consumption based on the historical (1960–1973) trend growth rate and actual consumption.

[b]This shortfall is based on the actual average rate of growth of GDP while holding rate of change of intensity of use (IU) constant at the 1960–1973 annual average.

[c]This shortfall is based on the actual average annual rate of change of IU, with the rate of growth of GDP held at the 1960–1973 annual average.

[d]These effects include the effects of GDP and IU working together.

[e]The historical trend growth rates of consumption and IU cover the 1965–1973 period.

[f]The historical trend growth rates of consumption and IU include China.

growth and a marked fall in IU joined forces to pull down the growth rate of metal consumption. It is clear that in comparison with the 1973–1979 period, a strong shift occurred between 1979 and 1987, with the decline in IU accounting for most of the downward turn in growth of metal demand. In that most recent period the decline in IU was substantial and particularly important, as its large drop was associated with a comparatively small decrease in the growth of GDP vis-à-vis the previous period.

Table 5-4 shows the relative contributions of the slowdown in GDP growth and changes in IU to the shortfall in metal consumption relative to the projected level (the latter based on historical rate of growth in consumption). Although the slowdown or income effect is self-explanatory, the IU effect captures the combined influence of various factors such as conservation (including the price effect), technological progress, and changes in the output structure. The joint (or interactive) effects capture that part of the shortfall which cannot be attributed to either GDP or IU taken individually because of their interaction. The table reveals that in the 1973–1987 period, slowdown of GDP growth has been the major factor in the consumption shortfall in steel, copper, and lead, whereas in the case of aluminum the reduction in IU has been the relatively more important factor. In zinc, changes in GDP and IU have been of roughly equal importance. (Here we ignore nickel and zinc because the dominance of the joint effects does not allow a meaningful isolation of the GDP and IU effects.) It is to be noted that the relative weight of the IU effect is rather significant (one-third or higher) even in those cases where GDP is the main force behind consumption shortfall.

Index (1973 = 100)

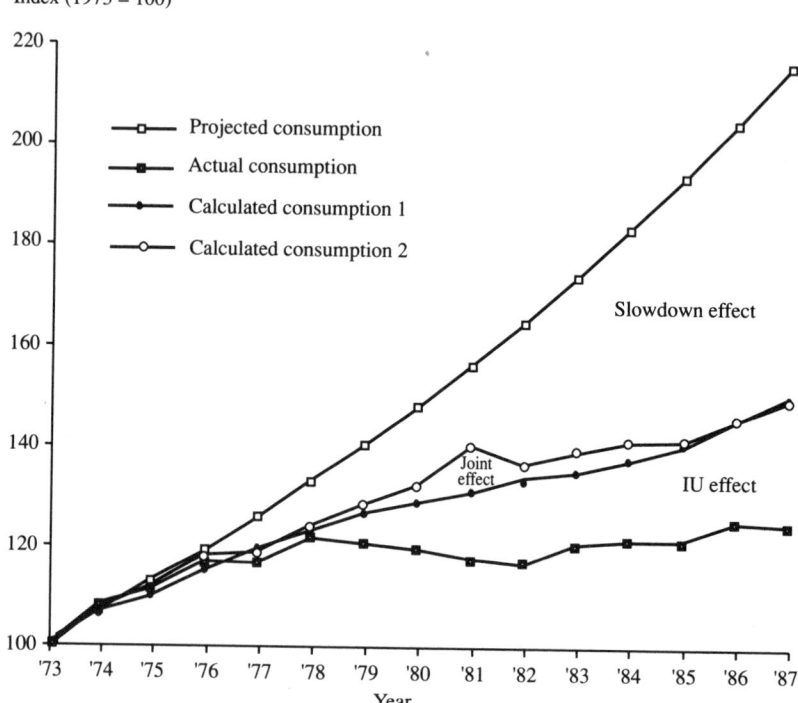

Figure 5-3. Decomposition of shortfall in CMEA-7 steel consumption.
Notes: Projected consumption is based on the 1960–1973 rate of growth. Calculated consumption 1 is based on the actual annual rate of growth in GDP, holding the rate of change in IU constant at the 1960–1973 annual average. Calculated consumption 2 is based on the actual rate of change in IU, holding the rate of GDP growth at the 1960–1973 annual average.

Figures 5-3 through 5-5 illustrate the relative importance of the various determinants of the consumption shortfall on a year-to-year basis for three major metals. From these figures it is apparent that over time, reductions in IU have become a progressively more important factor in causing the shortfall in consumption via-à-vis levels predicted on the basis of historical growth trends.

The foregoing raises the possibility of an irreversible downturn in IU trends in the CMEA countries. As figure 5-6 shows, the turnaround for most metals occurred at a level of economic development where per capita income was between $4,800 and $5,300 (in constant 1980 dollars). In an international cross-sectional perspective, the possibility of a peaking in IU in the CMEA group puts the latter in an intermediate position between the newly industrialized and the OECD countries, as illustrated by an idealized version of the familiar inverted U-shaped IU curve in figure 5-7. (A similar curve is con-

Index (1973 = 100)

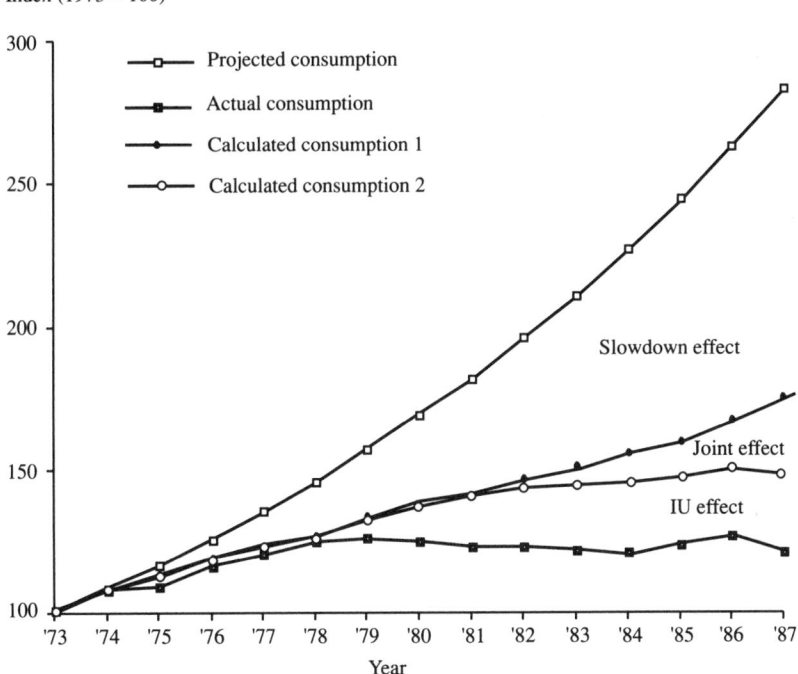

Figure 5-4. **Decomposition of shortfall in CMEA-7 aluminum consumption.**
Notes: Projected consumption is based on the 1960–1973 rate of growth. Calculated consumption 1 is based on the actual annual rate of growth in GDP, holding the rate of change in IU constant at the 1960–1973 annual average. Calculated consumption 2 is based on the actual rate of change in IU, holding the rate of GDP growth at the 1960–1973 annual average.

structed by Dresher [1986, p. 31] without an explicit identification of the position of the CMEA countries.)

POSSIBLE FACTORS CONTRIBUTING TO THE DECLINE IN IU

As the recent debate suggests, it is difficult to discern the various forces behind trends in IU (see chapter 3 and Tilton [1986, 1988]). Until very recently, the dominant view, initiated by Malenbaum (1978), explained the decline in IU in terms of per capita income, accompanied by a shift in overall economic activity away from large absorbers of metals, such as basic infrastructure and heavy industry, toward less material-intensive manufacturing and, particularly, services. In explaining the primary forces behind falling IU trends in the developed Western countries, a newly emerged view attributes greater importance to the changing material composition of income as a result of higher "metal productivity" brought about by the introduction of

Index (1973 = 100)

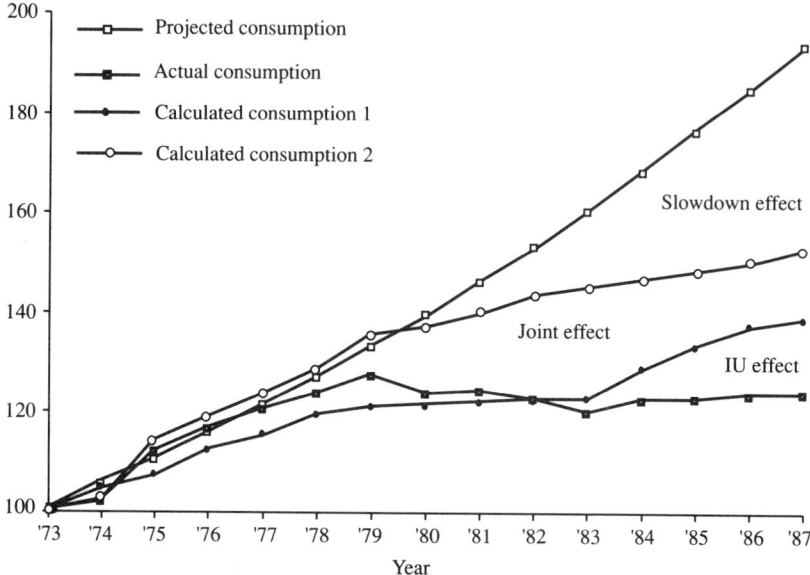

Figure 5-5.   Decomposition of shortfall in CMEA-7 copper consumption.
Notes: Projected consumption is based on the 1965–1973 rate of growth. Calculated consumption 1 is based on actual annual rate of growth in GDP holding the rate of change in IU constant at the 1965–1973 annual average. Calculated consumption 2 is based on the actual rate of change in IU holding the rate of GDP growth at the 1960–1973 annual average.

new materials-saving technologies, intermaterial substitution, government regulation, and so forth.

How relevant are these factors in explaining the underlying causes of the recent break in IU trends in the CMEA countries? What follows is an essentially qualitative assessment of the potential causal factors.

Product Composition of Income: Have CMEA-7 Entered the Postindustrial Era?

Intersectoral shifts in the economy toward less material-intensive activities such as services and high-technology manufacturing—in response to changing consumer preferences, levels of development, and technological progress—constitute a major force in reducing specific metal consumption. The potentially large effect of intersectoral shifts in GDP becomes evident when one considers the enormous differences in specific consumption across sectors. For instance, in 1980 in the CMEA countries the steel intensity of the

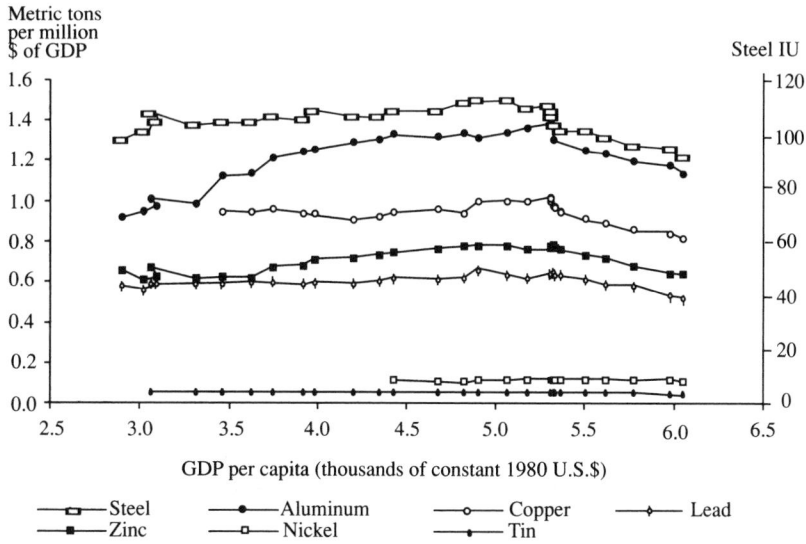

Figure 5-6. Intensity of use (IU) versus GDP per capita for CMEA-7, 1960–1987.

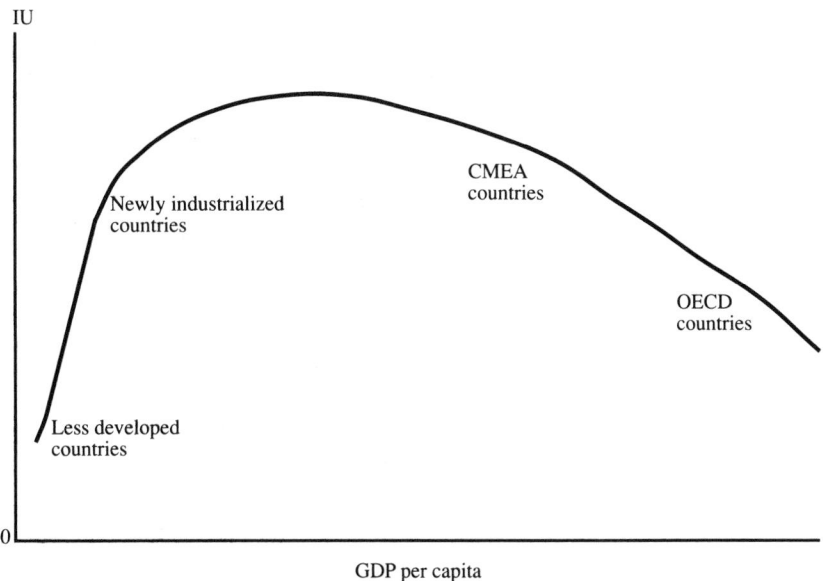

Figure 5-7. Idealized cross-sectional intensity of use (IU) curve for less developed, newly industrialized, CMEA, and OECD countries.

service sector was only about 15 percent of that of the industry as a whole (Economic Commission for Europe, 1984, p. 36).

Table 5-5 indicates broad sectoral changes in the composition of gross national product (GNP) of the individual CMEA countries. Unfortunately, comparable time-series data were accessible only until 1982 (until 1980 for the Soviet Union). There is no uniform pattern of growth in the share of GNP that the earlier-much-neglected service sector constitutes. In fact, in East Germany and Hungary that share declined, and the increased share in the case of Poland should be discounted because to a considerable extent it is simply a statistical reflection of the decline in industry caused by the political crisis rather than a break in the underlying trend. In other CMEA countries the share of services in GNP rose; the increase was rather marginal, however, particularly after the mid-1970s when IU first peaked and then subsequently turned down.

The general picture emerging from table 5-5 is the continued primacy of industry—indeed, the persistent increase in industry's share of GNP even in most of those countries where services registered some increase. Thus, at least through the early 1980s the CMEA countries were not going through deindustrialization. Nor does the available evidence, though limited, indicate a change in this situation in more recent years.

One clearly identifiable macroeconomic change that may have affected the composition of final outputs is the considerable fall in the rate of growth of total gross investment since the mid-1970s and especially since 1979. As table 5-6 shows, in CMEA-6 total gross investment, after growing very fast in the early 1970s, took a downturn in two steps: a decline in the rate of growth following the first oil shock and then a much more pronounced additional fall after the second oil shock. The drastic decrease in Poland's total gross investment, the result of political turmoil in that country during the early 1980s, has accentuated the underlying regional trend of severe investment cuts and rapidly falling investment ratios that lasted until the mid-1980s. Only recently has there been a moderate upturn in investment activity.

Because the investment sector is a major consumer of base metals,[3] the sharp and protracted decline in the growth of investment presumably contributed somewhat to the break in historical IU trends. The modest decline in the relative importance of the construction sector within most CMEA countries shown in table 5-5, however, suggests that the decline in the growth of investment has not been of great importance.

The conclusion drawn from this part of the statistical evidence would appear to be that the reversal in IU trends has not been caused by broad changes in the output structure. In fact, these shifts may have acted in the

---

[3]In the CMEA countries the relative IU of steel for the construction sector is more than 40 percent higher than the industrial average. See Economic Commission for Europe (1984), p. 36.

Table 5-5. Composition of GNP by Sectors of Origin (in constant prices), 1970, 1975, 1980, 1982

(percent)

Country and sector	1970	1975	1980	1982
Bulgaria				
Industry	34.1	35.1	39.2	39.2
Agriculture	28.4	27.6	22.2	22.9
Construction	6.8	6.7	6.8	6.4
Services	30.7	30.6	31.9	31.5
Total, GNP	100.0	100.0	100.0	100.0
Czechoslovakia				
Industry	41.5	38.1	39.2	40.1
Agriculture	18.4	16.7	16.2	14.5
Construction	5.3	9.1	8.8	8.7
Services	34.9	36.1	35.8	36.8
Total, GNP	100.0	100.0	100.0	100.0
East Germany				
Industry	42.5	42.8	44.1	45.4
Agriculture	13.8	14.6	13.6	12.7
Construction	5.8	5.2	5.3	5.2
Services	38.0	37.4	36.8	36.6
Total, GNP	100.0	100.0	100.0	100.0
Hungary				
Industry	34.3	31.4	31.7	31.3
Agriculture	22.4	25.6	25.0	25.5
Construction	5.6	7.4	6.9	6.5
Services	37.5	35.5	36.4	36.7
Total, GNP	100.0	100.0	100.0	100.0
Poland				
Industry	35.7	34.2	33.9	31.3
Agriculture	24.4	26.8	24.7	27.4
Construction	8.4	7.2	6.6	5.9
Services	31.5	31.8	34.8	35.4
Total, GNP	100.0	100.0	100.0	100.0
Romania				
Industry	35.5	38.9	39.7	38.7
Agriculture	31.3	25.8	24.9	26.1
Construction	7.5	7.2	7.4	6.7
Services	25.7	28.1	28.1	28.5
Total, GNP	100.0	100.0	100.0	100.0
USSR				
Industry	32.0	35.5	36.8	N.A.
Agriculture	21.1	15.7	13.9	N.A.
Construction	7.3	8.0	7.9	N.A.
Services	37.4	38.8	39.5	N.A.
Other	2.2	2.0	1.9	N.A.
Total, GNP	100.0	100.0	100.0	

Note: N.A. = not available.

Sources: **For CMEA-6 (Bulgaria, Czechoslovakia, East Germany, Hungary, Poland, Romania):** See Thad P. Alton, "East European GNP's: Origins of Product, Final Uses, Rates of Growth, and International Comparisons," in U.S. Congress, Joint Economic Committee, *East European Economies: Slow Growth in the 1980s,* vol. 1: *Economic Performance and Policy* (Washington, D.C., U.S. Government Printing Office, 1985) pp. 89–90. **For USSR:** See U.S. Congress, Joint Economic Committee, *USSR: Measures of Economic Growth and Development, 1950–80* (Washington, D.C., U.S. Government Printing Office, 1982) p. 61.

Table 5-6. Total Gross Investment in CMEA Countries: Annual Percentage Change in Real Terms, 1970-1987

Country/group	1970	1971	1972	1973	1974	1975	1976	1977	1978	1979	1980	1981	1982	1983	1984	1985	1986	1987
Bulgaria	10.6	1.7	10.0	6.9	7.8	17.3	0.6	14.2	0.6	-2.2	7.5	10.5	3.6	0.7	0.3[a]	8.6[a]	8.0[a]	7.2[a]
Czechoslovakia	5.8	5.7	8.9	9.0	9.1	8.3	4.4	5.7	4.1	1.8	1.4	-4.6	-2.3	0.6	-4.2	5.4	1.4	4.4
East Germany	6.8	1.7	5.0	8.4	5.4	4.6	7.3	5.3	2.8	1.2	0.1	2.4	-5.1	-0.3	-4.9	3.4	5.3	8.0
Hungary	16.9	10.6	-1.1	3.2	10.9	11.5	4.5	12.1	4.8	0.7	-5.8	-4.3	-1.6	-3.4	-3.7	-3.0	6.5	9.8
Poland	4.0	7.4	23.0	25.4	22.3	10.7	1.0	3.1	2.1	-7.9	-12.3	-22.3	-12.1	9.4	11.4	6.0	5.7	4.2
Romania	11.6	10.5	10.4	8.2	13.4	15.1	8.5	11.7	16.0	4.1	3.0	-7.1	-3.1	2.4	6.0[a]	1.6[a]	1.2[a]	0.9[a]
CMEA-6	8.0	6.4	11.7	12.5	13.4	10.8	3.9	7.3	5.7	-1.0	-2.2	-7.2	-4.4	2.3	2.3	3.9	3.9	4.7
USSR	11.4	7.2	7.0	4.6	7.0	8.6	4.3	3.5	5.8	0.7	2.2	3.7	3.5	5.6	1.9	3.0	8.3	5.7
CMEA-7	10.4	6.9	8.2	6.9	8.9	9.3	4.2	4.7	5.7	0.1	0.8	0.3	1.2	4.7	2.0	3.2	7.7	5.4

Note: National data aggregated by means of 1975 weights for total investments based on CMEA investigations.

Sources: Economic Commission for Europe, *Economic Survey of Europe in 1988-1989* (New York, United Nations, 1989); Hungarian Statistical Office, *Statistical Pocket Book of Hungary, 1987* (Budapest, Statistical Publishing House, 1988).

[a]Nominal.

Table 5-7. Share of Metal-Intensive Subsectors of Four CMEA Countries in Total Manufacturing Value Added, 1973-1975 and 1983-1985

(percent)

Country	1973-1975	1983-1985
Bulgaria[a]	24.6	29.9
Czechoslovakia	38.5	43.0
Hungary	31.6	37.0
Poland	28.6	34.1

Note: Metal-intensive subsectors are the following: metal products (ISIC 381), nonelectrical machinery (ISIC 382), electrical machinery (ISIC 383), and transportation equipment (ISIC 384).

Source: Data from United Nations Industrial Development Organization, *Handbook of Industrial Statistics 1986* (Vienna, UNIDO, 1986), and *Handbook of Industrial Statistics 1988* (Vienna, UNIDO, 1988).

[a]Share in total manufacturing employment.

opposite direction because in many of the CMEA countries, including the USSR, industry accounted for a larger share of GNP in the early 1980s than in the early 1970s, and the decline of construction has been relatively modest.

The highly aggregated economic sectors just examined may hide important changes in the mix of goods produced *within* individual sectors. To be sure, even the influence of a steadily increasing industry share of GDP can be offset by significant intrasectoral shifts toward activities that are less material-intensive. Indeed, differences in IU between subsectors within the same sector can be very large. In Czechoslovakia, for example, the specific steel consumption of the office, computing, and accounting machinery sector is 20 times smaller than that of the manufacturing engines and turbines sector (Economic Commission for Europe, 1984, p. 120).

Do the CMEA countries exhibit important intrasectoral shifts in the period under investigation? The following examination of this question focuses on the industrial sector as it accounts for a large part of total metal consumption. Table 5-7 shows the share of four countries' metal-intensive subsectors in the total value added of the manufacturing (industrial) sector. The high metal-absorbing subsectors increased their share of total manufacturing in all four countries, namely, Bulgaria, Czechoslovakia, Hungary, and Poland (the ones for which comparable data were accessible). There is reason to believe that these countries are broadly representative of the CMEA-7 as a whole. In East Germany, Romania, and the USSR, the rate of growth of the most material-intensive sector—engineering and metal working—was higher than the overall growth rate of the gross industrial output by 32 to 82 percent (taking the two extreme values) in the 1976-1980 period and by 37 to 70 percent in the 1981-1985 period (Economic Commission for Europe, 1983, pp. 142-143; 1987, pp. 143 and 148).

The foregoing discussion suggests that intrasectoral shifts in the mix of goods produced do not explain the break in IU trends in the middle and late 1970s. In fact, some partial evidence suggests the contrary.

Of course, even the three-digit industrial classification might be too aggregated for the purpose of our analysis. This possibility is suggested by a recent Soviet study that found, on the basis of an input–output analysis, that in the 1976–1984 period in the Soviet machinery sector, 12.1 percent of the total reduction in aggregate metal intensity is attributable to intrasectoral structural changes. Although this percentage is relatively small when compared with Japan (60 percent) or the United States (21.8 percent), it points to some limited significance of intrasectoral shifts in the Soviet IU decline (Nechaev, 1989, p. 252).

Does Technological Progress Explain Declining IU?

There is little or no empirical evidence indicating that technological progress has accelerated in the CMEA countries in recent years. Available indicators suggest instead that technological change in these countries has slowed down during this time. Except for East Germany, capital productivity continued to decrease in the CMEA countries at a rate of more than 3 percent a year during the first half of the 1980s (in the USSR, at a rate of 2.7 percent) (Economic Commission for Europe, 1987, p. 120). The decline in the level of total factor productivity in the Soviet industry greatly accelerated in the 1976–1982 period.[4]

Another crude proxy of the pace of technological change is the age structure of the capital stock. The slowdown in growth and declining levels of investment since the late 1970s have resulted in an aging capital stock overburdened with worn-out, obsolete machinery and equipment and with a historically low share of modern plant. (For specific data on the age structure

---

[4]The average annual rate of total productivity change was −2.2 percent in 1966–1970, and it deteriorated to −2.6 percent in 1971–1975, to −4.2 percent in 1976–1980, and to −4.7 percent in 1981–1982. The percentages for the machinery sector are −2.3, −2.5, −4.2, and −4.6, respectively. These factor productivity figures were calculated using a Cobb-Douglas (linear-homogeneous) production function; see Schroeder (1985, pp. 43–46). For further suggestive evidence on the declining rate of technological change, see Gomulka (1986, p. 170) who claims that after 1975 there was a drop in the fairly constant rate of the long-run trend of innovation in Soviet industry in the post–World War II period. Desai (1986, p. 176), using a production function technique, shows that the rates of technological change in Soviet industry declined from year to year in the 1950–1980 period and, when averaged over the period, were generally low. Kontorovich (1986, pp. 182–183) demonstrates that the growth in the number of innovations slowed down over the 1970s and probably came to a halt in 1981–1982. He also shows that the number of new industrial products and new types of equipment put into series production grew by between 100 and 200 percent in 1971–1975 relative to the 1966–1970 period but only 3 to 5 percent in 1976–1980 relative to 1971–1975 and only 3 to 5 percent in 1981–1982 compared to 1976–1980.

of individual CMEA countries' fixed assets, see Economic Commission for Europe [1987, p. 165]).

The possibility of raising the technological level of the capital stock through a rapid increase in imports of modern Western materials-saving equipment has been limited by balance-of-payments considerations. In fact, in the CMEA-6 the volume of machinery and equipment imports from the nonsocialist sources declined by an annual rate of 5.5 percent between 1976 and 1980, followed by a modest 1.1 percent increase between 1981 and 1987. In contrast, these imports were expanding by 18.5 percent a year between 1966 and 1970 and by 14.5 percent in the 1971–1975 period. Between 1981 and 1987, because of balance-of-payments constraints caused by the fall in oil prices, the volume of machinery imported from the West by the USSR declined by 2.8 percent a year (United Nations, 1986, p. 57; 1988, pp. 47–48).

Although these aggregate trends are suggestive, they do not necessarily reflect fully the underlying trends in technology at a greater degree of disaggregation. In particular, materials-saving innovation may have accelerated despite the overall slowdown of technological change as a result of recent policy initiatives by the CMEA governments stressing material conservation.[5] These programs, enjoying top priority in several countries, have generally called for an accelerated introduction of materials-saving technologies.

Although information on various material-producing and -consuming sectors of the CMEA countries is not sufficient to make a definitive judgment regarding whether technology has been a major factor in the maturation of IU for base metals, it does suggest that technology has played a role in improving "material productivity".[6]

The adoption of continuous casting (CC) in steelmaking provides an interesting example of technological change. The global spread of this advanced, energy-efficient technology has been very rapid, particularly since the mid-

[5]This suggestion of the possibility of differential technological change contrasts with the position taken on this matter by Gomulka and Rostowski (1988, p. 490), who assert that since the mid-1970s the rate of technological change generally fell in centrally planned economies, "and one would expect that, with it, the role of material and energy saving innovations would also have fallen."

[6]This suggestion, although not based on firm empirical evidence, is in concert with econometric estimates for the developed Western countries that indicate that metal-saving technological trends—embodied predominantly in the improved technical performance (productivity) of metals—have accelerated moderately subsequent to the oil price shocks of 1973–1974 and 1979–1980 and have thus contributed to the downward trend in IU. Soladay (1988, pp. 326–327) uses time trend as a proxy for technological change and interaction dummy variables to determine whether significant changes in the time coefficients occurred after the oil price increase. For aluminum, nickel, tin, and zinc, he found statistically significant evidence for accelerating technological change, whereas for copper he found that the negative coefficients were not statistically significant.

1970s. CC technology, apart from its lower capital requirement per unit of capacity and lower processing costs compared with traditional technologies, significantly improves yields for finished (cast, rolled, drawn, or forged) steel products per ton of crude steel. (For example, according to Brown and McKern [1987, p. 60], traditional casting processes can result in up to 20 percent of scrap, whereas with CC the share may be as low as 3 percent.) The adoption of CC thus increases steel productivity and reduces crude steel IU.

Figure 5-8 shows the CC diffusion curves for the individual CMEA countries and for the CMEA-7 compared with Western market-economy countries. Although lagging behind that of the West, the share of CMEA-7 crude steel production continuously cast increased by a factor of 3.7 between 1974 and 1987. In East Germany, Hungary, and Rumania, the spread of CC was particularly rapid.

As table 5-8 reveals, the speed of diffusion of CC technology has considerably accelerated in four of the CMEA countries. In the last one and one-half decades, a progressively greater percentage of total crude steel output was generated by a new technology; this had the effect of reducing IU in steel.

For the USSR there is specific evidence that the increasing application of continuous casting and the modernization of production engineering have resulted in improved yields for finished steel products per ton of crude steel. The saving coefficients (in terms of tons of crude steel saved per ton of finished steel product) recently achieved are substantial (0.25 or above) in various rolled-steel plates and sections (United Nations, Committee on Natural Resources, 1987). There are also some recent indications that metal savings resulting from improvements in product quality and a broadening of the more sophisticated product assortment—both made possible by modernization of the metallurgical industries—have been of some significance (Economic Commission for Europe, 1984, pp. 68–70).[7]

Ceramics, polymers and advanced plastics, superconductive and controlled crystallization alloys, composite materials, and other new materials have recently received increased attention in the CMEA countries. These new

---

[7]For instance, as a result of research, design, and experimental work over the past ten years, the mass of load-bearing structures of freight trucks in the USSR has been reduced by 20 to 25 percent, and the corrosion resistance of individual truck parts and units has been improved considerably. The use of new types of steel for lining truck walls and roofs has reduced the input of rolled steel to 200 kilograms per truck as a result of reductions in plate thickness. The potential of quality improvements for reducing demand in materials is certainly great. According to a Soviet estimate (Sachko, 1984, p. 119), improvements in the structural properties and quality of metals would be equivalent to between 16 million and 25 million tons of aggregate metal supply—an astonishing volume. This appears to be in line with another Soviet assessment (Rozenfeld, 1982, p. 35) that places the quality-driven share of overall savings in rolled-steel products at between 50 and 75 percent. For some specific technology-induced and recent material reduction in the USSR, see *Planovoe khoziastvo* (1987).

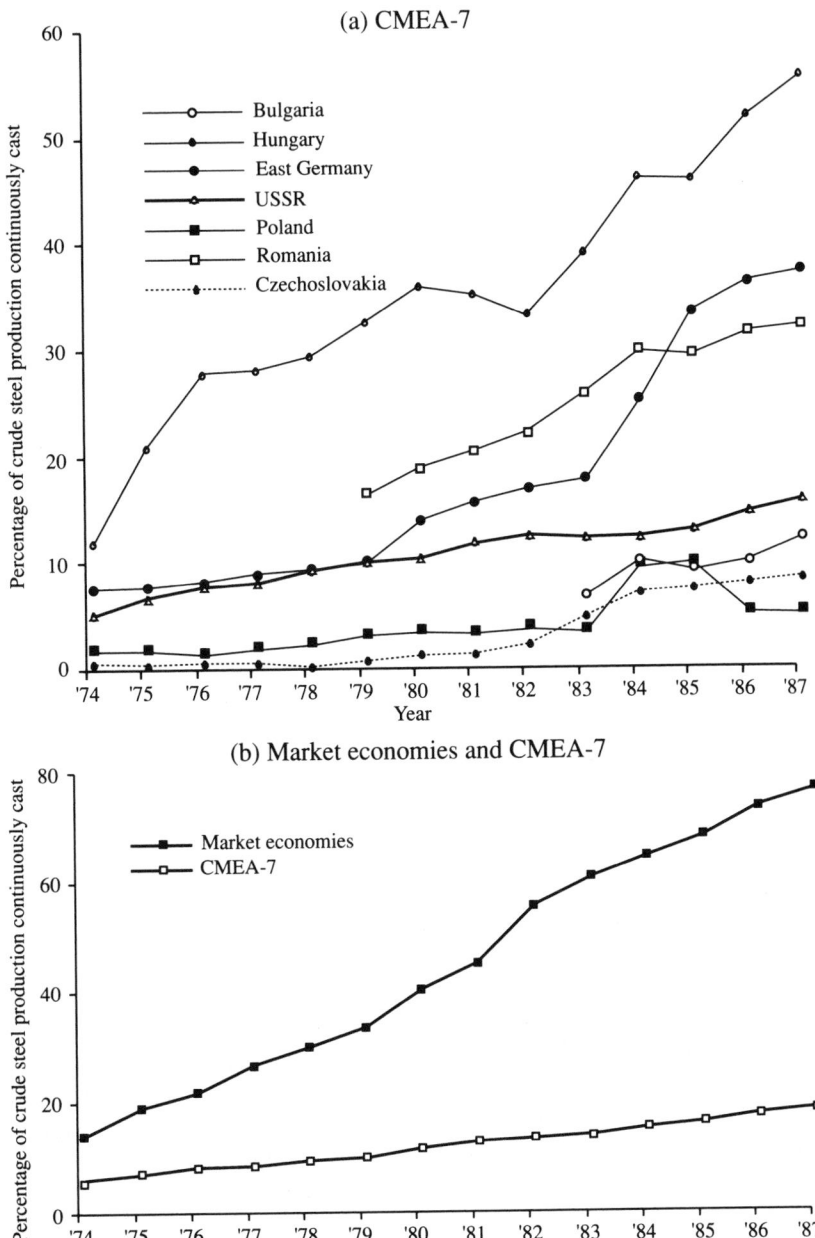

Figure 5-8. Share of crude steel production continuously cast in (a) the CMEA-7 and (b) market economies and the CMEA-7, 1974–1987.

Note: Market economies include the OECD countries, Yugoslavia, South Africa, Argentina, Brazil, Chile, Mexico, Venezuela, South Korea, and Taiwan.

Source: Calculated from International Iron and Steel Institute, *Steel Statistical Yearbook* (Brussels, IISI, 1988).

Table 5-8. Average Number of Years in CMEA-7 and Western Countries Required to Increase the Share of Continuously Cast Steel in Total Crude Steel Production by One Percentage Point, 1974–1979 and 1979–1987

Country or group	1974–1979	1979–1987
Bulgaria	a	0.65
Czechoslovakia	25.00	1.05
East Germany	1.85	0.30
Hungary	0.24	0.35
Poland	3.57	4.00
Romania	a	0.25
USSR	1.02	1.38
Western countries[b]	0.28	0.18

Source: Calculated from International Iron and Steel Institute, *Steel Statistical Yearbook* (Brussels, IISI, 1988).

[a]Continuous casting had not yet been introduced.

[b]In addition to the OECD countries, this group includes Yugoslavia, Argentina, Brazil, Chile, Mexico, Venezuela, South Korea, and Taiwan.

materials may eventually bring about substantial conservation in the use of metals. Experts in the CMEA countries, however, express serious concern over the slow rates at which these materials are being introduced.[8]

Is Improved Materials Management a Factor in IU Decline?

Although socialist country planners have always been interested in the conservation of materials, their interest has become significantly more intense since the second oil shock. The adverse effect of persistent and widespread shortages of basic material inputs has been strongly felt in most CMEA countries (Economic Commission for Europe, 1987, p. 143; Schroeder, 1985, p. 52). Moreover, the importance of demand-side initiatives has appeared to make good business sense from a macroeconomic cost–benefit point of view; as indicated by national sources, outlays for materials-saving technologies amount to only between 20 and 30 percent of the outlays needed to provide additional supplies of the same materials, as reported in the Soviet weekly *Ekonomicheskaya gazeta* (1985, p. 13). Severe investment and import constraints have further induced planners to shift from a traditional, supply-oriented materials policy toward demand management. In every country, comprehensive conservation ("rationalization") programs have been adopted, and in several countries, particularly East Germany and Czechoslovakia, reductions in the material intensity of industrial output have become a crucial

---

[8]When making this statement, I draw particularly on my interviews with researchers and government officials in Hungary, Czechoslovakia, and the USSR. For the USSR on this point, see Shumaev (1987, p. 79).

element of "intensive," resource-efficient industrial development strategies.[9] In some countries metal conservation has been motivated to a considerable extent by the need to save energy—an important complementary input to materials. (For East Germany in this context, see Braun [1987, p. 126].) Energy has enjoyed a high priority in global rationalization programs, and reduction in the use of materials of high energy content has become part of energy conservation design.

The salient features of government policy regarding material conservation are as follows:

• In some countries material conservation has become a key indicator for evaluating overall enterprise performance. In East Germany material expenditure per unit of production has become one of the three basic indicators that state authorities consider when evaluating performance.

• More realistic and significantly lower material norms have been imposed on users (a de facto method of rationing). In some countries there has been a tendency toward setting norms in each user sector that reflect specific material input requirements in the most efficient enterprises ("progressive" norms, in Soviet parlance).

• The range of materials and users for which specific conservation targets were included in the annual and five-year plans sent to ministries and enterprises has been expanded. In East Germany, where conservation programs are the most sophisticated among the CMEA countries, more than 95 percent of material consumption is regulated by norms imposed from above on decentralized users (Oleinik, 1984, p. 117). In the USSR the range of materials for which central recycling targets and tasks were specified increased from 23 in 1981 to 62 in 1987 (Pirogov, 1987, p. 95).

• Stronger negative and positive financial incentives have been combined to reduce material consumption. Fines for exceeding the administratively determined norms were raised considerably (in some cases more than ten times). In some countries a predetermined percentage of the financial resources saved as a result of more efficient use of materials may be set aside for raising enterprise wages and salaries. In Romania, for example, reportedly between 30 and 50 percent of the financial resources saved can be used for paying bonuses (Oleinik, 1984, p. 117).

---

[9]On the conservation programs and their specific provisions, see Oleinik (1982, pp. 105–109; 1984, pp. 113–122); Braun (1987, pp. 113–131); and Hewett (1984, pp. 130–139). It is worth mentioning that in some socialist countries, the degree of material use efficiency is considered a special indicator of the "intensification" (i.e., efficiency) level of aggregate economic activity. In regard to recycling, for example, a Soviet expert (Pirogov, 1987, p. 98) goes so far as to suggest that the transition of the national economy to the path of predominantly intensive development is simply impossible without solving the problems associated with the utilization of secondary materials.

Table 5-9. Recovery Ratios for Iron and Steel in Selected CMEA
Countries, 1971–1973, 1977–1979, and 1982–1984
(percent)

Country	1971–1973	1977–1979	1982–1984
Czechoslovakia	36	44	45
East Germany	58	57	68
Hungary	24	24	29
Poland	26	29	27
USSR	11	16	N.A.

Notes: N.A. = not available.
The recovery ratio is defined as the sum of blast furnaces' and steelworks' consumption of scrap divided by the sum of the blast-furnace consumption of iron ore, concentrates, and agglomerated products and the steelwork output of steel produced from pig iron and iron ore. These data are net of trade.
Source: Data from International Institute for Environment and Development and the World Resources Institute, *World Resources 1987* (New York, Basic Books, 1987), p. 308.

• The enforcement of existing regulations concerning fines for the overuse of materials has been strengthened. In connection with this, the scope of bargaining among enterprises, ministries, and central planning authorities with regard to the specific magnitude of norms has been reduced.

• In several countries concessional credits have been provided to encourage materials-saving measures.

• Pricing has been used more actively than ever before to discourage the use of materials by reducing distortions such as underpricing and by bringing domestic producer prices more in line with world prices. In some countries pricing has been more extensively used as an incentive to encourage quality improvements, which implies a reduction in specific consumption of materials. In the USSR, for example, the quality-related upward adjustment in material prices in recent years has been in principle as high as 30 percent, whereas the downward adjustment has been between 5 and 15 percent (Ivantsova, 1987, p. 143). (Unfortunately, there is little information about how consistently this pricing principle is applied in practice.)

• Recycling of used materials has been encouraged in every country through a variety of organizational and economic measures. The recycling ratios, as shown in table 5-9 for iron and steel, increased considerably in the case of some materials. The policy emphasis by planners on recycling is well illustrated by East Germany (historically a superperformer in recycling); there the central national plan called for doubling the aggregate recycling ratio (which covers all metals) between 1980 and 1985 (Oleinik, 1982, p. 107). (Factual information on the achievement of this target was not available; scattered reports in East German publications suggest good progress, however.)

• In some countries special institutions were established for the management and supervision of central conservation programs. In East Germany a

Table 5-10. Total Change in Intensity of Use (IU) in CMEA Countries Between 1979 and 1987

(percent)

Country/group	Steel	Aluminum	Copper	Zinc	Lead	Nickel	Tin
Bulgaria	4.6	−0.9	0.0	0.4	−16.6	−15.7	71.3
Czechoslovakia	−14.3	−25.3	0.0	−26.6	−28.5	3.1	−16.4
East Germany	−27.1	−18.2	−11.2	0.0	−26.5	−7.9	−8.1
Hungary	−14.5	12.5	1.0	0.1	9.0	32.6	−12.2
Poland	−25.1	−38.9	−0.6	−17.9	−3.3	−24.0	−36.7
Romania	−24.2	−37.5	−60.9	−31.2	−18.0	9.8	−60.4
CMEA-6	−21.8	−18.4	−12.5	−16.3	−19.8	−2.8	−22.9
USSR	−13.0	−22.0	−23.3	−18.4	−19.7	−14.3	−2.3
CMEA-7	−15.1	−21.0	−20.2	−17.8	−19.7	−11.2	−0.4

Sources: Those cited in table 5-3 in this chapter.

Ministry of Materials Management was established with a mandate to establish programs for the rational use of materials, the coordination of research and development in this area, the setting of scientifically based material norms, and so on.

No systematic data or references are available for assessing the net effects of measures introduced to reduce materials consumption. There does seem to be, however, a correlation between the comprehensiveness and sophistication of the materials-saving programs as well as the degree of enforcement of existing conservation regulations, on the one hand, and the size of reductions in IU, on the other. (Here we ignore the Polish figures, which were significantly affected by politically caused economic dislocations.) It is evident that of the CMEA countries, East Germany has developed the most complex and sophisticated conservation programs and supporting institutions. As table 5-10 shows, despite relatively low IU values in 1979, East Germany was able to substantially reduce its IU for several commodities between 1979 and 1987. In terms of the stringency of the savings targets pursued, Romania is equally committed to saving materials, sometimes even by adopting draconian measures to achieve (or rather force) conservation. In the 1979–1987 period Romania exhibited the best performance in reducing metal intensity. With the existence of large inherent conservation potentials (that have accumulated over time as a result of "wasteful" habits), spectacular reduction in metal intensity can be generated for a temporary period by stringent and consistently implemented savings programs.

A comparison between Bulgaria and Romania also suggests the relevance of policy actions in promoting and stimulating the economizing of materials. Although the two countries are roughly on the same level of economic development, their conservation performance is very different. Romania, which most aggressively pursued the "conservation by decree" approach, exhibited the greatest drop in IU in the case of most metals. Bulgaria, not being particularly conservation-conscious, showed a sharply contrasting pattern as its IU kept growing for three of the seven metals covered by our analysis. In contrast, Hungary's relatively poor performance may also be rooted in the lack of sophistication and stringency of public conservation policies (for example, there are no imposed input norms) and in the documented lack of sufficiently strong cost-minimization pressure on metal-using enterprises, despite market-oriented reform efforts.

To sum up, the assessment of various potential forces behind the recent IU decline in the CMEA countries provides some evidence that macrostructural shifts along with changes in the product composition of industrial output have generally tended to act against the fall in IU. A similar influence may also have been exerted by the apparent deceleration in technological progress, which is in large part the result of the very significant drop in investment activity and in imports of Western machinery and equipment. In contrast, the following factors have been working to reduce material consumption: (a) the increase in the price of oil, (b) the decline in the construction sector and overall investment activity, (c) shifts in the product mix within individual subsectors, (d) government material conservation programs, (e) improvements in product quality and a broadening in the range of high-quality metals, and (f) more efficient materials management.

There is no way to measure the relative importance of these factors. The lack of firm, empirically substantiated knowledge of the fundamental microeconomic forces behind the IU path, along with the temporary nature of some of the factors identified as IU-reducing, make a judgment concerning the long-term versus the transitory character of the break in IU tentative. Despite this caveat, we are inclined to believe that a permanent change has occurred. As was pointed out earlier, material conservation policies can claim some portion of the credit for the material savings in the CMEA countries that arose during the mid-1980s. These savings may have a reversible component. Policy reversals—such as a reduction in the role of material use per unit of industrial output as a major indicator of successful enterprise performance, weaker financial or fiscal incentives for conservation investments, less central pressure to adhere to "user norms" of materials, and less emphasis on exhortations as a means of boosting savings—would act in themselves to increase IU. Such reversals seem unlikely, however, at least on a broad scale.

ARE THE CMEA COUNTRIES OVERCONSUMING METALS?

Despite the apparent peaking of IU in the CMEA countries in the recent past, the metal intensity per unit of GDP remains high by international standards throughout the region. Figure 5-9 illustrates intensity of metal use of selected metals for the CMEA-7, the OECD countries, and the Third World, and table 5-11 provides more specific information regarding inter-

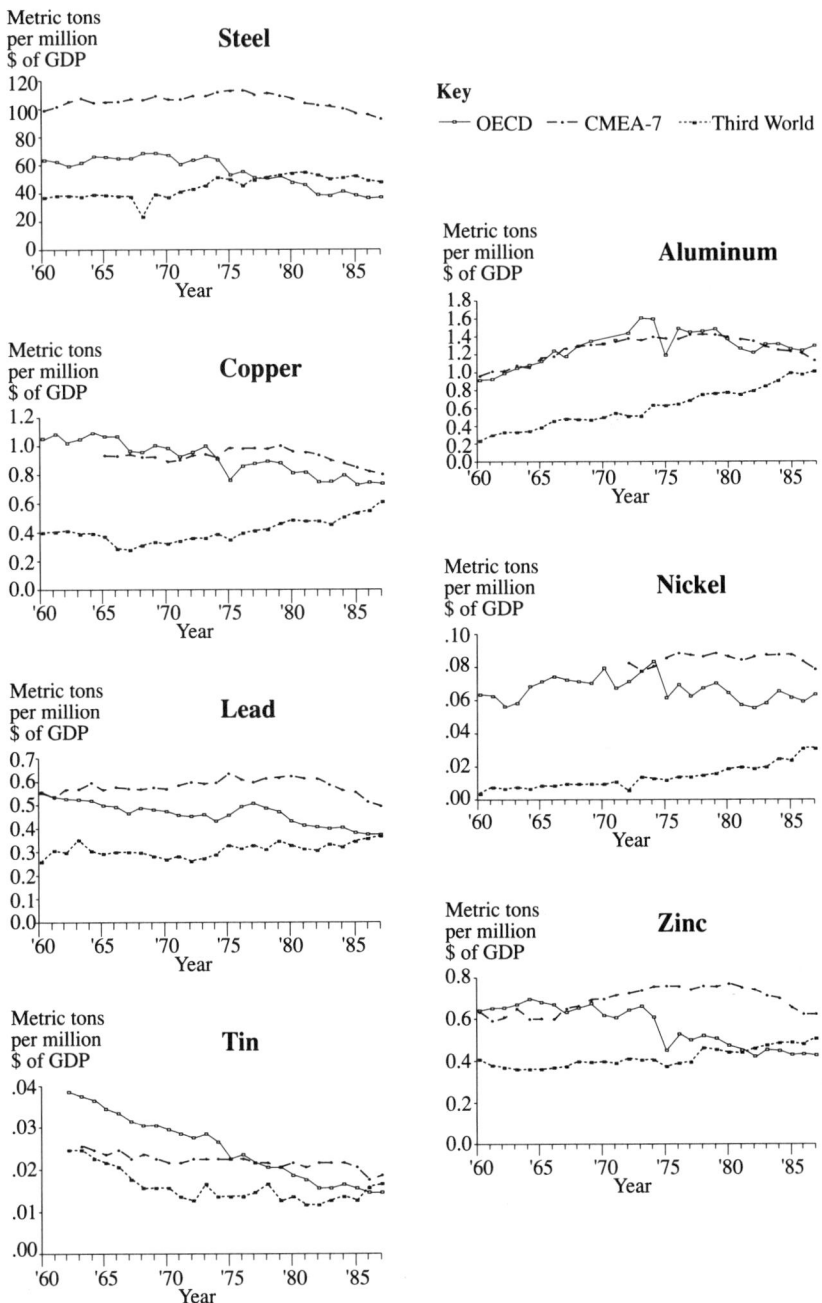

Figure 5-9. Intensity of use (IU) of selected metals in CMEA-7, OECD, and Third World countries, 1960–1987.

Source: Statistical appendix in this volume.

Table 5-11. Intensity of Use (IU) for the CMEA and Selected Third World Countries in 1960, 1973, and 1987 as a Percentage of the Average IU of the OECD Countries (IU for the OECD countries = 100)

(percent)

Metal and country/group	1960	1973	1987
Steel			
Bulgaria	75.6	85.2	174.2
Czechoslovakia	183.1	185.8	255.7
East Germany	143.4	127.4	156.5
Hungary	105.3	98.0	140.5
Poland	108.8	154.0	200.9
Romania	146.4	190.7	276.8
CMEA-6	133.3	148.0	222.3
USSR	164.4	171.4	270.8
CMEA-7	154.9	164.4	256.7
India	95.6	101.1	192.8
Brazil	74.1	93.5	136.2
South Korea	19.8	116.7	381.7
Third World	58.1	67.2	129.6
Aluminum			
Bulgaria	9.8[a]	60.8	78.2
Czechoslovakia	90.1	105.9	70.2
East Germany	123.9	111.0	107.6
Hungary	141.4	168.1	231.4
Poland	56.9	53.2	48.1
Romania	37.1[b]	85.8	77.3
CMEA-6	80.7[b]	90.6	95.6
USSR	113.7[b]	80.1	83.4
CMEA-7	110.2[b]	83.2	86.9
India	34.7	63.5	113.1
Brazil	60.4	74.6	109.4
South Korea	61.6[b]	60.7	147.1
Third World	23.5	30.5	77.2
Copper			
Bulgaria	90.6	124.6	177.0
Czechoslovakia	72.5[c]	79.0	109.9
East Germany	92.3	101.3	112.2
Hungary	52.8	45.4	53.1
Poland	59.8	87.5	138.0
Romania	43.5	83.8	47.6
CMEA-6	69.7[c]	86.8	117.5
USSR	100.8	104.3	105.3
CMEA-7	86.2[c]	93.2	108.8
India	74.6	51.0	70.2
Brazil	46.7	81.1	115.8
South Korea	3.6	36.3	322.7
Third World	37.4	34.7	82.4

Table 5-11 (continued)

Metal and country/group	1960	1973	1987
Zinc			
Bulgaria	85.9[b]	168.8	312.1
Czechoslovakia	124.6	101.0	113.4
East Germany	81.8	82.4	124.5
Hungary	54.2	65.2	95.9
Poland	189.2	141.8	172.7
Romania	45.6[b]	92.7	104.4
CMEA-6	115.0[b]	110.3	157.2
USSR	81.3	110.4	143.3
CMEA-7	92.0[b]	110.4	147.3
India	118.1	95.1	138.5
Brazil	79.7	78.1	137.4
South Korea	27.0	93.6	386.5
Third World	64.1	60.1	119.1
Lead			
Bulgaria	249.3[b]	286.9	525.5
Czechoslovakia	96.2	129.7	111.5
East Germany	175.0	184.5	134.0
Hungary	61.7	56.5	56.5
Poland	118.9	121.6	111.9
Romania	82.4	134.3	110.4
CMEA-6	133.0[b]	159.6	154.4
USSR	94.2	114.3	125.7
CMEA-7	105.8[b]	128.0	134.0
India	56.3	73.5	81.9
Brazil	55.2	86.6	82.6
South Korea	70.0[b]	64.6	278.4
Third World	46.1	58.0	98.0
Nickel[d]			
Bulgaria	N.A.	18.3	43.5
Czechoslovakia	N.A.	111.0	153.1
East Germany	N.A.	103.1	124.1
Hungary	N.A.	37.9	83.8
Poland	N.A.	41.8	54.7
Romania	N.A.	64.0	118.7
CMEA-6	N.A.	66.6	106.1
USSR	N.A.	113.6	131.0
CMEA-7	N.A.	99.2	123.9
India	N.A.	15.8	137.1
Brazil	N.A.	44.5	76.1
South Korea	N.A.	15.0[e]	78.3
Third World	N.A.	16.4	46.3
Tin			
Bulgaria	N.A.	105.5	253.3
Czechoslovakia	94.9[a]	152.7	180.2

(Continued)

Table 5-11 (continued)

Metal and country/group	1960	1973	1987
Tin (*continued*)			
East Germany	51.4[a]	113.4	147.3
Hungary	75.4[a]	109.5	135.9
Poland	67.8[a]	96.0	86.1
Romania	N.A.	154.2	86.3
CMEA-6	81.4[a]	121.4	142.3
USSR	60.8[a]	60.0	120.4
CMEA-7	67.3[a]	78.0	126.8
India	134.6[a]	82.6	80.3
Brazil	80.5[a]	115.9	178.9
South Korea	N.A.	139.3	366.2
Third World	64.3[a]	57.2	112.0

Note: N.A. = not available.

Sources: Those cited in table 5-3 in this chapter.

GDP data for the OECD countries and the Third World countries: World Bank, *World Bank Data Tape: National Accounts, Prices, Exchange Rates and Population for the Period 1960–1984* (Washington, D.C., 1986), and World Bank, *World Development Report 1988* (Washington, D.C., 1988).

[a]1963.

[b]1962.

[c]1965.

[d]1960 data not available for the CMEA countries.

[e]1974.

country group and cross-country differences in metal intensity. The general picture emerging from these data is the high level of metal consumption of the CMEA countries per unit of GDP compared with these levels in the OECD countries, except for aluminum and copper. In the case of steel, IU in the CMEA-7 is especially excessive; in 1987 it was almost 2.6 times higher than the OECD average. Another important conclusion to be drawn from table 5-11 is the consistent tendency for IU differences to grow over time, even in the case of steel, where IU of the CMEA nations was already high as early as 1960.

The dominant perception among analysts in both the East and the West is that high material IU in the CMEA countries is a systemic feature of Soviet-type centrally planned economies. It is suggested that the traditional focus on gross (as opposed to net) output success indicators, relatively weak managerial incentives in minimizing costs, low price sensitivity, relatively strong bias against technological change and quality improvements in products, disequilibrium input prices, and other systemic traits create a fertile ground for the excessive use of all inputs. (For these or similar views in the Eastern literature, see, among others, Arbatov and Mukhin [1987, pp. 66–67]; Rozenfeld [1982, p. 34]; Ivantsova [1987, pp. 141–143]; Vintrova [1986]; and Dobozi [1983, pp. 201–216]. In the Western literature, see, for example,

Nove [1984, pp. 57–61]; Wallace and Clarke [1986, pp. 121–125]; and Hewett [1980a, p. 283; 1984, pp. 139–143].)

Those who hold the view just described generally refer to high material consumption per capita and high material intensity per unit of GDP in the centrally planned economies as an indication of their propensity for overconsumption. Although this approach can be suggestive, in the strict sense it is inadequate because it fails to separate the effect of system-related forces from that of nonsystemic factors such as economic environment and policy. High material intensity can be caused by forces other than the nature of the economic system. For instance, as table 5-11 indicates, South Korea shows even more "profligate" metal consumption than the CMEA countries; in 1987 its copper and zinc IU was 3.6 times higher than the OECD average, while its steel IU was 3.1 times greater. In some cases (e.g., steel, aluminum, nickel, zinc) in 1987, even India has a higher IU than the OECD average.

In what follows, we will make an attempt to isolate empirically the distinctive effect of systemic factors on the level of metal consumption.

Isolation of the Economic System–Metal Consumption Link

Following an approach used in the field of comparative economic systems, we assume that variation in observed economic outcomes in different economies is the result of differences in three sets of factors: (1) the nature of the economic system, (2) economic policy, and (3) the environment of the system. (See, for example, Koopmans and Montias [1971], Gregory and Stuart [1985], and Hewett [1980a, b].) The *economic system* is understood as a set of mechanisms, rules, and institutions for decision making and the implementation of economic decisions. For our purpose the most basic system distinction relates to market economies and centrally planned economies. *Policies* within the system are those economic decisions that seek to change outcomes without changing the underlying system. For instance, in market-oriented economic systems, governments can pursue different industrial policies—those, for example, promoting heavy industry or emphasizing exports—with potentially important implications for the pattern and level of material consumption. The *environment* of the economic system includes the level of economic development, natural resource endowments, the size of the economy, the stock of human and physical capital, traditional consumer preferences, random events, and so on. (For a fuller discussion of these definitions, see Hewett [1980b, pp. 54–67].)

One cannot isolate systemic effects without first controlling for the effects of the environment and policies. Methodological problems arise in any procedure to disentangle the effects of systems from environmental and policy influences because the three sets of explanatory variables are to some extent interconnected.[10] Econometrically, this difficulty is recognizable as a case of multicollinearity between environment, policy, and system. Generally, it is easier to control for environment than policy because the interconnections between environment and system tend to be less significant than those between policy and system. Also, it is normally easier to find good proxy variables for environment than for policy.

We will use two econometric techniques, the forecasting and dummy-variable approaches, to estimate the systemic effect on resource use. Both rely on cross-sectional data for market economies and CMEA countries. (In the methodological discussion of these techniques, we draw on Hewett [1980a], who applied them in the context of energy consumption.)

The *forecasting* approach first estimates the relationship of metal consumption and environmental and policy variables for Western countries. With this relationship we then estimate metal consumption values for the CMEA countries. These values tell us the expected level of material consumption of the centrally planned economies, assuming that they follow the "normal" Western relationship of material consumption and the various explanatory variables. We then compare the actual and forecasted CMEA values. Assuming that the forecasts capture the "normal" Western relationship, differences between actual and forecasted values provide an indication of the effects of the economic system (including central planning), and the extent to which the centrally planned systems are underconsuming or overconsuming metals as compared with their Western counterparts.

The *dummy-variable* approach introduces a distinct variable to account for the systemic effect. (This variable is assigned a value of 1 for the Western countries and *"e"* for the CMEA countries, which makes them 0–1 in natural logarithms.) The dummy variable reflects the extent to which the system variable shifts CMEA metal consumption upward or downward.

Using the dummy variable in this way reveals a potential danger in this approach—namely, the implicit assumption that the two economic systems act in the same manner with regard to metal consumption, except for the shift. However, it may be that the relationship between the dependent variable and the independent variables is altered as well. In this case somewhat more complicated dummy-variable models are needed.

Cross-Sectional Estimation of Steel and Aluminum Consumption

In an attempt to enhance the reliability of empirical estimation, we applied both the forecasting and the dummy-variable approach to test the hypothesis that central planning induces an overconsumption of materials.

---

[10]Obviously, some policies tend to be closely intertwined with a given economic system. Some policies, however, are much less system-specific or system-determined. For example, a

Data for 1980 were collected for the CMEA-7 countries (Bulgaria, Czechoslovakia, East Germany, Hungary, Poland, Rumania, and the USSR) and several Western market-economy countries (the size of the Western sample is not identical because of data availability problems) covering two metals, steel and aluminum.[11]

Tables 5-12 and 5-14 report the regression results using the ordinary least squares estimation technique. All variables are expressed in natural logarithms. The log-log specification allows us to interpret the estimated coefficients as elasticities. The t-ratios are given in parentheses under the corresponding coefficient estimates. Four summary statistics are provided: the coefficient of determination corrected for degrees of freedom, $\overline{R}^2$; the F-statistic measuring the overall significance of the regression model; the standard error of the estimate, SE; and the sample size, n.

Steel Consumption   The dependent variable in table 5-12 is specified in three ways: total steel consumption (TSC), steel consumption per unit of GDP (SCGDP), and steel consumption per capita (SCCAP). For the Western sample, equation (1) posits a link between total GDP (TGDP) and total consumption, thus treating the demand for steel as derived demand resulting from aggregate demand for GDP. OMIX is introduced as a policy variable to account for differences in the output mix. It is hypothesized that steel use per capita tends to be higher, other things being equal, in those countries where high steel-consuming activities account for a greater share of aggregate economic activities (the proxy for OMIX is the percentage share of metal products, machinery, and transportation equipment in manufacturing value added). The third explanatory variable, the investment-GDP ratio (IRATE), serves as another policy variable, on the assumption that high investment-GDP ratios imply high demand for steel products both through construction and equipment.

Except for OMIX, the variables have the expected sign and are statistically significant at the 5 percent level. The independent variables explain 95 percent of the cross-country variations in total steel consumption. The output

---

vigorous material conservation policy can be applied across systems. Similarly, a heavy-industry-centered industrialization policy (with implications for material consumption) can characterize both market-oriented and centrally planned economies.

[11]The countries in the steel models are as follows: Australia, Austria, Belgium-Luxembourg, Canada, Czechoslovakia, Denmark, East Germany, the Federal Republic of Germany, Finland, France, Greece, Hungary, Ireland, Italy, Japan, The Netherlands, Norway, Poland, Portugal, Romania, Spain, Sweden, Switzerland, Turkey, the United Kingdom, the United States, and the USSR. In the aluminum models they are Canada, the United States, Belgium-Luxembourg, the Federal Republic of Germany, France, Greece, Italy, The Netherlands, the United Kingdom, Austria, Finland, Norway, Portugal, Sweden, Switzerland, Spain, Japan, Australia, New Zealand, Argentina, Brazil, South Korea, Turkey, Bulgaria, Czechoslovakia, East Germany, Hungary, Poland, Romania, and the USSR.

Table 5-12. Regression Results for Steel Consumption in CMEA and Western Countries, 1980

Sample[a]	W	W	W	C+W	C+W	C+W
Equation no.	(1)	(2)	(3)	(4)	(5)	(6)
Dependent variable	TSC	TSC	SCGDP	SCCAP	TSC	TSC
Constant	−8.510	−8.998	0.165	3.160	−9.701	−4.204
	(4.16)	(4.76)	(0.10)	(1.15)	(5.32)	(4.91)
TGDP	1.186	1.163			1.186	1.080
	(16.46)	(18.73)			(20.31)	(15.37)
GDPC			−0.214	−0.237		
			(2.11)	(1.42)		
OMIX	−0.205					
	(0.68)					
IRATE	1.151	1.186	1.001	0.842	1.316	
	(2.48)	(2.62)	(3.17)	(1.49)	(2.96)	
SYSTDUM			0.326	0.477	0.395	−1.182
			(6.40)	(2.17)	(2.27)	(0.89)
TGDPDUM						0.000
						(0.86)
IRATEDUM						0.057
						(1.33)
$\bar{R}^2$	94.9	95.0	70.2	40.9	94.4	92.4
F	124.6	192.4	22.2	7.2	152.9	76.7
SE	0.33	0.33	0.27	0.44	0.34	0.38
n	21	21	28	28	28	28

Notes: All variables are in natural logarithms. TSC = total steel consumption; SCGDP = steel consumption per unit of GDP; SCCAP = steel consumption per capita; TGDP = total GDP; GDPC = GDP per capita; OMIX = share of high steel-using activities in manufacturing value added; IRATE = investment-GDP ratio; SYSTDUM = dummy variable for CMEA countries; TGDPDUM = TGDP multiplied by SYSTDUM; IRATEDUM = IRATE multiplied by SYSTDUM.

Figures in parentheses are *t*-ratios.

Sources: **GDP and steel consumption data:** Statistical appendix to this volume. **Population data:** Derived from World Bank, *World Development Report 1982* (Washington, D.C., Oxford University Press, 1982). **Output mix data:** United Nations Industrial Development Organization, *Industrial Statistics Yearbook, 1982,* vol. 2 (New York: UNIDO, 1984). **Investment ratios:** International Monetary Fund, *International Financial Statistics Yearbook 1988* (Washington, D.C., IMF, 1988) and World Bank, *World Development Report 1982* (Washington, D.C., Oxford University Press, 1982).

[a]W = Western countries; C = CMEA countries; C+W = all countries.

mix variable has the opposite of the expected sign and is statistically insignificant. It is likely that the proxy we have chosen is too aggregative and thus cannot capture the structural effect on steel use. Therefore, in equation (2) we drop the OMIX variable.

We use equation (2), reflecting Western relationships, to forecast hypothetical values for the CMEA countries in order to determine if there is any statistically significant deviation of actual CMEA values from the predicted ones which is attributable to the effect of central planning. The results are presented in table 5-13. This table reports a range of values constructed around the forecasted value, a point estimate. Because we should expect some degree of forecast error in the estimates of the hypothetical

Table 5-13. Actual and Forecasted Steel Consumption in the CMEA-7 Countries, 1980

Country	Actual steel consumption (1)	Forecasted steel consumption (2)	Lower edge, 95% confidence band (3)	Upper edge, 95% confidence band (4)	Standard error of prediction (5)
Bulgaria	7.616	7.481	7.228	7.734	0.12
Czechoslovakia[a]	9.364	8.400	8.049	8.751	0.17
East Germany	8.663	8.645	8.367	8.924	0.13
Hungary	7.928	7.942	7.692	8.193	0.12
Poland[a]	9.814	9.004	8.783	9.225	0.10
Romania[a]	9.385	8.550	8.034	9.066	0.24
USSR[a]	11.921	11.438	11.023	11.852	0.20

Note: All data in natural logarithms.
[a]Actual consumption is above the upper bound of the confidence band.

values, the latter are not a single value but a range of values defined by a predetermined (in our case, 95 percent) confidence band.

A comparison of columns 1 and 2 shows that, with the exception of Hungary, the CMEA countries consume more steel than forecasted on the basis of the Western sample. Moreover, four countries (Czechoslovakia, Poland, Romania, and the USSR) lie outside the upper edge of the 95 percent confidence band constructed around the predicted values. The other three are within the confidence band, their steel consumption levels being compatible with those of similar Western countries. Thus, according to the forecasting approach, the majority of the centrally planned economies are overconsumers of steel relative to the market economies that serve as a reference group.

Equations (3) through (5) in table 5-12 introduce a dummy variable in the intercept to control directly for systemic differences in the pooled East-West sample. In equations (3) and (4), GDP per capita (GDPC) is included as an independent variable measuring the overall level of economic development. GDPC is taken as perhaps the most comprehensive environmental variable.

The dummy coefficient has the hypothesized positive sign and is statistically significant regardless of the specification of the dependent variable. Equation (5) shows that, other things being equal, on average the steel consumption of the centrally planned economies is 1.48 (= $e^{0.395}$) times that of Western market-oriented economies given similar environmental conditions and economic policies. However, in a strict sense the appropriate econometric answer is not a point estimate but a confidence band that accommodates, at a given level of probability, the error in the estimate. The lower edge of the confidence band is 1.048, and the upper edge is 2.102; thus, the range of CMEA country overconsumption lies somewhere between 1.048 and 2.102. A more precise estimate results from equation (3), in which the systems coefficient indicates that on average the steel consumption of the centrally planned economies (per unit of GDP) is 1.39 times that of Western market-oriented economies (the lower edge of the 95 percent confidence band is 1.32, and the upper edge is 1.46).

Equation (6) represents the full dummy-variable approach, as all interaction effects between the dummy variable and the nondummy explanatory variables are included. None of the interaction terms is statistically significant. The presence of very severe multicollinearity renders this model useless. Overall, however, the dummy-variable approach, like the forecasting approach, supports the conclusion that the centrally planned economies overconsume steel for systemic reasons.

Aluminum Consumption   Table 5-14 reports the regression results for aluminum consumption. The hypothesized relationship of the dependent variables—total aluminum consumption (TAC) and consumption per capita (ACCAP)—and the independent variables is basically the same as in the case of steel consumption. (Aluminum consumption per unit of GDP was tried as a dependent variable, but these models performed poorly.) The proxy for the output mix variable (OMIX) is the percentage share of the nonferrous metals sector in the manufacturing industry's value added.

Equations (1) through (3) show the parameter estimates for the Western sample. The level of development and the output mix variables are significant, but the investment ratio variable is insignificant. Equation (2) was used to forecast hypothetical consumption values for the centrally planned economies. Table 5-15 shows the actual and predicted values along with a 95 percent confidence band around the forecast. In five cases the actual value is greater than predicted, with two countries (East Germany and Hungary) lying above the upper bound of the confidence interval.

Equations (4) and (5) incorporate an intercept dummy variable to determine if there is an upward shift in the value of the dependent variable for systemic reasons, after controlling for level of development, an environmental variable, and the structure of output (considered a policy variable). The systems variable has the expected sign but is statistically insignificant. Equation (6) adds dummy variables to the slope, but, as earlier, severe multicollinearity makes this model of little use.

In summary, the regression analysis presents strong evidence of the overconsumption effect of central planning with respect to steel and weaker evidence with respect to aluminum, after controlling (at least partially) for non-system-related influences. The weaker evidence for aluminum may be related to the fact that most centrally planned economies have historically lagged behind in the use of this "progressive" metal. The results obtained for copper, not reported here, provide further indications regarding what seems to be an inherent material intensity bias under central planning.[12]

---

[12]The important question of how material intensity relates to economic efficiency is beyond the scope of the present study. In theory, intercountry (or intersystem) variations in material-

Table 5-14. Regression Results on Aluminum Consumption in CMEA and Western Countries, 1980

Sample[a]	W	W	W	C+W	C+W	C+W
Equation no.	(1)	(2)	(3)	(4)	(5)	(6)
Dependent variable	TAC	TAC	ACCAP	ACCAP	TAC	TAC
Constant	−10.300	−7.440	−6.965	−7.043	−7.295	−7.410
	(4.38)	(8.46)	(6.41)	(6.88)	(9.53)	(9.45)
TGDP	1.070	1.032			1.019	1.029
	(13.80)	(14.27)			(16.26)	(15.99)
GDPC			0.990	0.998		
			(8.05)	(8.61)		
OMIX	0.383	0.381	0.380	0.396	0.399	0.378
	(2.50)	(2.44)	(2.40)	(2.68)	(2.72)	(2.49)
IRATE	0.749					
	(1.32)					
SYSTDUM				0.134	0.136	−1.196
				(0.74)	(0.77)	(0.99)
TGDPDUM						0.000
						(0.85)
OMIXDUM						0.268
						(0.93)
$\bar{R}^2$	90.7	90.3	77.6	74.9	90.1	89.8
F	72.2	103.6	39.2	29.9	89.2	52.3
SE	0.41	0.42	0.42	0.40	0.40	0.41
n	23	23	23	30	30	30

Notes: All variables are in natural logarithms. TAC = total aluminum consumption; ACCAP = aluminum consumption per capita; TGDP = total GDP; GDPC = GDP per capita; OMIX = share of nonferrous metals sector in manufacturing value added; IRATE = investment-GDP ratio; SYSTDUM = dummy variable for CMEA countries; TGDPDUM = TGDP multiplied by SYSTDUM; OMIXDUM = OMIX multiplied by SYSTDUM.

Figures in parentheses are *t*-ratios.

Sources: **GDP and steel consumption data:** Statistical appendix to this volume. **Population data:** Derived from World Bank, *World Development Report 1982* (Washington, D.C., Oxford University Press, 1982). **Output mix data:** United Nations Industrial Development Organization, *Industrial Statistics Yearbook, 1982,* vol. 2 (New York: UNIDO, 1984). **Investment ratios:** International Monetary Fund, *International Financial Statistics Yearbook 1988* (Washington, D.C., IMF, 1988) and World Bank, *World Development Report 1982* (Washington, D.C., Oxford University Press, 1982).

[a]W = Western countries; C = CMEA countries; C+W = all countries.

output ratios should not themselves be taken as indicators of economic efficiency or even of material use efficiency. As Darmstadter, Dunkerley, and Alterman (1978, p. 222) state with regard to energy, "economic efficiency depends on how energy is used in combination with other resources—particularly capital and labor—and the relative costs of all of these." Elsewhere (Dobozi, 1988b, p. 89), we have suggested that in the context of the centrally planned economies, high material IU indicates problems with overall economic efficiency, as these economies have a system-driven tendency to overuse input factors in general (relative to a market-economy reference group).

Table 5-15. Actual and Forecasted Aluminum Consumption in the CMEA-7 Countries, 1980

Country	Actual aluminum consumption (1)	Forecasted aluminum consumption (2)	Lower edge, 95% confidence band (3)	Upper edge, 95% confidence band (4)	Standard error of prediction (5)
Bulgaria	3.912	3.921	3.657	4.186	0.13
Czechoslovakia	4.875	4.756	4.564	4.948	0.09
East Germany[a]	5.394	5.014	4.827	5.200	0.09
Hungary[a]	5.112	4.481	4.163	4.799	0.15
Poland	5.063	5.510	5.288	5.733	0.11
Romania	4.990	4.766	4.534	4.998	0.11
USSR	7.523	7.427	7.049	7.805	0.18

Note: All data in natural logarithms.
[a]Actual consumption is above the upper bound of the confidence band.

An in-depth inquiry of the underlying systemic factors promoting overconsumption in the centrally planned economies is beyond the scope of this chapter. We have investigated them elsewhere in the context of energy consumption, where an even greater margin of system-related overconsumption was found (63 percent in per capita GDP and 84 percent in per unit of GDP terms).[13] There appear to be several plausible causes. First, the centrally planned economies tend to favor supply-oriented solutions to their supply-demand gaps. These economies are designed to produce rather than save resources; they provide an incentive structure in which enterprises facing soft budget constraints are typically not given strong incentives to minimize resource costs, including material inputs. In fact, historically there has been some counter-incentive effect because material conservation has had the paradoxical effect of reducing growth rates measured in terms of gross production value, the traditionally dominant indicator of success for enterprise performance.[14] In spite of piecemeal economic reforms in some of the centrally planned economies, managerial incentives are still geared

---

[13]For estimation results on primary energy consumption, see Dobozi (1986, pp. 359–364); see also Hewett (1980a) and Slama (1986). For more extensive discussion of the system-related causes of overconsumption in centrally planned economies, see Dobozi (1985), Dienes and Merkin (1985), Hewett (1984), Gomulka and Rostowski (1988), and Kornai (1986).

[14]For specific Soviet examples of how output volume-oriented enterprise incentives act against reduction in metal intensity, see Ivantsova (1987, pp. 141–142). For example, the manufacturer of the home refrigerator "Saratov" requested that the producer of the compressor motor reduce the motor's weight. The request was rejected because weight reduction would have been contrary to the motor-producing firm's interest, as performance evaluation is based on volume indicators (p. 141). As a result of the interest in volume at the enterprise level and the narrow assortment and low quality of metals, manufactured goods of the CMEA countries tend to be significantly heavier than similar products in the West. For the USSR, Shumaev (1987, pp. 79–80) lists a number of machines and equipment whose weight is considerably (up to 20 percent) higher than that of the comparable "best-practice" items in foreign countries. Shumaev puts the "conservation reserve" associated with the weight gap at several million tons of metals in the machine-

predominantly toward fulfillment of short-term production plans rather than toward operational profitability. The resource-pricing system normally does not reflect relative scarcities; and input price increases, because of the relatively weak price sensitivity of users, do not necessarily result in reduced consumption. (Even Hungary, the most extensively marketized CMEA country, was found to be rather insensitive to changes in domestic energy price even when accounting for the possibility of delayed response in dynamic models. Both the short-run and long-run price elasticity turned out to be significantly lower than in the OECD market economies [see Dobozi, (1988a)].) For ideological reasons, in some centrally planned economies natural resources were treated as semifree or free goods, which resulted in the underpricing of these commodities for a long time. In the typical centrally planned economy, such systemic properties as uncontrolled expansion drive and relatively strong bias against technological change are also responsible in part for the excessive use of material inputs.

Our empirical analysis reveals, however, that only part of the considerable margin of CMEA country overconsumption (compared with that of the Western reference group) is attributable to specific system traits of the centrally planned economies. Policy-related factors, such as the relatively large industrial sector and the highly material-intensive branches within it, along with the startlingly low share (by international standards) of services in GDP, may also be instrumental in generating high material/GDP ratios.[15]

---

building industry alone. According to another Soviet source, the application of best-practice foreign technologies would allow a 10 to 15 percent reduction in metal use and an extension of the service life of machines by 20 percent in the Soviet machinery sector (Sachko, 1984, p. 129).

There is evidence for the material-intensity bias of the centrally planned economies in the area of manufacturing exports as well. In 1975, for example, to obtain $1 of export revenue in the OECD-Europe market, the CMEA countries exported construction and mining machinery that was 34 percent heavier and domestic electrical equipment that was 80 percent heavier than that observed in intra-OECD-Europe trade (calculated from OECD [1976].) For 1980, Poznanski found similar results for a wide range of manufactured products. The material content of the centrally planned economies' exports to the OECD-Europe market was shown to be significantly—in some cases, two to three times—higher not only vis-à-vis the developed Western exporters but also vis-à-vis such newly industrializing countries as Brazil, Mexico, South Korea, and Taiwan. See Poznanski (1986, pp. 70–71).

[15]On this issue there is no consensus in the limited empirical literature. Drabek (1988), in an input-output comparison between Austria and Czechoslovakia, concludes that the higher intensity of use of natural resources in Czechoslovakia cannot be explained by the technologies used in production because they are "highly similar" for the two countries. He suggests that the real problem lies in the structure of final output, which has been "heavily biased" toward high natural resource IU sectors. An opposite conclusion emerges from a broader cross-country input-output analysis by Gomulka and Rostowski (1988, p. 487), whose results contradict the view that the high material intensity of the centrally planned economies is due to the broad sectoral composition of their final demands. They argue (without proving) that "the main cause of the problem must lie with the technologies used in production processes and with the detailed product composition of the final demands."

CONCLUSIONS

Following a marked deceleration in the mid-1970s, the growth of metal demand has become negative during the 1980s for the smaller CMEA countries and stagnant for the USSR. A considerable drop in IU explains most of the recent slowdown; the earlier deceleration was a more balanced combination of declining trends in GDP and IU in the case of steel, aluminum, and zinc, and of slower economic growth alone in the case of copper, lead, and nickel.

Apart from the deterioration of macroeconomic performance, it is not entirely clear what forces are causing this striking departure from past trends. Intersectoral shifts in the composition of GDP generally tended to act against the decline in IU, at least until the early 1980s. The CMEA countries have not yet entered the postindustrial era, as demonstrated by the continued above-average growth and dominance of the industrial sector and the low share of the service sector. Similarly, changes in the composition of industrial output toward highly metal-absorbing branches have tended to raise rather than lower material intensity. No evidence could be found for a recent acceleration in technological progress; in fact, there is some evidence to the contrary.

Nonetheless, the following factors seemed to have worked in a combined fashion to reduce metal intensity of GDP: the oil price increase, the recent decline in the construction sector and investment, product mix shifts within highly disaggregated industrial branches, targeted innovative activity promoted by government and enterprise "rationalization" programs, technologically based improvements in product quality and broadening of the range of high-quality materials, and more efficient materials management. The reversal in IU trends of the CMEA countries appears to be permanent or long term, although more information is needed to confirm this conclusion.

Perhaps the most distinctive feature of metal consumption in the CMEA countries is its high IU by international standards. One widely held hypothesis claims that a Soviet-type centrally planned economy inherently encourages the profligate use of material inputs. Tests of this hypothesis do indicate a considerable margin of system-driven overconsumption after policy and environmental influences have been taken into account. These findings, along with other evidence, strongly suggest that the centrally planned systems suffer from a structural metal-intensity bias relative to the market economies. To make matters worse, it seems that this bias became progressively stronger over the 1960–1987 period, thus widening the East–West "material efficiency gap."

Only part of the overall margin of overconsumption, however, can be attributed to the systemic nature of these economies. Policy-related factors, such as imbalances in structural policy in the form of an overgrown industrial sector (which has a high share of material-intensive activities) and a weak service sector, are also involved. It thus seems clear that any serious attempt in the CMEA countries to reduce the present margin of material overuse on a long-term basis (and thus to alleviate associated economic difficulties that go much beyond the boundaries of the materials sector) must simultaneously address both system- and policy-related impediments to a more sustainable level of material consumption. It remains to be seen how much further the presently unfolding economic reforms in the CMEA countries—and the recent policy deemphasis, in several countries, on the highly material-absorbing industrial branches—can take these countries in their necessary transition to a more resource-efficient growth trajectory.

An important implication of the recent downturn in IU concerns the long-standing material consumption–production gap in the CMEA countries. Although the marked reduction in IU has in the West contributed importantly to the emergence of a large capacity overhang in several mineral industries during most of the past fifteen years, a similar IU trend in the CMEA countries has had an equilibrating effect by narrowing the persistent gap between the output of and demand for materials, thereby easing a traditional constraint on growth.

ACKNOWLEDGMENT

The author is indebted to John E. Tilton, Hans H. Landsberg, and anonymous referees for helpful suggestions, and to Kee Hwang for assistance in collecting a large portion of the data.

REFERENCES

Alton, Thad P. 1985. "East European GNP's: Origins of Product, Final Uses, Rates of Growth, and International Comparisons," in U.S. Congress, Joint Economic Committee, *East European Economies: Slow Growth in the 1980s*, vol. 1: *Economic Performance and Policy* (Washington, D.C., U.S. Government Printing Office) pp. 81–132.

_____, Krysztof Badach, Elizabeth M. Bass, Joseph T. Bombelles, Gregor Lazarik, and George J. Staller. 1985. Occasional Papers nos. 85–89 of the Research Project on National Income in East Central Europe (New York, L. W. International Financial Research).

Arbatov, A. A., and A. V. Mukhin. 1987. "K formirovaniiu dolgosrochnoi strategii obespecheniia ekonomiki SSSR toplivno-syrevymi resursami" (Toward the Formulation of Strategy to Secure the USSR with Fuels and Raw Materials), *Ekonomika i matematicheskiie metody* vol. 23, no. 1, pp. 61–73.

Bond, Daniel, and Lawrence R. Klein. 1985. "Impact of Changes in the Global Environment on the Soviet and East European Economies," in U.S. Congress, Joint Economic Committee, *East European Economies: Slow Growth in the 1980s*, vol. 1: *Economic Performance and Policy* (Washington, D.C., U.S. Government Printing Office) pp. 7–21.

Braun, M. 1987. "Domestic Raw Materials and Sources of Energy in the GDR," in Nansen Behar, ed., *Natural Resource Problems and the Ecological Challenge in East European Region* (Sofia, Union of Scientific Workers) pp. 113–131.

Darmstadter, Joel, Joy Dunkerley, and Jack Alterman. 1978. "International Variations in Energy Use: Findings from a Comparative Study," *Annual Review of Energy* vol. 3, pp. 201–224.

Desai, Padma. 1986. "Soviet Growth Retardation," *The American Economic Review* vol. 76 (May) pp. 175–180.

Dienes, Leslie, and Victor Merkin. 1985. "Energy Policy and Conservation in Eastern Europe," in U.S. Congress, Joint Economic Committee, *East European Economies: Slow Growth in the 1980s*, vol. 1: *Economic Policy and Performance* (Washington, D.C., U.S. Government Printing Office) pp. 332–355.

Dobozi, Istvan. 1983. "The 'Invisible' Source of 'Alternative' Energy: Comparing Energy Conservation Performance of the East and the West," *Natural Resources Forum* vol. 7, no. 3, pp. 201–216.

———. 1985. "Access to and Utilization of Natural Resources in Eastern Europe: A Regional Resource Management System in World Perspective" (mimeo) (Tokyo, United Nations University).

———. 1986. "Are the Centrally Planned Economies Over-Consuming Metals? A Cross-Sectional Analysis," *Materials and Society* vol. 10, no. 3, pp. 351–367.

———. 1988a. "The Responsiveness of the Hungarian Economy to Changes in Energy Prices," in Josef C. Brada and Istvan Dobozi, eds., *The Hungarian Economy in the 1980s: Reforming the System and Adjusting to External Shocks* (Greenwich, Conn., JAI Press) pp. 237–265.

———. 1988b. "Energiapolitika es gazdasagi mechanizmus a KGST-orszagokban" (Energy Policy and Economic Mechanism in the CMEA Countries), *Propagandista* no. 6, pp. 82–89.

Drabek, Zdenek. 1988. "The Natural Resource Intensity of Production Technology in Market and Planned Economies: Austria vs. Czechoslovakia," *Journal of Comparative Economics* vol. 12, no. 2, pp. 217–227.

Dresher, William H. 1986. "Copper Applications and Markets: Then, Now and Tomorrow," *CIPEC Quarterly Review* (April–June) pp. 10–42.

Economic Commission for Europe. 1983. *Economic Survey of Europe in 1982–1983* (New York: United Nations).

———. 1984. *The Evolution of the Specific Consumption of Steel* (New York: United Nations).

———. 1987. *Economic Survey of Europe in 1986–1987* (New York, United Nations).

———. 1988. *Economic Survey of Europe in 1988–1989* (New York, United Nations).

Ekonomicheskaya gazeta no. 40 (1985).

Gomulka, Stanislaw. 1986. "Soviet Growth Slowdown: Duality, Maturity, and Innovation," *The American Economic Review* vol. 76 (May) pp. 170–174.

———, and Jacek Rostowski. 1988. "An International Comparison of Material Intensity," *Journal of Comparative Economics* vol. 12, no. 4, pp. 475–501.

Gregory, Paul R., and Robert C. Stuart. 1985. *Comparative Economic Systems* (Dallas, Tex., Houghton Mifflin).

Hewett, Edward A. 1980a. "Alternative Econometric Approaches for Studying the Link Between Economic Systems and Economic Outcomes," *Journal of Comparative Economics* vol. 4, no. 4, pp. 274–294.

_____. 1980b. "Foreign Trade Outcomes in Eastern and Western Economies," in Paul Marer and John Michael Montias, eds., *East European Integration and East-West Trade* (Bloomington, Indiana University Press) pp. 41–69.

_____. 1984. *Energy Economics and Foreign Policy in the Soviet Union* (Washington, D.C., Brookings Institution).

Hungarian Statistical Office. 1988. *Statistical Pocket Book of Hungary 1987* (Budapest, Statistical Publishing House).

Hutchison, Roger S., and John E. Tilton. 1987. "Is the Intensity of Copper Use Still Declining in the USA?" *Natural Resources Forum* vol. 11, no. 4, pp. 325–334.

International Institute for Environment and Development, and the World Resources Institute. 1987. *World Resources 1987* (New York, Basic Books).

International Iron and Steel Institute, *Steel Statistical Yearbook* (Brussels, various issues).

International Monetary Fund, *International Financial Statistics Yearbook 1988* (Washington, D.C., IMF).

Ivantsova, N. 1987. "Khoziastvennii mekhanizm i ekonomia materialnykh resursov" (Economic Mechanism and Conservation of Material Resources), *Voprosy ekonomiki* no. 3, pp. 141–143.

Jack Faucett Associates. 1986. *Changes in Worldwide Demand for Metal Minerals* (Bethesda, Md., Jack Faucett Associates).

Keeling, Bernard. 1982. *The World Steel Industry: Structure and Prospects in the 1980s* (London, Economist Intelligence Unit) pp. 10–11.

Kontorovich, Vladimir. 1986. "Soviet Growth Slowdown: Econometric vs. Direct Evidence," *The American Economic Review* vol. 76 (May) pp. 181–185.

Koopmans, Tjalling C., and John Michael Montias. 1971. "On the Description and Comparison of Economic Systems," in Alexander Eckstein, ed., *Comparison of Economic Systems: Theoretical and Methodological Approaches* (Berkeley, University of California Press).

Kornai, Janos. 1986. "The Hungarian Reform Process: Visions, Hopes, and Reality," *Journal of Economic Literature* vol. XXIV (December) pp. 1687–1737.

Malenbaum, Wilfred. 1978. *World Demand for Raw Materials in 1985 and 2000* (New York, McGraw-Hill).

Marer, Paul. 1986. "Economic Policies and Systems in Eastern Europe and Yugoslavia: Commonalities and Differences," in U.S. Congress, Joint Economic Committee, *East European Economies: Slow Growth in the 1980s*, vol. 3: *Country Studies on Eastern Europe and Yugoslavia* (Washington, D.C., U.S. Government Printing Office) pp. 595–633.

Metallgesellschaft Aktiengesellschaft. Annual. *Metal Statistics* (Frankfurt am Main, Metallgesellschaft Aktiengesellshaft).

Nechaev, A. A. 1989. "Sopostavlenie potreblenie materialnyh i energeticheskikh re sursov v SSSR i razvityh kapitalisticheskikh stran" (A Comparison of Materials on Energy Consumption Between the USSR and the Developed Capitalist Countries), in *Sorevnovanie dvukh sistem* (*Competition of the Two Systems*) (Moscow, Nauka) pp. 244–259.

Nove, Alec. 1984. "Some Observations on Intersystem Comparisons," in Andrew Zimbalist, ed., *Comparative Economic Systems: An Assessment of Knowledge, Theory, and Method* (Boston, Kluwer-Nijhoff) pp. 47–63.

Organisation for Economic Co-operation and Development. 1975. *Trade by Commodities* vol. II (January–December) (Paris, OECD).

Oleinik, I. 1982. "Napravleniia deiatelnosti stran SEV po uluchsheniiu ispolzovaniia i ekonomiia topliva, energii, syria" (Directions in Improving Utilization and Conservation of Fuel, Energy and Raw Materials in the CMEA Countries), *Planovoe khozaistvo* no. 8, pp. 105–109.

―――. 1984. "Opyt stran SEV v ekonomii materialnikh resursov" (Experience of the CMEA Countries in Savings of Material Resources), *Voprosy ekonomiki* no. 5, pp. 113–122.

Pirogov, N. 1987. "Vtorichnie resursi i effektivnost" (Secondary Resources and Efficiency), *Planovoe khoziastovo* no. 6, pp. 95–100.

Poznanski, Kazimierz. 1986. "Competition Between Eastern Europe and Developing Countries in the Western Market for Manufactured Goods," in U.S. Congress, Joint Economic Committee, *East European Economies: Slow Growth in the 1980s*, vol. 2: *Foreign Trade and International Finance* (Washington, D.C., U.S. Government Printing Office) pp. 62–90.

Planovoe khoziastvo. 1987. "Rezervi i puti snizhenia sebestoimosti promishlennoi produktzii" (Reserves and Ways of Reducing Costs of Industrial Production), *Planovoe khoziastvo* no. 4, pp. 31–37.

Rozenfeld, S. 1982. "Puti ekonomii topliva, syria i materialov" (Ways to Save Fuel and Raw Materials), *Voprosy ekonomiki* no. 2, pp. 32–42.

Sachko, N. S. 1984. "Materialoiomkost produktsii: rezervi ekonomia" (Material Intensity of Production: Sources of Conservation), *Ekonomika i organizatsia promishlenogo proizvodstva* no. 10, pp. 118–130.

Schroeder, Gertrud E. 1985. "The Slowdown in Soviet Industry," *Soviet Economy* vol. 1 (January–March) pp. 42–74.

Shumaev, V. 1987. "Snizheniie metalloiomkosti mashin" (Reduction of the Metal Intensity of Machinery), *Planovoe khoziastvo* no. 1, pp. 78–80.

Slama, Jiri. 1986. "An International Comparison of Sulphur Dioxide Emissions," *Journal of Comparative Economics* vol. 10, no. 3, pp. 277–292.

Soladay, J. 1988. "Structural Change in the Metals Industry" (mimeo) (Washington, D.C., International Monetary Fund).

Staatsverlag der Deutschen Demokratischen Republik. 1975. *Statistische Jahrbuch der Deutschen Demokratischen Republik 1975* (*Statistical Yearbook of the German Democratic Republic*) (Berlin: State Publishers of the German Democratic Republic).

Tilton, John E. 1986. "Beyond Intensity of Use," *Materials and Society* vol. 10, no. 3, pp. 245–250.

―――. 1988. "Mineral Investment in Developing Countries in the Wake of Slower Growth in World Metal Demand," in G. Jaenicke, C. Kirchner, H.-J. Mertens, E. Rehbinder, and E. Schanze, eds., *Studies in Transnational Law of Natural Resources*, vol. 11: *International Mining Investment: Legal and Economic Perspectives* (Frankfurt am Main: Alfred Metzner Verlag) pp. 11–22.

United Nations, Committee on Natural Resources. 1987. "Mineral Resources and Salient Issues: Report of the Secretary-General" (New York, UN).

United Nations Industrial Development Organization. 1986. *Handbook of Industrial Statistics 1986* (Vienna, UNIDO).

_____. 1988. *Handbook of Industrial Statistics 1988* (Vienna, UNIDO).

United Nations. 1972. *Yearbook of National Account Statistics 1970* vols. 1 and 2 (New York, UN).

_____. 1986. *Economic Bulletin for Europe* vol. 38, no. 4 (Geneva, UN).

_____. 1988. *Economic Bulletin for Europe* vol. 40, (New York, UN).

U.S. Congress, Joint Economic Committee. 1982. *USSR: Measures of Economic Growth and Development, 1950–80* (Washington, D.C.: U.S. Government Printing Office).

van Brabant, Jozef M. 1987. "Economic Adjustment and the Future of Socialist Economic Integration," *Eastern European Politics and Societies* vol. 1, no. 1, pp. 75–112.

Vintrova, Ruzhena. 1986. "Strukturnye izmeneniie pri perekhode k intensifikatsii ekonomiki i ikh vliianie na mezhdunarodnoe razdelenie truda" (Structrual Changes During the Transition to the Intensification of the Economy and Their Impact on the International Division of Labor), paper presented at a conference on "Problems of Modernizing the Pattern of Industrial Production in the USSR and Czechoslovakia under the Conditions of the Intensification of the Economy" Moscow, June 2–6, 1986.

Wallace, William V., and Roger A. Clarke. 1986. *Comecon, Trade and the West* (London, Frances Pinter).

World Bank. 1986. *World Bank Data Tape: National Accounts, Prices, Exchange Rates and Population for the Period 1960–84* (Washington, D.C., IBRD).

_____. 1988. *World Development Report 1988* (Washington, D.C., IBRD).

6

The Passenger Car Industry: Faithful to Steel

RODERICK G. EGGERT

The motor vehicle industry is an important consumer of metals. In the United States since 1960, this industry—which produces passenger cars, trucks, and buses—has consumed approximately one-tenth of the aluminum and copper, one-fifth of the steel, one-third of the zinc, and one-half of the lead and malleable iron (see table 6-1). The motor vehicle industry is also an important consumer of metals in the other countries that produce large numbers of vehicles. Among the countries in the Organisation for Economic Co-operation and Development (OECD), these producers include Japan, the Federal Republic of Germany, France, Canada, Italy, Spain, and the United Kingdom. The Soviet Union is the most important producer of motor vehicles among the centrally planned economies; among the developing countries, Brazil, Mexico, and South Korea are important producers (see table 6-2).

The material composition of the typical passenger car has changed substantially since the 1960s and could change even more dramatically by the early part of the next century. Although iron and steel continue to account for more than two-thirds of a typical new car's weight, cast iron and plain carbon steels are less important, whereas high-strength steels—nonexistent in the early 1960s—are now more important. Plastics, composite materials, and aluminum together accounted for only about 1 percent of the weight of new cars in the early 1960s; in the late 1980s they accounted for well over 10 percent. In particular, plastics and composites have replaced steel in instrument panels, some bumpers, a limited number of outer-body panels, and other applications. Cast aluminum has replaced cast iron in many engine blocks. Zinc die castings have all but disappeared from automobile grilles.

Table 6-1. Share of the Motor Vehicle Industry in Total U.S. Consumption of Selected Metals, 1960–1987

(percent)

Metal	1960	1970	1980	1987
Aluminum	11	8	11	16
Copper	6	8	9	10
Iron (malleable)	70	41	46	43
Lead	47	N.A.	59	55
Steel	21	16	15	15
Zinc	35	29	27	30[a]

Note: N.A. = not available.

Source: Motor Vehicle Manufacturers Association, *Motor Vehicle Facts & Figures* (Detroit, MVMA, various years).

[a]1986 data.

Many if not most radiators now are made of aluminum rather than brass (an alloy of copper and zinc). All these changes could seem minor if, as some observers predict, plastic-bodied cars are produced in large quantities in the future.

Thus, the passenger car industry—the largest segment of the motor vehicle industry—is an obvious place to look when trying to understand slower growth in demand for the major metals since the early to mid-1970s (see chapter 1 in this volume for an overview). This chapter analyzes changing materials use in the passenger car industry and evaluates this industry's role in the stagnation of growth in metal consumption. The first section documents changes in materials consumption since 1960. The second and third sections then assess the forces behind these changes. The focus is on the three largest producers of passenger cars in the 1970s and 1980s: the Federal Republic of Germany, Japan, and the United States. The fourth section looks, in less detail, at the world as a whole. The focus is on three families of materials—iron and steel, aluminum, and plastics and composites—that account for three-quarters or more of the weight of a typical new car.

Methodologically, material consumption is analyzed in terms of two factors: passenger car production and pounds of material per car. When multiplied together these factors, by definition, yield the total weight of materials consumed by the automobile industry in the production of new cars. Changes in the first factor are largely determined by changes in the economy as a whole; changes in the second factor reflect technological changes in automobile design and construction. The task of this analysis, therefore, is to identify and assess the forces behind changes in the production of new cars and in pounds of material per car, and in so doing to explain changes in overall materials consumption.

This methodology is analogous but not identical to the methodology described in chapter 2, which evaluates metal consumption in terms of changes

Table 6-2. World Production of Motor Vehicles, 1960–1988

Group and countries	1960 No. of vehicles (thousands)	1960 Percentage	1970 No. of vehicles (thousands)	1970 Percentage	1980 No. of vehicles (thousands)	1980 Percentage	1988 No. of vehicles (thousands)	1988 Percentage
OECD countries								
Canada	398	2.4	1,160	3.9	1,374	3.5	1,960	4.0
Germany, Federal Republic of	2,055	12.5	3,842	12.9	3,879	10.0	4,625	9.5
France	1,369	8.4	2,750	9.3	3,378	8.7	3,698	7.6
Italy	645	3.9	1,854	6.2	1,612	4.2	2,111	4.3
Japan	482	2.9	5,289	17.8	11,043	28.4	12,700	26.1
Spain	58	0.4	536	1.8	1,182	3.0	1,866	3.8
United Kingdom	1,811	11.1	2,098	7.1	1,313	3.4	1,545	3.2
United States	7,905	48.3	8,284	27.9	8,010	20.6	11,262	23.2
Other OECD	606	3.7	1,438	4.8	1,475	3.8	1,343	2.8
Total OECD	15,329	93.6	27,251	91.7	33,266	85.7	41,110	84.6
Centrally planned economies (CPE)								
USSR	524	3.2	916	3.1	2,199	5.7	2,180	4.5
Other CPE	191	1.2	449	1.5	894	2.3	1,895	3.9
Total CPE	715	4.4	1,365	4.6	3,093	8.0	4,075	8.4
Developing countries								
Brazil	133	0.8	416	1.4	1,165	3.0	1,069	2.2
Mexico	50	0.3	193	0.6	490	1.3	512	1.1
South Korea	0	0.0	28	0.1	123	0.3	1,084	2.2
Other developing countries	156	1.0	455	1.5	734	1.9	766	1.6
Total developing countries	339	2.1	1,092	3.7	2,512	6.5	3,431	7.1
WORLD TOTAL	16,383	100.0	29,708	100.0	38,838	100.0	48,616	100.0

Sources: Motor Vehicle Manufacturers Association, *Motor Vehicle Facts & Figures* (Detroit, MVMA, various years) and *World Motor Vehicle Data* (Detroit, MVMA, various years); *Automotive News 1989 Market Data Book* (special annual issue of weekly *Automotive News*).

in gross domestic product (GDP), the product composition of income, and the material composition of products. The production of new cars in any country is strongly influenced by both the overall level of economic activity (that is, GDP) and the importance of the passenger car industry to the country's overall economy (product composition of income). The analysis of changes in passenger car production in the second section of this chapter thus embodies changes in both GDP and the product composition of income. The third section then focuses on changes in pounds of material per new passenger car or, in other words, changes in the material composition of products. This chapter does not explicitly look at intensity of use, which would be measured as the number of pounds of material used in new passenger cars per unit of GDP.

CHANGES IN MATERIALS CONSUMPTION

Figure 6-1 presents estimates over time (since 1960) of the amounts of materials used in the production of passenger cars in the Federal Republic of Germany (referred to in this chapter as West Germany), Japan, and the United States.[1] U.S. consumption of iron and steel by the car industry in the 1960s dwarfed consumption by the Japanese and West German industries. By 1986, however, the gap between U.S. and Japanese consumption was essentially closed, and the West German industry was using about one-half as much iron and steel as the industries in the United States and Japan. Over this period iron and steel used in U.S. cars rose slightly between 1960 and the late 1970s and then fell sharply, whereas consumption grew steadily in both Japan and West Germany. Growth was more substantial in Japan (a fivefold increase) than in West Germany (a threefold increase). (Data for Japan are unavailable before 1967.)

Table 6-3 indicates that most of these increases in iron and steel consumption in West Germany and Japan can be attributed to growth in the production

---

[1]Several words of caution are in order about these data. They are estimates generated by the author from other data (on production of new cars and on pounds of material per car) rather than independent estimates of consumption. The estimates do not account for materials used in spare and replacement parts; if these were included, consumption estimates would be higher (on the order of 10 percent), although the actual percentage increase would vary from material to material (personal communication from Masahiro Watanabe, Mazda, Tokyo, May 13, 1987). The estimates also do not include scrap generated during car production; the amount of scrap generated varies considerably from material to material, from almost none for cast metal parts to between 30 and 35 percent of the total amount of sheet steel purchased by automakers (Gjostein, 1986). Finally, the data are not completely comparable across countries, and data for some years are missing. Despite these limitations the data provide a starting point for the remainder of the analysis. (The reader considering using these data for other purposes should bear in mind the definitions in tables 6-A-1 through 6-A-4 in the appendix to this chapter, from which the figures were generated.)

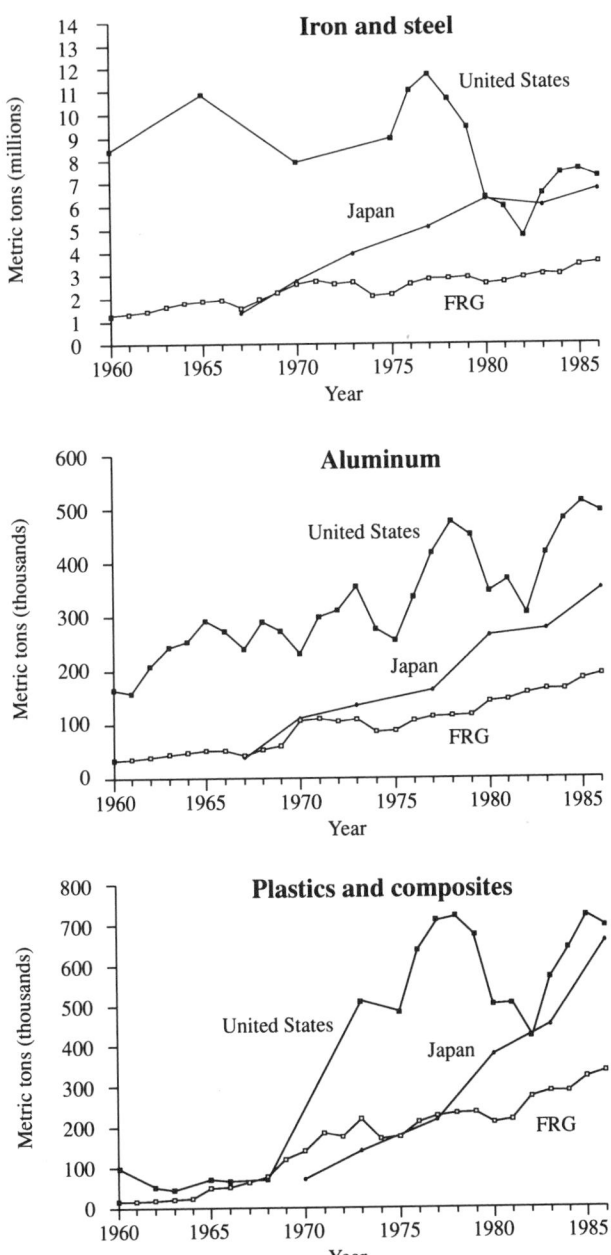

Figure 6-1. Material consumption by the passenger car industries of the Federal Republic of Germany (FRG), Japan, and the United States, 1960–1986.

Source: Tables 6-A-1 through 6-A-3 in the appendix to this chapter.

Table 6-3. Growth Rates of Material Consumption by the Passenger Car Industry, of Car Production, and of Pounds of Material per Car in the Federal Republic of Germany (FRG), Japan, and the United States, 1960–1986
(percent)

Country and years	Iron and steel		Aluminum		Plastics and composites	
	Growth rate	Share of consumption growth attributable to changes in car production or pounds of material per car	Growth rate	Share of consumption growth attributable to changes in car production or pounds of material per car	Growth rate	Share of consumption growth attributable to changes in car production or pounds of material per car
FRG (1960–1986)						
Consumption	4.1		7.0		12.4	
Car production	3.4	83	3.4	49	3.4	15
Pounds per car	0.7	17	3.5	51	8.6	85
Japan (1967–1986)						
Consumption	9.0		12.2		15.0	
Car production	9.6	104	9.6	89	9.6	34
Pounds per car	−0.6	−4	2.4	11	8.8	66

United States						
1960–1977						
Consumption	2.0		—		11.9	
Car production	1.9	96	—	—	1.9	9
Pounds per car	0.1	4	—	—	9.8	91
1977–1986						
Consumption	−5.2		—		−0.2	
Car production	−1.8	36	—	—	−1.8	747
Pounds per car	−3.5	64	—	—	1.6	−647
1960–1986						
Consumption	−0.6		4.3		7.5	
Car production	0.6	−111	0.6	10	0.6	4
Pounds per car	−1.2	211	3.7	90	6.9	96

Notes: Dash (—) = not applicable.

The calculation in the right-hand column for each material is based on the following identity: materials consumption in any year = (car production in that year) × (pounds of material per car in that year). The number in the column represents the percentage of the total change in consumption over the period (e.g., 1960–1986) that would have occurred if only that particular factor (e.g., car production) had changed. The multiplicative effect is distributed to each factor in proportion to the direct effects.

Source: Calculations by the author on the basis of data from figure 6-1 and from tables 6-A-1 through 6-A-3 in the appendix to this chapter.

of passenger cars. In fact, Japanese consumption would have grown even more were it not for the decline in the number of pounds of iron and steel per car between 1967 and 1986. In the United States nearly all the growth in consumption of iron and steel between 1960 and 1977 can be attributed to growth in car production; between 1977 and 1986, some two-thirds of the decline in consumption is attributable to the use of fewer pounds of iron and steel per car. (Two periods are considered for the United States in table 6-3 because of the break in the trend for consumption in about 1977.)

For aluminum a different picture emerges. In all three countries the amount of aluminum used in new cars grew substantially between the 1960s and 1986. This growth was most dramatic in Japan, where aluminum use increased by a factor of close to 10. West German use increased by a factor of about 6 and U.S. consumption by a factor of 3. Despite faster consumption growth in Japan and West Germany, U.S. aluminum use in 1986 continued to exceed Japanese and West German use by a wide margin. Table 6-3 indicates that the sources of growth varied significantly among the three countries. In Japan 89 percent of the growth in aluminum use is attributable to higher car output; in West Germany about half of the increase is attributable to each factor; and in the United States 90 percent of the increase is attributable to more pounds of aluminum per car.

For plastic and composite materials, still another picture emerges. Although use of these materials increased significantly in all three countries, as did aluminum use, differences also are apparent. In the United States consumption grew by a factor of 7 between 1960 and 1978, fell by some 40 percent by 1982, and then returned to its previous highs by the mid-1980s. In Japan and West Germany, in contrast, the use of plastic and composite materials increased more smoothly over the entire period. By 1986, as in the case of iron and steel, the United States and Japan were using about the same amounts of plastics and composites, and West Germany was using about half as much. For all three countries, table 6-3 indicates that most of the increase in the use of plastics and composites in car production is attributable to more pounds per car. (As with iron and steel, two periods are considered for the United States because of the break in consumption trend in about 1977.)

For all three families of materials, Japanese consumption rose more dramatically than did consumption in either of the other two countries. For iron–steel and aluminum in Japan, most consumption growth is attributable to increases in car production, whereas for plastics and composites, about two-thirds of the growth is attributable to more pounds per car.

U.S. consumption exhibits considerable fluctuation from year to year, primarily because of fluctuations in car production. Over the entire 1960–1986 period, however, increased use of aluminum and plastics is attributable largely to more pounds of material per car. West German consumption of all three families of materials changed more gradually than Japanese consumption and more steadily than U.S. consumption.

Although this section of the chapter has attributed changes in the amounts of materials used in passenger cars to changes in passenger car production and pounds of material per car, the story is far from complete. What is now required is a careful examination of the forces behind changes in these two factors.

PASSENGER CAR PRODUCTION

Changes in passenger car production over time, as noted earlier, are largely the result of changes in macroeconomic factors. To assess the relative importance of these factors, it is useful to divide total car production into two groups: (1) cars destined for the domestic market and (2) exports.

Changes over time in the number of cars produced for the domestic market reflect changes in demand in the home market. Demand for new cars, in turn, is largely a function of seven factors (adapted from factors cited in OECD, 1983). The first is income. Growth in income is likely to lead to greater demand for new cars. The absolute level of income also is apt to be important. When income growth occurs at low levels of income, many consumers will purchase a car for the first time or perhaps purchase a second car for the family. When income growth occurs at higher levels of income, however, many consumers will replace relatively inexpensive cars with more expensive ones. At higher levels of income, in other words, much of the growth in demand will be "replacement" demand rather than "new" demand. This phenomenon is sometimes referred to as product saturation. If product saturation occurs, the number of new cars sold in the home market is likely to be tied more closely to population than to income. The implication is that the fastest growth in sales of new cars is more likely to be in the industrializing, less developed countries than in the industrialized, OECD countries. The level of income at which saturation occurs is unknown and moreover is likely to vary from country to country because of differences in the availability of public transportation, the extent of road infrastructure, and other factors.

The second factor affecting demand for new cars is demographic trends, which influence the number of new cars produced for the home market. As the number of people of driving age increases, sales of new cars also are likely to increase except in those instances where population growth impedes economic growth. In the developed countries, the number of individuals who are fifteen and older is expected to increase by 11 percent between 1985 and 2000; in the less developed countries this portion of the population is expected to increase by 41 percent over the same period (United Nations, 1986). These less developed countries, incidentally, are also the countries in which "new" demand will be more important than "replacement" demand. In the OECD countries socioeconomic factors may be just as important as

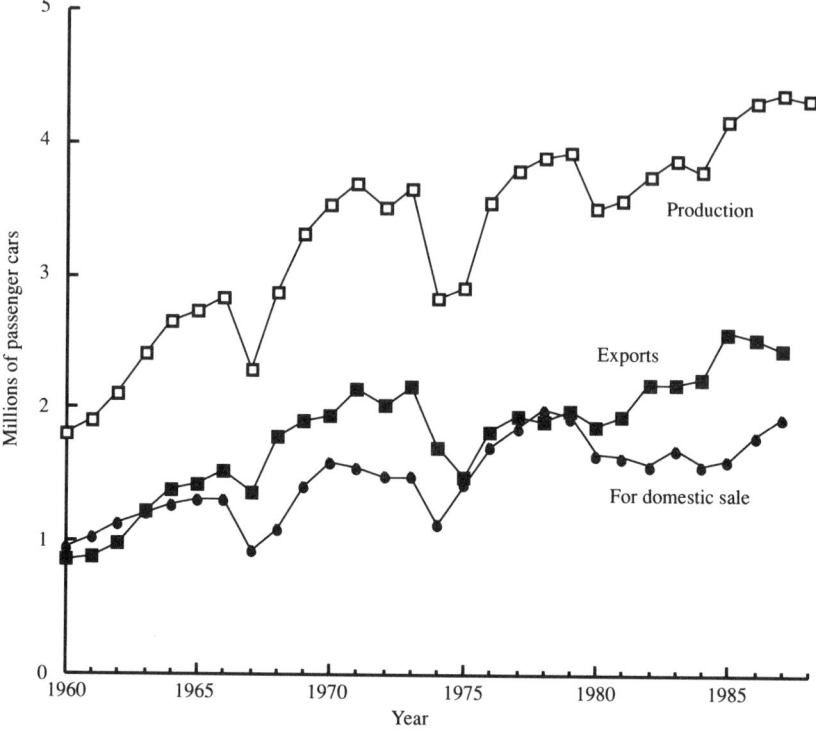

Figure 6-2. Passenger car production in the Federal Republic of Germany, 1960–1988.

Notes: The figures are for passenger cars plus *Kombinationswagen* (loosely translated as station wagons); domestic sales are estimated as production minus exports.

Sources: Automotive News 1989 Market Data Book; Motor Vehicle Manufacturers Association, *World Motor Vehicle Data* (Detroit, MVMA, 1988); Verband der Automobilindustrie, *Tatsachen und Zahlen aus der Kraftverkehrswirtschaft* (Frankfurt am Main, Verband der Automobilindustrie, 1986).

absolute increases in population. In the United States, for example, both smaller households and increases in leisure time are likely to stimulate an increasing demand for new cars because of reduced vehicle sharing and desire for greater mobility.

The third factor to influence the demand for new cars is costs of vehicle ownership. Two kinds of costs need to be considered. Fixed costs—such as the price of a new car, registration fees, and insurance—are independent of the number of miles driven. The most important of these costs undoubtedly is the car price. The higher the price, the lower the number of new cars demanded (other factors remaining the same). Variable costs, which depend on the number of miles driven, include such costs as those of gasoline and repairs. These costs are likely to have a smaller effect on the number of new cars sold than will fixed costs. If gasoline prices increase, for example, consumers are most likely to respond by driving less and purchasing more fuel-efficient cars rather than by delaying purchases of new cars.

Fourth, geography will affect the demand for new cars. More urbanized areas are likely to have lower ownership per capita than do rural areas because of problems with traffic and congestion. Fifth, institutional factors are important. The availability of public transportation, for example, influences car ownership and thus sales of new cars; areas with well-developed systems of public transportation are likely to have lower ownership per capita than areas with less extensive systems. The infrastructure of roads also influences car ownership: the better and more extensive the system of roads, the higher ownership per capita will be. The sixth factor is the life of the automobile: the longer the average life, the lower the level of replacement sales in a given year. Finally, the seventh factor is the availability and level of imported cars: the greater the level and availability of imports, the smaller the number of automobiles produced for the home market.

In addition to being influenced by demand for new cars in the home market, total car production in a country also is influenced by the level of exports. The demand for exports will be determined largely by the same seven factors just identified, but as they apply to foreign markets rather than to home markets. The third factor, ownership costs, needs to be expanded to include (1) foreign exchange rates, (2) government policies in foreign markets aimed at discouraging imports, and (3) domestic government policies designed to encourage exports (to the extent that these policies lower the costs to producers of exported cars and, in turn, car prices for consumers in foreign markets).

The rest of this section examines changes in the production of new cars in West Germany, Japan, and the United States in terms of these potential determinants of change.

The Federal Republic of Germany

West German car production more than doubled between 1960 and the late 1980s, the result of growth in both exports and domestic sales (figure 6-2). Exports accounted for 55 to 60 percent of production in the 1980s.

The most important cause of the rise in production for the home market was rising income. Between 1960 and the late 1980s, GDP more than doubled in terms of 1980 U.S. dollars (see the statistical appendix in this volume). Over the same period, the portion of the population that is at least fifteen years old also increased, but only by some 20 percent (OECD, 1972, 1988); thus, growth in the number of people of driving age contributed only slightly to increased car production for the home market.

Table 6-4. Imports as a Share of Domestic Sales of Passenger Cars in the Federal Republic of Germany (FRG), Japan, and the United States, 1960–1988
(percent)

Year	FRG	Japan	United States
1960–1964	11	2	6
1965–1969	24	1	9
1970–1974	35	1	15
1975–1979	38	2	18
1980–1984	43	1	26
1985–1988	46[a]	3	29

Note: Sales in FRG and Japan are estimated on the basis of registrations of new cars.

Sources: Calculated from data in Motor Vehicle Manufacturers Association, *Motor Vehicle Facts & Figures '89* and *World Motor Vehicle Data* (Detroit, MVMA, 1989); Japan Automobile Manufacturers Association, *Motor Vehicle Statistics of Japan 1989* (Tokyo, JAMA, 1989); Verband der Automobilindustrie, *Tatsachen und Zahlen aus der Kraftverkehrswirtschaft* (Frankfurt am Main, Verband der Automobilindustrie, 1986).

[a] Data from 1985 to 1987.

Several factors discouraged growth in production for the home market. In other words, were it not for the following factors, German car production for the domestic market likely would have increased more than it actually did. First, imports rose as a share of domestic car sales from about 10 percent in the early 1960s to over 40 percent in the 1980s (table 6-4). Second, the life of a West German automobile appears to have increased (table 6-5). Among the possible explanations for the longer life, two appear most plausible: (1) the cars are of better quality, especially with respect to rustproofing; and (2) each car is driven fewer kilometers per year as an increasing number of households acquire more than one vehicle, thereby reducing the demands on each vehicle.

There is no evidence of passenger car saturation in West Germany. Between 1960 and 1987 the number of car registrations per person of driving age increased steadily from about 100 to 550 cars per 1,000 persons as per capita income doubled (figure 6-3). If saturation had occurred, the number of cars per capita would have leveled off at the level of income at which every person desiring a car was able to afford one. Certainly, West Germany

Table 6-5. Median Life of Selected West German Cars in Sweden, 1965–1980
(years)

Car type	1965	1971	1975	1977	1978	1979	1980
Audi/DKW	8.3	9.9	11.9	12.0	12.4	12.6	12.5
BMW	9.1	10.5	12.8	13.3	13.5	14.0	14.4
Mercedes-Benz	10.2	12.4	14.7	15.5	15.2	16.0	16.6
Opel	8.8	11.4	13.1	13.0	13.5	14.0	14.4
Volkswagen	10.6	13.2	14.2	14.0	14.3	14.9	15.4

Source: OECD, *Long-Term Outlook for the World Automobile Industry* (Paris, OECD, 1983). Based on data from AB Svensk Bilprovning.

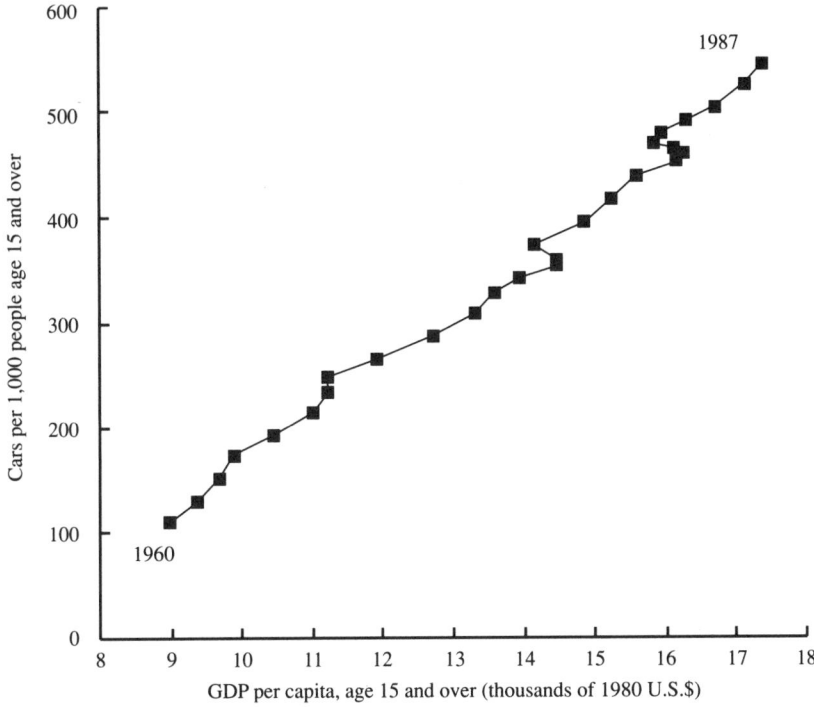

Figure 6-3. Passenger car registrations per capita versus income per capita in the Federal Republic of Germany, 1960–1987.
Note: Population figures for 1986 and 1987 are estimated.
Sources: OECD, *Labour Force Statistics 1959–1970* (Paris, OECD, 1972), and *Labour Force Statistics 1966–1986* (Paris, OECD, 1988); Motor Vehicle Manufacturers Associations, *World Motor Vehicle Data* (Detroit, MVMA, 1988); Verband der Automobilindustrie, *Tatsachen und Zahlen aus der Kraftverkehrswirtschaft* (Frankfurt am Main, Verband der Automobilindustrie, 1986); statistical appendix in this volume.

may reach saturation eventually, but undoubtedly at a lower level of income than in the United States. Because West Germany is more densely populated, its drivers face more congested driving conditions than their U.S. counterparts; by the late 1980s, however, there was little to indicate that physical congestion had discouraged car ownership in West Germany. Between 1960 and 1987, car ownership per capita increased with increases in the population density of people at least fifteen years old—that portion of the population forming individual households and more likely to contribute to physical congestion than will the density of the entire population (figure 6-4). If physical congestion had been a deterrent to car ownership, the number of cars per person of driving age would have leveled off at some degree of congestion. Aggregate measures of car ownership per capita and degree of

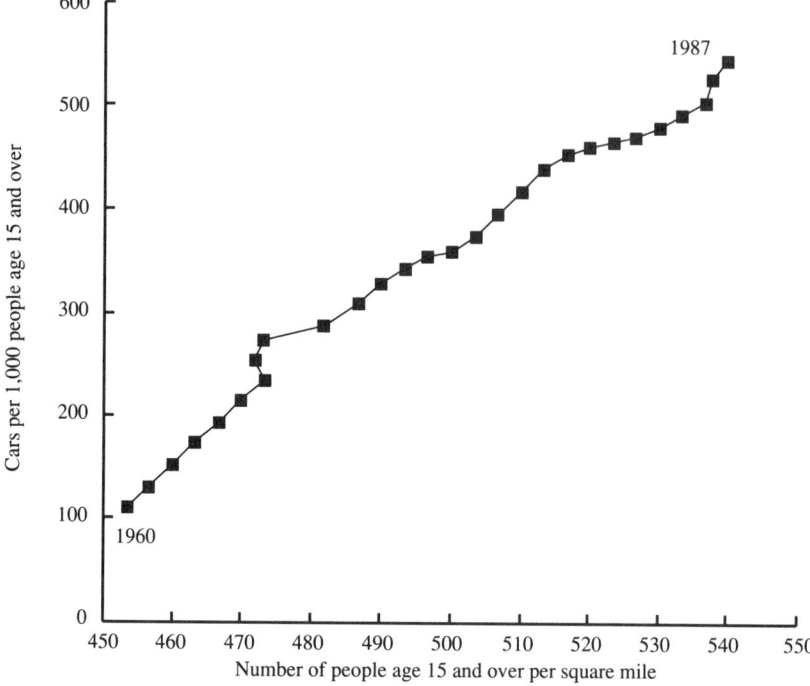

Figure 6-4. Passenger car registrations per capita versus population density in the Federal Republic of Germany, 1960–1987.

Note: Population figures for 1986 and 1987 are estimated.

Sources: OECD, *Labour Force Statistics 1959–1970* (Paris, OECD, 1972), and *Labour Force Statistics 1966–1986* (Paris, OECD, 1988); Motor Vehicle Manufacturers Association, *World Motor Vehicle Data* (Detroit, MVMA, 1988); Verband der Automobilindustrie, *Tatsachen und Zahlen aus der Kraftverkehrswirtschaft* (Frankfurt am Main, Verband der Automobilindustrie, 1986).

congestion, of course, mask differences between urban and rural areas. Increased congestion in urban areas could have discouraged car ownership, but there is no evidence to support that speculation.

Prices of new cars and operating costs apparently had little effect on car sales and production. Producer prices remained remarkably steady between 1970 and 1985, as did operating costs between 1979 and 1985 (in terms of constant 1980 deutsche marks; see table 6-6).

West German car exports increased somewhat more than car production for the home market between 1960 and the late 1980s (figure 6-2). The net effect on West German car production of changes in international trade, however, has been relatively small; net car exports—exports minus imports—have been about the same in the 1980s as in the 1960s: an average of between 1.0 million and 1.2 million cars per year (Motor Vehicle Manufacturers Association, *World Motor Vehicle Data,* various years).

Table 6-6. Producer Price Index for Passenger Cars and Typical Operating Costs for Car Owners in the Federal Republic of Germany, 1970–1985

Year	Producer price index for passenger cars (1980 DM)	Monthly operating costs (1980 DM)
1970	103.5	N.A.
1971	102.0	N.A.
1972	101.3	N.A.
1973	100.3	N.A.
1974	102.6	N.A.
1975	103.3	N.A.
1976	102.7	N.A.
1977	102.5	N.A.
1978	101.5	N.A.
1979	101.2	241.95
1980	100.0	246.21
1981	98.5	251.19
1982	100.4	239.92
1983	100.0	245.16
1984	102.0	236.54
1985	103.7	242.43

Notes: N.A. = not available.

Nominal figures adjusted to constant 1980 Deutsche marks (DM) using the West German GDP deflator from International Monetary Fund, *International Financial Statistics: Supplement on Price Statistics* (Washington, D.C., IMF, 1986).

Source: Verband der Automobilindustrie, *Tatsachen und Zahlen aus der Kraftverkehrswirtschaft* (Frankfurt am Main, Verband der Automobilindustrie, 1986).

Japan

Passenger car production in Japan increased from fewer than 200,000 cars in 1960 to more than 8 million in 1988 (see figure 6-5), a much more substantial increase in production than in West Germany. Until the late 1960s car exports accounted for a very small portion of total production; it was not until 1976 that exports exceeded production for the home market. Since 1970, production for the home market has stagnated (compared to its more significant growth in the 1960s), whereas exports have increased by a factor of 6. In the 1980s exports have accounted for 55 to 60 percent of production—about the same as in West Germany. Unlike West German exports, however, Japanese exports became an important part of total production only in the early 1970s; West German exports accounted for nearly half of total production over the entire 1960–1988 period. Further in contrast with West Germany, the net effect of international trade on car production has been substantial in Japan. Net exports of cars virtually equal gross exports because of the very small number of imported cars.

Cars produced for the home market were thus responsible for most of the increase in Japanese passenger car production from 1960 to the early 1970s. During this period Japanese income more than tripled (as measured by GDP

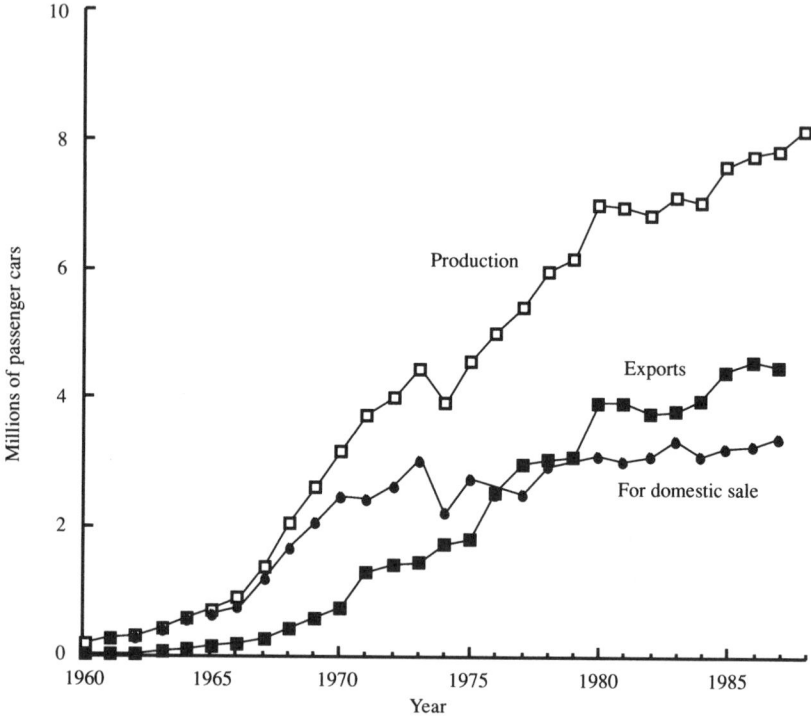

Figure 6-5. Passenger car production in Japan, 1960–1988.
Note: Domestic sales are estimated as production minus exports.
Source: Japan Automobile Manufacturers Association, *Motor Vehicle Statistics of Japan 1989* (Tokyo, JAMA, 1989).

in constant 1980 U.S. dollars; see the statistical appendix in this volume), certainly stimulating the first-time purchase of cars by many consumers. Almost all purchases of new cars were from Japanese car producers; imports accounted for only 1 to 2 percent of sales (table 6-4). Government policies, particularly tariffs, restricted car imports. From 1960 to 1967, imported cars with engine displacements greater then 2,000 cubic centimeters faced duties of 34 percent or more. Imports with smaller engines were taxed at the lower rate of 15 percent, but almost no U.S. cars and only some European cars were of this size. As a result Japanese automakers expanded production of small cars to be sold in Japan with only minimal competition from U.S. and European cars. Beginning in the late 1960s, as Japanese firms began to export cars in large numbers, tariffs on imported cars were lowered to 8 percent in 1972 on imports of all sizes and removed entirely in 1978 (Cusumano, 1985).

Since 1970, as noted earlier, the number of Japanese cars produced for the domestic market has grown much more slowly than in the 1960s (figure

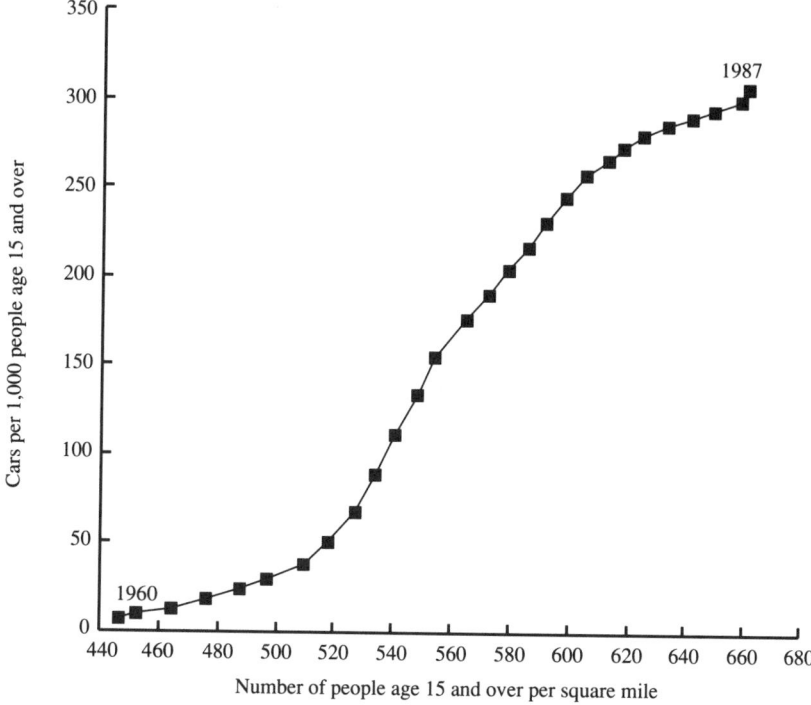

Figure 6-6. Passenger car registrations per capita versus population density in Japan, 1960–1987.

Note: Population figures for 1987 are estimated.

Sources: Japan Automobile Manufacturers Association, *Motor Vehicle Statistics of Japan 1989* (Tokyo, JAMA, 1989); OECD, *Labour Force Statistics 1959–1970* (Paris, OECD, 1972), and *Labour Force Statistics 1966–1986* (Paris, OECD, 1988).

6-5). The cause of slower growth was not a rise in imports, which might have been expected following the removal of tariff barriers (as discussed earlier); imports as a share of total sales fluctuated between about 1 and 2 percent from 1970 to 1985, virtually the same as in the 1960s. Instead, congestion is the most likely cause. The number of cars in use appears to be leveling off at about 300 cars per 1,000 persons of driving age as population density has risen to more than 600 persons (at least fifteen years old) per square mile (see figure 6-6). (The population density data given in figure 6-6 actually understate the extent of congestion in which the vast majority of Japanese people live. A large portion of the population lives on the coastal plain stretching from Tokyo to Osaka—a small part of the country.)

The implication is that saturation of the passenger car market is occurring in Japan at a level of per capita GDP (for those at least fifteen years old) of between $12,000 and $13,000 (1980 U.S. dollars; see figure 6-7). Nevertheless, congestion could be relieved—and, in turn, car ownership per capita

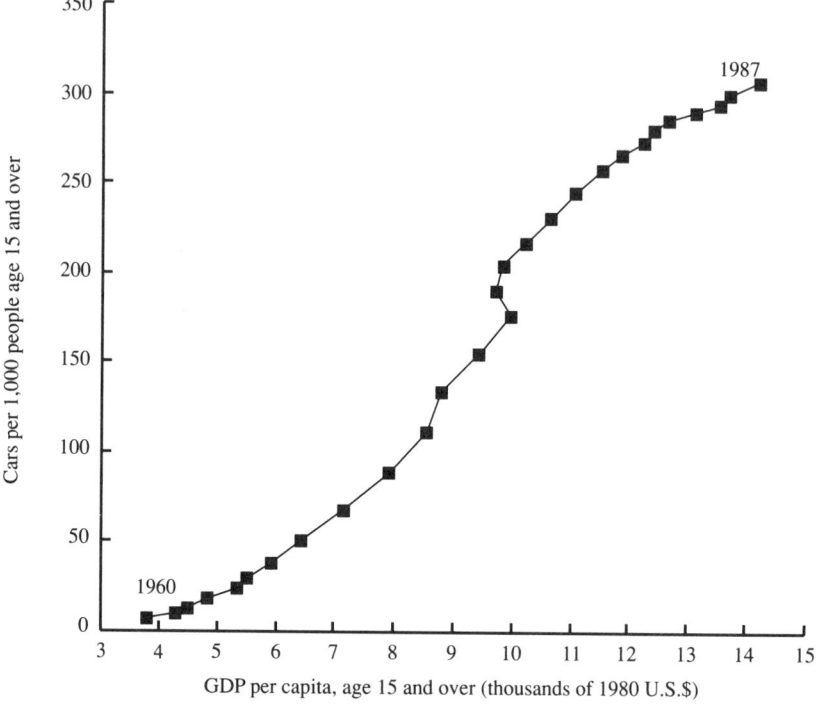

Figure 6-7. Passenger car registrations per capita versus income per capita in Japan, 1960–1987.

Note: Population figures for 1987 are estimated.

Sources: Japan Automobile Manufacturers Association, *Motor Vehicle Statistics of Japan 1989* (Tokyo, JAMA, 1989); OECD, *Labour Force Statistics 1959–1970* (Paris, OECD, 1972), and *Labour Force Statistics 1966–1986* (Paris, OECD, 1988); statistical appendix in this volume.

could rise—with the construction of new roads as Japan moves to spread its population over a larger portion of its land area.

Since the early 1970s exports have accounted for more of the increase in Japanese car production than has production for the domestic market. The United States has been and continues to be the most important single export market for new Japanese cars. Although exports to the United States accounted for more than 40 percent of Japanese car exports in as early as 1970 (see table 6-7), exports to the United States were given a big push by the oil price shocks of 1973–1974 and 1979–1980. U.S. consumers, facing dramatically higher gasoline costs, replaced many of their larger and less fuel-efficient cars with smaller and more fuel-efficient cars. U.S. car manufacturers traditionally had not manufactured large numbers of small cars; thus, U.S. consumers were forced to look elsewhere, and Japanese firms benefited.

Table 6-7. Japanese Car Exports to the United States, 1960–1988

Year	Japanese cars exported to the United States (number)	Total Japanese car exports (number)	U.S. share of total exports (percent)
1960	942	7,013	13.4
1965	22,127	100,703	22.0
1970	323,671	725,586	44.6
1975	711,902	1,827,286	39.0
1980	1,819,092	3,947,160	46.1
1985	2,215,811	4,426,762	50.1
1988	2,051,321	4,431,890	46.3

Sources: Motor Vehicle Manufacturers Association, *World Motor Vehicle Data* (Detroit, MVMA, 1988); Japan Automobile Manufacturers Association, *Motor Vehicle Statistics of Japan 1989* (Tokyo, JAMA, 1989).

Having gained a foothold in the U.S. market, Japanese firms have maintained their presence by offering cars with reputations for high quality and workmanship as well as for fuel economy. In coming years Japanese car exports to the United States are unlikely to grow as swiftly as they have over the past decade, largely because all the major Japanese automakers now are manufacturing cars in the United States or have plans to do so in the near future, either alone or in cooperation with a U.S. car manufacturer.

The United States

In contrast with the situation in West Germany and Japan, car production in the United States did not experience significant, long-term growth between 1960 and 1988 (see figure 6-8). To be sure, production increased from 6.7 million cars in 1960 to 9.6 million in 1973, an increase of over 40 percent. But production fell to 5.1 million in 1982, recovering to between 7 million and 8 million per year between 1984 and 1988. More generally, production experienced substantial ups and downs between 1960 and 1988, fluctuating around a nearly horizontal trend.

A second important difference between the United States and both West Germany and Japan concerns exports. U.S. exports have accounted for a much smaller share of production. In the United States exports rose from less than 2 percent of production in 1960 to only some 9 percent in the 1980s, whereas (as noted previously) exports have accounted for half or more of car production in Japan (since the mid-1970s) and in West Germany (since 1963). In addition, the net effect of international trade on car production has been to discourage U.S. production; net imports grew from 200,000–300,000 vehicles per year in the early 1960s to an average of about 3 million per year in the 1980s (Motor Vehicle Manufacturers Association, *World Motor Vehicle Data,* various years). (In West Germany the overall effect of trade has been small because net exports have remained essentially the same,

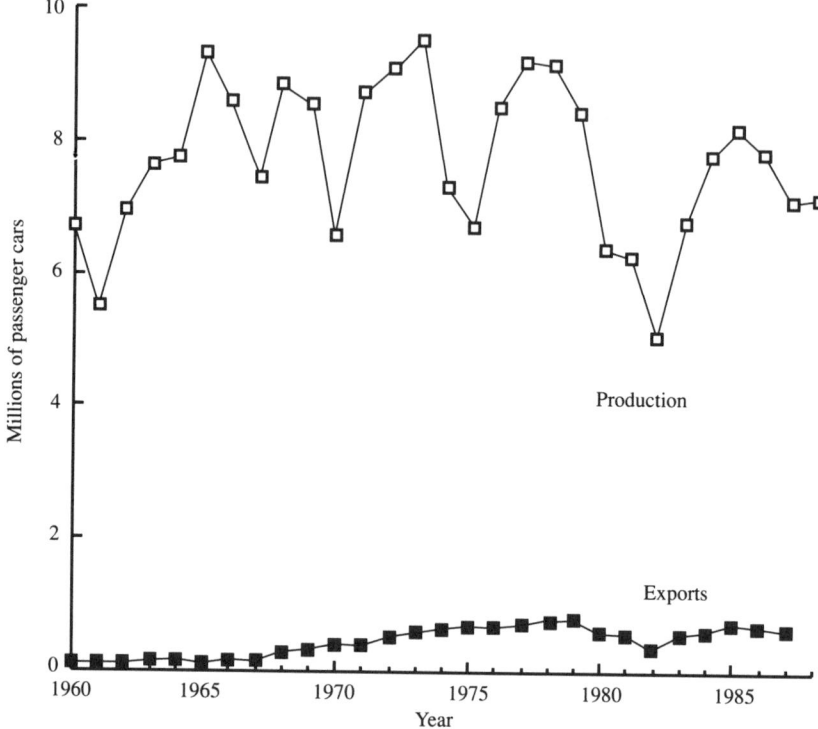

Figure 6-8. Passenger car production in the United States, 1960–1988.
Sources: Motor Vehicle Manufacturers Association, *Motor Vehicle Facts & Figures* (Detroit, MVMA, various years); *Automotive News 1989 Market Data Book.*

whereas in Japan trade has provided a strong stimulant to domestic car production because of dramatic growth in net exports.)

The absence of long-term growth in U.S. car production is not what one would expect on the basis of changes in several of the determinants of demand for passenger cars. Income, for instance, more than doubled between 1960 and the late 1980s as measured in terms of U.S. GDP in constant 1980 dollars (see the statistical appendix in this volume). There is little to suggest that the passenger car market in the United States is saturated (see figure 6-9)—especially because light trucks and vans (which throughout this study are not counted as passenger cars and thus are absent from the figure) have become increasingly popular vehicles for individuals and families.

If these determinants of demand for passenger cars—level and growth of income—do not explain the lack of long-term growth in U.S. car production, what does? The rise in imports is probably the most important factor. Imports as a share of sales of new cars in the United States grew from less than 10 percent in the 1960s to more than 25 percent in the 1980s (see table 6-4).

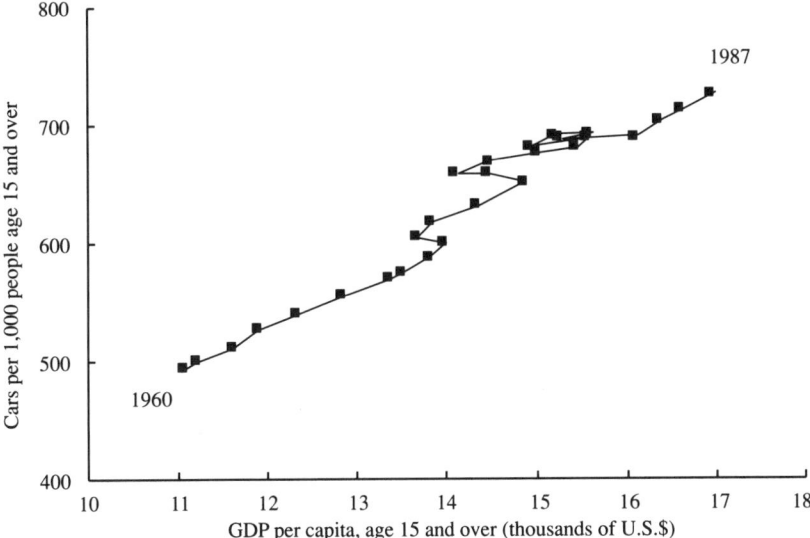

Figure 6-9. Passenger car registrations per capita versus income per capita in the United States, 1960–1987.

Note: Population figures for 1987 are estimated.

Sources: Motor Vehicle Manufacturers Association, *Motor Vehicle Facts & Figures* (Detroit, MVMA, various years); OECD, *Labour Force Statistics 1959–1970* (Paris, OECD, 1972), and *Labour Force Statistics 1966–1986* (Paris, OECD, 1988); statistical appendix in this volume.

Prior to the mid-1960s imports were unimportant in the U.S. market because U.S. consumers faced substantially different conditions than did most other car consumers. Gasoline prices were lower and driving conditions were less crowded (especially compared to Europe, with its typically narrow and winding city streets and its higher population density). As a result U.S. consumers tended to demand larger—and consequently less fuel-efficient—cars than those offered by foreign producers.

The first significant rise in imports occurred between 1965 and 1970, when imports grew to more than 10 percent of new-car sales. Robert Crandall and coauthors (1986) attribute this increase to lower import prices and improved quality of imported cars. The second significant increase in imports occurred between 1975 and the early 1980s, when imports as a share of sales of new cars increased to more than 25 percent. This increase can be attributed directly to higher gasoline prices in the latter half of the 1970s, which motivated consumers to purchase more fuel-efficient (hence smaller) cars. U.S. producers traditionally had not competed in the small-car market, which allowed foreign producers to satisfy the limited demand for small cars.

The average age of passenger cars in the United States increased from 5.6

years in 1970 to 7.6 years in 1987 (Motor Vehicle Manufacturers Association, *Motor Vehicle Facts & Figures,* 1988). This contributed to the stagnation of growth in U.S. production of new cars and, more generally, of growth in sales (including imports) between 1973 and the mid-1980s. An increase in average age implies that consumers are waiting longer to replace aging vehicles with new ones. One explanation for this is that the quality of vehicles is improving; evidence for this includes improved corrosion resistance and longer warranties. Another explanation is that safety and emissions regulations have added to the costs of purchasing a car in the United States and as a result have encouraged consumers to keep their cars longer. Crandall and coauthors (1986) estimate that safety and emissions regulations added between $1,300 and $2,200 to the costs of purchasing and operating a car between the late 1960s and the early 1980s. A third possible explanation is that consumers are driving their cars fewer miles per year, thereby stretching the useful life of their cars over more years. A fourth possibility is that consumers wait longer to replace their cars during periods of low economic growth such as that which the United States experienced between the mid-1970s and early 1980s.

It is likely that changes in prices of new cars have influenced the sales of new cars in the United States and, in turn, U.S. production of cars. The available data, however, provide a mixed picture of the effects of prices on sales and production. The average transaction price per new car (in constant 1980 dollars) fell from $7,777 to $7,150 between 1967 and 1974, then increased to $9,990 in 1988 (see table 6-8). It might be inferred from these data that falling prices stimulated sales in the earlier period, and rising prices discouraged sales in the more recent period. However, these inferences ignore changes in the quality of cars over time. In other words, a typical 1988-model car has more options, safety features, and emissions-control equipment than a typical car of the 1960s; thus, price differences reflect differences in quality as well as changes over time in the cost to consumers of purchasing a standardized product. Estimates of what a hypothetical 1967-comparable car would cost in 1988 suggest that the price of this standardized product fell by about 10 percent over this period (table 6-8).

Finally, it would be surprising to find that congestion had discouraged car ownership in the United States and, in turn, car production, in view of the widely held perception that the United States, perhaps more than any other industrialized country apart from Canada and Australia, is the land of wide-open spaces. The evidence, however, is inconclusive. The number of cars per person (at least fifteen years old) has grown more slowly than has population density since the late 1970s (see figure 6-10). In contrast, the number of motor vehicle registrations per mile of surfaced road, another measure of congestion, increased steadily over the entire 1960–1985 period. If congestion had been a deterrent to car ownership, the number of registrations per mile should have leveled off at some point.

Table 6-8. Various Costs of Vehicle Ownership in the United States, 1967–1988
(1980 U.S.$)

Year	Operating costs (¢/mile)	Insurance, license, registration ($)	Average transaction price ($/car)	Estimated price of a 1967 comparable car ($/car)
1967	9.2	722	7,777	7,802
1968	N.A.	N.A.	7,903	7,828
1969	8.7	714	7,835	7,617
1970	N.A.	N.A.	7,364	7,478
1971	8.4	766	7,410	7,471
1972	N.A.	N.A.	7,361	7,176
1973	8.4	700	7,184	6,910
1974	9.2	580	7,150	6,812
1975	9.4	600	7,184	6,788
1976	N.A.	N.A.	7,483	6,877
1977	7.6	774	7,600	6,881
1978	6.9	604	7,742	6,887
1979	6.5	636	7,599	6,829
1980	7.6	572	7,574	6,771
1981	7.5	547	8,144	6,950
1982	7.2	435	8,548	6,895
1983	7.1	511	9,010	6,986
1984	6.2	486	9,045	6,814
1985	6.2	475	9,140	6,823
1986	4.9	479	9,438	6,950
1987	5.2	486	9,782	6,943
1988	5.3	513	9,990	6,680

Notes: N.A. = not available.
Operating costs include the costs of gas, oil, maintenance, and tires. Nominal dollar values are adjusted using the U.S. gross national product (GNP) implicit price index (1980 = 100).
    Source: Motor Vehicle Manufacturers Association, *Motor Vehicle Facts & Figures '89* (Detroit, MVMA, 1989).

Future Car Production

Forecasts of long-term growth for the car industry in particular countries tend to focus on sales rather than production. Forecasting long-term growth in production thus requires adjusting sales forecasts for net imports.

For the United States, analysts of the auto industry generally expect sales of new cars to increase on the order of 1 percent per year over the rest of this century, roughly in line with forecasts of GDP and population growth. (These predictions are based on off-the-record conversations with several analysts.) Car imports are expected to remain steady or decline slightly over this period, implying relatively little growth in U.S. car production in the foreseeable future. This aggregate analysis, however, masks the anticipated increase in so-called transplant production—that is, cars produced in the United States at plants owned by foreign companies (for example, Honda

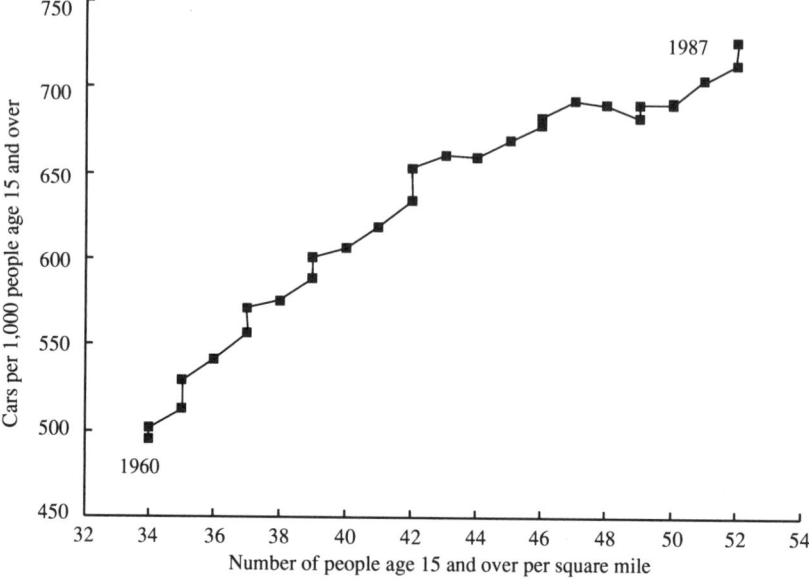

Figure 6-10. Passenger car registrations per capita versus population density in the United States, 1960–1987.

Note: Population figures for 1987 are estimated.

Sources: Motor Vehicle Manufacturers Association, *Motor Vehicle Facts & Figures* (Detroit, MVMA, various years); OECD, *Labour Force Statistics 1959–1970* (Paris, OECD, 1972), and *Labour Force Statistics 1966–1986* (Paris, OECD, 1988).

Accords manufactured in Marysville, Ohio). Transplant car production already has more than tripled from 213,357 to 822,495 cars between 1984 and 1988 (Motor Vehicle Manufacturers Association, *Motor Vehicle Facts & Figures,* 1987; *Automotive News, Market Data Book,* 1989); it is expected to increase to more than 1.3 million cars by 1991 (U.S. Department of Commerce, 1988).

The message for U.S. material suppliers is that transplant producers are likely to be the major growth market, especially as several of these producers strive to increase the domestic content of their cars, that is, the amount of materials purchased from suppliers in the United States. (The goal of Honda North America, for example, is to increase the domestic content of its U.S.-built cars to 75 percent by 1991 from 60 percent in 1987; *Automotive News,* 1987.)

In Western Europe sales of new cars and production are expected to increase slightly more per year than in the United States, on the order of 1.5 percent per year between the late 1980s and the end of the century. Compared to the United States, Western Europe is expected to have slower growth in both GDP and population but more first-time purchasers of cars.

Finally, in Japan sales of new cars are expected to grow faster than in either the United States or Western Europe—at a rate of approximately 2 percent per year because of more substantial growth in GDP. Almost all cars sold in Japan are made in Japan, and there is little to suggest that this situation will change substantially in the next few years. Japanese car exports are unlikely to grow appreciably, especially because increasing numbers of Japanese transplants are built in the United States and other countries. (Relatively few auto industry analysts have sophisticated mathematical models for forecasting future car sales over the longer term; most analysts are interested only in the next several years. Two academic studies, however, have examined the last two decades of the twentieth century from the perspective of the early 1980s. The OECD [1983] and Altshuler and coauthors [1984] have developed models to forecast sales of new cars largely on the basis of per capita income and population. Both studies predict that sales of new cars for the world will increase by approximately 2 percent per year, with the highest growth rates in the developing countries and the centrally planned economies.)

POUNDS OF MATERIAL PER CAR

Figure 6-11 illustrates changes in the pounds per car of iron and steel, aluminum, and plastics and composites in the three countries under study. In table 6-9 these changes are attributed to changes in (1) the average weight of a car and (2) the material composition of the car. For iron and steel, substantial differences exist among the trends for West Germany, Japan, and the United States. In West Germany pounds of iron and steel per car rose gradually from the mid-1970s to the mid-1980s; this rise is attributable entirely to an increase in the average weight of a car (table 6-9). In Japan, pounds of these metals per car fluctuated around a generally horizontal trend, falling slightly from 1967 to 1986; this decrease is attributable largely to iron and steel's smaller share of the weight of a car. In the United States pounds of these metals per car dropped sharply in the middle to late 1970s, largely because of declines in the average weight of a car.

In absolute terms typical U.S. cars in the 1960s contained about twice as many pounds of iron and steel as West German cars, with Japanese cars intermediate between U.S. and West German cars. By the mid-1980s, however, these differences had nearly disappeared as cars from all three countries became more nearly equal in weight.

For aluminum, pounds per car rose for all three countries between the 1960s and the 1980s, more than doubling in the United States and West Germany and increasing slightly less in Japan. These increases are attributable almost entirely to aluminum's increased share of the weight of a car (table 6-9). In absolute terms U.S. cars have contained more pounds of

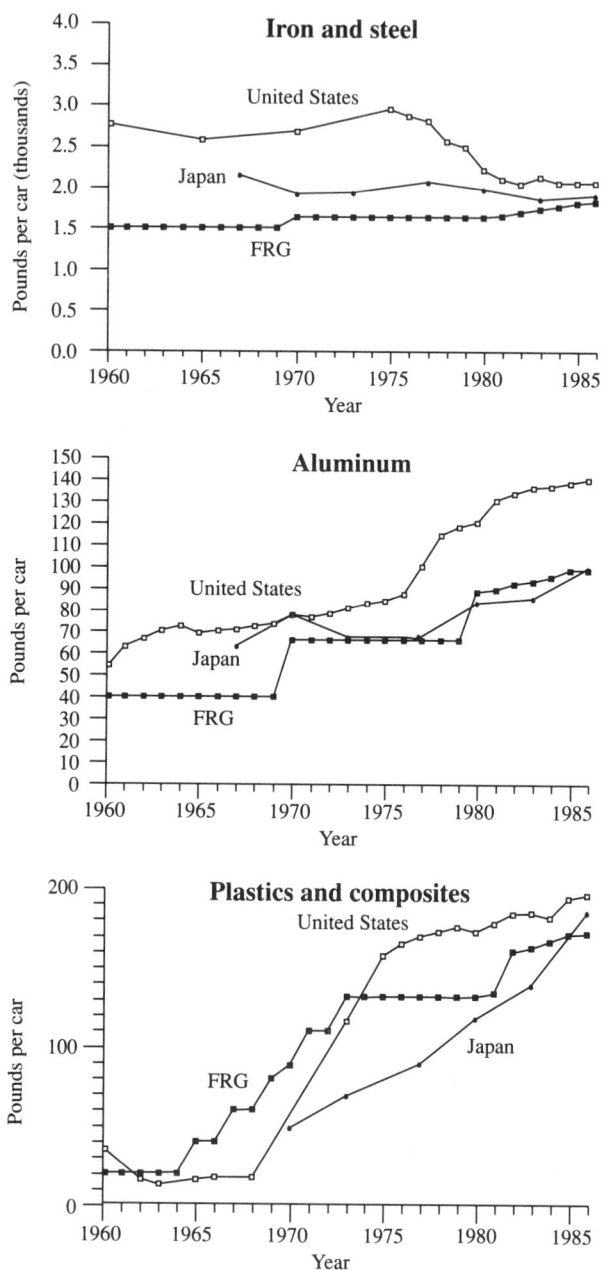

Figure 6-11. Changes in the number of pounds of iron and steel, aluminum, and plastics and composites per car in the United States, Japan, and the Federal Republic of Germany (FRG), 1960–1986.

Source: Tables 6-A-1 through 6-A-3 in the appendix to this chapter.

Table 6-9. Changes in the Number of Pounds of Material per Car and Percentage of Those Changes Attributable to Changes in Average Car Weight and Material Composition, 1960–1986

Material, country, and years	Changes in pounds per car	Percentage share attributable to changes in	
		Average car weight	Material composition
Iron and Steel			
Federal Republic of Germany, 1960–1986	313	107	−7
Japan, 1967–1986	−240	23	77
United States, 1960–1986	−718	81	19
Aluminum			
Federal Republic of Germany, 1960–1986	58	18	82
Japan, 1967–1986	36	−5	105
United States, 1960–1986	85	−17	117
Plastics and composites			
Federal Republic of Germany, 1960–1986	152	4	96
Japan, 1967–1986	138	−2	102
United States, 1960–1986	161	−6	106

Note: The calculations of percentage changes attributable to changes in car weight and material composition are based on the following identity: pounds of material per car = (car weight) × (material's percentage share in total car weight). The numbers in the right-hand columns represent the percentage of the total change in the number of pounds per car that would have occurred if only that particular factor (either car weight or material composition) had changed. The multiplicative effect is distributed to each factor in proportion to the direct effects.

Source: Calculated by the author with data in tables 6-A-1 through 6-A-3 in the appendix to this chapter.

aluminum than West German and Japanese cars over almost the entire period. For plastic and composite materials, pounds per car also rose for all three countries between the 1960s and the 1980s, again almost entirely because of increased shares of the weight of a new car (table 6-9). But the magnitude of change has been much greater for plastics and composites than for aluminum, increasing five to ten times over the period. In addition, only since the early to mid-1970s have U.S. cars contained more pounds of plastics and composites per car than their West German and Japanese counterparts.

The following sections examine the forces behind changes in the average weight and the material composition of a car. The purpose of this examination is to increase understanding of why the number of pounds of material per car change over time and differ among countries.

Average Weight of a Car

The weight of a typical U.S. car was approximately 3,500 pounds in the 1960s, rising to some 3,700 pounds in the early and mid-1970s and then falling to some 2,800 pounds in the first half of the 1980s (figure 6-12).

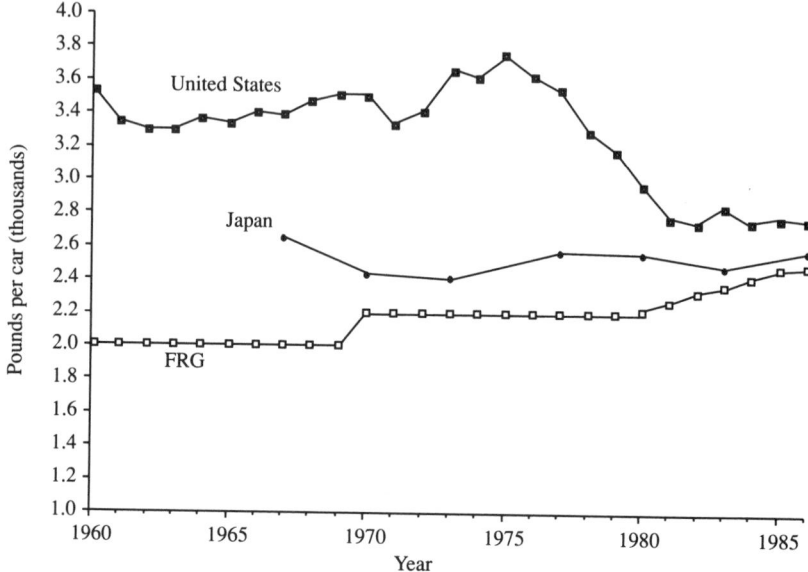

Figure 6-12. Average weight of a new car in the United States, Japan, and the Federal Republic of Germany (FRG), 1960–1986.

Source: Tables 6-A-1 through 6-A-3 in the appendix to this chapter.

During the same period, in contrast, the weights of typical German and Japanese cars remained more nearly constant, with German cars actually rising in weight in the 1970s and 1980s. In the 1960s typical U.S. cars weighed 40 to 75 percent more than German and Japanese cars. By 1986, differences in weight were less than 20 percent.

Why have U.S. cars been significantly heavier than West German and Japanese cars? An important explanation concerns differences in driving and living conditions. The West Germans and Japanese live closer together and drive on more congested roads than do U.S. residents; hence space is a much scarcer resource in these two countries than in the United States. There is less space for parking as well as driving. Many West German cities, for example, have narrow, winding streets built prior to the invention of the automobile. As a result West German and Japanese drivers prefer smaller, lighter cars. A complementary explanation is that West German and Japanese drivers pay substantially higher gasoline prices than do U.S. drivers and thus prefer smaller, more fuel-efficient cars.

The next question is why the weight of U.S. cars rose slightly in the late 1960s and early 1970s and then fell sharply in the late 1970s, whereas the weight of West German and Japanese cars remained more nearly constant. In the United States in the late 1960s and early 1970s, car weight rose for two reasons: consumers demanded more options (such as air conditioning and automatic transmissions) and larger, more comfortable cars, all of which add to the weight of a car; and the government and its Federal Motor Vehicle Safety Standards required safer vehicles, which prompted automakers to add new features (such as side-door intrusion beams and head restraints) and to strengthen existing ones.

In the latter half of the 1970s, however, U.S. car weights fell in response to significantly higher gasoline prices. Consumers demanded more fuel-efficient cars. Because small cars typically are more fuel efficient than large cars, the subcompact and compact share of new-car registrations (including imports) increased from 35 percent in 1970 to 52 percent in 1975 and to 64 percent in 1980 (*Automotive News, Market Data Book,* various years). (By 1988, however, the share of subcompact and compact cars had fallen to between 50 and 60 percent of the sales of new cars. Fuel prices had fallen, and the average weight of larger cars fell in response to greater use of lightweight materials such as aluminum and plastics.)

Moreover, government policy encouraged production of lighter cars with the fuel-economy requirements of the Energy Policy and Conservation Act of 1975. The act required each car manufacturer to meet a fuel-economy standard of 18 miles per gallon (mpg) averaged over its fleet by 1978; the requirements rose to 27.5 mpg in 1985; however, the standards for 1986, 1987, and 1988 were reduced to 26 mpg. The so-called gas-guzzler tax also promoted higher fuel efficiency by taxing all cars not achieving 18 mpg by 1980; this minimum requirement rose in subsequent years.

U.S. automakers pursued three strategies to meet the increased fuel-economy requirements of U.S. consumers and the government (Niemczewski, 1984). The first focused on vehicle design and materials and included substituting light materials for heavy materials, reducing the size and weight of the car, improving aerodynamic design, reducing rolling resistance, and improving lubrication. The second strategy concentrated on improving the drive train (or transmission) by, for example, adding fourth and fifth gears and building more cars with transverse front-wheel drive. The third strategy focused on improving engine performance with fuel-injection systems, exhaust-gas recirculation, and different compression ratios. Weight reduction either with smaller cars or lighter materials was simply one of the faster methods of increasing fuel economy.

Why did West German and Japanese car manufacturers not respond to the oil price hikes of the 1970s as U.S. firms did, by producing lighter cars? Most important, in West Germany and Japan fuel economy had been an important goal of automotive design throughout the entire post-World War II period; thus, West German and Japanese cars already were lighter and more fuel efficient than U.S. cars (table 6-10). Having already pursued weight reduction (an important element of the first strategy just described) to a much greater extent than U.S. producers, West German and Japanese car makers placed greater emphasis on transmission and engine improvements (the sec-

Table 6-10. Average Fuel Economy for New Passenger Cars in the Federal Republic of Germany (FRG), Japan, and the United States, 1970–1988

(miles per gallon of gasoline)

Year	FRG	Japan	United States
1970	23.3	N.A.	N.A.
1973	N.A.	22.6	N.A.
1974	N.A.	22.2	13.2
1975	N.A.	22.2	14.8
1976	N.A.	22.6	16.6
1977	N.A.	24.9	17.2
1978	24.0	26.6	18.7
1979	24.5	27.3	19.3
1980	25.6	28.2	22.6
1981	27.0	28.9	24.2
1982	27.7	30.6	25.0
1983	29.0	30.1	24.6
1984	30.2	30.1	25.6
1985	31.0	N.A.	26.3
1986	N.A.	N.A.	26.6
1987	N.A.	N.A.	27.0
1988	N.A.	N.A.	27.3

Notes: N.A. = not available.

The FRG and U.S. figures refer to the domestic fleet of new cars (imports are excluded), whereas the Japanese figures refer to new cars offered in the domestic market. In view of the relative unimportance of Japanese car imports, the Japanese data should be roughly comparable to the U.S. and FRG data.

The FRG figures represent the so-called VDA mix, the weighted average of European city driving, driving at 90 kilometers per hour (km/hr), and driving at 120 km/hr (each type of driving has a weight of one-third). The U.S. figures represent the so-called U.S. combined cycle, the weighted average of city driving (55 percent weight) and highway driving (45 percent). In general, the same car gets better fuel economy in the U.S. combined cycle than in the VDA mix. (Personal communication from P. Walzer of Volkswagen, November 24, 1987.)

Sources: Calculated with data from A. Diekmann, The Automotive Industry in Germany (Cologne, Deutscher Instituts-Verlag, 1985); Japan Automobile Manufacturers Association, 1986 Motor Industry of Japan (Tokyo, JAMA, 1986); Motor Vehicle Manufacturers Association, Motor Vehicle Facts & Figures '89 (Detroit, MVMA, 1989).

ond and third strategies). West German cars increased in weight between the late 1970s and mid-1980s as a result of demands for more options, more powerful engines, and more comfortable cars.

Material Composition of Passenger Cars

Changes in a material's percentage share in the total weight of a car reflect material substitution defined in the broadest possible sense. The most obvious type of substitution is material-for-material substitution, in which one material replaces another in a particular application. A second type is doing-more-with-less substitution, in which less of a material is needed to obtain a product of similar or better quality. (This type of substitution often is moti-

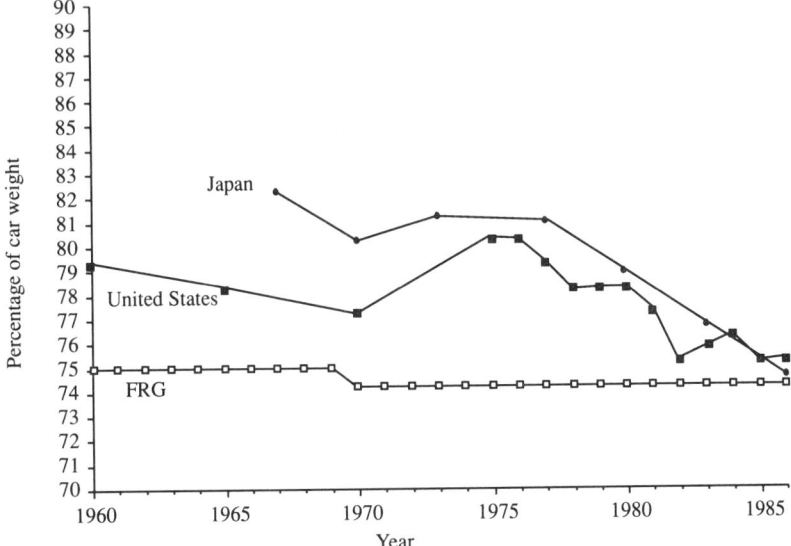

Figure 6-13. Share of iron and steels in the weight of new cars in the United States, Japan, and the Federal Republic of Germany (FRG), 1960–1986.

Source: Calculated from data in tables 6-A-1 through 6-A-3 in this chapter.

vated by the threat of material-for-material substitution.) A third type is functional substitution, which is substitution only in a broad sense; changes in the design of a product either create or eliminate the need for a particular material by creating or eliminating the function of that material.

Materials compete with one another to provide certain chemical and physical properties (or performance) at lowest cost. The tradeoff is always between performance and costs. One material wins out over a competing material only when it provides the same properties or performance at lower cost or better performance at the same cost. It is not the cost of raw materials alone that matters, but rather the cost per installed part. In car manufacturing the important costs include those of engineering and of equipment for fabrication, installation, and finishing, as well as raw material costs. The important properties for automotive materials are weight, volume, strength, stiffness, corrosion resistance, and tolerance to heat and cold.

Changes over time or among countries in the material composition of a car therefore reflect changes in (1) the relative costs of using alternative materials to provide certain properties, and (2) the mix of properties desired or required by car manufacturers and consumers.

Iron and Steel Iron and steel's share in the total weight of a car declined between the 1960s and the middle to late 1980s (see figure 6-13), but these materials continue to account for some three-quarters of the weight of a car.

This picture of gradual decline for iron and steel in general, however, masks significant changes in the use of specific types of iron and steel.

Automotive steels include cold- and hot-rolled sheets, hardenable-alloy bars, rods, wires, and high-strength (HS) steels. The HS steels are a family of materials with tensile strengths of 50,000 to 80,000 pounds per square inch (psi), compared to strengths of 30,000 psi or less for conventional steels (Compton and Gjostein, 1986). Types include (1) high-strength, low-alloy steels, introduced in the 1960s, strengthened through precipitation hardening, and microalloyed with niobium, vanadium, or titanium, and used as reinforcement in car bodies, wheels, and engines; (2) rephos steels, introduced in the 1970s, strengthened through solution hardening, and used in some body applications; and (3) dual-phase steels, introduced about 1980, strengthened with a microstructure of ferrite, requiring continuous-annealing lines for manufacture, and used in body panels (Gunnarson, Ericsson, and Steen, 1986).

It is useful to distinguish between HS and other steels. Other steels fell as a share of total car weight in the United States from 64 percent in 1975 to less than 60 percent in 1986, and in Japan from over 75 percent in 1967 to some 65 percent in 1986. Comparable data are not available for West German cars.

Changes in the use of cold-rolled sheet steel account for most of the decline in the share of other steels. The most important type of steel in this category, it is the dominant material in outer-body panels. It represented some two-thirds of the weight of a U.S. car in the 1960s, but only about half of a U.S. car's weight in the mid-1980s (Gjostein, 1986). Part of the explanation is doing-more-with-less substitution. Thinner sheets are now used. At Nissan, for example, only 21 percent of the steel sheet used in 1967 in new cars was between 0.5 millimeters (mm) and 0.79 mm in thickness; the remaining 79 percent ranged from 0.8 to 1.2 mm; in 1983, 56 percent of the steel sheet was between 0.5 and 0.79 mm in thickness, and only 44 percent was between 0.8 and 1.2 mm in thickness (personal communication from Fujihiko Deguchi of Nissan, Yokosuka, Japan, May 11, 1987).

An equally important explanation for the decline in cold-rolled steel's share of total weight is material-for-material substitution. Aluminum, plastic and composite materials, and HS steels replaced cold-rolled sheet steel in numerous applications, including hoods, trunk lids, and door panels.

The driving force behind both types of substitution was the desire for greater fuel economy through weight reduction, motivated by high fuel prices. In West Germany and Japan the drive for greater fuel economy through weight reduction was important throughout the entire 1960–1987 period. In the United States, however, weight reduction was not an important goal of car manufacturers until the mid-1970s, when consumers demanded and the government required more fuel-efficient cars.

Although steel's total share of the weight of a car declined between the early 1970s and the mid-1980s, HS steel's share increased from 0 to over 7 percent in the mid-1980s, at least in Japanese and U.S. cars. Japanese firms were the first to use HS steels in automotive applications in the early 1970s, largely because of proximity and cooperation with the Japanese steel industry. Japanese steel producers were the first to have the continuous-annealing lines necessary to reduce variability in the quality of HS steels.

U.S. automakers began to use HS steels shortly thereafter. They first used these materials in engine mounts, as bumper reinforcements, and as side-door intrusion beams, in response to the Federal Motor Vehicle Safety Standards. In the mid-1970s U.S. firms began to use HS sheets to save weight in outer-body panels and thus improve fuel economy in response to consumer demands and government requirements. Since the mid-1970s HS steels have been used in an increasing number of applications, including body panels, structural parts, wheels, and suspension arms (Magee, 1984).

In contrast, West German car manufacturers—and European firms in general—have used little HS steel in their cars. Part of the explanation is lack of supply: in the mid-1980s only two of the necessary continuous-annealing lines existed in Europe, one in Sweden and the other in The Netherlands. Furthermore, European car makers lack two motivations that drove U.S. companies to begin using HS steels heavily in the 1970s: the government safety requirement of side-door intrusion beams, and the desire to reduce weight quickly as a means of improving fuel economy.

Another significant change in automotive steel use is the increase in usage of zinc-coated steels to improve corrosion resistance. In Japanese cars, for instance, although coated steel sheets represented only 1.4 percent of total car weight in 1973, they accounted for 8.2 percent in 1986 (personal communication from Takao Sanaki, Japan Automobile Manufacturers Association, Tokyo, May 13, 1987). Concern about corrosion resistance increased in the mid-1970s, when consumers rebelled against the corrosion of body panels that in many instances meant that a car body rusted through before the engine wore out. Corrosion problems were caused by increased use of road salt to melt snow and ice, by the use of thinner steel sheets (which rust through more quickly than thicker ones), and—at least on some U.S. cars—by poor paint jobs. Concern about corrosion was a bigger issue among U.S. consumers than among Europeans except for those living in mountainous areas and coastal regions (where salty air was perhaps a larger cause of corrosion than road salt, and where such concern dated back to the 1960s).

Japanese consumers have been much less concerned about corrosion for two reasons. First, most do not face winters as harsh as those in much of the United States and Europe and thus do not subject their cars to much road salt. Second, their cars must pass an expensive inspection program when they are five years old and as a result Japanese car owners tend to sell their new cars in advance of this age, before corrosion becomes a problem. Many of these cars are exported to other Asian countries (personal communication from Leif Olsson of Saab, Helsinki, Finland, October 13, 1987).

Car makers raced to improve corrosion resistance, following several strategies: improved paint jobs (the simplest solution), treating parts of a car's body with hot wax, improving underseals, placing plastic (corrosion-resistant) skirts around the bottom of cars, and using zinc-coated metals in areas particularly prone to perforation and rust. Different companies followed different strategies; some, such as Saab, have relied chiefly on better paint jobs, whereas others, such as Audi, have emphasized coated steels.

Some of the movement to coated steels has occurred over the objections of certain engineers who believe that coated steels are an inferior solution to some corrosion problems. Coated steels are more difficult to form, paint, and weld than conventional, uncoated steel sheet. In addition, coated steels have less value as scrap because of zinc impurities. Some engineers argue that companies have jumped on the bandwagon to provide corrosion resistance and are using coated steels as a marketing ploy, even though reduced reliance on coated steels and greater reliance on better paint jobs and hot-wax treatments would provide more corrosion protection at lower cost.

Cast iron, yet another material in the iron and steel family, is used for engine blocks, other engine components, and crankshafts; it represents 5 to 15 percent of a car's weight. Cast iron's share in car weight lies near the upper end of this range for cars with cast iron engine blocks (the vast majority of U.S. cars), whereas cast iron's share is much lower for cars with cast aluminum blocks (typical of many European cars). Between 1960 and the late 1980s, cast iron's share in total weight declined as cast aluminum replaced iron in numerous engine parts. At Ford Motor Company (in the United States), cast iron's share in total car weight fell from between 16 and 17 percent in 1975 to some 13 percent in 1985 (Gjostein, 1986). Counter to this trend, however, in BMW's 3-series cars the share of cast iron increased from between 4 and 5 percent in 1978 to between 12 and 13 percent in 1987 as iron replaced unalloyed-carbon steel in the crankshaft (personal communication from Harald Franze of BMW, Munich, West Germany, June 24, 1987).

Aluminum   Aluminum's share of the total weight of a car increased from some 2 percent in the 1960s to between 3 and 5 percent in the 1980s for cars produced in the United States, Japan, and West Germany (see figure 6-14). Despite the overall similarity of the trends for all three countries, important differences exist in how aluminum gained its increased share.

In U.S. cars prior to the mid-1950s, aluminum was restricted essentially to castings in pistons and clutch housings and accounted for less than 1 percent of total car weight. Between the mid-1950s and the mid-1960s, aluminum increased its share gradually to about 2 percent as wrought aluminum was used for the first time in grilles and interior and exterior trim,

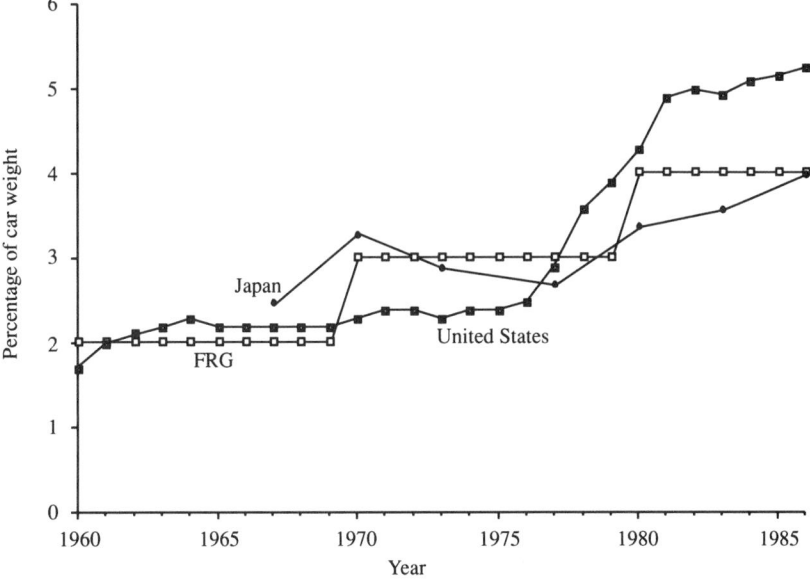

Figure 6-14. Share of aluminum in the weight of new cars in the United States, Japan, and the Federal Republic of Germany (FRG), 1960–1986.

Source: Calculated from data in tables 6-A-1 through 6-A-3 in the appendix to this chapter.

and as use of cast aluminum was expanded to (for example) transmission housings, master cylinders, water pumps, and intake manifolds. Over the next decade aluminum lost some of its newfound uses in grilles and trim to plastics, which were cheaper to produce and more corrosion resistant; but aluminum benefited from the increasing popularity of automatic transmissions and air conditioning, which used significant quantities of aluminum. The net result was that by the mid-1970s, aluminum's share of the weight of a car had increased slightly to between 2.0 and 2.5 percent.

During this entire period from the mid-1950s to the mid-1970s, aluminum substitution was a slow, evolutionary process. Part of the evolution represented material-for-material substitution. Cast and wrought aluminum gradually replaced cast iron and steel, respectively, as aluminum became cost-effective in specific applications. Part of the evolution also represented functional substitution; the increasing popularity of air conditioning and automatic transmissions created an opportunity for aluminum where none had existed previously. In both types of substitution, aluminum became cost-effective when (1) its cost per installed part fell below the costs for competing materials, or (2) it provided better performance at the same or lower costs than those of competing materials.

Over the latter half of the 1970s, aluminum's share increased swiftly from slightly more than 2 percent to almost 5 percent of the weight of a typical U.S. car. Cast aluminum continued to replace cast iron in engine parts, transmission housings, brake drums, and elsewhere. Wrought aluminum substituted for steel in hoods and other outer-body panels and in bumpers. But in contrast to the previous twenty years, aluminum's increasing share of the weight of a car was revolutionary rather than evolutionary. As we have seen, weight reduction became an important goal of U.S. car producers, and substituting lightweight aluminum for heavier steels and cast iron was an important element of weight reduction. In some cases this apparently led to the use of aluminum in applications for which it was more expensive per installed part than a competing material. The oil price hikes of the 1970s were therefore ultimately responsible for the swiftness of aluminum's rising share in the weight of U.S. cars in the late 1970s. Since the early 1980s aluminum's share has risen only slightly.

In West Germany and Europe in general, aluminum's share in the total weight of a car increased more gradually and steadily than in the United States. In Europe weight reduction as a path to greater fuel economy has been an important goal for several decades, not just since the mid-1970s as in the United States. As a result, European car makers used aluminum for engine blocks, cylinder heads, intake manifolds, radiators, and other purposes earlier and to a greater extent than did U.S. producers.

An important example of differences in aluminum use among countries is the radiator. In the mid-1980s up to 80 percent of new Western European cars had aluminum radiators, compared to some 30 percent of U.S. cars and less than 25 percent of new Japanese cars (Pennington, 1986). The Europeans switched quickly in the early 1970s from copper-brass to aluminum radiators. This switch was the result of the interplay of several factors. First, aluminum radiators provided significant weight savings over copper-brass radiators—an advantage for aluminum, in light of the ongoing European concern about fuel economy and weight reduction. Second, aluminum prices were more stable than copper prices. Price volatility was a greater problem for European firms than for U.S. companies, because European copper prices were based on London Metal Exchange (LME) prices and were more volatile than the producer prices paid by U.S. companies. Third, the sulfeca process of mechanically joining aluminum radiator fins was developed by the French and available to European car makers. In the early 1970s U.S. automakers were less concerned about weight reduction and price volatility, so the availability of a mechanical joining process was of less interest to them. When General Motors and Ford began to use aluminum radiators later in the 1970s, they used a fluxless, vacuum-brazing technique developed by General Electric for joining the aluminum fins, rather than the European mechanical method. Japanese companies did not switch to aluminum radiators in the 1970s because they considered aluminum a higher-cost material than copper. By the early 1990s, however, the majority of new U.S. and Japanese cars are expected to have aluminum radiators because they are lighter and more corrosion resistant than copper-brass radiators.

West German cars and European cars in general had a lower share of aluminum than U.S. cars in the 1980s (figure 6-14). The reason for this is that European cars use very little wrought aluminum, whereas wrought aluminum accounts for about one-fifth of the aluminum in U.S. cars. Wrought aluminum accounted for a significant portion of aluminum's rising share of the total weight of a U.S. car in the late 1970s, as part of the drive for weight reduction and increased fuel economy. There was less pressure for quick weight reduction in Europe, hence less pressure for quick fixes—which sometimes took the form of replacing sheet steel with aluminum in trunk lids, hoods, and other outer-body panels in U.S. cars.

Europeans used less wrought aluminum because this material was more difficult than steel to weld, more expensive to fabricate because the dies and presses designed for steel could not be used, and more expensive to finish because it required fine-grit sandpapers and special lubricants (Wrigley, 1976). Furthermore, wrought aluminum had lower strength and stiffness than steel, which meant that more aluminum was required per application than steel; these disadvantages offset some of the weight-reducing advantages of aluminum (Niemczewski, 1984).

Aluminum's increasing share in the weight of a car between the 1960s and the 1980s reflected the net effect of various costs—of materials, fabrication, installation, and finishing—in relation to aluminum's chemical and physical attributes. For some time automotive engineers had been interested in aluminum because of its low density and consequent weight-reducing potential. In many applications, however, aluminum was more expensive per installed part because of higher costs for raw materials and production. Aluminum also suffered from certain technical problems in manufacturing, installation, and finishing. Gradually, between the 1960s and the 1980s, aluminum overcame many of its economic and technical disadvantages.

Plastic and Composite Materials Automotive plastics generally are one of three types. First, sheet-molding compounds (SMC), known more generically as fiberglass, are manufactured by compression molding and used where stiffness is required, such as in horizontal panels (for example, hoods or "bonnets" and roofs). Second, reaction-injection moldings (RIM) are used where flexibility and dent resistance are required, such as in bumpers and vertical panels (for example, door panels). Third, thermoplastics are manufactured by injection molding and can be remelted and used again (unlike SMC and RIM). They are used for instrument panels, bumpers, and trim, among other applications. Composites are plastic materials reinforced with fibers of, for example, glass or graphite (Gunnarson, Ericsson, and Steen, 1986; Lowell and Winter, 1987). The share of plastic and composite materials in the weight of a car increased from about 1 percent in the early

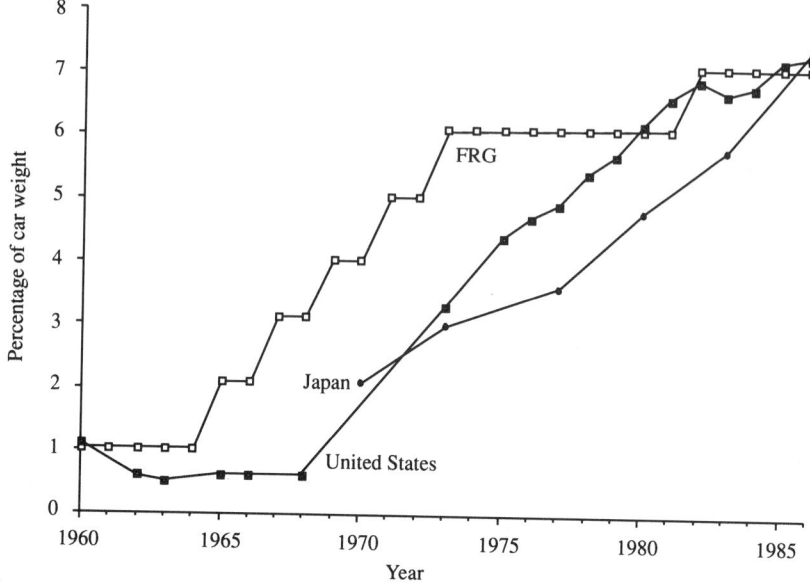

Figure 6-15. Share of plastic and composites in the weight of new cars in the United States, Japan, and the Federal Republic of Germany (FRG), 1960–1986.
Source: Calculated from data in tables 6-A-1 through 6-A-3 in the appendix to this chapter.

1960s to 7 percent in the mid-1980s for U.S., Japanese, and West German cars (see figure 6-15). Most of the increasing share is the result of material-for-material substitution.

Plastics were first used in the early 1960s for window cranks, knobs, heater ducts, and other nonstructural applications, in many cases replacing zinc die castings. Later in the 1960s and then in the early 1970s, plastics appeared elsewhere, in interior door panels, grilles, fan shrouds, wheel-well liners, instrument panels, and other applications that benefit from plastic's superior corrosion resistance and lower density as compared to competing metallic materials (Niemczewski, 1984). Furthermore, plastics incur less damage in minor accidents, and manufacturing costs are often lower because the manufacture of a one-piece plastic part requires fewer steps than that of a comparable metal part.

The earlier plastics were at a disadvantage, however, for several reasons. Molded plastics often required tedious manual trimming. More importantly, many plastics suffered from lack of a sufficient supply base; that is, manufacturing capacity was insufficient to supply plastic components to the automobile industry in quantities large enough for wider use of these materials.

Between the mid-1970s and mid-1980s, plastics and composite materials found an ever-increasing number of uses, including bumpers, exterior trim and grilles, headlamp housings (replacing zinc die castings), engine components, and luggage load floors. The initial motivation for the increasing use of plastics in this period was the push for weight reduction. U.S. auto makers responded initially by replacing steel and zinc die castings with plastics in relatively simple applications such as bumper covers and front-end panels. Over time, the desire for corrosion resistance became another motivation, and improved production methods allowed for more significant substitutions. Plastics became more durable, were able to receive better-quality finishes, and benefited from improved production processes that reduced molding times, used robots for trimming, and used computer-controlled manufacturing techniques.

In the aggregate there has been little difference among West German, Japanese, and U.S. cars in the use of plastic and composite materials. (Figure 6-15 suggests that plastics rose to importance sooner in West German cars than in Japanese and U.S. cars, but this probably reflects poor data rather than an actual difference among these countries.) However, U.S. producers (particularly General Motors) took the lead in using plastic and composite materials for outer-body panels. The Pontiac Fiero (no longer produced) and the Corvette have bodies made entirely of fiber-reinforced polymers, a type of composite material formed into sheets that hang on a steel frame.

The Future The future for iron and steel, aluminum, and plastic and composite materials in passenger car production will depend on the same factors that have shaped past trends: the tradeoffs between costs and desired performance. Costs change as the result of changing costs of raw materials and changing technologies of manufacturing, installation, and use. Desired performance—that is, the chemical and physical properties desired by producers and consumers—is a function of a variety of factors: ownership and operating costs, operating conditions such as the degree of congestion associated with driving and parking, and consumer tastes and preferences. Furthermore, the properties desired by producers and consumers will change over time as it becomes technologically possible to produce materials with an increasingly wide range of physical and chemical characteristics.

The share of iron and steel in the weight of a new car is unlikely to change significantly over the next five to ten years, although it may decline slightly as thinner steel sheets and iron castings are developed. Iron and steel undoubtedly will remain the most important family of automotive materials for the foreseeable future. Simple substitutions of aluminum and plastics for iron and steel have been made already. The major area of competition, and the only one that would significantly reduce the share of iron and steel in the weight of a car, is now outer-body panels.

Steel has several advantages. It has a broad range of strengths. Automotive engineers are familiar with this material, and the specifications for its use are well documented. Steels are easier to manufacture (in the sense that they are easier to form, join, and paint with existing equipment) than are aluminum and plastics. As a result, steel use is often cheaper per installed part.

Moreover, steel companies have not stood idly by as aluminum and plastics have mounted their challenge. Thinner steel sheets, some of which belong to the family of high-strength steels, overcome at least some of steel's problems with high density that initially spawned the use of aluminum and plastics. Zinc-coated steel sheets satisfy much of the concern about corrosion resistance that also encouraged the use of plastics for outer-body panels and bumpers.

A remaining problem for the conventional sheet-steel car, however, is the high cost of retooling each year for new car models. One way to reduce tooling costs is to increase automation through the use of robots and to reduce minor assembly by designing modular steel structures. Another solution is to manufacture the skin and ultimately the entire body of the car from plastic and composite materials. Most current use of plastic and composite materials for outer-body panels simply involves material-for-material substitution; in other words, plastics or composites substitute for sheet steel in hoods, trunk lids, or doors. Citroen, for example, already is using plastics extensively for hoods and deck lids. Fiat plans to replace its Strada/Ritmo model with a car featuring a plastic tailgate, hood, and door panels, using a production technique that will shorten molding-cycle times.

The next step is to make all outer-body panels from plastics or composites and to hang these panels on specially designed frames of steel or perhaps aluminum. The discontinued Pontiac Fiero is a recent example of this type of design with a steel frame. The ultimate and much more radical step is to eliminate the metal frame and make the entire body from fiber-reinforced composites.

Such a radical change in the design of a car could reduce retooling costs by perhaps as much as 80 percent and reduce the weight of metal in a car by 50 percent (personal communication from Mervin Rowbotham of Ford, Basildon, England, June 11, 1987). Such a cost savings might justify the use of materials that cost more per pound than sheet steel. Perhaps just as important, such a change would give auto makers greater flexibility to produce many models in smaller quantities, thereby satisfying consumer demands for a variety of options.

Any change to an all-composite-bodied car will occur gradually if at all. It will occur gradually if for no other reason than that it would require completely new plants and equipment. Existing facilities for conventional sheet-metal cars will continue to be used until they wear out. Any switch is likely to start with the small-volume production of specialty cars so that problems can be ironed out on a small scale before production commences on a large scale, and so that production can begin on more expensive cars for which cost minimization is not so important. (More expensive cars compete with each other as much on the basis of quality and image as on price.) Even if decisions were made now to produce all-composite-bodied cars, production in significant quantities could not occur before the mid-1990s. But during the first decade of the next century, such cars could be produced in large quantities if certain problems or barriers (aside from necessary large investments in plants and equipment) were overcome.

The most obvious problems with plastics and composites concern lack of experience with these materials. Little is known about how they age: how will they hold up over time at high and low temperatures? Corrosion, a problem for steels, certainly is not a problem for plastics and composites, but will there be other problems associated with wear, such as bubbles around glass fibers? Little is known about the ability to control quality during high-volume production of plastics and composites for automotive panels and frames; in other words, the problem is how to convert the technology of plastics and composites into high-volume production. Other difficulties have already been encountered in manufacturing. Painting of plastic or composite body panels, for instance, has been a problem in terms of both quality of the finish and matching the finish of plastic panels with metal panels. In addition, manufacturing-cycle times for SMC plastics (used for horizontal panels) typically are three to four minutes per panel—much too slow if this type of material is to compete with steels. Even if cycle times are reduced to a minute or less—as some plastics suppliers now claim is possible—these times might still be too slow for plastics to compete with steels.

All these problems, however, may well be solved as manufacturers gain experience with these new materials. This reinforces our earlier conclusion that any switch on a large scale to plastics and composites will occur gradually and slowly.

Two other problems loom for automotive plastics and composites. First, some observers are concerned that the fibers in fiber-reinforced composites could have effects on human health similar to those of asbestiform minerals. Second, the recycling and disposal of plastics and composites are more difficult than for metals. European car manufacturers in particular are concerned that they may be required to pay for recycling or disposal if particular materials give problems. Of the three main types of automotive plastics (SMC, reaction-injected moldings, and thermoplastics), only thermoplastics currently offer the possibility of reuse (they can be remelted). There are no good options for disposal. Burning is a possibility, but toxic-gas emissions may be a problem. Dumping these materials in landfills is another possibility, but this option uses valuable space (a significant concern in Europe and Japan and a growing one in an increasing number of localities in the United States) and could lead to contamination of soils or groundwater.

An area of the car where plastics could be used sooner is the engine. Plastics are being considered and, in a few cases, have already been used for intake manifolds, pistons, and drive shafts. Plastics are lighter in weight and potentially less noisy (an important characteristic in view of the noise standards of Japan and many European countries). In addition, plastics could be used for oil pans, water pumps, and fuel tanks.

Aluminum's share of the weight of a typical car is likely to increase but only gradually over the next five to ten years. It is likely that aluminum will gain new applications in engine blocks and cylinder heads, replacing cast iron and bringing about a reduction in weight. Although some European car makers switched to aluminum blocks in the 1970s, only a few U.S. models had aluminum blocks in the late 1980s. Aluminum also will be used more extensively in radiators in U.S. cars primarily because its corrosion resistance is higher than that of copper brass. (Most European cars have had aluminum radiators for a decade or more.) However, aluminum is being replaced by thinner steels and in some cases by plastics in hoods, doors, and other body panels; it was a short-term solution for U.S. companies to the problem of meeting fuel-economy standards in the late 1970s and early 1980s. Over the longer term, aluminum could account for a significantly higher share of the weight of a new car if its use as a space frame develops; in this, aluminum would replace steel. The primary advantage would be weight savings, which have been estimated at some 200 pounds per car as compared to a steel frame. Moreover, tooling costs could be as low as 20 to 30 percent of the costs for steel because fewer parts would be required. Such cost savings would more than make up for aluminum's higher raw-material costs. Aluminum space frames might be used in conjunction with plastic outer-body panels, but new forming techniques would be needed to implement these space frames; more generally, their economic viability has not yet been demonstrated. These frames would not become widespread until the middle to late 1990s at the earliest (Zoia, 1987).

CAR MANUFACTURING AND GLOBAL TRENDS IN METAL CONSUMPTION

Chapter 1 in this volume described sharp breaks in the growth of world metal consumption that occurred in the early to mid-1970s (see figure 1-1). Actual consumption from 1973 to 1985 was compared with projected trends on the basis of an assumption of continued growth at the same rates as for the 1950–1973 period. Sizable gaps appeared between actual consumption and projected trends.

How much of these gaps can be attributed to the car industry? Rough estimates are possible by calculating similar gaps for the car industry between actual and projected consumption, and then comparing the sizes of these gaps with the gaps for total global consumption of these metals.

The first step requires estimates of world consumption of steel and aluminum in passenger car manufacturing. Rough estimates are given in figures 6-16 and 6-17.[2] The amount of steel consumed in the manufacture of passen-

---

[2]The estimates of world steel and aluminum consumption by the car industry are based on several assumptions. Total consumption in any year equals the product of world car production

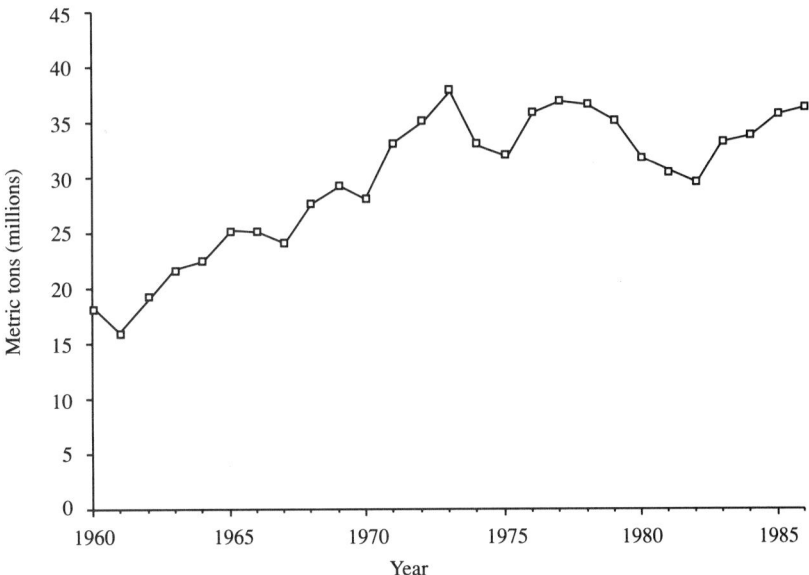

Figure 6-16. World steel consumption by the passenger car industry, 1960–1986.
Source: Table 6-A-4 in the appendix to this chapter.

ger cars grew at an average rate of 6.0 percent per year between 1960 and 1973; it declined by 0.5 percent per year between 1973 and 1985 (see table 6-11). Aluminum use in car production displays no similarly sharp break in trend; nevertheless, the rate of growth fell from 9.9 percent per year between 1960 and 1973 to 4.9 percent per year between 1973 and 1985. These figures suggest that trends in the use of steel and aluminum in car production are similar to trends in total world consumption for these metals—more so for steel than for aluminum (table 6-11). Slower growth in car production certainly contributed to slower growth in steel and aluminum consumption by the car industry; car production grew at an average rate of between 0 and 1 percent per year between 1973 and 1985, as compared to between 6 and 7 percent per year between 1960 and 1973. Changes in rates of growth for pounds of steel and aluminum per car were not nearly as large.

The next step is to calculate what steel and aluminum consumption by the car industry would have been in 1985 if such consumption had continued to grow after 1973 as it had between 1960 and 1973 (on the basis of the growth

and the number of pounds of steel or aluminum per car. Estimates of pounds of steel and aluminum per car assume that the world average is the same as crude weighted-average values for West German, Japanese, and U.S. cars. These estimates of pounds of metal per car also include a factor that accounts for scrap generated during manufacturing; estimates of the pounds of material in a finished car are multiplied by a factor of 1.5 for steel and 1.2 for aluminum. No allowance is made for steel and aluminum used in spare and replacement parts.

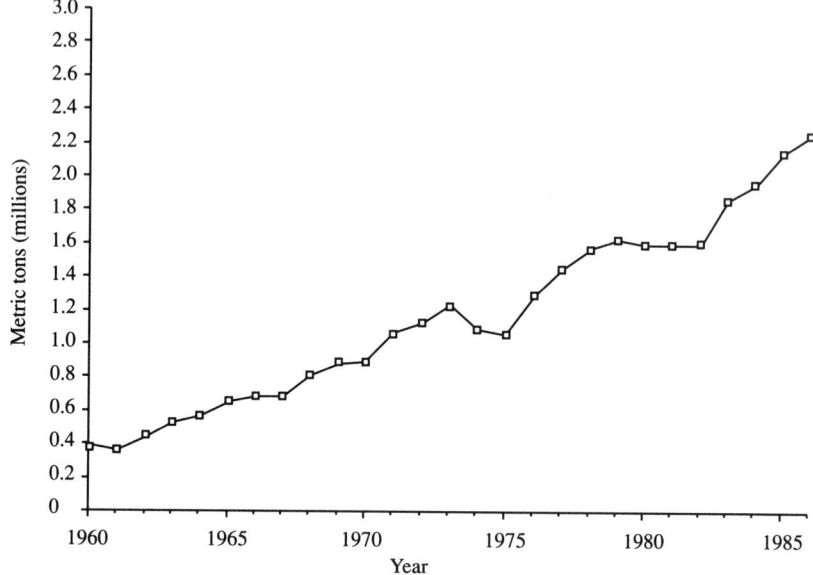

Figure 6-17. World aluminum consumption by the passenger car industry, 1960–1986.
Source: Table 6-A-4 in the appendix to this chapter.

rates in table 6-11). Steel consumption by the car industry would have been some 40 million tons higher, representing between 6 and 7 percent of the gap between actual and projected consumption of 608 million tons for total world steel consumption. Aluminum consumption by the car industry would have been some 1.6 million tons higher than actual consumption, representing (as in the case of steel) between 6 and 7 percent of the gap of 23 million tons for total world aluminum consumption.

CONCLUSIONS

Slower growth in the use of steel and aluminum in the passenger car industry contributed to slower growth in total world consumption of these metals. However, other industries must be important in explaining trends in world consumption of steel and aluminum, because the car industry accounts for only between 5 and 10 percent of the slowdown.

Slower growth in the consumption of steel and aluminum by the world car industry is predominantly the result of slower growth in the production of passenger cars rather than the result of the use of fewer pounds of steel and aluminum per car. (The number of pounds of aluminum per car actually rose considerably between 1960 and 1986.)

Table 6-11. World Rates of Growth for Steel and Aluminum Consumption, Car Industry Consumption of These Metals, Car Production, and Pounds of Steel and Aluminum per Car, 1960–1985
(annual average percent per year)

Metal and years	World consumption	Car industry consumption	Car production	Pounds per car
Steel				
1960–1973	5.8	6.0	6.7	−0.7
1973–1985	0.3	−0.5	0.6	−1.1
Aluminum				
1960–1973	9.6	9.9	6.7	3.0
1973–1985	1.3	4.9	0.6	4.2

Source: Calculated with data from the statistical appendix in this volume and from tables 6-A-1 through 6-A-4 in the appendix to this chapter.

Within the three most important car-producing countries—the Federal Republic of Germany, Japan, and the United States—the story of materials consumption over the last three decades is difficult to generalize. In West Germany the car industry used ever-larger quantities of iron and steel, aluminum, and plastics and composites because of increases in both car production and the pounds of each type of material per car. In Japan consumption increased to an even greater extent than in West Germany because of larger increases in car production. In the United States iron and steel use declined because fewer pounds of material per car were used, whereas the use of aluminum and plastics increased because of an increase in pounds of material per car. Rates of growth of consumption vary considerably from country to country.

What are the implications of this study for metal-producing companies and countries, mineral economists, and other observers of the metal and mineral industries? The first implication is that two different crystal balls are needed to forecast metal consumption by the car industry. One crystal ball must focus on future trends in passenger car production, which will depend on the level of income and its rate of growth; on demographic, geographic, and institutional factors; on the costs of vehicle ownership; and on the average life of a vehicle. Furthermore, when analyzing car production in a particular country, the levels of imports and exports are also important. There is no magic formula; different forces will be important in different countries over time. The second crystal ball must focus on the amount of a material used per car, which depends on various technological aspects of vehicle design and construction (which in turn are influenced by economic and political as well as purely technological factors).

Significant year-to-year fluctuations in material consumption by the car industry are largely a function of changes in car production; changes in the amount of a particular material used per car do not occur quickly, especially when the industry is viewed as a whole. Over the longer term, however, changes in the total consumption of a material are strongly influenced by changes in the material composition of a car and in technologies of manufacturing that reduce the amount of scrap generated during production.

The second implication of this analysis is that although no revolutionary changes in the material composition of a car are likely over the next decade or so, and although gradual or evolutionary changes are certain to occur, the extent of change over the longer term is not at all clear. Iron and steel are likely to account for ever smaller shares of the weight of a car, in part because of material-for-material substitution and in part because of thinner steel sheets and iron castings. But the absolute decline of iron and steel in terms of both pounds per car and their percentage share of car weight may be small if iron and steel are able to feed off the challenge of aluminum and plastics. Aluminum is likely to account for more pounds per car ten years from now, but further into the future the number of pounds could either grow or decline, depending on competition from plastics and iron and steel. Plastic and composite materials will almost certainly grow in terms of both pounds per car and percentage share of car weight because of their greater use in hoods, trunk lids, and door panels. But will plastic-bodied cars ever replace metal-bodied cars in large quantities? No one knows.

The third and final implication of this study follows from the second. If there is a lesson for material suppliers in the recent history of automotive materials, it is that material substitution does not move inexorably toward new families of materials (such as plastics) at the expense of more traditional materials (such as steel). Several years ago plastics and composite materials seemed destined to replace steel in the bodies of cars. Yet today steels are considered to have a good chance of staving off many of the challenges from plastics, not only because of recently appreciated problems with plastics (such as scrap disposal) but also because of renewed efforts by the steel industry to counter the advantages offered by plastics, particularly in the areas of retooling costs, weight, and corrosion resistance. Materials compete with one another to provide certain chemical and physical properties at lowest cost, and the ability of a particular material to provide certain properties changes over time as a result of technological advances in production and use.

ACKNOWLEDGMENTS

I am indebted to many individuals and organizations for their help in preparing this study. For their careful reading of an earlier version of the chapter, I thank the participants at the World Metal Demand Workshop held in Helsinki, Finland, on October 11–13, 1987. I also am grateful to the automotive engineers and economists who gave so much of their time and information, especially Norman Gjostein and E. M. Rowbotham at Ford Motor Company, Takao Sanaki at the Japan Automobile Manufacturers Association, Kazuo

Sawa and Masami Yasujima at Nissho Iwai, and Hakan Kappelin and Leif Olsson at Saab. I alone, of course, am responsible for any errors of fact or judgment.

REFERENCES

Altshuler, Alan, Martin Anderson, Daniel Jones, Daniel Roos, and James Womack. 1984. *The Future of the Automobile* (Cambridge, Mass., MIT Press).

Automotive News. 1987. "Honda: 2nd Ohio Assembly Plant to Spark Quest for Domestic Automaker Status," September 21, pp. 1, 52.

Automotive News Market Data Book (special annual issue of the weekly *Automotive News*, various years).

Compton, W. Dale, and Norman A. Gjostein. 1986. "Materials for Ground Transportation," *Scientific American* vol. 255, no. 4, pp. 92–100.

Crandall, Robert W., Howard K. Gruenspecht, Theodore E. Keeler, and Lester B. Lave. 1986. *Regulating the Automobile* (Washington, D.C., Brookings Institution).

Cusumano, Michael A. 1985. *The Japanese Automobile Industry: Technology and Management at Nissan and Toyota* (Cambridge, Mass., Harvard University Press).

Diekmann, Achim. 1985. *The Automotive Industry in Germany* (Cologne, Deutscher Instituts-Verlag).

Gjostein, N. A. 1986. "Automotive Materials Usage Trends," *Materials and Society* vol. 10, no. 3, pp. 369–404.

Gunnarson, S., R. Ericsson, and A. Steen. 1986. "Automotive Materials," pp. 246–261 in Michael B. Bever, ed., *Encyclopedia of Materials Science and Engineering*, vol. 1 (Cambridge, Mass., MIT Press).

International Monetary Fund. 1986. *International Financial Statistics: Supplement on Price Statistics* (Washington, D.C., IMF).

Japan Automobile Manufacturers Association. Annual. *The Motor Industry of Japan* (Tokyo, JAMA).

_____. Annual. *Motor Vehicle Statistics of Japan* (Tokyo, JAMA).

Lowell, John, and Drew Winter. 1987. "The State of Materials '88," *Ward's Auto World* vol. 23, no. 9, pp. 50–61.

Magee, Christopher L. 1984. "Recycling of Iron and Steel from Automotive Vehicles," pp. 99–118 in R. Andrew Blelloch, ed., *The Impacts of Material Substitution on the Recyclability of Automobiles* (New York, American Society of Mechanical Engineers).

Motor Vehicle Manufacturers Association. Annual. *Motor Vehicle Facts & Figures* (Detroit, MVMA).

_____. Annual. *World Motor Vehicle Data* (Detroit, MVMA).

Niemczewski, Christopher M. 1984. "The Changing Materials Content of Automobiles," pp. 11–37 in R. Andrew Blelloch, ed., *The Impacts of Material Substitution on the Recyclability of Automobiles* (New York, American Society of Mechanical Engineers).

Organisation for Economic Co-operation and Development. 1972. *Labour Force Statistics 1959–1970* (Paris, OECD).

_____. 1983. *Long-Term Outlook for the World Automobile Industry* (Paris, OECD).

_____. 1988. *Labour Force Statistics 1966–1986* (Paris, OECD).

Pennington, Neiland. 1986. "Auto Radiators: Aluminum Still Gains; Chrysler Bets on Copper," *Modern Metals* (January) pp. 80–85.

United Nations, Department of International Economic and Social Affairs. 1986. *World Population Prospects: Estimates and Projections as Assessed in 1984*, Population Studies no. 98 (New York, United Nations).

U.S. Department of Commerce. 1988. *U.S. Industrial Outlook 1988* (Washington, D.C., U.S. Government Printing Office).

Verband der Automobilindustrie. 1986. *Tatsachen und Zahlen aus der Kraftverkehrswirtschaft* (Frankfurt am Main, Verband der Automobilindustrie).

Ward's Communications. Annual. *Ward's Automotive Yearbook* (Detroit, Ward's Communications).

Winter, Drew. 1987. "Plastics," *Ward's Auto World* vol. 23, no. 9, pp. 81–87.

World Bank. 1986. *World Bank Data Tape: National Accounts, Prices, Exchange Rates and Population for the Period 1960–84* (Washington, D.C., World Bank).

Wrigley, A. 1976. "Materials and Processes: Industry Solves Old and New Problems," pp. 57–67 in Ward's Communications, *Ward's Automotive Yearbook* (Detroit, Ward's Communications).

Zoia, David E. 1987. "Aluminum: The Lightweight Material Is Suiting Up for the Space-Frame Age," *Ward's Auto World* vol. 23, no. 9, pp. 76–77.

Appendix to Chapter 6

Table 6-A-1. Passenger Car Production Data for the Federal Republic of Germany, 1960–1986

Year	Car production	Average weight per car (pounds)	Iron and steel		Aluminum		Plastics and composites	
			Pounds per car	Total consumption (thousands of metric tons)	Pounds per car	Total consumption (thousands of metric tons)	Pounds per car	Total consumption (thousands of metric tons)
1960	1,816,779	2,000	1,500	1,236	40	33	20	16
1961	1,903,975	2,000	1,500	1,295	40	35	20	17
1962	2,109,166	2,000	1,500	1,435	40	38	20	19
1963	2,414,107	2,000	1,500	1,643	40	44	20	22
1964	2,650,183	2,000	1,500	1,803	40	48	20	24
1965	2,733,732	2,000	1,500	1,860	40	50	40	50
1966	2,830,050	2,000	1,500	1,926	40	51	40	51
1967	2,295,714	2,000	1,500	1,562	40	42	60	62
1968	2,862,186	2,000	1,500	1,947	40	52	60	78
1969	3,312,539	2,000	1,500	2,254	40	60	80	120
1970	3,527,864	2,200	1,628	2,605	66	106	88	141
1971	3,696,779	2,200	1,628	2,730	66	111	110	184
1972	3,521,540	2,200	1,628	2,600	66	105	110	176
1973	3,649,880	2,200	1,628	2,695	66	109	132	219
1974	2,839,596	2,200	1,628	2,097	66	85	132	170
1975	2,907,819	2,200	1,628	2,147	66	87	132	174
1976	3,546,900	2,200	1,628	2,619	66	106	132	212
1977	3,790,544	2,200	1,628	2,799	66	113	132	227
1978	3,890,176	2,200	1,628	2,873	66	116	132	233
1979	3,932,556	2,200	1,628	2,904	66	118	132	235
1980	3,520,934	2,200	1,628	2,600	88	141	132	211

(Continued)

Table 6-A-1 (continued)

Year	Car production	Average weight per car (pounds)	Iron and steel		Aluminum		Plastics and composites	
			Pounds per car	Total consumption (thousands of metric tons)	Pounds per car	Total consumption (thousands of metric tons)	Pounds per car	Total consumption (thousands of metric tons)
1981	3,577,807	2,234	1,653	2,683	89	145	134	218
1982	3,761,436	2,295	1,698	2,898	92	157	161	274
1983	3,877,642	2,332	1,726	3,035	93	164	163	287
1984	3,790,164	2,385	1,765	3,034	95	164	167	287
1985	4,166,686	2,438	1,804	3,410	98	184	171	323
1986	4,310,828	2,450	1,813	3,545	98	192	172	335

Notes: Car production data include passenger cars and *Kombinationskraftwagen* (vehicles designed to hold either passengers or goods or both). Total consumption of a material = (car production) × (pounds of material per car). Data for the earlier years (other than for car production) do not change significantly from year to year and represent only best guesses by the industry representatives identified below.

Sources: **Car production data:** Motor Vehicle Manufacturers Association, *World Motor Vehicle Data* and *Motor Vehicle Facts & Figures* (Detroit, Motor Vehicle Manufacturers Association, 1987).

Data on average vehicle weights and pounds per car of iron and steel, aluminum, and plastics and composites: Estimated by the author on the basis of partial data from a variety of sources, including:

1. Joachim Bloedorn, *Bauweisen und Werkstoffe im Automobilbau* (Berlin, Verlag Dr. Ruediger Martienss, 1987) (estimates of material mix of West German cars, 1973–1981).

2. Personal communication from Harald Franze, BMW, Munich, West Germany, June 25, 1987 (estimates of the weight and material mix of selected BMW cars, 1978–1987).

3. Personal communication with Mervin Rowbotham, Ford Motor Company, Basildon, England, June 11, 1987.

4. Personal communication from Peter Mast, Porsche, Weissach, West Germany, June 24, 1987 (estimates of material composition of an average West German car in 1973, an average European car in 1983, and selected Porsche models in 1953, 1975, 1977, 1980, 1983, and 1985).

5. Personal communications with F. K. Boersch, E. Loeffler, and J. E. Siebels, Volkswagen, Wolfsburg, West Germany, June 29, 1987.

6. Personal communication with B. Felzer, GM Europe, Ruesselsheim, West Germany, June 26, 1987.

7. Personal communications with Mr. Kappelin and L. R. Olsson, Saab, Trollhaettan, Sweden, June 9, 1987.

8. R. G. Eggert, "Changing Patterns of Materials Use in the U.S. Automobile Industry," *Materials and Society* vol. 10, no. 3, pp. 405–431 (estimates of the average weight of European cars for 1961 and selected years between 1970 and 1985).

9. Personal communication from P. Walzer, Volkswagen, letter of November 24, 1987.

210

Table 6-A-2. Passenger Car Production Data for Japan, 1967–1986

Year	Car production	Average weight per car (pounds)	Iron and steel		Aluminum		Plastics and composites	
			Pounds per car	Total consumption (thousands of metric tons)	Pounds per car	Total consumption (thousands of metric tons)	Pounds per car	Total consumption (thousands of metric tons)
1967	1,375,755	2,610	2,130	1,329	63	39	N.A.	N.A.
1970	3,178,708	2,395	1,906	2,749	77	111	48	69
1973	4,470,550	2,375	1,926	3,906	67	135	69	140
1977	5,431,045	2,530	2,047	5,042	66	162	89	218
1980	7,038,108	2,515	1,969	6,287	83	265	118	377
1983	7,151,888	2,440	1,854	6,016	85	277	139	451
1986	7,809,809	2,540	1,890	6,694	99	351	185	657

Notes: Total consumption of a material = (car production) × (pounds of that material per car).

N.A. = not available.

Sources: **Car production data:** Japan Automobile Manufacturers Association, *Motor Vehicle Statistics of Japan 1986* (Tokyo, Japan Automobile Manufacturers Association, 1986); Motor Vehicle Manufacturers Association, *Motor Vehicle Facts & Figures* (Detroit, Motor Vehicle Manufacturers Association, 1987).

Other data: Based on survey information collected by the Japan Automobile Manufacturers Association (JAMA) and supplied by Takao Sanaki of JAMA, May 13, 1987. JAMA collects information every three to four years on materials purchased for use in passenger cars. Raw data are in the form of percentage shares of the total weight of materials purchased per car. These data are sales-weighted averages based on between three and six models in each of four size categories. The data are broadly representative of materials purchased for use in exported and domestically sold cars. Estimates of the average weight per car were made by the author on the basis of (a) JAMA index numbers of the total weight of materials purchased per car, and (b) a JAMA estimate that the average dry (or shipping) weight per car in 1986 was 1,150 kilograms (2,540 pounds).

211

Table 6-A-3. Passenger Car Production Data for the United States, 1960–1986

Year	Car production	Average weight per car (pounds)	Iron and steel Pounds per car	Iron and steel Total consumption (thousands of metric tons)	Aluminum Pounds per car	Aluminum Total consumption (thousands of metric tons)	Plastics and composites Pounds per car	Plastics and composites Total consumption (thousands of metric tons)
1960	6,703,108	3,487	2,762	8,397	54.4	165	35	106
1961	5,522,019	3,301	N.A.	N.A.	62.7	157	N.A.	N.A.
1962	6,943,334	3,253	N.A.	N.A.	66.5	209	16	51
1963	7,644,377	3,256	N.A.	N.A.	70	243	13	45
1964	7,745,492	3,321	N.A.	N.A.	72.4	254	N.A.	N.A.
1965	9,335,227	3,290	2,566	10,866	69.1	293	16	70
1966	8,604,712	3,358	N.A.	N.A.	70	273	17	66
1967	7,412,659	3,352	N.A.	N.A.	71	239	N.A.	N.A.
1968	8,848,620	3,430	N.A.	N.A.	72.2	290	17	69
1969	8,224,392	3,472	N.A.	N.A.	73.3	273	N.A.	N.A.
1970	6,550,128	3,462	2,666	7,920	77.6	231	N.A.	N.A.
1971	8,583,653	3,291	N.A.	N.A.	76.8	299	N.A.	N.A.
1972	8,828,205	3,375	N.A.	N.A.	78	312	N.A.	N.A.
1973	9,667,152	3,629	N.A.	N.A.	81	355	116	509
1974	7,324,504	3,575	N.A.	N.A.	83	276	N.A.	N.A.

Year	Car production	Average weight	Iron and steel	Aluminum			
1975	6,716,951	3,684	8,957	84	256	158	483
1976	8,497,893	3,586	11,003	87	335	165	636
1977	9,213,654	3,546	11,722	100	418	170	711
1978	9,176,635	3,269	10,654	114	475	173	721
1979	8,433,662	3,141	9,420	118	451	176	673
1980	6,375,506	2,838	6,385	120	347	173	501
1981	6,253,138	2,732	5,951	130	369	178	504
1982	5,073,496	2,702	4,689	133	306	184	423
1983	6,781,184	2,804	6,512	136	418	185	569
1984	7,773,332	2,716	7,240	136.5	481	182	642
1985	8,184,821	2,733	7,600	138	512	194	720
1986	7,828,783	2,722	7,259	139.5	495	196	696

Notes: N.A. = not available.

Data on pounds of material per car are estimates, not production-weighted averages based on engineering data for the entire fleet of cars.

Sources: **Car production data:** Motor Vehicle Manufacturers Association, *Motor Vehicle Facts & Figures* (Detroit, Motor Vehicle Manufacturers Association, 1987).

Average weight of a car (production-weighted average dry weight): J. Weinberg, K. L. Harris, and G. White, "Steel in Motor Vehicles—A 35-Year Perspective." Manuscript.

Iron and steel data: Total consumption = (car production) × (pounds per car); data on pounds per car based on information in Ward's Communications, *Ward's Automotive Yearbook* (Detroit, Ward's Communications, various years).

Aluminum data: Total consumption = (car production) × (pounds per car); data on pounds per car from J. J. Tribendis, C. N. Cochran, and R. H. G. McLure, "Aluminum Alloys," pp. 119–145 in R. A. Bielloch, ed., *The Impacts of Material Substitution on the Recyclability of Automobiles* (New York, American Society of Mechanical Engineers, 1984), and Ward's Communications, *Ward's Automotive Yearbook* (Detroit, Ward's Communications, various years).

Plastics and composites data: Total consumption = (car production) × (pounds per car); data on pounds per car from Ward's Communications, *Ward's Automotive Yearbook* (Detroit, Ward's Communications, various years).

213

Table 6-A-4. World Consumption of Steel and Aluminum in the Production of Passenger Cars, 1960–1986

Year	World car production	Pounds of steel per finished car	Total steel consumption (thousands of metric tons)	Pounds of aluminum per finished car	Total aluminum consumption (thousands of metric tons)
1960	12,838,910	2,000	17,471	50	349
1961	11,390,629	1,980	15,345	52	322
1962	14,011,817	1,960	18,686	54	412
1963	15,941,095	1,940	21,042	56	486
1964	16,734,646	1,920	21,861	58	528
1965	18,951,914	1,900	24,500	60	619
1966	19,151,634	1,880	24,497	62	646
1967	18,574,476	1,860	23,506	64	647
1968	21,613,654	1,840	27,058	66	776
1969	23,103,996	1,820	28,610	68	855
1970	22,494,258	1,800	27,549	70	857
1971	26,447,611	1,810	32,570	71	1,022
1972	27,886,168	1,820	34,532	72	1,093
1973	29,984,605	1,830	37,334	73	1,191
1974	25,946,555	1,840	32,483	74	1,045
1975	24,958,731	1,850	31,416	75	1,019

1976	28,793,648	1,800	35,264	80	1,254
1977	30,474,089	1,750	36,285	85	1,410
1978	31,183,666	1,700	36,069	90	1,528
1979	30,774,627	1,650	34,549	95	1,591
1980	28,577,518	1,600	31,110	100	1,556
1981	27,457,792	1,600	29,891	104	1,554
1982	26,626,660	1,600	28,986	108	1,565
1983	29,966,497	1,600	32,622	112	1,827
1984	30,478,607	1,600	33,180	116	1,924
1985	32,233,228	1,600	35,090	120	2,105
1986	32,849,675	1,600	35,761	124	2,217

Notes: The figures for steel per car are estimated by the author as crude weighted average values for West German, Japanese, and U.S. cars (see tables 6-A-1 through 6-A-3 in the appendix to this chapter). The number of pounds per car is estimated to have fallen from 2,000 pounds in 1960 to 1,800 pounds in 1970 because of increased car production in West Germany and Japan. Pounds per car rose to 1,850 in 1975 because of the increased weight of U.S. cars. Pounds per car fell to 1,600 by 1980 because of steel's declining percentage share in car weight in the United States. Pounds per car remained relatively constant between 1980 and 1985 because the declining pounds per U.S. car were offset by increasing pounds per West German car.

Total steel = (car production) × (pounds per car) × (1.5). The factor of 1.5 is to account for scrap.

The figures for aluminum per car are estimated by the author as crude weighted average values for West German, Japanese, and U.S. cars (see tables 6-A-1 through 6-A-3 in the appendix to this chapter and figure 6-15, which suggests that trends in each country paralleled one another).

Total aluminum = (car production) × (pounds per car) × (1.2). The factor of 1.2 is to account for scrap.

Sources: Motor Vehicle Manufacturers Association, *World Motor Vehicle Data* and *Motor Vehicle Facts & Figures* (Detroit, MVMA, 1987).

7

The Food and Beverage Container Industries: Change and Diversity

CARMINE NAPPI

The food and beverage container industries provide an interesting laboratory for studying the shrinking global demand for metals and, in particular, for assessing the relative importance of the variables influencing that demand. The intense rivalry among materials used in making food and beverage containers—metals, glass, cardboard, plastic, and composite products—and among metals—aluminum, chromium, lead, tin, and steel—has given rise to major technological changes that have obviously influenced relative demand. Consumer life styles and market imperfections or distortions in the form of pressure groups, tariffs, and environmental costs must be added to the standard economic variables such as prices and income if one is to understand the evolution of the demand for metals in the food and beverage container market.

The influence of these variables differs among countries. A preference for aluminum over steel cans for beer and soft drinks, for instance, has thus far developed only in the United States, Sweden, Austria, and Greece. In every other industrialized country the reception of aluminum cans has been mixed. Because the competition among substitutes leads to different results in different countries, it is appropriate to examine the evolution of metal demand in the food and beverage container industries in Canada, Japan, and the major Western European countries as well as in the United States.

The first section of this chapter evaluates the merits of the many containers that the food and beverage industries use. The purpose is to identify the metals likely to be affected by the substitution of one container for another as well as the major reasons for such substitutions. The second section focuses on the United States, assessing the effects on the demand for aluminum, steel, and tin arising from the competition among container materials. This exercise is repeated in the third section (within the limits imposed by the availability of statistics) for Western Europe, Japan, and Canada. The chapter's concluding section summarizes the findings and suggests possible implications for researchers investigating the demand for metals beyond the end-use market, at the aggregate level.

COMPETING FOOD AND BEVERAGE CONTAINERS

The metal food can dates from the Napoleonic wars, when French industrialist Nicolas Appert invented a food-preserving technique using metal containers sterilized at high temperatures. Metal cans are now used extensively in both the food and the beverage industries, where they compete with containers made of glass, plastic, cardboard, or composites.

Although remaining the principal container markets, the food industry and the beverage industry impose very different technological constraints on the containers used. Metal cans for food must be resistant enough to compensate for the loss of internal pressure resulting from high-temperature sterilization. This constraint is much less important for metal cans for beer and soft drinks. These beverages contain a gas dissolved under pressure; by exerting pressure on the walls of the can, the gas adds to the container's resistance. Because of this difference, the two markets are examined separately here.

Food Containers

For a long time the soldered three-piece tinplate can was the only can used in food processing. Tinplate is a low-carbon steel strip coated with tin. It is still the metal most often used in metal cans, but its market share declined a few years ago when health concerns arose over the lead used in side-seam soldering. New welding techniques solved the lead problem but created a new one for tin: it was found that the welding process could be adapted to cans made of electolytic chromium-coated steel or, as it is commonly known, tin-free steel.[1]

Retort pouches (three-layered containers with a polyester film on the out-

---

[1]The demand for tin-free steel (TFS) seems to be particularly strong when the three-piece containers are cemented. When the three pieces of the container are welded together, tinplate remains as popular as chromium-coated steel. The introduction of two-piece containers has not negatively affected the demand for tinplate when the container is manufactured by the draw and ironed (D&I) method. (TFS cannot be used because of its abrasiveness, which results in significant tooling wear, and aluminum's lower strength has prevented it from being widely used.) However, the demand *is* affected when other production methods are employed; chromium-coated steel and aluminum then have higher growth rates than does tinplate.

side, an aluminum foil in the middle, and a polypropylene film on the inside), plasticans, glass jars, and, to a limited extent, aluminum cans, also have shares in the food container market. (Figure 7-1 illustrates, for each container type, whether the use of each technology and material is stable, expanding, or declining. The figure also provides technical descriptions.) Aluminum is a minor player; its resistance to soldering and welding restricts its use to two-piece cans that cannot withstand high-temperature sterilization. Nor has aluminum penetrated the lid market, where tin-free steel and plastic (for glass and flexible containers) are making gains. Tin-free steel is expected to continue its gains in the near future in lid and small two-piece can products.

The past good performance of steel in the food can market is not a guarantee of an equally promising future. First, aluminum producers are not sitting idly by. One promising development for strengthening the aluminum can involves adding liquid nitrogen to the filled can which, after the can is sealed, expands and exerts pressure on the can body. (Aluminum producers have also tried to strengthen the aluminum can by developing new aluminum alloys tailored for specific can-making techniques, such as draw and redraw [DRD], so as to achieve the same can strength by using less material.) Second, tin-mill products in the future will experience greater competition from other packaging materials. Retort pouches have been introduced increasingly to the American market after having enjoyed considerable success in Japan. Their major drawbacks are that they cannot be filled and handled at the high speeds possible for cans, and there are problems with reliable sealing (see Standard & Poor's, 1982). Glass containers do not represent a great threat. They are confined to a very limited range of products (e.g., fruit, jams, sauces), and several disadvantages limit their use for other products: their weight, fragility, and the fact that the color of some types of foods fades on exposure to light.

Beverage Containers

The beverage industry, too, has its share of container choices. Figure 7-2 shows the five technologies involved: nonreturnable and returnable glass bottles, plastic bottles, and two-piece and three-piece metal cans. In most industrialized countries returnable glass bottles are losing their market share, as are three-piece soldered tinplate and cemented tin-free steel cans. The move is toward two-piece draw and ironed (D&I) cans (see note 2 of figure 7-1) made of aluminum or of tinplate, and plastic containers made of polyethylene terephtalate (PET). (The D&I technique has quickly spread among can producers and independent bottlers despite the substantial capital investment it requires. The pressurized nature of the contents permits considerable thinning of the can wall and thus substantial material savings, which obvi-

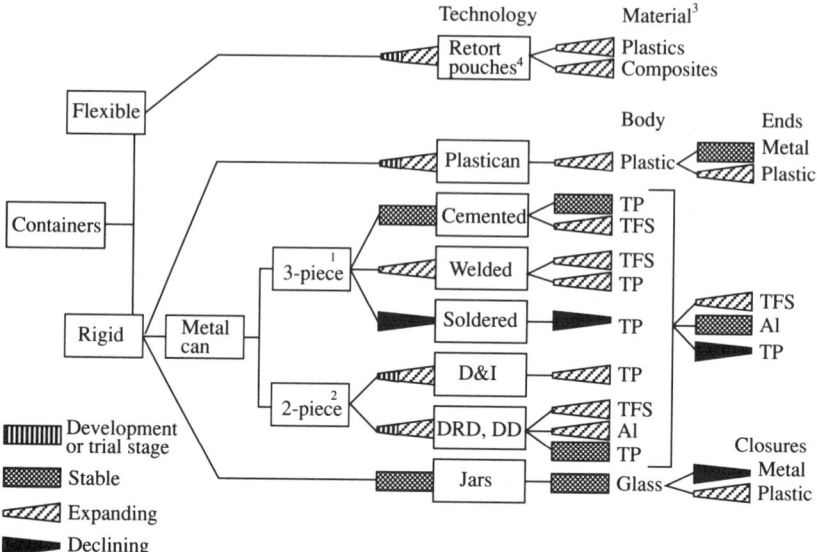

[1]There are two types of metal cans. The majority of open-top food cans are three-piece (i.e., the can is made from three pieces of plate, two ends and a body). The can body is made from a flat sheet, the opposite ends of which are seamed together to form a cylinder. The body side seam may be secured by soldering, cementing, or welding. The bottom end of the can is mechanically crimped and sealed to the body, forming a container open at one end, to be delivered to the canners. After the can has been filled, the top end is mechanically crimped and sealed to the body.

[2]There are other open-top food cans made of two pieces of metal sheet, a body and an end. Three methods of making two-piece, open-top food cans are available: draw (DD), draw and redraw (DRD), and draw and ironing (D&I) techniques. In all three methods a disc is stamped from a metal sheet and formed into a cup. In the DD method the cup is drawn only once and therefore remains shallow. In the DRD method the cup is then redrawn by means of successively smaller diameter punches and dies so that the walls gain in height while essentially retaining the thickness of the original metal sheet. In the D&I method the cup walls are reduced in thickness and increased in height by passing the cup between a punch and several ironing dies of successively smaller diameter.

[3]Apart from glass, plastics, and composites, the other materials are Al (aluminum), TP (tinplate—a low-carbon steel strip coated with tin either by electrodeposition or by dipping in molten tin), and TFS (tin-free steel, also known as electrolytic chromium-coated steel or ECCS, is a low-carbon, mild steel strip electroplated with a chromium/chromium oxide coating).

[4]"Retort pouches" are flexible three-layered containers with a polyester film on the outside, an aluminum foil in the middle, and a polypropylene film on the inside. Retort pouches are thinner and lighter than cans, and cooking the food within the package is quicker and requires lower temperatures, thus retaining more nutrition and using less energy (and also it requires no refrigeration).

Figure 7-1. Competing technologies and materials for containers for food conserved by high-temperature sterilization.

Source: Adapted, with permission, from International Tin Council, *Study on Consumption: United States of America, Tin in Tinplate* (London, ITC, 1983), p. 40.

220

ously helps reduce production costs. Also, the production scale is often large enough, especially in the case of beer, to reduce significantly the average fixed costs.)

Ideally, the choice of material for beverage containers is made by comparing systematically the advantages and disadvantages of each. A document of the International Tin Council sums up the situation in the following way:

Tinplate is cheaper, but causes greater tooling wear, requires more expensive body-

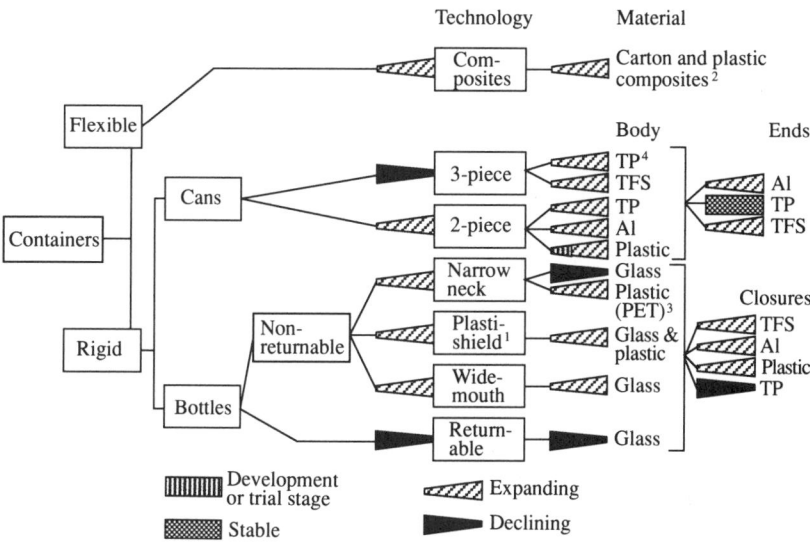

[1]Plasti-shield bottles are single-service bottles introduced in 1977 in 7-, 10-, and 16-ounce sizes. These packages generally consist of plastic-sheathed, uniform-shaped bottles held together by a single plastic holder, and they come in packs of six or eight. The phenomenal success with this package has enabled glass producers to replace most of the tonnage it lost to the 2-liter plastic (PET) bottle. These bottles eliminate the need for costly mold changes, making them more cost-competitive with cans and plastic bottles.

[2]A good example of the combined use of carton and plastic is the aseptic box. This type of packaging, which is used extensively in Europe and other areas overseas, is essentially a paperboard (usually in a brick shape) coated with polyethylene film and lined with aluminum foil. It is used to store milk and fruit juices for extended periods without refrigeration.

[3]PET is polyethylene terephtalate, a plastic used in the packaging industry.

[4]As observed by a referee, it is strange that in this figure (taken from the International Tin Council study) both materials (TP and TFS) are growing when three-piece cans are declining.

Figure 7-2. Competing technologies and materials for beer and soft drink containers.

Note: For definition of Al, TP, and TFS, see note 3 in figure 7-1.

Source: Adapted, with permission, from International Tin Council, *Study on Consumption: United States of America, Tin in Tinplate* (London, ITC, 1983), p. 43.

making machinery and tinplate cans need thicker internal lacquer coatings. Aluminum's scrap value is higher, cans are lighter and cheaper to transport, but being non-magnetic, cans cannot be processed using magnetic can handling equipment or be magnetically separated from municipal scrap. (International Tin Council, 1984, p. 38.)

In reality, however, variables such as government regulation and the determination of certain pressure groups (such as producer associations, unions, and local chambers of commerce) add to the technical and economic considerations.

In some countries, notably the United States, the success of aluminum can collection and recycling programs must be added to the variables that have allowed aluminum to dominate the metal container market in just a few years. This penetration should prompt aluminum producers to be cautious, even in the United States, since marginal gains are becoming more and more difficult to achieve and, additionally, since metal containers are now threatened by competition from other kinds of packaging. For example, glass is managing to preserve a stable market share because of the popularity of nonreturnable bottles, especially plasti-shield bottles. Flexible containers such as aseptic boxes (composed of layers of paper, aluminum foil, and polyethylene) are being introduced into the U.S. market following their success in Europe. Finally, despite their serious problems—short shelf life, recycling difficulties, inadequate gas barrier, and low carbonation retention among others—plastic bottles continue to register growth rates superior to those of other substitutes. Apparently, consumer satisfaction is a more important variable than technical problems. (The use of plastic in the production of containers will be even greater in the future as the problems of short shelf life and low carbonation retention are resolved and the price decreases by way of lighter bottles and more productive machinery.)

Competition among metals extends beyond the production of container bodies to the manufacture of ends and lids. At this level aluminum and tin-free steel lids have grown at faster rates than have tinplate lids.

Competing Materials: The Driving Force

Three general trends emerge from observing the technical evolution that has taken place in the food and beverage container market since 1950 and the effect that this evolution has had on the relative demand for metals and other materials.

1. For foods preserved by high-temperature sterilization, steel is the metal of choice, with tin-free steel gaining on the market share of tinplate—a substitution expected to continue through the midterm. The three-piece open-top can is the most widely used construction.

2. In the same market aluminum, plastic, and various forms of flexible

packaging in the form of two-piece metal cans, plasticans, and retort pouches are making breakthroughs, although not yet strongly enough to impair steel's market position.

3. The move in beer and soft drink containers is toward two-piece aluminum and tinplate cans and, increasingly, to plastic. These forms have largely replaced three-piece soldered tinplate and cemented tin-free steel cans. Nonreturnable glass containers, in particular plasti-shield bottles, remain popular despite laws to eliminate or reduce their use. Flexible and plastic containers, although handicapped by technical and economic problems, have enjoyed consumer acceptance.

We will see later that these general trends can be observed only in varying degrees in our grouping of major industrialized countries; their adoption rate is far from synchronized. But before examining these differences, we need to identify the reasons for this proliferation of containers.

The technological dynamics can be explained by the competition among materials that characterizes the food and beverage container and packaging industries. This competition has forced producers to invest heavily in an effort to reduce relative costs. Where have they directed this effort? Table 7-1 indicates that the focus has been on reducing the amount of raw materials used in each kind of container. Indeed, this table shows that in 1985 the cost of these materials (aluminum, hot-rolled coil and tin ingots, glass melt and/or plasti-shield, and the raw materials of PET bottles) accounted in most cases for more than one-half of total manufacturing costs. This effort has been particularly visible in the metal can market, where cost reductions have focused on the following:

1. Gauge reductions in the can body and lid stock.

2. The development of containers with narrower necks that in turn reduce the diameter and thus the cost of ends (each additional step in the necking process reduces the diameter of the can end).

3. The development of high-strength alloys that allow for further light-weighting of both body and ends.

Figure 7-3 illustrates the results of the effort to reduce the amount of raw materials per container. The number of pounds of steel per thousand cans has decreased by almost 60 percent since 1960. Between 1950 and 1977 the tin content of the average tinplate beer can decreased by 93 percent; of the soft drink can, by 74 percent. The decrease in tin content is not just a North American phenomenon; it can be observed in Japan, in member countries of the European Economic Community, and generally in the rest of the world (Demler, 1983, pp. 17–18; International Tin Council, 1983, p. 74). The effort aimed at improving tinplate's productivity is also aimed at steel. Thus, the increase in the production of thinner but stronger tinplate, offering savings in both materials and transportation costs to can makers, has allowed

Table 7-1. Cost Structure of Aluminum and Tinplate Can Manufacturing and Glass and PET Bottle Manufacturing, 1985

(percent)

Cost element	Two-piece can (12 oz)		Nonreturnable glass bottle				PET bottle (16 oz)
	Aluminum	Tinplate	10 oz[a]	16 oz[a]	16 oz[b]	12 oz[c]	
Raw material cost[d]	65.8	63.1	49.7	51.3	37.2	41.0	57.1
Direct labor and supervision cost	8.5	14.3	13.4	12.2	13.6	13.2	10.8
Other conversion costs[e]	12.6	10.8	25.1[f]	25.7[f]	37.2[f]	33.0[f]	19.6
Capital servicing costs[g]	13.1	11.8	11.8	10.8	12.0	12.8	12.5
Calculated cost	100.0	100.0[h]	100.0	100.0	100.0	100.0	100.0

Notes: Cost data apply to 1985 except for tinplate; tinplate data are for 1982.

Sources: Derived from Chase Econometrics, *Materials Competition in the Beverage Container Industry to 1995* (Bala Cynwyd, Pa., Chase Econometrics, January 1986), pp. 4.6, 5.24, 5.26, 5.28, 5.30, and 6.21; Frederick R. Demler, "Beverage Containers," p. 25 in John E. Tilton, ed., *Material Substitution: Lessons from Tin-Using Industries* (Washington, D.C., Resources for the Future, 1983); International Tin Council, *Study on Consumption: United States of America, Tin in Tinplate* (London, ITC, 1983), p. 47, and *Study on Consumption: European Economic Community, Tin in Tinplate* (London, ITC, 1981), p. 21.

[a]Nonreturnable plasti-shield soft drink glass bottle.

[b]Nonreturnable pre-labeled soft drink glass bottle.

[c]Nonreturnable glass beer bottle.

[d]This cost element covers the following items: total aluminum (body stock, body stock scrap credit, shell stock, shell stock scrap credit, tab stock, tab stock scrap credit, and spoilage credit); tinplate materials (hot-rolled coil, 50 percent; tin ingots, 10 percent; other, 3 percent); plasti-shield and/or glass melt: bottle (PET resin, labels and adhesive, reshipping, other packaging materials) and base cup (HDPE resin, base cup glue).

[e]These costs include the following items: natural gas, electricity, operating supplies, molds and maintenance, tooling and spare parts, coating and other materials, insurance and property taxes, packaging, freight, royalties, general sales and administrative (GSA) expenses, and other direct costs.

[f]Packaging, freight, and general sales and administrative expenses represent the most important items of this cost element.

[g]These costs have been derived using, in most cases, the following depreciation and useful-life assumptions: equipment, 5 years; building, 18 years; working capital, 5 years. In the case of the PET bottle, the following assumptions have been made: building and off-sites, over 18 years; equipment and on-sites, over 7 years; tooling, over 3 years; and working capital, over 5 years.

[h]Tinplate can made from tinplate containing 118 pounds of steel and 0.25 pound of tin per base.

tinplate producers to maintain and in some cases to improve their competitive position.

The situation is similar for aluminum. The number of pounds of aluminum per thousand cans has decreased by more than 40 percent since 1960 because of gauge reductions in the can body and lid stock. The average can body was 0.017 inch thick in 1970; it thinned to 0.0126 inch in 1987. According to industry representatives, further reductions in thickness of both bodies and lids are expected.

Production costs are not the only costs. To the cost of manufacturing an empty can or bottle must be added the cost of filling the container and the additional costs of materials and processing needed to complete the package—labels for certain bottles, closures for all bottles, and multipacking and shipping materials. These costs vary with each kind of container and, at least

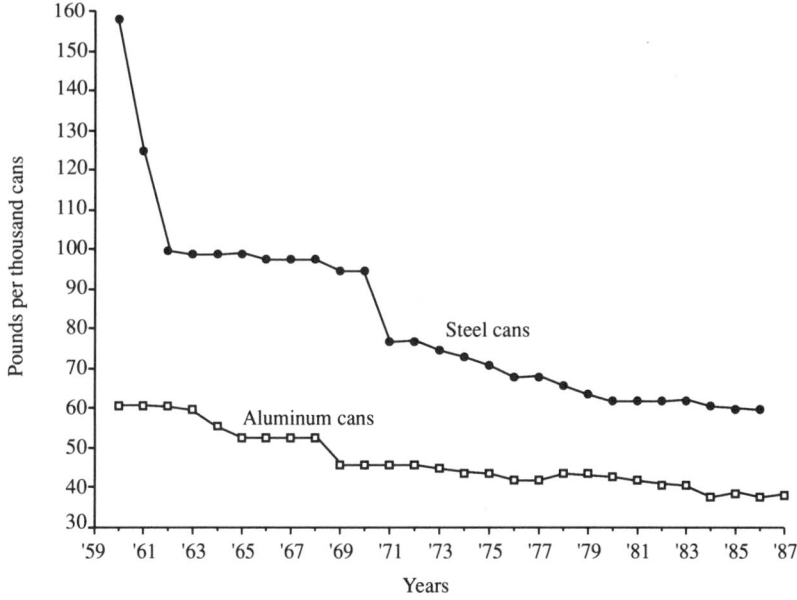

Figure 7-3. Aluminum and steel can weights (pounds per 1,000 cans), 1960–1987.
Source: Derived from Frederick R. Demler, "Beverage Containers," pp.17–18 in John E.
Tilton, ed., *Materials Substitution: Lessons from Tin-Using Industries* (Washington, D.C.,
Resources for the Future, 1983). F. R. Demler also provided the data on steel can weights.

for the most popular containers in the United States, serve to shrink the
overall differences in cost among competing containers. As Table 7-2 indicates, the currently higher cost of the aluminum can as compared to the
bottle is almost cancelled by the efficiency of filling cans versus bottles and
by the higher multipacking costs incurred with bottles. Moreover, the small
cost differences that might persist could disappear if the costs of warehousing, distribution, and handling, which are harder to assess, are taken into
account. One must also consider the recycling credits of each type of container and the external costs related to their disposal problems. The importance of these variables are evaluated in the following sections.

MATERIALS SUBSTITUTION IN THE U.S. FOOD AND BEVERAGE CONTAINER INDUSTRIES

Thus far, three general trends have been identified: (1) Three-piece steel cans
will dominate the food can market in the midterm, with tin-free steel gaining
on tinplate. (2) In the same market, two-piece metal cans, plasticans, and
retort pouches are growing contenders, not yet strong enough to impair
steel's advantage. (3) Aluminum and tinplate two-piece cans and plastic

Table 7-2. Costs of Filled Beverage Containers, 1985

(percent)

Cost	Soft drink containers			Beer containers	
	Aluminum can, 12 oz	Bottles[a]		Aluminum can, 12 oz	Bottles, 12 oz[b]
		10 oz	16 oz		
Filling	3.2	3.7	4.6	3.0	4.7
Completion of package					
Closures	—[c]	11.1	11.1	—[c]	4.4
Labels and glue	—[c]	—[c]	—[c]	—[c]	9.3
Multipacking	5.8	8.2	8.2	5.8	11.7
Shipping	6.3	—[c]	—[c]	6.3	—[c]
Subtotal	12.1	19.3	19.3	12.1	25.4
Container	84.7	86.2	103.2	84.7	65.8
TOTAL FILLED COST	100.0	109.2	127.1	99.8	95.9
Total filled cost per ounce[d]	8.33	10.92	7.94	8.32	7.99

Note: Total filled costs of a two-piece, 12-oz aluminum soft drink can = 100 percent.

Source: Derived from Chase Econometrics, *Materials Competition in the Beverage Container Industry to 1995* (Bala Cynwyd, Pa., Chase Econometrics, January 1986) p. 7.9.

[a]Nonreturnable plasti-shield soft drink bottles.

[b]Nonreturnable beer bottles.

[c]Dash (—) = included in container cost.

[d]Total filled cost divided by the number of ounces in each type of container.

containers are leaders in the beverage market, with plastic making gains in spite of technical and economic problems; the market share of steel has been declining over time.

We turn next to an investigation of how these general trends apply to the U.S. beverage and food container markets, first looking at the competition among materials for beer and soft drink containers.

Competing Materials for Beer and Soft Drink Containers

Figure 7-4 highlights the competition since 1950 among metals, glass, and plastic, and between aluminum and steel, for U.S. beer containers. Figure 7-5 presents the same information for U.S. soft drink containers.

Since 1950 beer consumption increased 3.4 percent per year, but it has stagnated since 1980 (table 7-3; Demler, 1983, p. 17). The American preference for packaged beer far outweighs that for draft beer. Although draft beer sales in 1950 accounted for more than one-quarter of total sales, that share dropped steadily until 1977 when they stabilized at a little over 11 percent.

The preference for packaged beer is clearly not for beer in glass bottles. The combined share of bottles (refillable and nonrefillable) decreased by half after 1950, standing in 1988 at just over one-quarter of the market. The metal (aluminum) can in 1988 claimed more than 60 percent of the market,

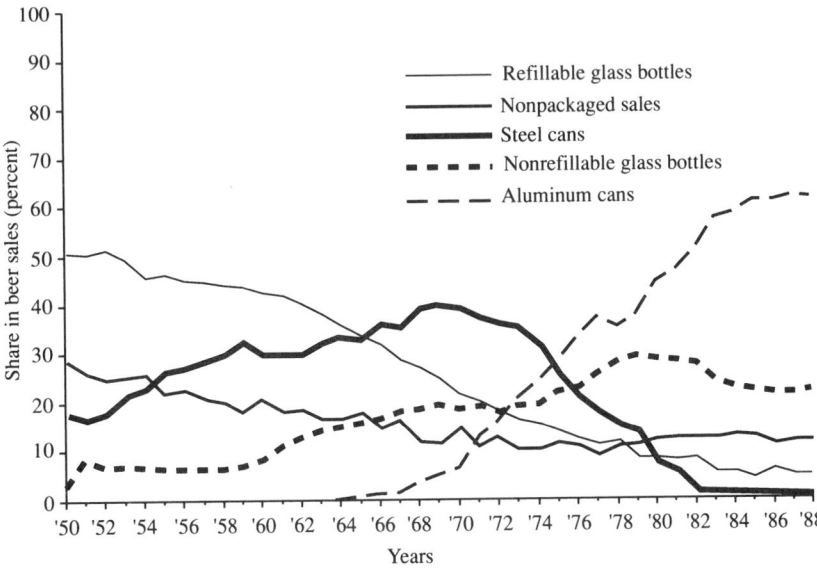

Figure 7-4. Breakdown of U.S. beer sales by container type, 1950–1988.

Sources: Beverage Industry (Duluth, Magazines for Industry, various issues); *Beverage World* (East Stroudsburg, Pa., Keller Publishing, various issues); Frederick R. Demler, "The Nature of Tin Substitution in the Beverage Container Industries" (Ph.D. thesis, Pennsylvania State University, University Park, August 1980) pp. 171–172; *The Food and Beverage Market* (Commack, N.Y., Business Trend Analysts, 1983) p. 103.

a startling gain considering its 18 percent share (for steel cans) in 1950. A look at events within both the bottle and can markets provides some clues that elucidate this shift. In 1950 the refillable beer bottle accounted for one-half of all sales; nonrefillable bottles, less than 3 percent. In 1988 the nonrefillable bottle was the significant share holder. The market for metal beer cans experienced a similar upheaval. Long the metal of choice, steel held a healthy 40 percent share of all beer sales by type of container in 1968. But with the advent of the aluminum can in the late 1960s, aluminum's share of the beer container market quickly surpassed that of steel. Today the dominance of aluminum is almost complete.

Consumption patterns in the soft drink market differ somewhat from those for beer. Since 1950 the annual increase in soft drink consumption has been more than twice that of beer (table 7-4; Demler, 1983, p. 18). And unlike consumption of unpackaged beer, consumption of unpackaged soft drinks has been growing—from less than 10 percent of all sales in 1950 to more than 23 percent in 1988.

The same phenomenon of less demand for bottles and more for cans has occurred in the soft drink market. Nonetheless, there are differences. Within the shrinking bottle market, the refillable bottle in 1988 had almost the same

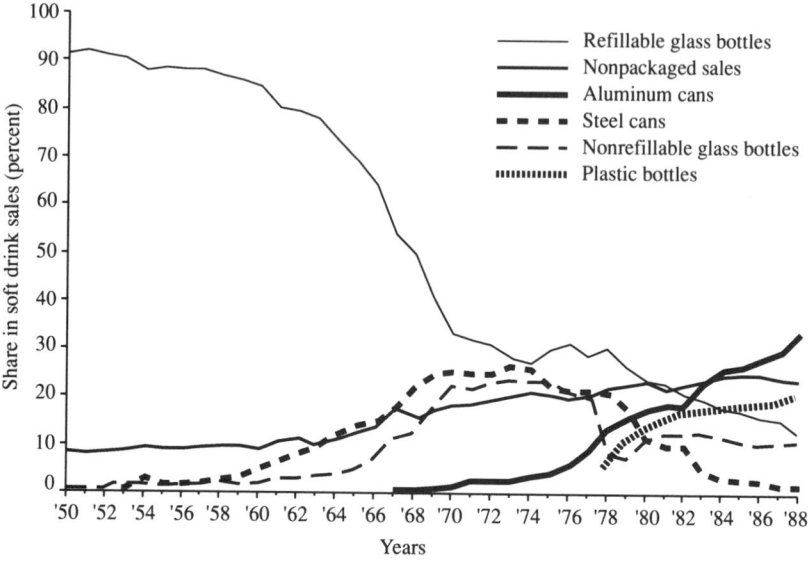

Figure 7-5. Breakdown of U.S. soft drink sales by container type, 1950–1988.

Sources: Beverage Industry (Duluth, Magazines for Industry, various issues); *Beverage World* (East Stroudsburg, Pa., Keller Publishing, various issues); Frederick R. Demler, "The Nature of Tin Substitution in the Beverage Container Industries" (Ph.D. thesis, Pennsylvania State University, University Park, August 1980) pp. 169–170; *The U.S. Soft Drink Market* (Commack, N.Y., Business Trend Analysts, 1984), and *The Food and Beverage Market* (Commack, N.Y., Business Trend Analysts, 1983) p. 103.

market share as the nonrefillable bottle. The former accounted for over 90 percent of all soft drink sales in 1950; it now accounts for less than 11 percent. Nonrefillable bottle sales peaked at 23 percent in the mid-1970s and now account for one-half that percentage.

As in the beer market, the appearance of the aluminum can in the soft drink market signaled the demise of the steel can. It is important to note, however, that although aluminum cans account for 93 percent of all soft drinks packaged in metal cans, they accounted for less than 35 percent of all soft drink sales in 1988. This is explained in part by the popularity of unpackaged sales at fast-food outlets and by the introduction of the glass industry's plasti-shield bottle. The overriding reason for this low market share, however, is the entrance of a new competitor absent from the beer market: the plastic bottle. Introduced in 1978, its share in 1988 was more than one-fifth of the market.

We have seen that metal cans are containers for a growing portion of beer and soft drink sales, making them an important product for metal producers. This favorable development, however, conceals the fierce competition between aluminum and steel products that after twenty years has edged out steel. The U.S. container and packaging sector has become the major outlet for aluminum shipments. Although sales to this sector represented only 8 percent of total aluminum shipments in 1964, they claimed almost 28 percent in 1987 (Aluminum Association, 1987, p. 12). In contrast, in 1974, steel shipments to the container and packaging sector totaled about 7.5 million tons; tin shipments totaled 23,000 tons. Twelve years later, steel shipments dropped by almost one-half and tin shipments by almost two-thirds (Commodity Research Bureau, 1986, pp. 136, 271).

These trends are easier to describe than to explain. The study by Demler (1983, pp. 15–35), of the underlying causes of the decrease in tin consumption in the U.S. beverage industry establishes the dominant role of technological change. Demler found that the quantity of tin contained in a beer can dropped by 93 percent between 1950 and 1977; the tin content of soft drink cans dropped by 74 percent during the same period. (Tin consumption in beer containers has declined from 6,278 tons in 1950 to 494 tons in 1977. In the case of soft drink containers, tin consumption, nonexistent in 1950, rose until 1969 when it reached 2,133 tons; eight years later it totaled only 1,128 tons.) According to Demler, if technological changes had not occurred during the 1950–1977 period, tin consumption in the manufacture of beer cans would have been thirteen times higher. For soft drink cans, tin consumption would have multiplied by nine. In both cases the comparison is valid only if one assumes that the higher costs would not have reduced the demand for tin cans.

Although the influence of technological change on tin consumption was felt during the entire period under study, the effects of other variables—the introduction of new containers and a decrease in sales of packaged soft drinks—began to be felt in the mid-1960s. These forces cancelled out what otherwise would have helped preserve tin's market share—the growth of beer and soft drink consumption and the drop in sales of draft beer.

These findings apply mostly to tin consumption in the manufacture of tinplate and not necessarily to steel consumption, the more important component. In the case of steel, the increased use of double-reduced steel—a method requiring less steel per can—in tinplate manufacture was a minor negative development for steel in comparison to the havoc wreaked by the introduction of the aluminum can.

How can the success of aluminum be explained? Despite its simplicity, the apparent-determinants method used by Demler (1983) provides some answers. The amount of aluminum used in any particular year to produce beer or soft drink containers depends on five apparent determinants, as the following identity indicates:

$$Q_t \equiv B_t\, a_t\, b_t\, c_t\, d_t$$

where Q_t = tons of aluminum consumed for the beverage considered
during year t;

B_t = millions of barrels of the beverage shipped in year t;

a_t = proportion of the beverage that is packaged in bottles or cans during year t (as opposed to being shipped in bulk containers);

b_t = proportion of the packaged beverage put into aluminum cans (as opposed to tinplate cans, tin-free steel cans, and glass or plastic bottles) during year t;

c_t = number of average-volume aluminum cans required per barrel of beverage in year t;[2]

d_t = weight in tons of aluminum contained in the average-volume aluminum can used to ship the beverage in year t.

The apparent determinants of aluminum consumption for the 1964–1987 period appear in tables 7-3 and 7-4. Thus, in 1987 (table 7-4) soft drink consumption rose to 364 million barrels (B_t), of which 76 percent (a_t) was shipped in packaged containers. Aluminum cans accounted for 40.9 percent (b_t) of all packaged soft drinks. Because the contents of each barrel fills 331 12-oz cans (c_t) and each of these cans in 1987 contained 1.65×10^{-5} ton of aluminum, 618,000 tons of aluminum were consumed in making cans for soft drinks in that year. The last figure is equal to (364.0×10^6) (0.76) (0.409) (331) (1.65×10^{-5}). Aluminum consumption for beer and soft drink containers, which was less than 3,000 tons when aluminum cans were introduced in the mid-1960s, surpassed the 1.2-million-ton mark during the 1980s.

Both positive and negative variables have influenced the level of aluminum consumption. On the positive side are the sustained growth of beer and soft drink consumption, the sustained increase in the proportion of shipments packaged in aluminum cans, and, in the case of beer containers, an increase in the proportion shipped in packaged containers. The negative variables are a 30 percent decrease in the aluminum content of the average-size can and, in the case of soft drinks, a drop in the market share of packaged sales. The number of average-size aluminum cans per barrel (331) has remained relatively constant over the period under study.

To assess the relative importance of the determinants that tend to increase aluminum use, individual effects were estimated by calculating the increase in aluminum consumption that each alone would have caused had all the other apparent determinants remained unchanged between 1964 and 1987 for beer cans, and between 1967 and 1987 for soft drink cans. The individual effect of each of the negative determinants was estimated by calculating the amount by which aluminum consumption in 1987 would have increased had

---

[2]The average size of aluminum cans used for beer and soft drinks in 1987 is the 12-ounce (oz) can (80 percent of all cans used). A barrel contains 31 gallons, or 3,968 oz. Therefore, each barrel holds the same amount contained in 330.67 12-oz cans.

Table 7-3. Apparent Determinants of Aluminum Consumption in Beer Containers, 1964–1987

Year	(B_t) Beer consumption (million barrels)	(a_t) Proportion of consumption shipped in packaged containers (percent)	(b_t) Proportion of packaged shipments in aluminum cans (percent)	(c_t) Number of average-size aluminum cans per barrel[a]	(d_t) Aluminum content of average-size aluminum cans[b] (10^{-5} metric tons)	(Q_t) Aluminum consumption by beer containers[c] (thousand metric tons)
1964	97.1	83.9	0.4	331	2.45	2.6
1965	101.2	82.7	1.4	331	2.30	8.9
1966	103.2	85.4	2.4	331	2.30	16.1
1967	109.3	84.0	3.7	331	2.30	25.9
1968	109.8	88.0	4.2	331	2.30	30.9
1969	114.9	88.5	6.4	331	2.02	43.5
1970	125.3	85.6	8.2	331	2.02	58.8
1971	126.3	88.9	14.8	331	2.02	111.1
1972	132.8	87.3	18.1	331	2.09[d]	145.2
1973	135.8	90.0	22.8	331	2.04	188.2
1974	144.4	89.4	27.8	331	2.00	237.6
1975	148.7	88.7	32.0	331	1.97	275.2
1976	150.6	89.1	37.3	331	1.95	323.1
1977	155.5	90.7	40.8	331	1.93	367.6
1978	165.7	89.2	39.4	331	1.92	370.1
1979	170.9	88.5	43.1	331	1.92	414.3
1980	177.4	88.1	50.7	331	1.87	490.5
1981	181.8	88.1	53.5	331	1.86	527.6
1982	181.8	87.7	58.8	331	1.80	558.6
1983	183.8	87.9	65.5	331	1.77	620.0
1984	182.8	87.0	67.4	331	1.68	596.1
1985	182.5	87.4	69.9	331	1.71	631.1
1986	187.5	88.6	69.9	331	1.68	645.7
1987[e]	187.8	88.3	70.0	331	1.65	634.0

Sources: Derived from *Beverage Industry* (Duluth, Magazines for Industry, various issues); *Beverage World* (East Stroudsburg, Pa., Keller Publishing, various issues); Frederick R. Demler, "The Nature of Tin Substitution in the Beverage Container Industries" (Ph.D. thesis, Pennsylvania State University, University Park, August 1980) pp. 14, 171–172; *The Food and Beverage Market* (Commack, N.Y., Business Trend Analysts, 1983) p. 103; personal interview with representatives of the Aluminum Association, Washington, D.C., 1988.

[a]The average-size beer can is assumed to remain at 12 oz over the 1964–1987 period. In determining the number of cans per pound of metal, the Aluminum Association also assumes that all aluminum cans are this size.

[b]Includes weight of closure, end, and body.

[c]Actual consumption underestimated largely because aluminum in scrap generated in production has been excluded.

[d]Data for the 1964–1971 period are from Demler (1980); for the 1972–1987 period, from the Aluminum Association (1988).

[e]Figures for this year are estimated.

a particular apparent determinant remained unchanged. The results are presented in figure 7-6.

The left-hand column of each of the two graphs in figure 7-6 indicates the quantity of aluminum consumed in 1964 and 1967 for the manufacture of beer and soft drink cans, respectively. The center column reveals the quantity

Table 7-4. Apparent Determinants of Aluminum Consumption in Soft Drink Containers, 1967–1987

Year	(B_t) Soft drink consumption (million barrels)	(a_t) Proportion of consumption shipped in packaged containers (percent)	(b_t) Proportion of packaged shipments in aluminum cans (percent)	(c_t) Number of average size aluminum cans per barrel[a]	(d_t) Aluminum content of average-size aluminum cans[b] (10^{-5} metric tons)	(Q_t) Aluminum consumption by soft drink containers[c] (thousand metric tons)
1967	119.5	82.7	0.3	331	2.30	2.3
1968	134.4	84.5	0.8	331	2.30	6.9
1969	141.8	82.8	1.0	331	2.02	7.9
1970	149.9	81.7	1.7	331	2.02	13.9
1971	162.3	81.0	2.8	331	2.02	24.6
1972	172.4	80.6	3.0	331	2.09[d]	28.8
1973	182.5	80.0	3.1	331	2.04	30.6
1974	183.8	79.0	4.6	331	2.00	44.2
1975	189.5	79.3	5.0	331	1.97	49.0
1976	212.8	80.1	8.0	331	1.95	88.0
1977	235.8	78.9	11.2	331	1.93	133.1
1978	245.2	79.2	16.4	331	1.92	202.4
1979	255.3	77.7	20.5	331	1.92	258.4
1980	264.9	76.9	22.8	331	1.87	287.5
1981	272.4	77.9	23.4	331	1.86	305.7
1982	295.2	77.2	23.6	331	1.80	320.4
1983	305.9	76.4	30.2	331	1.77	413.5
1984	317.7	75.7	33.6	331	1.68	449.4
1985	333.4	75.2	34.7	331	1.71	492.4
1986	348.4	75.0	36.9	331	1.68	536.2
1987[e]	364.0	76.0	40.9	331	1.65	617.9

Sources: Derived from *Beverage Industry* (Duluth, Magazines for Industry, various issues); *Beverage World* (East Stroudsberg, Pa., Keller Publishing, various issues); Frederick R. Demler, "The Nature of Tin Substitution in the Beverage Container Industries" (Ph.D. thesis, Pennsylvania State University, University Park, August 1980) pp. 14 and 169–170; *The U.S. Soft Drink Market* (Commack, N.Y., Business Trend Analysts, 1984); *The Food and Beverage Market* (Commack, N.Y., Business Trend Analysts, 1983) p. 103; interview with representatives of the Aluminum Association, Washington, D.C., 1988.

[a] The average-size soft drink can is assumed to remain at 12 oz over the 1967–1987 period. In determining the number of cans per pound of metal, the Aluminum Association also assumes that all aluminum cans are this size.

[b] Includes weight of closure, end, and body.

[c] Actual consumption underestimated largely because aluminum in scrap generated in production has been excluded.

[d] Data for the 1967–1971 period are from Demler (1980); for the 1972–1987 period, from interview with representatives of the Aluminum Association, Washington, D.C., 1988.

[e] Figures for this year are estimated.

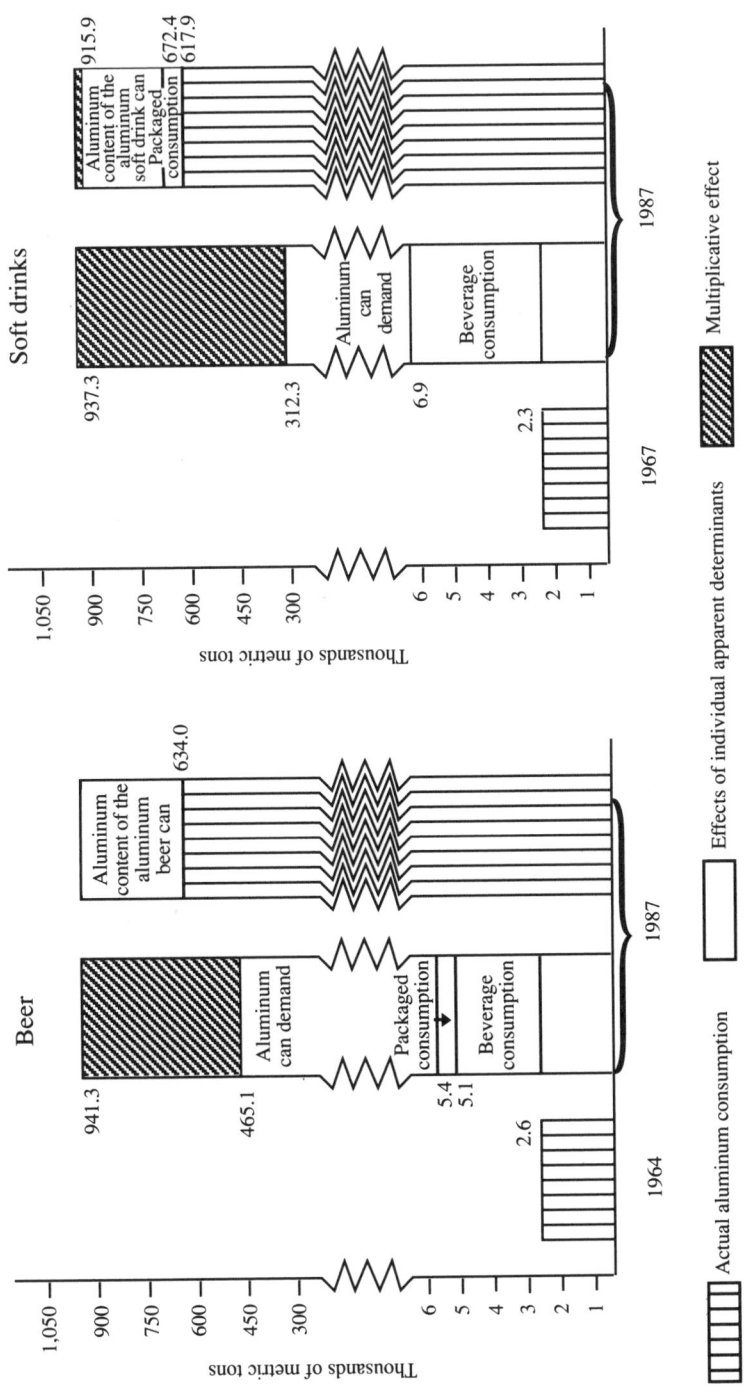

Figure 7-6. **Effects of changes in apparent determinants on aluminum consumption in beer and soft drink containers, 1964–1987 and 1967–1987, respectively (in thousands of metric tons). See discussion in text.**

233

of aluminum that would have been consumed in 1987 if only those apparent determinants having a positive influence on aluminum consumption had changed between 1964 (or 1967) and 1987. Aluminum consumption for beer containers would have reached 941,000 tons in 1987 instead of the 634,000 tons actually consumed. Data on soft drink containers show that consumption would have risen to 937,000 tons instead of the actual 618,000 tons.

In light of the individual effects of the apparent determinants, figure 7-6 indicates that the rise in beer consumption, had it alone changed, would have increased aluminum consumption by 2,500 tons, and the growth in the share of packaged sales, had it alone changed, would have expanded aluminum consumption by a mere 300 tons. In contrast, if only the market share of packaged sales claimed by aluminum cans had increased, aluminum consumption would have risen by 460,000 tons. When two or more apparent determinants tend to increase aluminum consumption, they produce a multiplicative effect that must be added to their individual effects. Here, the multiplicative effect for the three apparent determinants stimulating aluminum consumption in beer containers amounts to 476,000 tons. The right-hand column indicates the actual aluminum consumption in 1987 as well as the effect of apparent determinants having a negative influence on aluminum use in the manufacture of beer cans. Thus, aluminum consumption would have risen by approximately 310,000 additional tons if this metal's content in an aluminum can had remained unchanged since 1964.

For soft drink containers, figure 7-6 shows that the positive effect of the rise in soft drink consumption and the negative effect of the drop in the proportion of packaged sales on aluminum use have been rather marginal. This is not the case, however, for the other determinants. Indeed, if only the proportion of shipments packaged in aluminum cans had gone up, aluminum use would have increased by 305,000 tons. Similarly, aluminum consumption would have risen by 240,000 tons if the aluminum content of the average-size aluminum can had not changed since 1967.

From this analysis we now know that to understand the phenomenal growth of aluminum consumption in the production of cans for the beer and soft drink industries, we must comprehend the fundamental reasons for the substitution of aluminum for steel. The influence of the other apparent determinants (increases in beer and soft drink consumption, variations in the market share of packaged sales) seems relatively less important.[3] Finally, it must be emphasized that despite a strong increase in aluminum consumption, this

---

[3]It is the same for the explanatory variables of these apparent determinants, such as the evolution of disposable income and consumer preferences. The latter refers to the reasons that have led to a rise in the share of sales of unpackaged soft drinks since the mid-1970s. These preferences affect the demand for metals, as they imply a move away from metallic containers toward plastic and paper cups. The following factors are responsible for this structural change in the soft drink sector: the improvement of mixing and filling equipment, the phenomenal

growth might have been even stronger had there not been an effort to reduce the content of aluminum in can manufacturing—"might" because without such an effort the aluminum can would not have displaced the steel can so easily. (Because the cost of a metal sheet represents a high proportion of the total costs of can manufacturing [see table 7-2], manufacturers have a strong incentive to reduce material usage as much as possible. It is difficult to find a basis of comparison for such technological efforts aimed at reducing relative production costs. However, a review of the literature shows that efforts by the steel sector to find ways to reduce metal content are just as serious as those of the aluminum sector.)

Even though several reasons may be suggested for the substitution of aluminum for steel or for glass in the U.S. market, we believe that the fundamental reason lies in the fact that the aluminum can has increased its competitiveness over the other containers by closing the gap in production costs, which have always been to aluminum's disadvantage, and by developing other advantages, in particular, lower handling and shipping costs and higher recycling credits. Aluminum has also to some extent been favored by government regulation. Let us examine these reasons in more detail.

Data in table 7-2 indicate that the difference in total filled cost per ounce between the soft drink 12-oz aluminum can and 16-oz glass bottle is not very great—less than 5 percent to the latter's advantage. But this difference turns to aluminum's advantage if warehousing, distribution, and handling costs are taken into account. By making the same comparison of the total costs of producing two-piece, 12-oz cans from aluminum and tinplate, we come to the same conclusion: the difference in their total costs is small, has been decreasing over time, and turns to aluminum's advantage when warehousing and shipping costs are taken into account. Of course, aluminum has an initial material cost disadvantage compared with steel (at the end of 1987, with a price for the 0.0126-inch body stock of $1.04 per pound, this disadvantage was $5.65 per thousand cans). The cost of producing an aluminum can has been more than that for a tinplate can. In the United States this difference (12 percent in 1978)[4] has been declining over time. Contributing

growth of fast-food chains, and, to a certain degree, consumer response to governmental regulations concerning mandatory deposits.

The share of unpackaged beer sales has changed very little over time; it has been slightly declining since the mid-1970s, an effect of the greater consumption of beer at home instead of in bars and restaurants. The influence of all these variables can increase in the future, but for the moment they are relatively less important than those justifying the technological efforts aimed at reducing the metal content of cans or explaining the progressive and rapid substitution of the steel by the aluminum can.

[4]See Demler (1983, p. 25). The starting metal costs (and scrap credits) as well as the cleaning and treatment costs are more important elements in the cost structure for the aluminum can than they are for the tinplate can. The reverse is true for interior coating costs, tooling costs, labor costs, overhead costs, and depreciation.

to the decline is the development of a new aluminum alloy (the H19). By permitting higher-gauge reductions, this alloy provides the edge that neither the tin-free can, introduced in 1967, nor the two-piece steel can, developed later in response to aluminum's more efficient use of its H19 alloy, could overcome. Both the aluminum and steel industries continued to effect weight and cost reductions throughout the 1970s and 1980s, but in the end it was the H19 alloy that allowed the aluminum can not only to survive the competition but also to expand its market share continuously.

The increasing importance of recycling credits is another factor contributing to the competitiveness of the aluminum can. Recycling programs have expanded enormously. More than 50 percent of all aluminum cans are recycled—42 billion cans in 1988 weighing almost 700,000 tons. The International Tin Council (1983) cites several reasons for this success:

> Among the factors that have contributed towards the success of aluminum can recycling are the relatively high scrap value of aluminum which permits the payment to the public of a small sum for all aluminum cans returned (cans with tinplate bodies are commonly accepted but not paid for), the convenient siting of can collection centres in supermarkets and the appeal of the concept of recycling to the public. Aluminum can recycling has rapidly grown into a large industry, with recycling operations being carried out by aluminum companies, can makers and other companies, and a considerable amount of capital has been invested in recycling plants. As dominance of the aluminum beverage can in the US market is a prerequisite for the aluminum can recycling industry's existence, tinplate producers will encounter strong opposition should they attempt to recapture tinplate's former market share. (International Tin Council, 1983, p. 45.)

Access to this secondary supply is particularly important to high-cost, integrated primary aluminum producers or to beverage producers that manufacture their own cans. In both cases the difference between primary metal price and scrap may be significant, and access to the secondary supply may represent a real asset. This is not the case for low-cost primary aluminum producers, as the difference between the two prices is more modest, especially after the shipping and treatment costs of scrap have been taken into account.

The fact that aluminum has advanced so fast against tin-mill products (44.7 percent of the beer can market in 1974, 99 percent in 1988; 12.2 percent of the soft drink can market in 1974, 95 percent in 1988) suggests that the differences in the production and filling costs of these two cans have greatly diminished. Easier access to secondary aluminum supplies and the introduction of the H19 aluminum alloy and other technological improvements have led to important cost reductions. Moreover, as mentioned earlier, there are other costs to consider. For instance, steel cans weigh about twice as much as aluminum cans, and this difference affects transportation and handling costs. It is not easy to assess the relative contribution of each of these factors, but the suggestion that "total" production costs are still to a large extent to aluminum's disadvantage can be dismissed easily.

Another consideration is whether aluminum or steel consumption in metal can manufacturing would have been greater without government regulation. It is important to note here that currently there are only nine states with mandatory deposit laws (MDLs) (Connecticut, Delaware, Iowa, Maine, Massachusetts, Michigan, New York, Oregon, and Vermont). No other state has joined this list since July 1983 when New York adopted its bottle bill.[5] Attempts to impose similar laws have been defeated in California, the District of Columbia, and New Jersey, and proposed MDLs have been set aside in Florida and Pennsylvania.

The direct consequence of these environmental laws has been an increase in consumption of unpackaged beverages and an increased market share for returnable bottles (at the expense of nonreturnable containers). The laws' effect on metal cans has been rather mixed. In the beer sector, after an initial negative effect, can use almost returned to prior levels. In the soft drink sector the market share of metal cans dropped in the states that adopted MDLs and has not regained its lost ground.

At first glance it would appear that because of the small number of states involved, the effect of MDLs on the total U.S. market share of metal cans in general and aluminum cans in particular would have been rather limited. Upon closer examination of the matter, however, we suppose that even in states where MDLs were rejected, environmentalists have pressed for recycling and conservation of resources, a concern shared to some extent by the general public. If this is so, the adoption of MDLs was certainly a greater benefit to aluminum than to steel because of aluminum's lower transportation and recycling costs. Furthermore, aluminum scrap is worth more than steel scrap, an argument not to be disregarded. Far from reducing aluminum consumption in can manufacturing, MDLs may have contributed to its boost (Rathje, 1986, pp. 16–18).[6]

---

[5]The New York bill is a good example of the measures generally demanded by environmentalists: a five-cent deposit on returnable glass, metal, or plastic containers for beer, soft drinks, sparkling water, and other beverages; a one-cent-per-container retailer handling fee; a ban on the use of detachable pull tabs on metal cans; and a ban on plastic loops that hold six-packs together.

[6]The passing of MDLs has been highly controversial. On the one hand, government intervention is justified by environmentalists to bring about a decrease in the pollution of parks, rivers, and roadsides; to reduce the costs related to the recovery and disposal of refuse; and to conserve primary nonrenewable resources. On the other hand, it has been said that these laws have increased the cost of packaged beverages (hence their consumption, production, and related employment levels have decreased); that consumers' choice of containers and beverages is reduced; and that these laws are not going to reverse the drop in the market share of returnable bottles. This last argument has been explained in the following way:

"First, where deposit bills are in effect, there is no evidence that the return percentage of each bottle filled has been improved sufficiently to support the present 12 trips that are required to make a refillable bottle economically viable. Most reports indicate returns ranging from 75% to 90% (about 4 to 10 trips).

"The second reason is that brewers and soft drink bottlers are not equipped to handle

In addition to those mentioned above, many other reasons, well researched but perhaps playing a lesser role, have been advanced to explain aluminum's success (Demler, 1983, pp. 28–29; Chase Econometrics, 1986; Corplan Associates, 1966; and Weinberg, 1971). Producers of beverage can sheet have moved forward into can making, breaking the historical tie between can manufacturers and steel firms producing tinplate—a development favoring the aluminum can. Beverage producers in the 1970s also moved into can making, and this favored aluminum and tinplate over glass. Aluminum cans have particularly benefited from this move, as they weigh less than steel cans or glass bottles—a factor in transportation costs, which rise as distances increase. Also, U.S. consumers prefer cans over bottles because of their handiness, compactness, and easy cooling characteristics. In particular, they prefer aluminum over steel cans because aluminum minimizes taste distortion. And finally, aluminum cans caught on quickly in the beer market because most breweries are large operations that can spread the high capital costs of the new filling equipment over greater volumes than can bottling plants for soft drinks.

Competing Materials for Food Containers

Significantly fewer cans are used for food—both at home and in restaurants—than for beer and soft drinks, and the number is declining. Food can shipments dropped from 30 billion units in 1977 to 27 billion units in 1988, a 10 percent decrease (U.S. Department of Commerce, 1989). This drop is not surprising, considering the reduced number of meals prepared at home, the trend toward smaller families, the increased numbers of working women, and the greater use of frozen foods.

Steel holds the food container market. About 94 percent of food shipments in metal containers are in steel cans. The metals competition is principally between tinplate and other tin-mill products. Tinplate, used in the production of three-piece steel cans, has lost some ground in its market share (94 percent in 1979 versus 84 percent in 1986) to tin-free steel (2 percent in 1979 versus 10 percent in 1986), particularly when can ends and two-piece draw-and-redraw cans are considered (International Tin Council, 1983, p. 58; interview with representatives of the Can Manufacturers Institute, Washington, D.C., 1987). The increase in market share of the two-piece food can is expected to continue and will expand the demand for lacquered tin-free steel.

---

refillables within their plants in sufficient volume to replace present non-refillable glass. . . .

"Finally, . . . once the present controlled, closed system of delivering pristine glass from glass manufacturer to bottler is broken by allowing the consumer into the delivery system, anything can be added to the bottle which may or may not be removed in the soaking and rinsing operation" (Cavanagh, 1982, p. 266).

Aluminum, as noted earlier, is currently unsuitable for most food canning, as its resistance to soldering and welding restricts its use to two-piece cans that cannot withstand high-temperature sterilization. Another problem for aluminum is that food cans come in a variety of shapes and volumes, and canneries are usually too small to carry the high capital cost of new filling equipment; that is, the volume is not available to cover the one-time conversion costs. Also, in contrast to beverage can manufacturing, in the food can sector a greater proportion of cans are made by canners for their own use (not by integrated aluminum producers), which is likely to stand in the way of any rapid gain in market share by aluminum. Two food categories that do use aluminum cans are meat and poultry and dairy products. But these two product categories represent only 15 percent of the food market. Little aluminum is used in the important and expanding sectors of pet foods, fruits, vegetables, and juices.

Other packaging technologies are rapidly developing in the food container market. These include aseptic packaging, retort pouches, and composite containers made from laminates of paperboard, plastic, and aluminum foil.

MATERIALS SUBSTITUTION IN OTHER INDUSTRIALIZED COUNTRIES

In 1988, 81.2 billion metal cans were produced in the United States for the beer and soft drink industries (U.S. Department of Commerce, 1989, p. 7-1). More than 96 percent of these containers were made of aluminum. Another 27.0 billion metal cans were manufactured for the food industry, of which barely 6 percent were aluminum. This gives a total of 79.6 billion aluminum cans; steel-based containers (28.6 billion cans with steel bodies and aluminum lids) take up the rest of the metal can market. In comparison, aluminum can production in other industrialized countries seems rather meager. In 1986, aluminum can production in Western Europe reached 5.36 billion cans, while in Japan and Canada it amounted to 2.17 billion and 1.02 billion cans, respectively.

Aluminum can production for these industrialized countries in 1986 was barely 12 percent of U.S. production. Even if these markets seem less developed on a per capita basis than their American counterpart, they deserve examination. First, they are significant outlets for the production of steel containers. Second, it is important to find out why aluminum cans have had difficulty penetrating these markets. Finally, despite their actual size, these markets represent significant potential outlets for aluminum, especially when it is taken into account that aluminum in the U.S. beverage container industry can no longer increase at steel's expense. From now on aluminum's growth will be tied largely to increases in consumption of beer and soft drinks.

The Western European Market

In 1988 the Western European market for metal cans for beer and soft drinks reached 16.5 billion units. Almost 60 percent of metal containers produced (9.9 billion cans) were two-piece tinplate cans; the rest were aluminum (see table 7-5). The production capacity for three-piece tinplate cans has all but disappeared.[7]

It is difficult to find information to answer several critical questions: How is aluminum can production divided among major Western European countries? What is the relative importance of the various containers used in the Western European beer and soft drink industries? How can the weak market share held by aluminum cans be explained? Statistics are either unobtainable or too sketchy for comparison. Despite these problems, table 7-5 amasses the principal available information and presents a reasonable picture of the competition among container materials in eleven Western European countries (Austria, Belgium, Denmark, the Federal Republic of Germany, Finland, France, Greece, Italy, Norway, Sweden, and the United Kingdom).

Table 7-5 indicates a rather dismal position for metal beer cans, even in the larger markets—the United Kingdom, the Federal Republic of Germany, and Italy. Only in Sweden does the metal can dominate. The situation is slightly improved in the soft drink markets of Belgium, Italy, the United Kingdom, the Federal Republic of Germany, and Sweden. It can be legitimately concluded that most Western European markets are dominated by glass bottles. In two countries where statistics are available (the Federal Republic of Germany and, in particular, the United Kingdom), the plastic bottle is gaining in the soft drink market.

In the metal can market, aluminum's share is greater than that of steel in small countries, such as Austria, Greece, and Sweden. Its position is far lower in France and the Federal Republic of Germany. The aluminum can seems to be entrenched in only two countries with high gross domestic product, the United Kingdom and Italy. Despite the relatively unimpressive position of the metal can in general and the aluminum can in particular, their penetration of the Western European beer and soft drink markets is clearly increasing. This is particularly true in the most industrialized European countries: the Federal Republic of Germany, France, Italy, and the United Kingdom.

By American standards the contribution of the European market for metal containers to the demand for metals has been rather disappointing. Several

---

[7]Because 45 grams (g) are used to produce one tinplate can body, the beer and beverage can market represents 4.1 million metric tons to the tinplate industry. Similarly, because 18 g are used to manufacture one aluminum can body and 5 g are used to produce one aluminum easy-open end (all ends are in aluminum), the beer and beverage can market represents more than 1.5 million metric tons to the Western European aluminum industry.

Table 7-5. Materials Substitution and the Beverage Container Industry in Selected Countries in Western Europe, 1985–1988

Country	Metal can consumption (billions)	Aluminum can consumption (billions)	Proportion of cans in Aluminum (%)	Tinplate (%)	Soft drink market Cans (%)	Glass (%)	PET (%)	Beer market Cans (%)	Glass (%)
Austria	0.30	0.30	100.0	—	N.A.	N.A.	N.A.	N.A.	N.A.
Belgium	N.A.	N.A.	a	N.A.	30	N.A.	N.A.	1	N.A.
Denmark	N.A.	N.A.	N.A.	N.A.	N.A.	N.A.	N.A.	—b	N.A.
Finland	N.A.	N.A.	N.A.	N.A.	10c	N.A.	N.A.	10c	N.A.
France	0.40	0.02–0.04	5–10	90–95	7d	N.A.	N.A.	2e	35f
Greece	0.26	0.21–0.23	80–90	30	N.A.	N.A.	N.A.	N.A.	N.A.
Italy	1.40	0.98	70	30	26g	N.A.	N.A.	12h	N.A.
Norway	i	—	—	N.A.	15	N.A.	N.A.	N.A.	N.A.
Sweden	0.65	0.65	100	—	23j,k	l	N.A.	53	N.A.
United Kingdom	5.0	2.20	44	55	23j,k	N.A.	33m	13n,o	N.A.
West Germany	3.5	0.53	15	85	16p	66q	8	6r	66q
Western Europe	16.5	6.60	40	60	N.A.	N.A.	N.A.	N.A.	N.A.

Note: N.A. = not available.

Sources: Derived from International Tin Council, *Study on Consumption: European Economic Community, Tin in Tinplate* (London, International Tin Council, 1981); A. von Lewinski and A. H. Wirtz, "European Can Recycling Proves Feasible—At a Price," *Metal Bulletin Monthly* (February 1987) pp. 14–15; A. H. Wirtz, "Recycling: the Key to the Growth of the Aluminum Beverage Can in Europe," *Proceedings of the 45th Annual World Magnesium Conference* (Dayton, Ohio, International Magnesium Association, 1988) pp. 47–49; personal interviews.

[a]Very low.
[b]Beer cans are prohibited in Denmark.
[c]Cans are statutorily limited to a 10 percent share of the beverage market.
[d]1.5 percent in 1976.
[e]0.6 percent in 1977.
[f]Nonreturnable bottles.

[g]15 percent in 1977.
[h]8 percent in 1979.
[i]Share of metal cans in Norway is negligible because of high taxes.
[j]Over 70 percent of these are aluminum.
[k]20.4 percent in 1974.
[l]The market share of returnable glass bottles is falling and that of nonreturnable bottles is increasing in the United Kingdom.
[m]PET's share of packaged soft drinks was 3 percent in 1979.
[n]33 percent of these are aluminum.
[o]5.9 percent in 1974.
[p]0.8 percent in 1970.
[q]Returnable bottles.
[r]2.2 percent in 1977.

reasons for these results are based largely on information dealing with specific countries and not Western Europe as a whole. In several countries the beer industry is composed of hundreds of small, regional brewers whose production lines are much too small to justify the cost of installing high-volume can-filling lines. (In the Federal Republic of Germany, no less than 1,500 breweries are in operation, and only the ten most important are in the canning business.) Where the markets are not fragmented, downstream integration limits the metal can. In France, for example, the three major breweries are under the control of the glass industry. Shipping distances are short in Europe, making container weight a smaller cost consideration than in the United States.

The aggressive strategy of some competitors is another reason for the low contribution of the Western European market to the demand for metals. For example, to benefit from standardization of equipment and economies of scale, West German producers of returnable bottles are attempting to market a uniform half-liter bottle for the whole of Europe. Moreover, the increasing popularity of plastic bottles in the United Kingdom and the Federal Republic of Germany has slowed the aluminum can's penetration of these two major European markets. The competition between metals is no less fierce than that between materials. The collapse in tinplate prices in 1985 helped the steel can producers enhance their dominant position in Europe, but that factor was less important during the 1988–1989 period when the price of tin increased on world markets.

Another reason for metal's poor showing in Western Europe is the negative effect of legislation pertaining to the use of cans. Danish law prohibits the use of beer cans, and Finnish law limits metal beverage cans to 10 percent of the market. In Norway high taxes on metal containers discourage their use. A law was passed in Sweden in March 1984 requiring a deposit of 25 öre per can, a move to increase the recycling rate to at least 75 percent. When that did not work, a deposit of 50 öre per can was imposed. The result has been a total loss of the market for steel and a bonanza for aluminum. (In several other countries government policy concerning the choice of containers has not been as explicit. In the Federal Republic of Germany, for instance, there was, until the beginning of 1986, a "gentlemen's agreement" with the industry to keep the share of nonreturnable containers at a maximum of 25 percent. The new waste disposal law passed in 1986 aims at waste reduction by encouraging the use of returnable bottles. But even there, the Ministry of Environment, actually working on directives, asked the industry to come up with voluntary measures to reduce household waste.)

None of these reasons for the weakness of the metal cans should be minimized, especially when examining the competition among different containers in specific countries. However, when looking at the Western European market as a whole, we believe that the weakness of the metal can is best explained by the concept of "total" relative cost as defined earlier, which puts the can at a disadvantage in relation to the glass bottle. This also applies to the competition between metals, in which, in contrast to the situation in the United States, aluminum cans have not overcome the disadvantage of "total" costs. One reason for this liability is the absence of aluminum can collection and recycling networks. (We are not discussing here the influence of technological efforts, such as downgauging, on relative production costs, as these efforts seem at first glance rather comparable. Indeed, in 1973, 20.6 grams (g) of aluminum were used in the manufacturing of a can, as opposed to 17.8 g in 1987. In the case of the tinplate can, the corresponding figures were 60 g and 45 g, respectively.) Producers have responded to the disadvantageous aluminum situation with pilot projects to establish a Western European recycling network, but so far the effort has been greater than the results.[8]

The enormous differences between the U.S. and Western European beverage container industries are largely absent in the food industries. In both food sectors the open-top three-piece tinplate can is the one most used; tin-free steel products are making gains; the aluminum can market is small but growing; glass is not expected to erode metal's market share; and the retort pouch represents a potential threat to the can, especially for large containers for institutional use, food containers for the military, and packaging for pet foods.

The differences are found mostly at a more disaggregate level. In Western Europe the breakthrough of tin-free steel can be explained principally by its much wider use in ends and not, as in the United States, by its wider use in small two-piece food cans. The more noteworthy difference seems to be the greater use of the aluminum food can. Although it was a late entrant in the Western European market, by 1981 it outperformed U.S. sales.

The Japanese Market

In Japan steel consumption for food and beverage cans is rising, but according to 1985 figures provided by the Mitsubishi Research Institute, it represents less than 1 percent of total steel consumption. Aluminum cans in 1985 represented a 6.5 percent share of total aluminum consumption, about the same as in the major Western European countries but far less than in the United States. These two metals face the same stiff competition from glass and plastic observed elsewhere.

---

[8]The pilot projects have mostly taken place in the Federal Republic of Germany (West Berlin, Düsseldorf, and six other cities in the state of Nord-rheinwestfalen); the United Kingdom (the "cash-a-can" recycling scheme and the "vend-a-can" and "catch-a-can" programs in Birmingham, Edinburgh, Glasgow, Wallsall, Wolverhampton, Portsmouth, and Northampton); Italy (Milan, Lodi, and Verona); and Greece (three recycling centers have been started in Athens) (see von Lewinski and Wirtz, 1987, pp. 24–25).

Over the last fifteen years, Japanese beer consumption has grown at an annual rate of between 2.5 and 3 percent. As indicated in table 7-6, very little beer is consumed in cans, even though this share has doubled since 1982. The poor performance is a result of the entrenched returnable-bottle system in Japan, which gives the bottle 70 percent of the market. As in the United States, the can market is dominated by aluminum, which currently has a 90 percent share.

An increasing Japanese preference for noncarbonated beverages has fueled an intense rivalry among manufacturers of soft drink containers for the diminishing soft drink market. The share of soft drinks packaged in metal containers grew rapidly from 1971, peaked in 1982 at nearly 40 percent, and then dropped and leveled off at 30 percent in 1985. Introduced on the Japanese market in 1972, the aluminum can quickly penetrated the soft drink market; however, unlike in the United States, its growth peaked in 1980 and has since stalled.

The aluminum can claims only about 10 percent of the Japanese soft drink market, as compared to 28 percent in the United States. It holds an even weaker share of the noncarbonated beverage market. A turnaround could occur if current research on liquid nitrogen injection systems proves successful.

The market share of other containers used for soft drinks is hard to determine because of a lack of statistics on liquids. However, from data provided by the Japan Soft Drink Bottlers' Association and the Ministry of International Trade and Industry (MITI) (table 7-7), it is safe to say that in the past few years this share must have greatly increased for plastic and nonreturnable glass bottles. The market share for returnable glass bottles has decreased to a level near that of metal cans.

Looking at the Japanese beer and soft drink industries as a whole, and with the aid of data in table 7-6, we find that despite a strong increase in the consumption of aluminum cans since 1971, these containers have not managed to displace others, including the steel-based can. Two possible explanations are the consumer preference for beer bottles over cans and the short shipping distances, which reduce incentives to use aluminum cans. To these reasons must be added production costs that are higher for aluminum in Japan than in the United States. The higher aluminum production costs are a consequence of energy costs (25 percent of aluminum's production costs), which are twice as high as in the United States.[9] This competitive dilemma

---

[9]For a comparison of the production costs of a tinplate can versus an aluminum can, see Shida (1981, pp. 54–64), from which one learns that in the early 1980s in Japan, the production cost of an aluminum can was 17 percent higher than the cost of producing a steel-based can. Furthermore, the cost of a metal sheet represented 73.5 percent of the total cost of producing an aluminum can, whereas it represented only 40 percent in the case of a steel can. It must be noted that these cost data do not take into account the appreciation of the yen relative to the U.S. dollar which has occurred since the mid-1980s.

Table 7-6. Metal Consumption and the Japanese Beer and Soft Drink Industries, 1971-1985

Year	Beer consumption[a]	Beer industry			Soft drink consumption[a]	Soft drink industry			Total aluminum cans (billions)	Ratio of aluminum cans to total cans (%)
		Beer: proportion in cans (%)	Ratio of aluminum cans to total cans (%)	Proportion of beer produced in aluminum cans[b] (%)		Soft drinks: proportion in cans (%)	Ratio of aluminum cans to total cans (%)	Proportion of soft drinks produced in aluminum cans[b] (%)		
1971	3.1	2.5	15.7	N.A.	N.A.	10.9	N.A.	N.A.	0.03	2.8
1972	3.4	3.6	35.4	1.3	N.A.	16.8	2.0	N.A.	0.16	7.6
1973	3.6	4.6	61.2	2.8	N.A.	25.2	7.7	N.A.	0.54	15.0
1974	3.6	4.6	65.2	3.0	2.9	35.3	8.5	3.0	0.55	16.2
1975	3.9	5.2	64.8	3.3	2.8	32.8	9.6	3.2	0.60	19.0
1976	3.6	5.4	78.4	4.2	2.7	33.4	15.4	5.2	0.80	25.8
1977	4.1	6.3	85.9	5.4	3.1	33.2	24.4	8.1	1.30	35.0
1978	4.4	6.6	94.7	6.3	3.3	36.5	27.6	10.1	1.70	39.2
1979	4.5	7.4	95.0	7.0	3.3	36.4	31.4	11.4	1.88	43.1
1980	4.5	8.0	95.4	7.6	2.8	34.5	32.2	11.1	1.75	46.9
1981	4.6	8.4	89.2	7.4	2.7	37.3	31.1	11.6	1.74	45.1
1982	4.7	10.0	95.6	9.6	2.6	39.8	29.5	11.7	1.98	47.4
1983	4.9	13.0	93.3	12.1	2.7	36.4	30.7	11.2	2.28	53.0
1984	4.7	14.0	93.8	13.1	2.9	35.3	30.8	10.9	2.60	54.1
1985	4.8	17.0	91.0	15.5	2.9	30.0	30.8	9.2	2.70	N.A.

Note: N.A. = not available.

Sources: Derived from statistical data obtained from the following Japanese organizations: Tokei Jiho Sha, Inc., Japan Aluminum Federation, Japan Soft Drink Bottlers' Association, and the Ministry of International Trade and Industry (MITI).

[a]In millions of kiloliters.

[b]For each industry, the fourth column is the product of the first three columns divided by the first column.

Table 7-7. Production of Various Containers for the Japanese Soft Drink Industry, 1978–1985

(billions of bottles)

Container	1978	1979	1980	1981	1982	1983	1984	1985
Returnable glass bottle	5.6[a]	5.3[a]	4.3[a]	3.5	3.0	2.7	2.5	2.2
One-way glass bottle	N.A.	N.A.	N.A.	N.A.	0.2	0.6	0.7	0.8
PET container	—	—	—	—	—	0.04	0.09	0.2
Metal can	3.0	3.0	2.4	2.4	2.5	2.3	2.4	2.4

Source: Interviews with representatives of the Japan Soft Drink Bottlers' Association and MITI.
[a]Returnable and one-way glass bottles.

for the aluminum can exists despite access to a can collection and recycling network that rivals the American network in almost every respect except volume.

Aluminum can recovery in Japan has doubled since 1977. Most important, Japan achieved its 40 percent recycling rate largely through voluntary public cooperation (McBride, 1984, pp. 84–88). In Japan mandatory deposit laws are opposed by store owners and container manufacturers, who point to the economic drawbacks of these laws and question their necessity in view of the success of voluntary can collection. Despite the respectable recycling rate, opportunities for growth of aluminum can recycling are limited by the relatively small size of Japan's beer and soft drink markets. Consequently, aluminum can recycling will probably not become as important a factor in aluminum's competitive position as it is in the United States.

As in the United States and Western Europe, aluminum cans have not been successful in capturing a significant share of the Japanese food market. In recent years tinplate has lost significant ground to tin-free steel in both the bodies and ends of cans. Metal food cans face competition from glass jars and bottles, retort pouches and aseptic packaging systems, and plastic and paperboard containers. Although there has been a small drop in market share of cans to glass jars and bottles, there is no evidence of market-share loss for flexible containers. (For more information on the Japanese food market and container industry, see International Tin Council [1984].)

Canada

The belief that the U.S. and Canadian economies are similar in nature has led many market analysts to divide U.S. data by 10 to obtain Canadian data. Although this method is often successful, it does not work for the food and beverage container markets. One of the principal reasons is that Canada is essentially a refillable-container market. Several provinces have antilitter laws favoring the production and collection of returnable glass bottles.

In Canada beer consumption grew by 3 percent per year between 1970 and 1980 but has since stagnated (see table 7-8). Packaged beer sales outperform

Table 7-8. Metal Consumption and the Canadian Beer Industry, Selected Years

Year	Beer sales[a]	Bulk sales (%)	Proportion of beer sold in cans (%)	Ratio of aluminum to total cans (%)	Number of cans consumed (millions)	Proportion of beer sold in refillable glass bottles (%)
1970	1.55	N.A.	2.8	0	120	N.A.
1975	1.95	12	2.5	0	145	85.5
1980	2.05	8	2.0	0	125	90.0
1984	2.10	8	8.0	98.5	320	84.0
1985	2.00	N.A.	12.0	100.0	625	77.0

Note: N.A. = not available.
Sources: Derived from *The Food and Beverage Container Market* (Commack, N.Y., Business Trend Analysts, 1983), pp. 57–68; Chase Econometrics, *Materials Competition in the Beverage Container Industry to 1995* (Bala Cynwyd, Pa., Chase Econometrics, 1986), ch. 12; Commodities Research Unit, *Aluminum Can Sheet Study* (London, Commodities Research Unit, 1986) pp. 119–122.
[a]In millions of kiloliters.

bulk sales. In some provinces—Alberta, New Brunswick, and Prince Edward Island—beer sales have increased at a rate clearly superior to those of other provinces, but overall the beer industry is suffering. Part of the problem can be related to the poor performance of the Canadian economy, an unemployment rate above 10 percent for many years, and a weak rate of growth for personal income. But the low growth may also be attributed to life style changes that emphasize health and physical fitness.

A decline in draft beer sales is the only similarity between the Canadian and U.S. beer markets (see tables 7-8 and 7-9). The share of the metal can in the beer container market was slight until aluminum cans were introduced in 1982 in Quebec and, during the three following years, in the other provinces (except Saskatchewan), which improved the can market dramatically.

The refillable glass bottle has claimed a fluctuating share of 75 percent to 90 percent of the Canadian beer market for the past ten years. As recently as 1984, all Canadian brewers used the same stubby, 12-oz brown glass bottle—a practice that simplified packaging, distribution, and bottle collection and allowed for standardization of equipment. The lower costs have forestalled the advance of the nonrefillable container. Other reasons that this has happened are the antilitter and beverage container deposit laws, a consumer preference for the longer shelf life of glass bottles over steel cans, and lobbying by the steel industry, which delayed by eighteen years the introduction of the aluminum can. (To alleviate the effects of structural changes in the steel industry, many provinces decreed that only steel cans may be allowed for use as nonreturnable containers.)

Despite the continuing domination of the glass bottle, its market share has eroded since 1984. Since then the aluminum can has replaced the steel can and has gained ground over the glass bottle. The slight gains are attributable

Table 7-9. Metal Consumption and the Canadian Soft Drink Industry, Selected Years

| Year | Soft drink sales[a] | Bulk sales (%) | Soft drinks consumed in cans (%) | Ratio of aluminum to total cans (%) | Number of cans consumed (millions) | Proportion of soft drinks sold in | | Proportion of soft drinks sold in PET bottles (%) |
						Refillable glass bottles (%)	Nonrefillable glass bottles (%)	
1972	1.20	N.A.	21.0	0	885	N.A.	N.A.	0
1975	1.35	N.A.	25.0	0	1,160	N.A.	N.A.	0
1978	1.60	17	25.0	0	1,380	52	6	0
1984	1.90	20	30.0	33	1,930	35	7	8
1985	2.00	22	30.0	33	2,010	N.A.	N.A.	N.A.

Note: N.A. = not available.

Sources: Derived from *The Food and Beverage Container Market* (Commack, N.Y., Business Trend Analysts, 1983), pp. 57–68; Chase Econometrics, *Materials Competition in the Beverage Container Industry to 1995* (Bala Cynwyd, Pa., Chase Econometrics, 1986), ch. 12; Commodities Research Unit, *Aluminum Can Sheet Study* (London, Commodities Research Unit, 1986) pp. 119–122.

[a]In millions of kiloliters.

to the abandonment of the stubby bottle in favor of bottles specific to each company and brand, a strategy that has increased costs and diminished (but not eliminated) the relative advantage of glass. (This change owes to marketing considerations aiming to attract consumers and not to reasons related to production costs; in fact, packaging costs have increased. The change in strategy must be perceived as the breweries' adaptation to a much more competitive environment.)

The Canadian soft drink market is as large as the beer market, but its annual rate of growth is greater (4.7 percent). Moreover, the share of bulk sales has continuously increased and, in 1985, claimed 22 percent of the market—a percentage comparable to that of the American market (see table 7-9).

The glass bottle dominates the market for soft drink containers because of its advantage in production costs, ensured by the presence of a vast network of collection depots and by antilitter and deposit laws. However, this hold on the soft drink market is weaker (between 40 and 50 percent of total sales; see table 7-9) than in the beer market, a consequence of greater competition from other kinds of containers.

In Canada almost one-third of soft drinks are consumed from cans, three times more than for beer. Most metal cans are still made of steel. Aluminum's share was only 33 percent in 1985 (see table 7-9). This weakness is not surprising in light of the fact that Ontario, the most densely populated province, prohibited the aluminum soft drink can until September 1987. Now that this ban has been lifted, aluminum's share of the metal container market will probably surpass 50 percent. In British Columbia the aluminum soft drink can was introduced in 1983 and in most of the other provinces one year later. In Alberta the date of introduction was 1985; in Saskatchewan all cans are still prohibited.

Introduced in Canada in 1981 (three years later than in the United States), plastic bottles represent less than 10 percent of total soft drink sales (see table 7-9). In view of the PET bottle's advantages—it is light and durable and offers a competitively low cost per milliliter in its large-container size— one would have expected better results. It is worth noting that Ontario restricted PET bottles until December 1985.

Despite its late introduction in Canada, the aluminum can has been a success: 1.3 billion cans were sold in 1985. The steel can is again the big loser; it has been displaced from the beer can market and is in danger of losing the soft drink market as provincial laws defending its market share are abandoned.

Despite the breakthrough of aluminum cans and PET bottles, we do not believe that they will replace the glass bottle as quickly as in the United States. For Canadian consumers glass bottles are almost a part of the cultural environment. The vast network of collection depots for glass bottles will continue to benefit beer and soft drink bottlers even if the loss of the stubby beer bottle has somewhat diminished this advantage. The establishment of a recycling network for aluminum cans is in progress, but the effort is timid. Finally, in most Canadian provinces there is strong demand for environmental protection laws. The abolition or relaxing of antilitter and deposit laws is perceived by some provincial governments as political suicide.

Statistics on the Canadian food container market are too scattered to allow detailed comparisons with other countries. In general, what is available does not seem to contradict the trends observed in the United States, Western Europe, and Japan regarding the domination of three-piece tinplate steel cans. The hypothesis that Canadian data can be obtained by dividing American data by 10 seems more valid for the food container market than for the beverage container market.

CONCLUSION

This chapter has described the containers available to the food and beverage industries of the United States, Western Europe, Japan, and Canada; examined the evolution of their market shares; and, finally, evaluated the effects on the consumption of aluminum, steel, tin, and other materials.

In the beer market the United States has cut back on its use of returnable bottles, and despite mandatory deposit laws in nine states, the market share of the nonreturnable bottle still remains high. An even more important change has been the switch from steel to aluminum cans.

In the soft drink market, unpackaged sales have expanded and now constitute one-quarter of the U.S. market. Returnable bottles have suffered a decline, and their share is now about the same as that of nonreturnable bottles. Aluminum claims 93 percent of the metal can market, although its share of all soft drink sales is only 30 percent. Plastic bottle sales have risen dramatically since their introduction in 1978.

The effects of these developments on metal consumption are clear: a strong rise in the demand for aluminum (more than 1.2 million tons in 1987) coupled with a decrease in the demand for steel and tin. Using an apparent-determinants analysis to assess the causes of these trends, we have found that the rise in consumption of beer and soft drinks (caused in part by an increase in consumer disposable income) accounts for only a small part of the increase in aluminum consumption. The same is true for the sociodemographic trends in U.S. society and changes in consumer preferences that exert an influence on the evolution of unpackaged sales. The most important apparent determinants are those affecting intensity of use and, in particular, the material composition of products: namely, the proportion of shipments packaged in aluminum cans (the result of material substitution) and the decrease in the aluminum content of beer and soft drink cans (the result of material-saving technology). Demler (1980) has obtained similar results in his study of tin.

Table 7-10. Penetration of Cans in the Beverage Industry in the United States, Western Europe, Japan, and Canada, 1985–1988

(percent)

	Sales in cans		Share of aluminum cans in total cans	
	Beer	Soft drinks	Beer	Soft drinks
United States	63	31	99	93
Western Europe	6–13	15–30	35	35
Japan	17	30	91	31
Canada	12	30	100	33

Changes in the product composition of income and in income variables such as gross domestic product are less important determinants of the demand for aluminum and steel in the beverage industry.

The switch from steel to aluminum since the mid-1970s has been driven largely by total production costs (total filled costs plus warehousing, distribution, and handling costs). Initially favoring the steel can, these cost differences first narrowed and then turned to aluminum's advantage. Thinner can body stock and can recycling programs are major contributors. Mandatory deposit laws have had less impact; perhaps their effect is more indirect, as these laws may have favored recycling by helping to promote environmental objectives.

Finally, the situation is quite different in the U.S. food industry. The producers of three-piece tinplate cans are trying hard to defend this market from two-piece tin-free steel and aluminum cans and from containers made of plastic or composite products. There are two reasons for steel's continued dominance and aluminum's weakness in this market. First, food containers must be strong enough to hold their shape during high-pressure vacuum processing. Second, because the relative market size of canneries in the food market is small, the high capital cost of the new filling equipment cannot be spread over a large volume. Also, the volume is not sufficient to cover the one-time conversion costs.

Generalizations based on the U.S. experience are possible only in the case of the food industry. In the beverage industry, as table 7-10 indicates, penetration of cans in general and aluminum cans in particular varies greatly among countries.

The metal can has penetrated the soft drink markets of Canada, Japan, and major Western European countries as deeply as in the United States (30 percent), but this performance has not been repeated in the beer industry. Moreover, the steel can continues to dominate the beer market in Western Europe and the soft drink market in Japan, Canada, and Western Europe.

The difficulties encountered by the aluminum can in its struggle to replace the steel can and erode the share of glass bottles in Western Europe, Japan, and Canada are largely the result of higher total production costs (as defined earlier). This disadvantage persists in part because the recycling system remains far less developed than in the United States, where vast, efficient, closed networks of can collecting and recycling were established a number of years ago by producers of primary and secondary aluminum.

These findings have four important implications for the intensity of use and consumption of metal. First, the almost complete displacement of the steel can by the aluminum can has led to a drop in intensity of use of steel and tin on the American market. The decreases in aluminum's intensity of use over the last fifteen years cannot be attributed to the aluminum can. Indeed, without the rapid growth in the market for aluminum cans, the drop in intensity of use would have been greater. In the future the aluminum can cannot be expected to increase the intensity of aluminum use in the United States. It has already saturated the can market for beverages, and with competition from plastics and other materials, increases in market share are unlikely. This situation could be altered only if technological improvements make possible entry into the food can market. An intrusion of this kind would remove steel's last bastion in the metal can market.

Second, in Canada it is too early to assess the contribution of the aluminum can to the intensity of use of aluminum. Introduced in 1984, the aluminum can quickly conquered the beer market but has been slow to move into the soft drink market. The removal of the ban on the aluminum can may make a difference. The intensity of use of steel will probably fall, but if the PET bottle is as well accepted as in the United States, aluminum may not benefit.

Third, the success of the aluminum can in Japan during the 1970s contributed positively to aluminum's intensity of use, but during the 1980–1985 period its performance was rather disappointing. The share of total sales of soft drinks in metal containers dropped 10 percent between 1982 and 1985, and the share of the metal container market held by aluminum cans has stagnated at 30 percent since 1978. In the beer can market, aluminum's share held at around 90 percent. Consequently, during the first half of the 1980s, the aluminum can did not greatly stimulate this metal's intensity of use in Japan. This situation, however, may now be changing, as the demand for cans has been increasing by 25 percent annually since 1987 (Shroeder, 1989, p. 106).

Fourth, it is difficult to draw general conclusions with regard to the major Western European countries. Metal containers claim a weak share in sales of beer and soft drinks. While the aluminum can has increased the intensity of use of aluminum in the United Kingdom, Sweden, Austria, Italy, and Greece, nowhere in Europe does it appear that the intensity of use of steel increased because of the success of tinplate and tin-free steel cans.

These observations suggest that the demand for tinplate for metal cans will continue to decline during the next few years, and the demand for tin-free steel will experience greater stability. The growth in demand for aluminum will be weak for beer and soft drink containers and moderate for food containers. The potential demand for aluminum remains greater in industrialized countries other than the United States, but competition from the glass bottle, the plastic container, and the steel can may keep this potential from being realized.

We suggest this scenario even though the history of the food and beverage container industries calls for caution in predicting the future. This is particularly true in the U.S. beverage can industry, where the difference in the total production costs of an aluminum and steel can remains small. The installation of interchangeable production lines in recent years within the United States (Paprock, 1989a, p. 1; 1989b, p. 1) now allows many can makers to switch quickly from aluminum to steel or from steel to aluminum. This raises the possibility that the switch from steel to aluminum may be halted and a brighter future for steel may be envisioned, particularly if the price of aluminum can stock continues to rise as it did in 1988 and during the first half of 1989.

ACKNOWLEDGMENTS

The author is grateful to Phillip C. F. Crowson, Frederick R. Demler, Hans H. Landsberg, Bruce C. Netschert, and four anonymous referees. Their comments and suggestions contributed markedly to improving this chapter. Any remaining errors are, of course, my own.

REFERENCES

Business Trend Analysts. 1983. *The Food and Beverage Market* (Commack, N.Y., Business Trend Analysts).

_____. 1984. *The U.S. Soft Drink Market* (Commack, N.Y., Business Trend Analysts).

Cavanagh, J. 1982. "Modest Growth Rates to Prompt Major Savings," pp. 252–266 in Keller Publishing, *Beverage World 1882–1982, 100-Year History/Future Probe* (East Stroudsburg, Pa., Keller Publishing).

Chase Econometrics. 1986. *Materials Competition in the Beverage Container Industry to 1995* (Bala Cynwyd, Pa., Chase Econometrics).

Commodity Research Bureau. 1986. *Commodity Year Book* (New York, Commodity Research Bureau).

Commodities Research Unit, *Aluminum Can Sheet Study* (London, Commodities Research Unit) pp. 119–122.

Corplan Associates. 1966. *A Study of the Soft Drink Industry, 1965–1970* (Washington, D.C., American Bottlers of Carbonated Beverages).

Demler, Frederick R. 1980. "The Nature of Tin Substitution in the Beverage Container Industries," Ph.D. thesis, Pennsylvania State University.

_____. 1983. "Beverage Containers," pp. 15–35 in John E. Tilton, ed., *Materials Substitution: Lessons from Tin-Using Industries* (Washington, D.C., Resources for the Future).

International Tin Council. 1981. *Study on Consumption: European Economic Community, Tin in Tinplate* (London, International Tin Council).

———. 1983. *Study on Consumption: United States of America, Tin in Tinplate* (London, International Tin Council).

———. 1984. *Study on Consumption: Japan, Tin in Tinplate* (London International Tin Council).

Keller Publishing. *Beverage World* (East Stroudsburg, Pa., various issues).

Magazines for Industry. *Beverage Industry* (Duluth, Minn., Magazines for Industry, various issues).

McBride, J. R. 1984. "Recycling in Japan: Voluntary Efforts Recover 40% of Cans," *Modern Metals* vol. 39 (January) pp. 84–88.

Metal Bulletin Monthly (London, Metal Bulletin Ltd.).

Papcock, J. 1989a. "Aluminum May Lose Some Turf," *American Metal Market* vol. 97, no. 43 (March) p. 1.

———. 1989b. "Steel Cans Vie for Beer Market," *American Metal Market* vol. 97, no. 44 (March) p. 1.

Rathje, W. 1986. "A Clash of Good Intentions," *The Atlantic* (June) pp. 16–18.

Schroeder, M. 1989. "Has Aluminum Climbed Off Its Roller Coaster?" *Business Week* (May 1) p. 106.

Shida, O. 1981. *Packaging Japan* vol. 2, no. 6, pp. 54–64.

Standard & Poor's. 1982. *Containers: Basic Analysis* vol. 50, no. 34 (August 26) p. 131.

U.S. Department of Commerce. 1989. *U.S. Industrial Outlook* (Washington, D.C., U.S. Government Printing Office) p. 7-1.

Von Lewinski, A., and A. H. Wirtz. 1987. "European Can Recycling Proves Feasible—At a Price," *Metal Bulletin Monthly* (February) pp. 14–15.

Weinberg, R. S. 1971. "The Effects of Convenience Packaging on the Malt Beverage Industry 1947-1969," in the U.S. Brewers' Association, *Reference Source Book* (Washington, D.C., U.S. Brewers' Association).

Wirtz, A. 1988. "Recycling: The Key to the Growth of the Aluminum Beverage Can in Europe," pp. 47–49 in *Proceedings of the 45th Annual World Magnesium Conference* (Dayton, Ohio, International Magnesium Association).

8

The Outlook for World Metal Demand

JOHN E. TILTON

The first seven chapters in this book, concentrating on the past, sought answers to two important and perplexing questions initially raised in chapter 1. The first is why—even after controlling for economic size—such large differences in metal consumption have arisen among the three groups of countries studied here—OECD countries, the developing countries, and the centrally planned economies, as well as among individual countries within these groups. A second major area of inquiry has been why world metal demand has grown so much more slowly, and in some cases even stagnated, since the early 1970s. This final chapter, drawing on findings presented in previous chapters, focuses on the future of world metal demand. It considers where the major metal markets of tomorrow are likely to be and assesses the extent to which the developing countries or possibly the centrally planned economies will replace the OECD countries as the world's major metal consumers. It also addresses the related matters of the pace of future growth in metal demand and the factors that will govern this growth.

GEOGRAPHIC SHIFTS IN METAL MARKETS

In the early years after World War II, the OECD countries, and in particular the United States, accounted for the preponderant share of world metal consumption. Little industry existed in the developing countries, and war had shattered the economies of the Soviet Union, China, and the East European countries. Over the intervening decades a persistent shift in consumption has taken place, with the developing and centrally planned countries accounting for a growing share. This shift is due in part to faster economic growth and in part to heightened trends in intensity of use in these country groups (see tables 1-1 and 1-2 and figures 1-2 and 1-3 in chapter 1).

Important market shifts have also occurred within country groups. Among OECD countries the Federal Republic of Germany and especially Japan have expanded their share of the OECD market at the expense of the United States and the United Kingdom. Among the developing countries, nations such as South Korea that are emphasizing industrialization and liberal trade policies have become increasingly important metal markets. Within the centrally planned economies, metal consumption grew faster in the East European countries than in the Soviet Union during the 1960s and early 1970s, whereas the reverse has been the case in more recent years.

These shifts in consumption have encouraged the belief that the developing countries as a group and certain of these countries in particular could become the engine for the rapid growth in world metal demand that the OECD countries had been during the 1950s and 1960s. Yet, a careful examination of past trends also indicates that the shift toward a larger share of world metal consumption by the developing countries, although important and persistent, has been so gradual that many years would pass before the developing countries replaced the OECD countries as the world's principal market for metals if the shift continued at the present pace. Despite changes in recent years these countries still consume less than 20 percent of the world's production of major metals.

While the shift toward greater consumption by the developing countries could accelerate, the available evidence suggests that this is unlikely. Material substitution and new resource-saving technology are exerting downward pressure on the intensity of metal use (that is, on the tons of metal consumed per million dollars of real gross domestic product [GDP]) in these countries as elsewhere, and all countries have strong incentives to leapfrog obsolete techniques in favor of more modern and material-efficient technologies.

It is true that intensity of metal use among the developing countries has generally continued to rise, in marked contrast to its pervasive declines in the OECD and centrally planned countries. Indeed, were this not so, the shift toward a greater share of world metal consumption by the developing countries would probably have ceased in the early 1980s as the economic growth of these nations approximated the world average (see table 1-2). As Radetzki points out in chapter 4, however, the rising trends in intensity of use (IU) are the result of intersectoral shifts and, in particular, of the growth in manufacturing and gross domestic investment (GDI) as a percentage of GDP. Their continued expansion cannot be taken for granted, as the share of GDP already devoted to GDI is quite high in the developing countries as compared either to that of earlier periods or to that of the industrialized countries.

It is possible that economic growth in the developing countries will accelerate in the years ahead, given the modest growth rates of recent years, the slow but steady progress on the international debt problem, and the growing reliance on private incentives and markets in place of government direction in many developing countries. Even if that happens, however, the stimulus to metal consumption may well be partially or totally offset by less vigorous trends in intensity of use.

If the developing countries do not replace the OECD nations as the dominant world market for metals over the next decade, perhaps the centrally planned economies will. The inefficiencies of central planning are now widely recognized within these countries themselves, and economic reforms and restructuring are being discussed and introduced. If successful, these policies could greatly stimulate economic growth.

Moreover, Czechoslovakia, the German Democratic Republic, and other resource-deficient East European countries have long relied on the Soviet Union to meet many of their mineral needs. In recent years, however, the depletion of mineral deposits in the Soviet Union, particularly those west of the Ural Mountains, in combination with other production problems, has strained the ability of the Soviet Union to supply both its own needs and those of its allies. As a result, a surge in metal demand within the centrally planned countries could conceivably open new market possibilities for producers elsewhere. (See studies in Tilton [1986] on the changing supply conditions in the centrally planned countries and the future prospects for East–West mineral trade.)

The reforms needed to produce faster growth in these countries are, however, also certain to reduce intensity of metal use. As Dobozi points out in chapter 5, despite the efforts of the centrally planned countries in recent years to reduce IU, it remains unusually high compared with that of either the OECD or the developing countries. Economic incentives under central planning have emphasized output rather than profitable or efficient production. Meaningful economic reforms would improve productivity throughout the economies of these nations, and that would include the efficiency with which they consume metals. Hence, the stimulating effects on metal consumption of more rapid economic growth induced by reform and restructuring would be partially or totally offset by a reduction in intensity of use; comparisons with other country groups suggest that such a reduction could be substantial.

The possibility of reduced IU coupled with the fact that the consumption of most major metals in the centrally planned economies has in recent years been less than one-half that of the OECD countries (see figure 1-2), indicates that these countries are not likely in the near future to become the world's principal market for metals. A possible exception is steel, the one major metal whose market in the centrally planned countries approaches that of the

OECD countries. However, of the six major metals, which are steel, aluminum, copper, lead, zinc, and nickel, the use of steel in the centrally planned countries appears to be the most profligate. Because the intensity of use of steel is more than double that of the OECD countries, the opportunities for meaningful reform to reduce steel consumption in these countries appear substantial.

For these reasons the OECD countries are expected to remain the dominant market for metals at least for the rest of the twentieth century and possibly well into the twenty-first. The long erosion of the market share of the OECD countries, which goes back to the years right after World War II, will also probably continue, although at a gradual pace similar to the past. As a result, demand will expand faster in the developing and centrally planned countries, and much of the new growth in the world metal market will probably be concentrated in these countries.

LONG-RUN TRENDS IN DEMAND

During the 1950s and 1960s, world demand for all the major metals grew briskly. Then in the 1970s the growth of demand slowed in what appear to be two steplike reductions: the first about 1973, at the time of the first oil shock, and the second at the end of the decade, at the time of the second oil shock and as the first awareness of the international debt crisis was dawning. World metal consumption consequently grew slowly in the 1980s.

Underlying these global trends, one finds a myriad of complex forces at work. Some, such as higher world oil prices and the macroeconomic policies they engendered, date back only to the 1970s. Others, however, go back much further, and reveal that the seeds of the declines were planted some time ago. Their slow germination over many years cautions against exaggerating the discrete nature of the declines. Although the years 1973 and 1979 provide convenient turning points for analysis, they do not reflect abrupt discontinuities in the trends in metal consumption.

The initial decline was caused largely by the OECD countries, in which both economic growth and intensity of use trends deteriorated in the early 1970s. That decline was reinforced to some extent by slower growth of metal demand in the centrally planned countries. The developing countries contributed mostly to the second decline. In part because of substantial borrowing from abroad, they managed to maintain rapid economic growth during the 1970s, and their intensity of use of metals except for nickel increased. All this changed toward the end of the decade when economic growth stalled in the developing countries as a result of the international debt crisis and many other difficulties. Coupled with further declines in both economic growth and intensity of use in the OECD and centrally planned countries, the change in the developing countries led to the virtual stagnation in world metal demand during the early and middle 1980s.

This look at past trends leads naturally to questions about the future. Will the current sluggishness continue? Will another steplike reduction in growth occur, causing world metal consumption to actually fall? Or will world metal demand once again turn upward, perhaps even recapturing the brisk rates of growth of the 1950s and 1960s? While there are no certain answers to such questions, the insights of earlier chapters are helpful in allowing us to make some informed assessments.

Intensity of Use

In the future as in the past, resource-saving technology will relentlessly whittle away at material markets. For the minor metals whose consumption is concentrated in one or several major end uses, such technology can dramatically reduce demand within a few years. For the major metals with many end uses, however, the impact is more gradual. In either case the downward pressure on intensity of use from resource-saving technology can be offset or accentuated by material substitution. The latter by its very nature stimulates demand for one material while reducing demand for another.

In recent years many metals have been on the defensive in the competitive battle with polymers, advanced ceramics, composites, and other nonmetallic materials. Substitution, on balance, has presumably accentuated the downward pressure on intensity of use. This, however, need not be the case. In chapter 6, Eggert highlights the use of high-strength, low-alloy steels for traditional carbon steel in automobiles, a substitution that is stimulating the intensity of use of the former. As described by Nappi in chapter 7, the successful penetration of aluminum in the U.S. beverage container market at the expense of steel, tin, and glass is another example of substitution that fosters metal demand and intensity of use.

A hypothetical portrayal of the effects of resource-saving technology and material substitution on the intensity of use of a particular material over time is shown in figure 8-1. New materials, at least those destined to be important, first enter a growth stage during which they enjoy rising intensity of use. At this stage their developing technology is permitting their substitution for other materials in a number of existing products as well as their use in entirely new applications made possible by their special properties. Expanding uses more than offset the downward pressure on intensity of use exerted by new resource-saving technology. Aluminum and nickel alloys through the early 1970s are examples of materials in this stage of the life cycle.

As materials in the growth stage capture an increasing number of end uses, they face mounting competition, particularly from new materials, for their established markets. Substitution at this point can cut both ways, increasing demand in some cases and reducing it in others. Materials then move into the mature stage, when the effects of material substitution on demand roughly cancel out. Intensity of use declines gradually during this stage as a result of

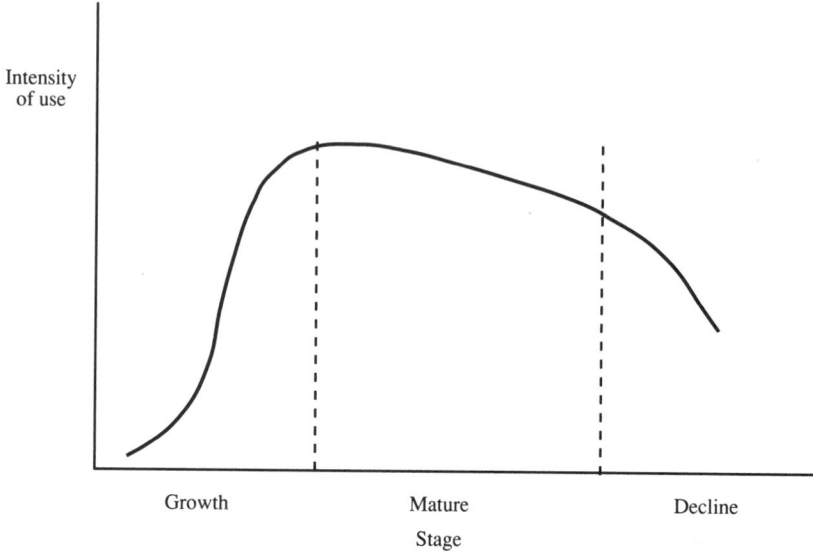

Figure 8-1. Hypothetical life cycle for major materials.

new, resource-saving technology. Consumption may continue to rise, stagnate, or decline, depending on the growth of the economy. When the effects of substitution on balance become negative, materials enter the stage of decline, and intensity of use can fall rapidly, as figure 8-1 illustrates.

Humphreys (1982) has shown, however, that material life cycles such as that shown in figure 8-1 are not inevitable. Unlike human beings, mature and even declining materials can reverse their aging process and return to the growth stage. Alternatively, they can pass quickly from youth to old age. Minor metals are particularly prone to such abrupt changes, since the gain or loss of one important market can greatly affect intensity of use. Major metals are less susceptible to dramatic change, as the gain or loss of even several end uses is less likely to have such a large effect on overall demand. Consequently, for the mature major metals, which now include all the metals under review, changes in the material composition of products (which reflect the combined effects of resource-saving technology and material substitution) are expected gradually to reduce intensity of use over the foreseeable future.

Shifts in the product composition of income caused by the rise of computers and other high-technology products within the manufacturing sector are expected to reinforce this tendency. This important intrasectoral shift, which has been most apparent and most thoroughly documented in the United States, is expected in the future to characterize not only other OECD countries but to some extent the developing and centrally planned countries as well. Per dollar of value added, high-technology products generally require far less of the major metals than do the more traditional manufacturing products.

Intersectoral shifts may also contribute to the decline in intensity of metal use, although this is less certain for several reasons. Such shifts—and in particular the rise of the service sector—have often been cited as the leading cause of falling intensity of use. Yet, the importance of the rise of the service sector can easily be exaggerated by focusing on its rapidly growing work force. In contrast, the service sector's contribution to total GDP, which is what affects intensity of use, has grown more modestly.

Moreover, there is some evidence to suggest that the simultaneous growth of other, more metal-intensive sectors may offset the depressing effect of the rise in services. As I note in chapter 3, according to Roberts (1985, 1986), intersectoral shifts have in the past actually increased the intensity of copper use in the United States, as the growth in consumer durables has more than neutralized the growth in services.

In the future the capital equipment and construction sectors, which also have relatively metal-intensive output, could similarly counter the effect of expanding services. With the unexpected decline in world economic growth in the early 1970s and the subsequent rise in excess production capacity, these sectors entered a prolonged period of stagnation. Since the late 1980s, however, mounting evidence suggests that less and less of this excess capacity remains and that major investments in new plants and equipment are needed now or will be soon, even if it is assumed that the modest rates of economic growth since 1973 will persist into the future.

There are also growing signs of infrastructure needs, even in the more-developed OECD countries. In the United States, which has an extensive and well-developed infrastructure, there is widespread concern over the need to replace antiquated bridges, to modernize water and sewer works, and to reconstruct large parts of the highway network. In Japan and other countries where per capita incomes have risen rapidly, higher living standards are producing a strong demand for better infrastructure.

For such reasons the future impact of intersectoral shifts is difficult to predict. It could reinforce the downward pressure on intensity of use exerted by other sources, or alternatively it could stimulate intensity of use. Even in the latter case, however, intensity of use for the major metals considered here is expected to decline over the next decade or two, as any upward pressure that intersectoral shifts might exert is not likely to offset entirely the combined effects of new, resource-saving technology, material substitution, and the growing contribution of high-technology products within the manufacturing sector.

World Economic Growth

World economic growth is the other variable that, along with trends in intensity of use, will determine the future course of metal demand. Confusion has arisen in recent years over the relationship between material needs and economic growth. In particular, as pointed out in chapter 1, some scholars have suggested that during the 1980s the demand for primary products, at least in the developed countries, became uncoupled from the industrial economy; that economic growth no longer depends on ever-increasing supplies of metals and other materials; and in turn that economic growth does not imply rising demand for the major metals.

Indeed, tables 1-1 and 1-2 in the first chapter appear to provide some empirical support for such beliefs. Worldwide, the consumption of steel and lead has stagnated since 1979 and the growth in consumption of the other metals has been sluggish, whereas the world economy has expanded at an average annual rate of almost 3 percent. The situation in the OECD countries is even more pronounced: GDP has increased at an average annual rate of over 2 percent, while the consumption of steel, copper, lead, and zinc has leveled off or declined.

It is easy, however, to misinterpret such figures. They clearly demonstrate that economic growth can occur without an increase in metal consumption, but this does not mean that the link or the relationship between these two variables of economic growth and metal consumption has been severed or no longer exists.

As noted earlier and as table 1-2 shows, intensity of use of metals for the world as a whole has been declining since 1979, on average between 1.0 percent (for nickel) and 2.7 percent (for steel) annually. If similar declines are experienced in the future, world metal consumption will fall if economic growth is 1.0 percent or less; it will experience little or no change if economic growth is between 1.0 and 2.7 percent; and it will rise if economic growth is above 2.7 percent. Of course, the average annual decline in intensity of use may become larger or smaller (although as noted earlier, it is expected to continue to decline). This, however, would simply raise or lower the level of economic growth required to keep metal consumption stable or rising.

Thus, economic growth and metal demand are linked, but the relationship is not simply that a rise or fall in the economy produces a corresponding rise or fall in metal demand. Rather, it is perhaps best expressed in terms of rates of growth for both the economy and metal consumption. As figure 8-2 illustrates, when the economy is growing slowly, metal consumption is stagnant or falling; however, when the economy is growing rapidly, metal consumption is also expanding.

Just where the curve, illustrated in the figure, will intersect the horizontal axis—that is, the point where growth in metal consumption is zero—depends on trends in intensity of use, which vary from one metal to another. In the case of steel, whose intensity of use worldwide has been declining on average by 2.7 percent annually since 1979, the economy must grow by this percentage to keep consumption constant. For nickel the intersection occurs closer to the origin, at the point where the economy is growing at 1.0 percent. The

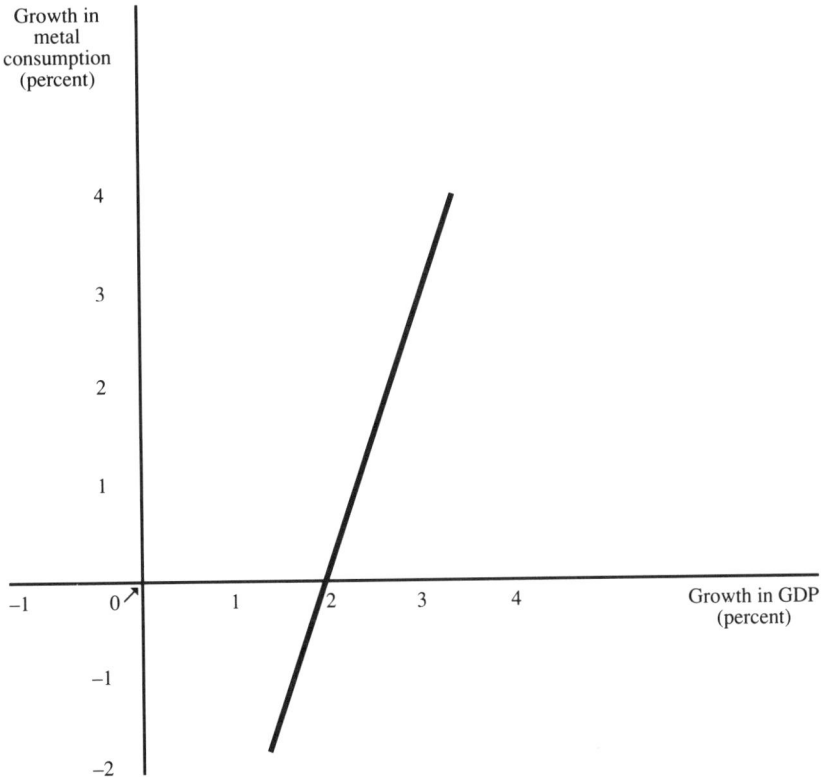

Figure 8-2. Postulated relationship between economic growth and metal consumption.

point of intersection on the horizontal axis may also shift over time with changes in trends in intensity of use. During the 1960s, for example, when world intensities of use for nickel and aluminum were rising, the intersection lay to the left of the vertical axis, indicating that the economy actually had to decline before metal consumption ceased to grow.

If economic growth and intensity of use trends were independent so that a change in one had no effect on the other, the curve shown in figure 8-2 would rise with a slope of 45 degrees, and a 1 percent increase in economic growth would produce a 1 percent increase in metal consumption. In fact, faster economic growth is likely to foster an increase in intensity of use, as rapidly expanding economies tend to devote a higher share of their total income to investment. As a result, the construction and capital equipment sectors are likely to constitute a larger portion of GDP than would otherwise be the case. For this reason the curve in figure 8-2 is shown with a slope of more than 45 degrees.

The implication, of course, is that rapid economic growth stimulates metal consumption directly, and also indirectly by raising intensity of use. Such a favorable situation from the point of view of metal producers existed during the 1950s and 1960s, the golden age of metal demand growth, when the world economy was expanding rapidly.

Growth during this period was unusually high, however, as the major industrialized nations both among the OECD and the centrally planned countries recovered from the Great Depression and World War II. Recent growth rates, although considered abnormally low by many, are really more typical of the twentieth century. This, together with the fact that the growth opportunities associated with shifting manpower out of agriculture and with catching up with the United States have largely been exploited, suggests that the rapid growth of the earlier postwar period will not soon return to the OECD countries.

In the less developed countries, the prospects for faster growth are more favorable, in part because their economies have suffered from such low growth rates since 1979. Furthermore, they still enjoy many opportunities for borrowing technology from the more industrialized countries. Yet, even a doubling of growth in these countries would not have a great effect on world metal demand for many years, as they still constitute such a small part of the world economy.

The centrally planned economies could also enjoy a surge in economic growth over the next decade or two if meaningful economic reforms take place, but such reforms will not be easy to carry out for a host of reasons. And even if they are successfully implemented, the stimulation to metal consumption from more rapid economic growth will largely be offset by greater efficiency in the use of metals and a decline in intensity of use.

Metal Demand

The macroeconomic scene, like changing trends in intensity of metal use, thus holds little promise of a return to the golden age of growth in world metal demand. It is important to understand, however, both what this means and what it does not mean.

What it means is that there is less need now for new investments in mines and metal-processing facilities than there was in the 1950s and 1960s. Expanding capacity at the old rates, which appears to have occurred during the latter half of the 1970s, is a sure formula for keeping world metal markets in a perpetual state of depression, as most mineral-producing companies have come to realize. It also represents a misallocation of scarce capital that from the point of view of the investor and society would be better invested elsewhere.

The fact that there is unlikely to be a return to earlier levels of metal demand growth also means that shifts in the comparative advantage of metal mining and processing will be more difficult to adjust to. Countries losing competitiveness will find their producers suffering more with slower demand growth. Countries gaining comparative advantage will find the shift of production capacity in their favor occurring much more slowly.

While the growth of metal demand characteristic of the fifties through the early seventies is not expected to be repeated, this does not mean that the era of materials, or even the era of metals, is over. Consumption of the metals whose growth has stagnated remains at or near historical highs, and for those whose growth has only slowed, consumption continues to rise.

Metal consumption over the next decade or two may decline slowly, remain stable, or rise modestly, depending on whether world economic growth is sufficient to offset the gradual but persistent decline anticipated in intensity of use. For most major metals we expect consumption to rise modestly.

SHORTAGES AND GLUTS IN METAL MARKETS

The unlikely return of the golden age of metal demand growth does not condemn the mineral markets to a future of perpetual oversupply, nor does it rule out the possibility of metal shortages. Metal markets are well known for their short-run instability, the result of sharp swings in demand over the business cycle caused by the concentration of metal use in four highly volatile end-use sectors—construction, capital equipment, consumer durables, and transportation. In most metal industries this instability causes pronounced swings in both prices and output—up when the economy is booming and down when it is depressed. Shortages occur during a boom period, because consumers cannot satisfy their demand except by paying unusually high prices. Where metal prices are controlled by the major producing firms or governments, instability takes the form of sharp fluctuations in output. In addition, during economic booms actual physical shortages may arise, because the metal demanded at the prescribed price exceeds the available supply. (For more on the causes and consequences of cyclical instability in the metal markets, see Tilton [1977, chapter 5] and Vogely and Tilton [1981].)

For over a decade following the mid-1970s and the slowdown in metal demand growth at that time, the huge overhang of excess capacity disrupted the traditional feast-or-famine swings typical of metal markets. Capacity was more than sufficient to satisfy metal demand at relatively low prices even during the booms of the business cycle. Consumers and others began to wonder if shortages were a thing of the past.

The surge in metal prices over the last several years has shaken this complacent view. Concerns over the future adequacy of metal supplies are rising, and fears of possible shortages are returning. In certain respects these concerns are valid and realistic. Much if not all of the overhang of excess capacity that has buffered metal markets from shortages over the last fifteen years may now be gone. Once this process is completed, the traditional pattern of cyclical instability will return, and metal prices will rise sharply during economic expansions or else physical shortages will occur.

Such shortages could raise broader concerns about the adequacy of mineral supplies and the world resource base over the long run. Shortages caused by the disappearance of excess capacity and the return of cyclical instability, however, will be temporary, lasting at most only several years until either the economy subsides or new capacity is built. Long-run or permanent scarcity, if it occurs, will come about for an entirely different reason—namely, the rising costs incurred in exploiting poorer-quality mineral deposits. On the basis of known information about existing deposits, mineral depletion does not appear to pose a significant threat over the next decade or two. Even over the longer term, new technology may continue, as in the past, to offset any upward pressure that depletion exerts on metal prices. (For more on the long-run threat of mineral depletion, see Fisher [1981, chapters 2 and 8]; Smith [1979]; Tilton [1977, chapter 2]; and Tilton and Skinner [1988].)

Shortages and higher metal prices may also foster another erroneous belief: that the strong exponential growth in world metal demand that characterized the 1950s and 1960s is returning. As noted earlier, and indeed throughout this volume, the long-run prospects for world economic growth and intensity of use trends simply do not justify this conclusion. When they occur, shortages and higher prices will reflect temporary or cyclical conditions, not a significant rise in secular metal demand.

This does not, however, imply the demise or even the decline of metal mining and processing. For most major metals, demand is expected to remain at or near historic highs and even to grow modestly. The golden age of growth may be gone, but the era of metals and materials is still very much with us.

REFERENCES

Fisher, Anthony C. 1981. *Resource and Environmental Economics* (Cambridge, England, Cambridge University Press).

Humphreys, David. 1982. "A Mineral Commodity Life Cycle? Relationships Between Production, Price and Economic Resources," *Resources Policy* vol. 8, no. 3 (September) pp. 215–229.

Roberts, Mark. 1985. "Theory and Practice of the Intensity of Use Method of Mineral Consumption Forecasting" (Ph.D. dissertation, University of Arizona).

_____. 1986. "An Aggregate Model of Long Term Mineral Requirements," *Materials and Society* vol. 10, no. 3, pp. 303–328.

Smith, V. Kerry, ed. 1979. *Scarcity and Growth Reconsidered* (Baltimore, Md., Johns Hopkins University Press for Resources for the Future).

Tilton, John E. 1977. *The Future of Nonfuel Minerals* (Washington, D.C., Brookings Institution).

_____, ed. 1986. *East-West Mineral Trade: Trends and Prospects* vol. 12, no. 3, special issue of *Resources Policy.*

_____, and Brian J. Skinner. 1987. "The Meaning of Resources," pp. 13–27 in Digby J. McLaren and Brian J. Skinner, eds., *Resources and World Development* (New York, Wiley).

_____, and William A. Vogely, eds. 1981. *Market Instability in the Metal Industries* vol. 5, no. 3, special issue of *Materials and Society.*

STATISTICAL APPENDIX

Acronyms

CMEA-6 Six countries in the Council for Mutual Economic Assistance: Bulgaria, Czechoslovakia, East Germany, Hungary, Poland, Romania

CMEA-7 CMEA-6 plus the USSR

CPE Centrally planned economies: Albania, CMEA-6 countries, China, Cuba, North Korea, North Vietnam, USSR, and other countries in Eastern Europe and Eastern Asia

DDR Deutsche Demokratische Republik (East Germany)

EEC-9 Nine countries in the European Economic Community: Belgium-Luxembourg, Denmark, Federal Republic of Germany, France, Greece, Ireland, Italy, The Netherlands, United Kingdom

FRG Federal Republic of Germany (West Germany)

LDC Less developed countries: All countries except OECD and CPE

OECD Organisation for Economic Co-operation and Development: Australia, Austria, Belgium, Canada, Denmark, Federal Republic of Germany, Finland, France, Greece, Iceland, Ireland, Italy, Japan, Luxembourg, The Netherlands, New Zealand, Norway, Portugal, Spain, Sweden, Switzerland, Turkey, United Kingdom, United States

Acknowledgment

Wendy Cropf Bailey, Denise M. Emmons, Kee Hyung Hwang, Phillip F. Roan III, Cheryl Womble Silverman, Daniel H. Silverman, and Karen E. Tramm, who served as research assistants for this volume, helped compile the statistical appendix.

Part A. Macroeconomic Data

Table A-1. Gross Domestic Product (GDP), 1960–1987 (millions of constant 1980 U.S. dollars)[1]

	1960	1961	1962	1963	1964	1965	1966	1967
A. World	5,116,101	5,334,495	5,592,204	5,848,249	6,266,268	6,613,094	6,966,078	7,229,432
B. OECD[2]								
1. Total	3,474,907	3,643,718	3,829,658	4,017,098	4,271,569	4,493,214	4,727,781	4,908,335
2. United States	1,375,585	1,410,838	1,489,013	1,549,192	1,630,908	1,730,028	1,830,917	1,881,510
3. Japan	247,633	283,686	303,701	335,604	379,941	399,443	441,766	487,612
4. EEC-9[3]	1,350,941	1,419,530	1,479,844	1,540,944	1,632,951	1,702,475	1,761,504	1,816,092
5. United Kingdom	338,593	349,699	353,067	366,930	386,182	395,191	403,237	413,674
6. France	266,808	281,520	300,335	316,336	336,968	353,087	371,491	388,900
7. FRG	392,150	412,183	430,386	443,192	472,921	499,540	512,072	511,158
C. LDC[4]								
1. Total	635,966	667,319	708,199	764,761	823,374	868,575	906,464	946,350
2. Brazil	60,211	66,399	69,856	70,469	72,922	75,152	78,274	82,121
3. India	79,465	82,759	85,216	90,365	97,327	93,612	93,290	101,101
4. Korea	12,629	13,398	13,683	14,934	16,379	17,318	19,428	20,573
D. CPE[5,6]								
1. Total	1,005,228	1,023,458	1,054,346	1,066,391	1,171,326	1,251,305	1,331,833	1,374,748
2. USSR	616,019	650,578	674,974	667,820	740,946	786,662	827,254	864,481
3. E. Europe (CMEA-6)[6]	277,033	293,020	304,766	315,954	334,171	352,133	372,803	388,157
4. China	112,176	79,860	74,606	82,617	96,208	112,510	131,776	122,109
5. CMEA-7[7]	893,052	943,598	979,740	983,774	1,075,117	1,138,795	1,200,057	1,252,638

See notes at end of table A-1 on page 274.

(continued)

Table A-1 (continued)

	1968	1969	1970	1971	1972	1973	1974	1975	1976	1977
A. World	7,629,609	8,060,698	8,458,863	8,802,363	9,236,700	9,836,334	10,050,058	10,141,104	10,612,459	11,072,880
B. OECD[2]										
1. Total	5,175,533	5,458,771	5,651,393	5,856,766	6,169,876	6,542,647	6,591,458	6,574,001	6,876,363	7,148,426
2. United States	1,957,620	2,013,080	2,007,327	2,068,688	2,188,458	2,312,358	2,292,002	2,274,745	2,382,125	2,512,957
3. Japan	548,953	615,247	673,115	701,576	760,386	820,274	810,288	831,355	871,126	917,198
4. EEC-9[3]	1,911,939	2,023,441	2,124,418	2,198,708	2,286,435	2,422,374	2,457,442	2,428,753	2,549,903	2,610,638
5. United Kingdom	430,815	437,186	446,902	458,929	469,124	504,373	499,335	496,417	514,327	520,803
6. France	405,487	433,797	458,708	483,501	512,046	539,477	556,944	557,940	586,837	604,714
7. FRG	543,356	585,892	620,927	640,959	664,377	696,850	700,601	687,703	723,195	745,148
C. LDC[4]										
1. Total	1,018,444	1,110,865	1,199,672	1,262,386	1,335,803	1,446,395	1,541,330	1,591,209	1,696,849	1,812,736
2. Brazil	91,487	100,407	109,328	122,485	136,088	154,542	169,539	178,738	196,132	207,394
3. India	104,611	111,281	117,784	120,514	119,651	123,948	124,144	136,247	137,855	149,244
4. Korea	22,907	26,078	28,362	30,970	32,811	37,544	40,514	43,571	49,104	54,414
D. CPE[5,6]										
1. Total	1,435,632	1,491,062	1,607,798	1,683,211	1,731,021	1,847,292	1,917,270	1,975,894	2,039,247	2,111,718
2. USSR	917,300	943,627	1,015,720	1,055,333	1,075,596	1,153,791	1,198,443	1,218,697	1,276,584	1,317,180
3. E. Europe (CMEA-6)[6]	404,213	411,381	424,227	448,319	470,579	493,173	516,383	538,011	555,313	570,893
4. China	114,119	136,055	167,850	179,559	184,846	200,327	202,443	219,186	207,350	223,645
5. CMEA-7[7]	1,321,513	1,355,008	1,439,947	1,503,652	1,546,175	1,646,964	1,714,826	1,756,708	1,831,897	1,888,073

Table A-1 (continued)

	1978	1979	1980	1981	1982	1983	1984	1985	1986	1987
A. World	11,497,168	11,873,299	12,049,782	12,275,004	12,307,918	12,587,186	13,122,706	13,488,016	13,993,244	14,528,249
B. OECD[2]										
1. Total	7,425,560	7,671,957	7,770,062	7,921,770	7,881,253	8,051,694	8,420,065	8,667,098	8,902,105	9,186,771
2. United States	2,631,843	2,699,988	2,688,188	2,779,785	2,697,038	2,776,392	2,975,223	3,060,183	3,144,620	3,255,049
3. Japan	963,979	1,014,006	1,059,060	1,099,940	1,131,161	1,166,814	1,225,237	1,280,588	1,312,219	1,368,761
4. EEC-9[3]	2,695,879	2,786,969	2,818,265	2,812,907	2,822,626	2,856,603	2,919,294	2,993,391	3,073,299	3,140,395
5. United Kingdom	537,995	545,425	533,129	526,865	531,969	551,921	563,753	584,864	598,346	625,439
6. France	627,163	648,850	655,180	658,228	670,419	674,991	683,959	691,755	706,420	720,233
7. FRG	769,115	803,417	818,785	819,060	811,742	819,883	841,013	866,077	887,556	904,590
C. LDC[4]										
1. Total	1,871,191	1,966,818	2,009,266	2,049,573	2,072,260	2,082,548	2,139,005	2,167,555	2,323,681	2,414,305
2. Brazil	217,763	231,701	248,370	244,524	246,865	239,004	249,759	267,749	294,700	310,631
3. India	159,161	150,944	161,182	170,526	175,385	188,813	197,314	211,563	222,184	227,741
4. Korea	59,926	64,319	62,419	67,042	70,849	78,600	85,397	89,796	100,473	111,615
D. CPE[5,6]										
1. Total	2,200,417	2,234,524	2,270,453	2,303,661	2,354,405	2,452,944	2,563,636	2,653,363	2,767,458	2,927,174
2. USSR	1,361,833	1,373,000	1,393,000	1,418,000	1,440,000	1,497,893	1,541,366	1,595,314	1,660,722	1,698,918
3. E. Europe (CMEA-6)[6]	586,915	592,565	590,738	584,860	590,373	599,911	617,463	640,309	670,404	691,857
4. China	251,669	268,959	286,716	300,801	324,032	355,140	404,806	454,606	493,066	536,399
5. CMEA-7[7]	1,948,748	1,965,565	1,983,738	2,002,860	2,030,373	2,097,804	2,158,829	2,235,623	2,331,126	2,390,775

(continued)

Notes to table A-1

[1]Source of GDP data: Data files of The World Bank for *World Tables 1987*, (Baltimore, Md., Johns Hopkins University Press for The World Bank, 1987); *World Tables 1988–89* (Baltimore, Md., Johns Hopkins University Press for The World Bank, 1989).

Source of GDP data for CPE: CMEA-6 (1965–82): Thad P. Alton, "East European GNP's" in Joint Economic Committee, *Economic Performance and Policy*, vol. 1 (Washington, D.C.: GPO, 1985), pp. 109–110, 126–127.

USSR, CMEA (1985–87): Derived using net material product indices from "Economic Survey of Europe in 1986–1987" (New York, United Nations, 1987), *Economic Bulletin for Europe*, vol. 40 (New York, United Nations, 1987).

CMEA-6 (1983–84): Thad P. Alton et al., Research Papers Nos. 85–89 of The Research Project on National Income in East Central Europe (New York, L. W. International Financial Research, 1985).

Hungary, Poland, Bulgaria (1960–64) and DDR (1960, 1963–64): World Bank Data Tape.

Czechoslovakia, Romania (1960–61): Derived using net material product indices from *Yearbook of National Account Statistics 1970*, vols. 1 and 2 (New York, United Nations, 1972).

DDR (1961): Estimated using official net material product index from *Statistisches Jahrbuch der Deutschen Demokratischen Republik 1975* (Berlin, Staatsverlag der Deutschen Demokratischen Republik, 1975).

Czechoslovakia (1962–64); DDR (1962); Romania (1962–64): Jack Faucett Associates, *Change in Worldwide Demand for Metal Minerals* (Bethesda, Md., Jack Faucett Associates, 1986).

USSR (1960–78): Derived from indices published in Joint Economic Committee "USSR: Measures of Economic Growth and Development 1950–1980 (Washington, D.C.: GPO, 1982), pp. 80–81.

USSR (1979–82): Daniel Bond and Lawrence R. Klein, "Impact of Changes in the Global Environment on the Soviet and East European Economies," in Joint Economic Committee, *Economic Performance and Policy*, vol. 1 (Washington, D.C., GPO, 1985) p. 17.

USSR (1983–84): Derived from indices in Jack Faucett Associates, *Change in Worldwide Demand for Metal Minerals* (Bethesda, Md., 1986), p. 113.

[2]OECD: Australia, Austria, Belgium, Canada, Denmark, Federal Republic of Germany, Finland, France, Greece, Iceland, Ireland, Italy, Japan, Luxembourg, The Netherlands, New Zealand, Norway, Portugal, Spain, Sweden, Switzerland, Turkey, United Kingdom, United States.

[3]EEC-9: Belgium-Luxembourg, Denmark, Federal Republic of Germany, France, Greece, Ireland, Italy, The Netherlands, United Kingdom.

[4]LDC: All countries except OECD and CPE.

[5]CPE: Albania, CMEA countries, USSR, China, North Korea, North Vietnam, Cuba, and other Eastern European and Eastern Asian countries.

[6]CMEA-6: Bulgaria, Czechoslovakia, German Democratic Republic, Hungary, Poland, Romania.

[7]CMEA-7: CMEA-6 and the USSR.

Table A-2.   Gross Domestic Investment (GDI), 1960–1987 (millions of constant 1980 U.S. dollars)[1]

	1960	1961	1962	1963	1964	1965	1966	1967
A. World[2]								
B. OECD[3]								
1. Total	757,080	814,127	853,194	910,368	1,003,331	1,083,081	1,141,366	1,168,301
2. United States	264,468	265,205	295,295	314,765	332,170	376,125	400,020	391,907
3. Japan	58,349	83,387	80,841	94,368	112,016	112,334	127,950	155,171
4. EEC-9	314,475	335,871	344,866	359,171	401,620	418,860	426,210	431,204
5. United Kingdom	63,406	65,342	62,239	65,029	81,752	82,359	82,264	88,242
6. France	60,723	66,643	70,395	80,886	83,348	91,437	95,481	101,225
7. FRG	108,580	113,702	116,904	115,532	131,906	141,785	140,870	125,868
C. LDC								
1. Total	118,364	125,964	127,990	135,305	153,019	165,626	173,389	179,524
2. Brazil	14,886	16,279	17,060	15,443	16,781	18,509	19,736	18,565
3. India	13,433	13,310	14,715	16,060	17,786	18,196	19,073	19,220
4. Korea	898	1,120	1,115	2,260	1,715	1,790	3,117	3,564
D. CPE[4]								
1. Total								
2. USSR								
3. E. Europe (CMEA-6)								
4. China	30,073	11,909	6,248	10,661	15,481	22,230	29,633	20,407

See notes at end of table A-2 on page 277.

(continued)

Table A-2 (continued)

	1968	1969	1970	1971	1972	1973	1974	1975	1976	1977
A. World[2]										
B. OECD[3]										
1. Total	1,256,913	1,358,269	1,405,499	1,450,961	1,533,139	1,683,502	1,594,331	1,434,354	1,537,350	1,608,258
2. United States	407,395	420,965	386,745	420,227	456,218	502,385	456,070	377,748	423,767	486,898
3. Japan	186,681	217,181	254,835	254,421	278,484	315,843	293,920	273,447	283,564	296,080
4. EEC-9	471,869	508,789	536,581	541,993	557,660	605,206	554,439	507,207	554,558	554,222
5. United Kingdom	94,196	94,756	96,127	94,983	93,954	112,333	104,149	89,822	100,923	102,228
6. France	114,589	119,630	122,502	133,404	143,720	145,361	126,077	139,910	137,448	137,272
7. FRG	140,047	158,799	170,416	170,691	175,722	180,570	157,701	142,059	163,647	163,830
C. LDC										
1. Total	195,207	217,972	237,016	257,683	265,184	302,343	354,296	414,961	467,290	524,710
2. Brazil	22,189	27,931	27,875	31,945	35,123	42,984	51,347	57,368	58,817	58,483
3. India	18,254	20,156	21,484	23,283	21,879	25,565	26,173	27,463	28,806	29,535
4. Korea	4,853	6,884	6,762	7,735	6,949	9,136	11,870	12,074	14,038	17,299
D. CPE[4]										
1. Total										
2. USSR										
3. E. Europe (CMEA-6)										
4. China	19,940	24,105	42,884	47,296	45,788	53,425	54,366	61,075	55,668	62,343

Table A-2 (continued)

	1978	1979	1980	1981	1982	1983	1984	1985	1986	1987
A. World[2]										
B. OECD[3]										
1. Total	1,676,301	1,758,109	1,688,902	1,684,313	1,605,047	1,636,863	1,799,684	1,862,967	1,932,528	2,077,756
2. United States	534,687	531,738	465,067	490,880	438,665	473,770	569,940	546,200	551,800	578,600
3. Japan	317,386	339,845	337,009	346,807	348,930	344,054	367,252	386,162	425,196	464,086
4. EEC-9	573,312	608,407	587,408	539,507	534,184	540,381	568,229	577,880	653,457	686,149
5. United Kingdom	102,802	106,279	89,110	80,725	89,903	98,253	104,633	106,851	111,953	121,860
6. France	148,761	152,336	138,269	147,002	143,017	141,434	143,954		149,574	159,244
7. FRG	168,587	189,534	188,345	166,391	157,976	167,489	171,880	172,154	181,374	187,478
C. LDC										
1. Total	542,684	552,457	577,293	638,683	590,059	609,693	613,971	609,474		
2. Brazil	59,877	60,936	68,295	57,479	55,026	45,437	47,568	43,471	50,887	45,962
3. India	34,031	33,610	35,368	35,742	37,123	39,814	41,628		52,890	53,840
4. Korea	21,250	25,443	19,408	20,638	20,666	24,274	28,797	29,253	32,353	37,289
D. CPE[4]										
1. Total										
2. USSR										
3. E. Europe (CMEA-6)										
4. China	81,709	84,913	85,981	84,446	93,658	107,877	130,240	151,695	163,465	187,170

Note: Data for blank cells not available.

[1]Source: For 1960–85: Data files of The World Bank for *World Tables 1987* (Baltimore, Md., Johns Hopkins University Press for The World Bank, 1987). For 1986–87: *World Tables 1988–1989* (Baltimore, Md., Johns Hopkins University Press for The World Bank, 1989).

[2]No CPE data were available, so World GDI was not calculated.
[3]OECD, LDC, CPE, and CMEA definitions: see list of acronyms on page 270 of the statistical appendix.
[4]Data not available except for China.

Table A-3. Manufacturing, 1960–1986 (millions of constant 1980 U.S. dollars)[1]

	1960	1961	1962	1963	1964	1965	1966	1967
A. World[2]								
B. OECD[3]								
1. Total	718,717	783,178	831,548	904,166	1,005,036	1,077,170	1,169,400	1,197,794
2. United States	319,337	320,075	346,772	374,797	401,642	437,485	471,262	470,378
3. Japan	53,430	64,128	69,543	77,579	90,124	93,629	106,145	127,280
4. EEC-9	323,217	339,456	353,427	367,078	400,981	424,347	462,751	465,658
5. United Kingdom	94,368	94,496	94,752	98,077	107,027	110,096	112,142	112,781
6. France	61,075	65,999	71,098	76,373	84,286	88,858	97,122	102,104
7. FRG	145,993	156,146	163,007	167,032	181,576	195,938	198,865	194,657
C. LDC								
1. Total	62,558	68,085	70,728	76,291	84,603	110,000	117,557	124,151
2. Brazil						16,279	18,231	18,621
3. India	9,171	10,005	10,941	11,877	12,784	12,959	12,784	13,018
4. Korea	897	933	1,042	1,209	1,330	1,602	1,878	2,285
D. CPE[4]								
1. Total								
2. USSR								
3. E. Europe (CMEA-6)								
4. China	38,211	21,562	19,126	21,582	27,370	33,899	41,976	36,288

See notes at end of table A-3 on page 280.

Table A-3 (continued)

	1968	1969	1970	1971	1972	1973	1974	1975	1976	1977
A. World[2]										
B. OECD[3]										
1. Total	1,289,550	1,394,617	1,446,895	1,488,909	1,595,714	1,751,519	1,741,386	1,649,851	1,779,778	1,858,322
2. United States	494,272	511,382	484,095	492,060	538,080	599,293	575,545	532,475	581,298	618,320
3. Japan	146,932	170,983	202,879	215,436	238,361	271,383	266,055	255,461	289,459	310,612
4. EEC-9	505,189	555,188	588,053	601,757	626,325	672,199	680,165	647,504	687,598	704,976
5. United Kingdom	120,863	125,312	125,824	124,418	127,486	139,123	137,460	127,870	130,428	132,857
6. France	108,083	120,978	131,880	140,320	149,171	159,546	164,703	161,304	172,675	179,122
7. FRG	215,422	241,858	256,128	259,604	267,013	283,295	284,119	269,208	288,509	296,559
C. LDC										
1. Total	135,273	152,189	167,785	179,661	194,909	215,365	228,531	236,823	256,864	269,582
2. Brazil	21,241	23,638	25,980	29,102	33,228	38,858	41,980	43,709	49,340	50,789
3. India	13,603	15,066	15,279	15,709	16,353	17,146	17,549	17,927	19,506	20,770
4. Korea	2,906	3,535	4,239	5,032	5,776	7,503	8,678	9,706	12,026	13,951
D. CPE[4]										
1. Total										
2. USSR										
3. E. Europe (CMEA-6)										
4. China	32,957	44,206	60,294	68,471	72,116	78,344	79,132	90,047	86,435	98,311

(continued)

Table A-3 (continued)

	1978	1979	1980	1981	1982	1983	1984	1985	1986
A. World²									
B. OECD³									
1. Total	1,933,209	2,020,167	2,014,436	2,034,515	2,004,254	2,062,248	2,167,316	2,233,132	2,084,521
2. United States	652,245	673,337	646,492	662,865	619,352	648,263	532,093	577,001	712,900
3. Japan	333,410	366,525	399,388	417,494	441,589	476,955			444,196
4. EEC-9	717,639	741,449	727,034	709,469	704,558	713,240	734,300	749,833	756,419
5. United Kingdom	133,496	133,752	121,221	113,572	113,572	116,229	120,657		131,047
6. France	183,987	189,790	187,563	182,522	188,032	190,200	193,365		155,863
7. FRG	301,865	316,501	317,324	313,848	303,054	305,066	314,763	330,588	280,000
C. LDC									
1. Total	283,677	300,070	316,672	318,165	317,616	319,352	354,005	355,451	
2. Brazil	54,357	57,981	62,385	58,371	58,483	54,803	79,172		72,337
3. India	23,055	22,628	23,011	23,780	25,392	26,709	28,171	30,073	44,005
4. Korea	16,925	18,667	18,462	19,852	20,675	23,205	26,650	27,588	34,493
D. CPE⁴									
1. Total									
2. USSR									
3. E. Europe (CMEA-6)									
4. China	114,286	122,497	137,517	140,654	150,868	168,024	195,928		144,600

Note: Data for blank cells not available.
¹Source: Data files of The World Bank for *World Tables 1987* (Baltimore, Md., Johns Hopkins University Press for The World Bank, 1987).
²No CPE data were available, so World Manufacturing was not calculated.
³OECD, LDC, CPE, and CMEA definitions: see list of acronyms on page 270 of the statistical appendix.
⁴Not available except for China.

Table A-4.   Services, 1960–1986 (in millions of constant 1980 U.S. dollars)[1,2]

	1960	1961	1962	1963	1964	1965	1966	1967
A. World[3]								
B. OECD[4]								
1. Total	1,344,459	1,483,391	1,560,036	1,664,839	1,805,455	1,904,576	2,066,679	2,160,778
2. United States	656,375	674,813	711,392	739,270	777,768	822,607	868,480	900,045
3. Japan	106,866	119,157	132,205	148,370	168,402	182,835	204,092	223,316
4. EEC-9	541,586	571,977	594,840	626,019	657,317	684,466	768,367	798,240
5. United Kingdom	169,909	178,610	180,896	190,435	197,391	201,658	206,810	213,949
6. France	105,270	111,248	119,044	127,191	134,635	141,024	148,057	155,032
7. FRG	147,090	154,591	160,171	166,117	175,722	185,052	190,449	194,474
C. LDC								
1. Total	172,474	180,270	185,334	197,704	213,828	261,660	273,189	283,699
2. Brazil	18,763	20,010	21,121	22,321	23,666	25,590	27,429	28,823
3. India						24,193	24,953	25,919
4. Korea	3,681	3,677	3,993	4,312	4,500	4,963	5,608	6,398
D. CPE[5]								
1. Total								
2. USSR								
3. E. Europe (CMEA-6)								
4. China	35,167	18,051	13,531	23,985	15,501	20,120	27,043	22,103

(continued)

See notes at end of table A-4 on page 283.

Table A-4 (continued)

	1968	1969	1970	1971	1972	1973	1974	1975	1976	1977
A. World[3]										
B. OECD[4]										
1. Total	2,287,283	2,420,951	2,561,041	2,696,193	2,868,954	3,042,150	3,097,532	3,172,739	3,323,306	3,479,807
2. United States	948,130	986,627	1,006,245	1,042,825	1,110,233	1,168,790	1,177,050	1,204,043	1,262,010	1,345,642
3. Japan	250,537	282,312	315,888	339,489	380,143	407,225	404,824	422,818	437,436	457,007
4. EEC-9	837,212	884,380	933,655	981,886	1,025,409	1,089,414	1,118,368	1,133,645	1,195,112	1,226,062
5. United Kingdom	222,158	225,671	234,804	246,364	252,432	273,397	274,801	283,441	298,237	296,887
6. France	161,363	173,847	182,815	193,834	206,553	220,621	232,050	234,571	248,052	258,426
7. FRG	203,987	218,898	230,606	239,479	250,731	261,067	265,732	269,757	284,759	297,565
C. LDC										
1. Total	322,737	353,887	403,043	431,346	459,535	499,285	538,680	573,243	610,771	672,690
2. Brazil	32,280	35,513	43,709	49,618	55,695	64,002	71,974	76,658	84,407	92,156
3. India	27,060	28,288	29,617	30,570	31,483	32,387	33,712	36,392	38,542	40,847
4. Korea	7,419	8,451	9,709	11,069	11,888	13,641	14,571	15,564	17,377	19,268
D. CPE[5]										
1. Total										
2. USSR										
3. E. Europe (CMEA-6)										
4. China	18,398	29,032	38,391	40,381	42,991	46,162	44,453	48,638	39,640	45,801

Table A-4 (continued)

	1978	1979	1980	1981	1982	1983	1984	1985	1986
A. World[3]									
B. OECD[4]									
1. Total	3,632,380	3,763,992	3,871,350	3,994,709	3,992,923	4,099,239	4,209,912	4,268,649	4,907,852
2. United States	1,413,197	1,454,202	1,473,378	1,544,915	1,514,972	1,577,660			2,034,200
3. Japan	477,282	510,212	545,963	562,893	581,838	610,623	635,377	665,808	695,925
4. EEC-9	1,277,768	1,320,157	1,356,469	1,375,210	1,381,221	1,412,215	1,447,263	1,462,431	1,750,857
5. United Kingdom	307,258	306,301	311,415	314,247	315,399	330,639	338,798		295,512
6. France	271,966	283,982	293,829	305,962	305,962	309,947	314,343		473,972
7. FRG	311,561	326,929	338,546	341,016	344,766	353,639	365,622		531,758
C. LDC									
1. Total	703,928	733,908	776,028	809,518	810,337	804,345	865,756	840,726	
2. Brazil	97,954	102,470	109,941	112,728	113,509	99,404	109,902		130,226
3. India	44,085	44,454	46,639	49,436	52,949	56,167	59,678	63,510	79,582
4. Korea	21,811	23,524	24,172	25,220	26,756	30,227	32,657	35,034	41,681
D. CPE[5]									
1. Total									
2. USSR									
3. E. Europe (CMEA-6)									
4. China	53,538	53,004	57,343	62,417	64,486	68,692	73,965		71,640

Note: Data for blank cells not available.

[1] Source: Data files of The World Bank for *World Tables 1987* (Baltimore, Md., Johns Hopkins University Press for The World Bank, 1987).

[2] Services defined as Utilities + Transportation + Trade + Banking + Dwellings + Services (as defined by the World Bank).

[3] No CPE data were available, so World Services was not calculated.

[4] OECD, LDC, CPE, and CMEA definitions: see list of acronyms on page 270 of the statistical appendix.

[5] Not available except for China.

Part B. Metal Consumption Data

Table B-1. Crude Steel, 1960–1987 (thousand metric tons)[1,2]

	1960	1961	1962	1963	1964	1965	1966	1967
A. World	334,741	350,635	359,520	386,912	428,939	452,228	472,274	495,698
B. OECD								
1. Total	215,163	221,129	220,822	241,583	276,350	289,765	299,339	310,158
2. United States	90,014	89,846	91,240	102,544	118,386	128,095	132,137	126,649
3. Japan	19,456	25,638	22,550	24,449	28,095	28,504	35,101	50,808
4. EEC-9	81,078	78,889	80,297	84,739	95,390	92,179	92,500	94,486
5. United Kingdom	22,051	18,650	17,692	19,824	23,098	22,975	21,106	21,296
6. France	13,689	13,964	14,770	15,461	17,098	15,963	17,024	17,841
7. FRG	28,889	27,255	27,501	27,036	33,496	31,608	30,075	28,025
C. LDC								
1. Total	22,398	24,340	25,739	27,209	30,621	32,170	32,713	33,908
2. Brazil	2,812	2,693	2,860	3,330	3,323	2,695	3,920	3,562
3. India	4,776	5,358	6,476	7,288	7,412	7,338	6,841	6,445
4. Korea	157	107	318	394	248	337	605	744
D. CPE								
1. Total	97,180	105,166	112,959	118,120	121,968	130,293	140,222	151,632
2. USSR	63,520	68,537	74,020	77,340	80,767	86,785	91,498	97,253
3. E. Europe (CMEA-6)	23,169	25,638	27,234	26,988	29,500	30,627	32,794	34,921
4. China	8,796	10,160	10,610	12,724	10,519	11,604	14,601	18,049
5. CMEA-7	86,689	94,175	101,254	104,328	110,267	117,412	124,292	132,174

See notes at end of table B-1 on page 286.

Table B-1 (continued)

	1968	1969	1970	1971	1972	1973	1974	1975	1976	1977
A. World	529,310	573,498	588,255	579,120	631,770	697,490	706,310	642,630	678,678	679,469
B. OECD										
1. Total	347,852	366,300	371,074	344,163	382,340	423,365	407,220	337,551	370,202	354,183
2. United States	137,751	138,680	127,304	127,663	138,410	149,595	144,120	116,821	129,044	133,108
3. Japan	49,908	61,655	69,882	57,700	68,890	87,180	75,750	64,740	65,220	63,205
4. EEC-9	118,474	119,170	123,830	108,920	121,660	128,100	122,500	99,000	119,411	106,303
5. United Kingdom	23,309	24,322	25,005	20,590	23,090	25,010	23,430	20,520	22,970	19,700
6. France	17,945	22,291	23,236	21,230	24,340	25,260	24,937	19,261	23,601	19,616
7. FRG	34,864	40,110	40,605	35,570	39,970	40,410	35,070	30,260	37,512	33,656
C. LDC										
1. Total	21,860	41,323	42,307	49,597	54,890	63,075	76,020	75,899	73,827	85,694
2. Brazil	4,494	5,530	6,090	7,390	7,660	9,510	12,800	11,240	10,265	11,958
3. India	5,861	6,000	6,432	7,710	9,230	8,220	8,550	8,500	7,938	9,336
4. Korea	811	1,110	1,280	1,475	1,500	2,860	3,230	2,960	3,877	5,434
D. CPE										
1. Total	159,598	165,875	174,874	185,360	194,540	211,050	223,070	229,180	234,649	239,592
2. USSR	101,813	104,837	110,234	115,360	121,240	129,390	137,550	141,030	147,406	146,577
3. E. Europe (CMEA-6)	36,702	40,569	41,370	42,590	44,720	47,740	51,310	54,010	56,631	57,567
4. China	19,613	18,350	20,960	24,950	25,950	30,750	30,650	31,070	26,220	30,006
5. CMEA-7	138,515	145,406	151,604	157,950	165,960	177,130	188,860	195,040	204,037	204,144

(continued)

Table B-1 (continued)

	1978	1979	1980	1981	1982	1983	1984	1985	1986	1987
A. World	719,498	750,920	719,230	710,107	652,194	662,311	711,795	721,380	724,975	740,527
B. OECD										
1. Total	364,827	388,173	355,074	350,147	294,262	294,226	332,028	321,071	309,978	324,987
2. United States	145,150	140,407	113,990	128,504	84,319	94,123	111,343	105,256	94,872	101,642
3. Japan	66,652	78,163	79,007	71,136	69,504	65,614	74,367	73,377	69,941	75,757
4. EEC-9	104,507	115,529	107,310	97,136	92,233	89,050	95,218	93,435	93,376	95,596
5. United Kingdom	19,530	20,160	13,960	15,040	14,360	14,280	14,620	14,530	14,350	15,021
6. France	19,740	20,728	20,159	17,461	17,197	15,298	15,492	14,755	14,541	14,817
7. FRG	33,288	37,850	34,791	32,592	27,955	30,278	31,089	30,789	30,508	29,100
C. LDC										
1. Total	92,820	100,249	104,864	108,301	105,239	100,372	104,445	108,956	108,977	110,986
2. Brazil	11,955	12,798	14,275	12,063	10,612	8,580	10,698	11,951	14,477	14,971
3. India	11,102	12,367	11,665	14,047	13,908	12,241	12,475	13,869	14,784	15,536
4. Korea	6,565	7,104	5,554	7,512	6,607	7,646	9,481	9,996	11,196	15,070
D. CPE										
1. Total	261,851	262,498	259,292	251,659	252,693	267,713	275,322	291,353	306,020	304,554
2. USSR	153,436	151,644	150,330	150,849	150,343	157,263	159,050	159,328	165,122	163,199
3. E. Europe (CMEA-6)	59,668	59,330	58,735	54,455	54,139	53,192	53,167	52,775	54,006	54,569
4. China	42,057	44,456	42,728	39,150	40,806	49,411	54,796	68,918	75,716	78,092
5. CMEA-7	213,104	210,974	209,065	205,304	204,482	210,455	212,217	212,103	219,128	217,768

[1]Source: International Iron and Steel Institute, *Steel Statistical Yearbook* (Brussels, IISL, various issues).

[2]OECD, LDC, CPE, and CMEA definitions: see list of acronyms on page 270 of the statistical appendix.

Table B-2. Primary Aluminum, 1960–1988 (thousand metric tons)[1,2]

	1960	1961	1962	1963	1964	1965	1966	1967	1968
A. World	4,166.3	4,496.0	4,965.1	5,469.6	5,985.5	6,648.5	7,615.7	7,780.2	8,863.8
B. OECD									
1. Total	3,096.2	3,278.0	3,691.0	4,115.7	4,533.1	4,945.1	5,746.8	5,658.4	6,577.9
2. United States	1,541.2	1,791.1	2,089.3	2,340.3	2,534.9	2,852.4	3,281.3	3,119.2	3,597.1
3. Japan	150.5	185.6	179.0	238.7	265.3	298.3	393.4	496.6	621.1
4. EEC-9	1,050.1	980.3	1,036.6	1,127.7	1,267.5	1,272.2	1,451.3	1,435.3	1,652.1
5. United Kingdom	357.2	282.6	285.4	317.5	356.2	350.6	362.9	356.6	388.4
6. France	212.7	201.2	235.6	242.5	249.3	248.5	298.3	294.0	293.5
7. FRG	313.0	297.0	301.9	315.4	385.9	287.4	419.5	416.8	539.3
C. LDC									
1. Total	130.1	181.0	214.7	233.6	260.3	312.2	390.0	429.7	452.8
2. Brazil	33.0	36.8	41.2	46.7	45.1	51.6	72.1	78.0	80.5
3. India	24.9	30.0	49.0	62.0	56.6	71.0	83.6	118.5	128.0
4. Korea			8.2	3.2	0.2	3.7	4.7	7.4	8.5
D. CPE									
1. Total	940.0	1,307.0	1,059.4	1,120.3	1,192.1	1,391.2	1,478.9	1,592.1	1,833.1
2. USSR	632.0	715.0	734.3	777.9	824.8	971.0	1,044.3	1,146.9	1,212.4
3. E. Europe (CMEA-6)	201.0	217.0	240.1	256.9	280.8	323.2	337.4	410.6	457.1
4. China	90.0	80.0	85.0	85.0	85.0	95.0	95.0	130.0	160.0
5. CMEA-7	833.0	932.0	974.4	1,034.8	1,105.6	1,294.2	1,381.7	1,557.5	1,669.5

(continued)

See notes at end of table B-2 on page 289.

Table B-2 (continued)

	1969	1970	1971	1972	1973	1974	1975	1976	1977	1978
A. World	9,673.5	9,982.7	10,702.6	11,751.4	13,646.0	14,061.3	11,457.2	14,123.5	14,538.0	15,340.0
B. OECD										
1. Total	7,240.1	7,326.2	7,811.7	8,711.8	10,366.2	10,368.1	7,661.0	10,054.4	10,173.8	10,668.0
2. United States	3,705.8	3,488.1	3,927.0	4,298.8	5,076.2	5,127.5	3,265.0	4,490.5	4,756.0	4,978.1
3. Japan	807.1	911.4	972.9	1,216.3	1,611.8	1,303.0	1,170.8	1,609.6	1,419.9	1,656.1
4. EEC-9	1,904.8	2,037.4	1,930.8	2,148.5	2,486.2	2,605.5	2,068.0	2,669.5	2,650.3	2,722.0
5. United Kingdom	387.7	404.2	325.6	408.2	487.8	498.6	392.7	444.5	418.7	402.3
6. France	367.1	413.3	377.4	398.3	450.1	480.0	399.2	492.6	533.8	532.8
7. FRG	642.3	669.8	684.4	724.4	855.7	872.3	703.7	954.4	912.3	952.3
C. LDC										
1. Total	593.0	564.7	657.0	642.3	701.7	930.4	956.2	1,045.5	1,189.4	1,356.0
2. Brazil	84.0	83.5	103.3	137.8	158.0	187.1	216.8	217.3	232.3	240.4
3. India	114.7	162.0	193.0	172.9	148.5	124.6	159.0	170.0	187.6	205.4
4. Korea	12.6	15.3	17.0	18.5	36.4	25.8	36.1	52.3	75.0	105.8
D. CPE										
1. Total	1,940.4	2,091.8	2,233.9	2,397.3	2,578.1	2,762.8	2,840.0	3,023.6	3,174.8	3,316.0
2. USSR	1,230.0	1,330.0	1,395.0	1,445.0	1,480.0	1,550.0	1,580.0	1,690.0	1,760.0	1,830.0
3. E. Europe (CMEA-6)	503.8	530.3	587.4	648.5	716.3	795.8	798.0	839.4	872.6	893.5
4. China	200.0	225.0	245.0	295.0	370.0	400.0	440.0	470.0	510.0	560.0
5. CMEA-7	1,733.8	1,860.3	1,982.4	2,093.5	2,196.3	2,345.8	2,378.0	2,529.4	2,632.6	2,723.5

Table B-2 (continued)

	1979	1980	1981	1982	1983	1984	1985	1986	1987	1988
A. World	15,992.9	15,298.8	14,613.6	14,296.3	15,391.5	16,022.6	16,252.5	16,601.8	17,506.2	
B. OECD										
1. Total	11,178.5	10,483.2	9,845.2	9,402.2	10,374.2	10,825.6	10,710.7	10,828.8	11,631.4	12,215.1
2. United States	5,017.7	4,453.8	4,156.1	3,581.0	4,221.0	4,457.0	4,282.0	4,143.0	4,536.0	4,598.9
3. Japan	1,803.4	1,639.0	1,570.2	1,639.3	1,802.6	1,766.9	1,818.0	1,849.9	2,055.0	2,315.0
4. EEC-9	2,964.4	2,953.4	2,679.7	2,755.9	2,916.2	3,074.0	3,033.0	3,192.5	3,231.5	3,430.4
5. United Kingdom	417.6	409.3	343.6	326.3	323.4	369.5	350.0	389.1	383.6	427.4
6. France	595.9	600.9	538.7	578.4	613.4	579.3	586.1	592.6	615.6	645.0
7. FRG	1,067.8	1,042.3	1,021.8	1,000.2	1,085.0	1,151.6	1,158.0	1,189.7	1,185.7	1,232.6
C. LDC										
1. Total	1,450.2	1,504.9	1,485.5	1,586.4	1,699.9	1,873.8	2,085.2	2,204.4	2,367.9	
2. Brazil	265.7	296.4	261.7	281.9	270.6	294.7	366.7	423.7	430.3	393.0
3. India	211.9	233.8	249.6	219.7	218.5	310.0	297.6	310.0	326.0	337.0
4. Korea	94.3	67.5	103.6	97.1	120.0	128.8	145.6	196.8	207.9	254.0
D. CPE										
1. Total	3,364.2	3,310.7	3,282.9	3,307.7	3,317.4	3,323.2	3,456.6	3,568.6	3,506.9	
2. USSR	1,865.0	1,850.0	1,860.0	1,880.0	1,850.0	1,800.0	1,850.0	1,885.0	1,800.0	
3. E. Europe (CMEA-6)	881.4	872.5	824.4	804.2	803.6	843.7	851.6	873.6	839.4	
4. China	580.0	550.0	560.0	580.0	620.0	630.0	700.0	750.0	800.0	
5. CMEA-7	2,746.4	2,722.5	2,684.4	2,684.2	2,653.6	2,643.7	2,701.6	2,758.6	2,639.4	

Note: Data for blank cells are not available.

[1]Source: Metallgesellschaft Aktiengesellschaft, *Metallstatistic* (Frankfurt am Main: Metallgesellschaft AG, various issues).

[2]OECD, LDC, CPE, and CMEA definitions: see list of acronyms on page 270 of the statistical appendix.

Table B-3. Refined Copper, 1960–1988 (thousand metric tons)[1,2]

	1960	1961	1962	1963	1964	1965	1966	1967
A. World	4,755.8	5,088.4	5,201.7	5,519.3	5,995.4	6,192.5	6,462.7	6,216.8
B. OECD								
1. Total	3,602.7	3,880.6	3,848.1	4,139.1	4,589.3	4,719.7	4,974.5	4,651.8
2. United States	1,224.6	1,348.1	1,458.8	1,590.0	1,690.0	1,844.3	2,155.7	1,799.5
3. Japan	304.0	372.9	301.0	352.1	457.5	427.5	482.5	616.0
4. EEC-9	1,626.3	1,664.9	1,592.5	1,649.3	1,843.2	1,830.0	1,684.8	1,649.8
5. United Kingdom	560.3	528.8	526.1	558.0	632.9	650.1	592.5	514.3
6. France	236.8	243.6	243.7	250.3	291.7	287.3	291.3	271.3
7. FRG	516.2	561.5	500.6	493.5	561.1	536.3	458.7	501.2
C. LDC								
1. Total	241.5	256.0	278.5	281.2	308.1	307.3	241.0	242.9
2. Brazil	29.7	36.4	39.3	38.3	36.6	30.7	38.0	41.0
3. India	62.4	68.0	77.7	78.6	65.4	62.1	32.7	42.3
4. Korea	N.A.	N.A.	0.5	1.8	2.8	2.1	3.1	4.9
D. CPE								
1. Total	911.6	951.8	1,075.1	1,099.0	1,098.0	1,165.5	1,247.2	1,322.1
2. USSR	651.6	681.8	735.1	736.0	740.0	783.0	817.0	867.0
3. E. Europe (CMEA-6)						261.5	279.0	294.0
4. China	110.0	120.0	120.0	120.0	120.0	120.0	140.0	150.0
5. CMEA-7						1,044.5	1,096.0	1,161.0

See notes at end of table B-3 on page 292.

Table B-3 (continued)

	1968	1969	1970	1971	1972	1973	1974	1975	1976	1977
A. World	6,547.9	7,137.1	7,290.5	7,295.5	7,941.3	8,739.3	8,309.7	7,444.2	8,538.9	9,056.8
B. OECD										
1. Total	4,882.0	5,399.3	5,472.1	5,329.5	5,807.8	6,431.1	5,898.5	4,893.3	5,792.0	6,165.0
2. United States	1,704.0	1,950.6	1,860.2	1,833.4	2,029.9	2,221.1	1,994.9	1,399.2	1,812.1	1,989.9
3. Japan	695.2	806.9	820.6	805.7	951.3	1,201.8	880.9	827.4	1,050.3	1,127.1
4. EEC-9	1,835.1	1,966.2	2,057.1	1,967.9	2,089.4	2,197.7	2,185.8	1,976.0	2,193.9	2,309.0
5. United Kingdom	539.2	546.8	553.7	517.3	534.6	541.2	496.9	450.5	457.6	512.0
6. France	292.9	334.8	330.7	343.6	390.2	407.8	414.2	364.5	367.1	326.1
7. FRG	608.8	655.7	697.5	630.5	672.1	727.2	731.0	634.6	744.6	779.9
C. LDC										
1. Total	297.6	346.3	362.5	403.7	456.0	495.1	564.9	530.4	635.6	710.2
2. Brazil	57.0	63.0	73.9	95.3	110.6	125.3	162.0	155.2	179.3	210.9
3. India	38.8	50.9	55.0	61.0	59.3	62.9	46.5	24.4	50.8	52.9
4. Korea	6.2	6.5	7.5	8.7	9.8	13.5	23.5	35.1	47.0	57.8
D. CPE										
1. Total	1,368.3	1,391.5	1,455.9	1,562.3	1,677.5	1,813.1	1,846.3	2,020.5	2,111.3	2,181.6
2. USSR	890.0	913.0	950.0	985.0	1,030.0	1,100.0	1,100.0	1,220.0	1,250.0	1,290.0
3. E. Europe (CMEA-6)	305.0	314.5	309.9	350.0	390.0	425.6	447.7	479.9	519.3	539.1
4. China	160.0	150.0	180.0	210.0	240.0	270.0	280.0	300.0	320.0	330.0
5. CMEA-7	1,195.0	1,227.5	1,259.9	1,335.0	1,420.0	1,525.6	1,547.7	1,699.9	1,769.3	1,829.1

(continued)

Table B-3 (continued)

	1978	1979	1980	1981	1982	1983	1984	1985	1986	1987	1988
A. World	9,527.2	9,848.5	9,389.2	9,547.9	9,015.6	9,100.1	9,885.9	9,612.8	10,082.8	10,425.8	
B. OECD											
1. Total	6,527.4	6,660.2	6,180.8	6,335.1	5,795.6	5,931.4	6,566.4	6,183.4	6,495.5	6,607.1	6,871.7
2. United States	2,196.9	2,164.5	1,867.7	2,071.0	1,675.6	1,813.9	2,122.7	1,905.6	2,136.5	2,135.4	2,273.0
3. Japan	1,241.4	1,330.1	1,158.3	1,254.1	1,243.1	1,216.3	1,368.3	1,230.8	1,219.2	1,284.2	1,343.5
4. EEC-9	2,291.5	2,359.9	2,327.0	2,178.9	2,144.2	2,110.0	2,239.3	2,198.3	2,271.2	2,299.3	2,355.5
5. United Kingdom	501.6	498.8	409.2	333.1	355.4	358.0	352.9	346.5	339.6	327.7	327.6
6. France	319.0	358.4	433.4	429.6	407.4	390.0	411.5	397.8	401.1	399.0	408.9
7. FRG	780.0	794.1	747.8	747.5	730.7	737.0	791.7	753.8	770.7	800.1	797.5
C. LDC											
1. Total	747.2	871.6	934.8	940.3	948.9	906.7	1,041.0	1,111.3	1,229.3	1,434.6	
2. Brazil	180.8	228.7	246.0	179.0	244.9	148.4	189.2	196.1	254.9	258.8	258.0
3. India	73.7	67.9	77.2	75.1	83.2	96.0	84.8	113.6	110.0	115.0	114.8
4. Korea	73.5	85.3	84.0	139.8	136.7	152.3	188.0	207.3	262.3	259.0	290.0
D. CPE											
1. Total	2,252.6	2,316.7	2,273.6	2,272.5	2,271.1	2,262.0	2,278.5	2,318.1	2,358.0	2,384.1	
2. USSR	1,330.0	1,360.0	1,300.0	1,320.0	1,320.0	1,300.0	1,280.0	1,305.0	1,300.0	1,290.0	
3. E. Europe (CMEA-6)	548.6	573.7	579.4	557.8	543.6	553.0	578.5	555.1	574.5	586.3	
4. China	350.0	360.0	370.0	370.0	380.0	380.0	390.0	425.0	450.0	470.0	
5. CMEA-7	1,878.6	1,933.7	1,879.4	1,877.8	1,863.6	1,853.0	1,858.5	1,860.1	1,874.5	1,876.3	

Note: Data for blank cells not available.

[1]Source: Metallgesellschaft Aktiengesellschaft, *Metallstatistic* (Frankfurt am Main: Metallgesellschaft AG, various issues).

[2]OECD, LDC, CPE, and CMEA definitions: see list of acronyms on page 270 of the statistical appendix.

Table B-4. Refined Lead, 1960–1988 (thousand metric tons)[1,2]

	1960	1961	1962	1963	1964	1965	1966	1967	1968
A. World	2,621.4	2,706.3	2,818.9	2,968.7	3,149.5	3,182.2	3,332.9	3,323.0	3,668.2
B. OECD									
1. Total	1,890.7	1,916.6	1,980.6	2,063.0	2,174.1	2,198.1	2,283.2	2,236.7	2,476.4
2. United States	646.6	640.8	689.6	718.3	727.9	753.5	821.8	770.2	912.0
3. Japan	99.6	125.7	117.7	130.3	164.2	147.3	147.9	163.3	180.7
4. EEC-9	892.0	888.6	899.0	911.9	954.7	955.0	954.5	960.7	1,032.4
5. United Kingdom	286.5	275.7	276.3	283.5	307.8	312.1	293.4	276.3	276.8
6. France	161.4	160.7	156.3	170.1	172.1	144.6	168.6	164.2	179.3
7. FRG	239.5	236.1	243.9	245.7	259.7	272.9	258.0	259.4	288.2
C. LDC									
1. Total	156.2	196.6	203.6	259.8	240.8	244.2	262.4	272.3	292.3
2. Brazil	18.4	26.2	21.6	30.4	18.8	17.5	22.9	23.3	16.4
3. India	24.7	31.5	36.0	40.0	37.8	37.3	44.0	37.0	36.5
4. Korea			5.0	5.0	6.0	2.3	5.2	3.7	7.0
D. CPE									
1. Total	574.5	593.1	634.7	645.9	734.6	739.9	787.3	814.0	899.5
2. USSR	320.0	312.0	332.0	343.6	380.0	385.0	420.0	425.0	450.0
3. E. Europe (CMEA-6)	168.5	180.1	212.2	206.8	249.1	248.7	260.3	277.1	287.5
4. China	70.0	85.0	85.0	90.0	100.0	100.0	100.0	100.0	150.0
5. CMEA-7	488.5	492.1	544.2	550.4	629.1	633.7	680.3	702.1	737.5

(continued)

See notes at end of table B-4 on page 295.

Table B-4 (continued)

	1969	1970	1971	1972	1973	1974	1975	1976	1977	1978
A. World	3,837.4	3,914.2	4,024.4	4,168.6	4,472.9	4,419.8	4,758.8	5,178.9	5,491.7	5,522.4
B. OECD										
1. Total	2,575.2	2,623.0	2,626.8	2,732.5	2,943.2	2,790.3	2,942.2	3,340.6	3,568.4	3,540.2
2. United States	911.3	943.3	941.6	1,009.6	1,093.2	1,055.1	1,122.7	1,272.3	1,417.9	1,404.5
3. Japan	187.7	210.5	209.7	231.0	267.3	217.4	260.7	309.7	333.9	352.1
4. EEC-9	1,096.4	1,102.5	1,115.6	1,126.3	1,167.4	1,116.7	1,113.0	1,264.2	1,315.0	1,304.3
5. United Kingdom	275.3	261.7	276.7	278.4	282.2	327.6	306.0	318.3	317.7	336.5
6. France	198.5	192.5	188.4	202.0	213.7	217.9	190.3	228.1	210.4	211.7
7. FRG	314.7	308.9	286.5	273.5	293.7	323.7	282.5	299.8	348.5	335.8
C. LDC										
1. Total	300.8	308.6	341.2	334.0	378.2	427.0	505.1	515.8	577.6	560.4
2. Brazil	18.7	19.5	25.7	55.2	61.9	50.8	75.2	79.4	92.1	81.2
3. India	30.2	41.5	33.0	42.1	41.5	42.7	36.0	52.2	54.0	55.0
4. Korea	8.0	8.0	9.0	10.0	11.0	11.4	10.3	10.6	17.8	27.4
D. CPE										
1. Total	961.4	982.6	1,056.4	1,102.1	1,151.5	1,202.5	1,311.5	1,322.5	1,345.7	1,421.8
2. USSR	460.0	490.0	530.0	560.0	600.0	630.0	700.0	700.0	720.0	760.0
3. E. Europe (CMEA-6)	304.3	314.4	333.2	348.9	358.3	372.8	396.5	398.7	391.8	415.6
4. China	185.0	160.0	170.0	170.0	170.0	175.0	185.0	190.0	200.0	210.0
5. CMEA-7	764.3	804.4	863.2	908.9	958.3	1,002.8	1,096.5	1,098.7	1,111.8	1,175.6

Table B-4 (continued)

	1979	1980	1981	1982	1983	1984	1985	1986	1987	1988
A. World	5,644.8	5,396.1	5,282.0	5,223.9	5,278.3	5,434.9	5,420.9	5,502.9	5,622.5	
B. OECD										
1. Total	3,547.4	3,293.0	3,208.7	3,146.7	3,149.9	3,323.8	3,226.1	3,265.0	3,323.2	3,398.6
2. United States	1,345.4	1,094.0	1,127.8	1,106.1	1,134.2	1,142.7	1,099.1	1,118.5	1,202.8	1,184.0
3. Japan	368.2	392.5	382.5	354.0	359.6	390.7	394.9	389.6	377.9	407.0
4. EEC-9	1,340.0	1,296.9	1,217.4	1,206.7	1,194.5	1,260.3	1,213.9	1,239.2	1,243.8	1,292.3
5. United Kingdom	333.2	295.5	265.8	271.9	292.9	295.3	274.3	282.1	287.5	302.8
6. France	211.4	212.0	210.7	194.5	196.1	209.1	208.0	205.3	207.5	215.6
7. FRG	361.3	333.1	331.6	333.2	318.3	357.0	345.0	358.8	344.6	373.5
C. LDC										
1. Total	660.2	639.7	616.8	609.2	671.5	664.8	721.1	802.5	858.8	
2. Brazil	96.8	88.2	60.9	40.4	51.0	63.7	73.3	87.6	92.8	94.5
3. India	58.4	54.0	56.8	67.5	60.0	62.0	70.0	80.5	67.5	65.0
4. Korea	33.1	33.0	37.9	31.5	48.0	46.0	63.2	88.3	112.4	146.0
D. CPE										
1. Total	1,437.2	1,463.4	1,456.5	1,468.0	1,456.9	1,446.3	1,473.7	1,435.4	1,440.5	
2. USSR	780.0	800.0	800.0	810.0	805.0	790.0	800.0	760.0	775.0	
3. E. Europe (CMEA-6)	410.7	418.9	409.5	411.0	403.4	405.8	418.0	45.4	387.5	
4. China	210.0	210.0	215.0	215.0	215.0	215.0	220.0	225.0	240.0	
5. CMEA-7	1,190.7	1,218.9	1,209.5	1,221.0	1,208.4	1,195.8	1,218.0	1,175.4	1,162.5	

Note: Data for blank cells not available.

[1]Source: Metallgesellschaft Aktiengesellschaft, *Metallstatistic* (Frankfurt am Main: Metallgesellschaft AG, various issues).

[2]OECD, LDC, CPE, and CMEA definitions: see list of acronyms on page 270 of the statistical appendix.

Table B-5. Zinc, 1960–1988 (thousand metric tons)[1,2]

	1960	1961	1962	1963	1964	1965	1966	1967
A. World	3,081.1	3,237.1	3,386.8	3,631.7	3,952.1	4,085.5	4,266.8	4,322.1
B. OECD								
1. Total	2,189.6	2,334.8	2,458.5	2,646.1	2,932.4	3,010.0	3,114.3	3,050.1
2. United States	790.4	838.0	929.3	996.2	1,088.5	1,221.3	1,284.8	1,129.5
3. Japan	150.5	234.3	242.8	304.7	364.3	329.5	388.7	461.8
4. EEC-9	973.9	999.7	1,001.5	1,008.4	1,108.7	1,087.3	1,067.7	1,059.9
5. United Kingdom	275.9	258.7	246.3	265.2	291.9	282.1	272.6	258.5
6. France	172.1	188.7	185.8	180.8	203.6	185.7	197.1	202.5
7. FRG	296.7	306.0	291.0	280.4	320.5	330.0	310.2	302.7
C. LDC								
1. Total	251.5	244.4	252.0	267.1	287.5	302.7	322.6	340.6
2. Brazil	30.8	32.7	42.2	38.9	30.7	31.6	41.4	38.7
3. India	60.0	74.9	84.6	81.1	66.4	69.5	60.0	59.8
4. Korea			2.4	7.1	4.3	9.2	5.2	8.5
D. CPE								
1. Total	640.0	657.9	676.3	718.5	732.2	772.8	829.9	931.4
2. USSR	370.5	359.2	358.6	392.6	390.0	430.0	450.0	530.0
3. E. Europe (CMEA-6)	184.5	188.7	227.7	235.9	242.2	242.6	254.4	270.8
4. China	70.0	90.0	90.0	90.0	100.0	100.0	120.0	120.0
5. CMEA-7	555.0	547.9	586.3	628.5	632.2	672.6	704.4	800.8

See notes at end of table B-5 on page 298.

Table B-5 (continued)

	1968	1969	1970	1971	1972	1973	1974	1975	1976	1977
A. World	4,714.0	5,116.3	5,041.8	5,204.1	5,728.2	6,238.0	6,033.9	4,980.4	5,775.5	5,787.2
B. OECD										
1. Total	3,332.4	3,623.3	3,429.4	3,483.5	3,902.9	4,265.6	3,945.2	2,886.9	3,558.7	3,500.3
2. United States	1,220.5	1,251.7	1,074.3	1,136.9	1,285.7	1,363.5	1,216.1	790.1	1,079.3	990.2
3. Japan	522.7	599.9	623.1	628.0	716.7	814.9	695.4	547.1	695.6	716.8
4. EEC-9	1,178.0	1,305.2	1,259.9	1,243.6	1,364.2	1,501.8	1,438.0	1,038.7	1,237.4	1,255.5
5. United Kingdom	280.7	288.9	277.8	273.7	277.3	305.4	268.5	207.1	242.8	244.8
6. France	202.3	239.0	220.2	225.4	264.1	290.4	306.1	222.5	265.1	257.7
7. FRG	361.5	398.4	395.7	387.5	413.0	438.2	398.1	297.4	325.6	333.9
C. LDC										
1. Total	391.1	425.0	461.1	475.2	531.9	568.0	604.7	573.7	638.3	692.7
2. Brazil	45.7	50.0	49.1	63.2	66.0	80.0	93.4	82.4	97.2	105.5
3. India	81.0	81.0	97.0	91.5	102.8	77.9	86.3	82.0	90.2	97.0
4. Korea	7.9	10.6	11.0	13.9	15.0	23.1	25.4	27.6	35.3	46.3
D. CPE										
1. Total	990.5	1,068.0	1,151.3	1,245.4	1,293.4	1,404.4	1,484.0	1,519.8	1,578.5	1,594.2
2. USSR	580.0	630.0	680.0	730.0	760.0	840.0	900.0	900.0	930.0	945.0
3. E. Europe (CMEA-6)	280.2	292.5	305.8	324.9	342.9	358.9	378.5	413.8	437.3	433.0
4. China	120.0	135.0	150.0	170.0	170.0	180.0	180.0	180.0	180.0	185.0
5. CMEA-7	860.2	922.5	985.8	1,054.9	1,102.9	1,198.9	1,278.5	1,313.8	1,367.3	1,378.0

(continued)

Table B-5 (continued)

	1978	1979	1980	1981	1982	1983	1984	1985	1986	1987	1988
A. World	6,303.0	6,370.4	6,191.9	6,083.3	5,939.0	6,318.6	6,544.9	6,492.1	6,679.8	6,862.4	
B. OECD											
1. Total	3,787.9	3,815.8	3,594.5	3,469.1	3,241.2	3,563.4	3,683.5	3,635.3	3,757.4	3,801.4	3,981.4
2. United States	1,112.0	1,057.0	878.6	939.0	794.6	933.5	980.2	940.6	998.6	1,052.2	1,100.0
3. Japan	732.5	778.6	752.3	699.1	703.1	770.8	774.6	780.1	753.0	728.2	774.1
4. EEC-9	1,359.3	1,386.7	1,386.3	1,265.6	1,212.0	1,301.0	1,337.0	1,312.0	1,360.3	1,371.4	1,441.4
5. United Kingdom	247.6	238.8	181.3	185.4	178.0	177.0	182.0	189.0	181.9	188.1	192.8
6. France	281.7	286.7	330.0	272.1	263.9	270.5	281.2	246.9	260.5	247.5	290.1
7. FRG	391.0	417.1	405.7	373.2	368.6	405.9	424.9	408.8	432.7	452.1	445.6
C. LDC											
1. Total	839.9	871.5	864.6	880.5	923.2	962.9	1,011.3	1,031.2	1,090.0	1,192.8	
2. Brazil	123.6	123.6	138.2	113.8	90.6	104.4	118.7	139.4	150.9	176.6	144.0
3. India	108.0	116.2	95.3	108.0	131.0	125.0	124.3	130.0	135.0	130.5	142.0
4. Korea	58.0	72.7	68.0	78.5	94.4	113.2	121.1	125.4	152.2	178.5	173.0
D. CPE											
1. Total	1,675.2	1,683.1	1,732.8	1,733.7	1,774.6	1,792.3	1,850.1	1,825.6	1,832.4	1,868.2	
2. USSR	990.0	1,000.0	1,030.0	1,040.0	1,050.0	1,050.0	1,050.0	1,000.0	990.0	1,010.0	
3. E. Europe (CMEA-6)	469.0	461.6	473.3	444.2	433.1	418.3	436.1	438.8	435.6	451.2	
4. China	185.0	190.0	200.0	220.0	260.0	290.0	330.0	350.0	360.0	360.0	
5. CMEA-7	1,459.0	1,461.6	1,503.3	1,484.2	1,483.1	1,468.3	1,486.1	1,438.8	1,425.6	1,461.2	

Note: Data for blank cells not available.

[1]Source: Metallgesellschaft Aktiengesellschaft, *Metallstatistic* (Frankfurt am Main, Metallgesellschaft AG, various issues).

[2]OECD, LDC, CPE, and CMEA definitions: see list of acronyms on page 270 of the statistical appendix.

Table B-6.   Nickel, 1960–1987 (thousand metric tons)[1,2]

	1960	1961	1962	1963	1964	1965	1966	1967
A. World	292.7	320.9	318.0	335.2	401.7	431.0	467.6	473.0
B. OECD								
1. Total	216.7	222.2	209.5	230.4	287.4	315.3	346.2	350.1
2. United States	98.1	107.5	107.7	112.9	133.3	156.1	170.4	157.7
3. Japan	17.6	20.6	15.6	22.6	32.4	28.6	36.3	50.0
4. EEC-9	79.8	73.6	66.4	73.4	94.8	99.9	107.6	106.5
5. United Kingdom	27.8	26.5	25.1	27.6	38.1	36.9	34.4	30.5
6. France	19.4	15.4	13.2	15.8	20.5	21.0	24.5	28.7
7. FRG	23.0	22.0	19.2	20.3	25.6	30.7	33.6	31.0
C. LDC								
1. Total	1.4	3.7	3.5	4.8	4.3	5.7	6.4	7.9
2. Brazil					0.8	0.8	0.9	0.9
3. India							1.0	1.2
4. Korea								
D. CPE								
1. Total	74.0	95.0	105.0	100.0	110.0	110.0	115.0	115.0
2. USSR								
3. E. Europe (CMEA-6)								
4. China								
5. CMEA-7								

See notes at end of table B-6 on page 301.

(continued)

Table B-6 (continued)

	1968	1969	1970	1971	1972	1973	1974	1975	1976	1977
A. World	490.4	502.8	576.6	526.4	580.1	657.5	711.3	577.4	666.7	640.6
B. OECD										
1. Total	361.8	374.1	441.5	385.6	430.0	495.8	540.6	394.6	467.5	437.1
2. United States	144.5	136.6	149.1	133.2	156.9	182.1	194.5	132.9	147.8	138.7
3. Japan	59.3	74.7	99.3	90.6	87.7	113.6	115.9	83.3	115.0	97.3
4. EEC-9	119.1	119.7	138.9	118.5	136.1	144.6	161.5	124.6	147.8	146.9
5. United Kingdom	33.1	32.5	37.5	31.0	30.0	31.5	33.5	27.0	30.5	30.5
6. France	30.7	31.8	36.1	32.2	31.3	29.6	40.5	31.9	33.5	35.8
7. FRG	35.4	36.8	40.3	34.1	42.8	54.8	61.2	42.8	56.4	53.6
C. LDC										
1. Total	8.6	8.7	10.1	10.8	4.8	18.0	16.4	16.0	20.8	21.7
2. Brazil	1.0	0.9	1.6	1.5	0.9	5.3	6.6	3.9	4.7	5.2
3. India	1.1	1.3	1.7	2.5	1.7	1.5	2.8	3.3	3.5	5.6
4. Korea							0.5	0.5	1.1	1.0
D. CPE										
1. Total	120.0	120.0	125.0	130.0	145.3	143.7	154.3	166.8	178.4	181.8
2. USSR					100.0	100.0	105.0	115.0	121.0	125.0
3. E. Europe (CMEA-6)					24.9	25.2	30.8	33.3	38.9	38.3
4. China					20.0	18.0	18.0	18.0	18.0	18.0
5. CMEA-7					124.9	125.2	135.8	148.3	159.9	163.3

Table B-6 (continued)

	1978	1979	1980	1981	1982	1983	1984	1985	1986	1987
A. World	700.6	749.0	711.2	665.8	652.3	700.0	790.7	787.4	798.2	846.8
B. OECD										
1. Total	490.4	531.0	489.3	442.2	426.0	461.5	535.5	523.9	520.0	568.0
2. United States	163.9	152.7	142.1	139.7	124.7	139.2	141.0	146.9	142.0	141.0
3. Japan	99.0	132.0	123.8	106.4	108.4	118.0	144.6	136.1	126.6	153.9
4. EEC-9	163.8	184.3	161.1	142.7	141.5	146.6	178.6	171.7	176.5	192.9
5. United Kingdom	32.0	35.0	22.8	22.3	22.5	21.7	26.1	24.8	27.4	33.1
6. France	35.5	38.9	38.4	33.6	31.8	32.5	38.9	32.3	31.9	39.3
7. FRG	66.4	76.5	67.6	62.0	57.8	63.0	78.0	76.3	77.3	81.1
C. LDC										
1. Total	24.2	28.4	35.0	37.4	34.4	38.3	48.6	48.7	66.9	69.2
2. Brazil	6.5	7.9	11.2	9.8	7.1	7.1	10.3	11.5	13.4	14.6
3. India	6.0	6.5	7.0	9.5	11.0	13.0	15.7	14.0	16.0	19.3
4. Korea	0.8	0.8	3.0	3.9	2.8	2.6	3.1	3.5	6.6	5.4
D. CPE										
1. Total	186.0	189.6	186.9	186.2	191.9	200.2	206.6	214.8	211.1	209.6
2. USSR	127.5	130.0	130.0	130.0	138.0	145.0	150.0	156.0	146.0	138.0
3. E. Europe (CMEA-6)	39.0	40.1	38.3	36.6	34.3	35.6	36.1	37.2	45.0	45.5
4. China	19.0	19.0	18.0	19.0	19.0	19.0	20.0	21.0	19.0	25.0
5. CMEA-7	166.5	170.1	168.3	166.6	172.3	180.6	186.1	193.2	191.0	183.5

Note: Data for blank cells not available.

[1]Source: Metallgesellschaft Aktiengesellschaft, *Metallstatistic* (Frankfurt am Main, Metallgesellschaft AG, various issues).

[2]OECD, LDC, CPE, and CMEA definitions: see list of acronyms on page 270 of the statistical appendix.

Table B-7.   Tin, 1962–1988 (thousand metric tons)[1,2,3]

	1962	1963	1964	1965	1966	1967	1968	1969
A. World	198.6	204.5	210.9	209.3	214.6	209.1	215.7	223.1
B. OECD								
1. Total	146.1	148.7	153.8	151.6	154.2	151.4	155.2	162.3
2. United States	55.5	56.1	59.5	59.5	61.2	58.8	59.8	58.7
3. Japan	14.0	16.1	18.2	17.0	19.1	21.1	23.1	26.0
4. EEC-9	60.4	60.0	59.5	57.4	55.3	55.1	56.0	60.9
5. United Kingdom	22.8	22.1	21.4	21.0	20.0	19.5	19.5	19.7
6. France	11.4	11.2	11.2	10.3	10.5	10.2	9.5	10.7
7. FRG	13.1	12.5	13.7	13.0	12.1	11.8	12.3	14.4
C. LDC								
1. Total	17.2	18.2	18.5	17.9	17.7	16.3	15.7	16.7
2. Brazil	1.9	2.1	1.7	1.8	1.6	2.0	2.5	2.4
3. India	4.6	4.5	5.1	4.7	5.0	5.0	4.1	4.5
4. Korea								
D. CPE								
1. Total	35.3	37.6	38.6	39.8	42.7	41.4	44.8	44.1
2. USSR	15.0	15.0	15.5	15.5	16.0	16.0	16.5	16.5
3. E. Europe (CMEA-6)		9.5	10.0	11.1	12.6	11.8	14.4	13.7
4. China	10.5	13.0	13.0	13.0	13.5	13.0	13.0	13.0
5. CMEA-7		24.5	25.5	26.6	28.6	27.8	30.9	30.2

See notes at end of table B-7 on page 304.

Table B-7 (continued)

	1970	1971	1972	1973	1974	1975	1976	1977	1978	1979
A. World	225.5	225.9	232.3	254.0	244.3	212.2	234.0	224.9	232.7	229.3
B. OECD										
1. Total	162.0	162.6	167.9	180.8	171.4	143.0	161.5	150.0	151.0	154.0
2. United States	53.9	52.8	54.4	59.1	52.4	43.6	51.8	47.6	48.4	49.5
3. Japan	28.6	30.4	32.5	38.8	33.6	28.1	34.7	29.7	29.6	31.2
4. EEC-9	61.0	59.8	61.4	64.5	63.0	52.6	55.1	53.7	54.3	52.4
5. United Kingdom	18.6	18.1	17.9	18.4	16.7	14.4	15.2	14.9	13.9	13.2
6. France	10.5	10.5	11.0	11.7	11.7	10.0	10.5	9.8	9.9	9.7
7. FRG	15.1	15.4	15.9	16.9	15.7	13.0	15.7	14.9	15.1	15.2
C. LDC										
1. Total	18.5	17.0	16.5	22.9	20.0	19.9	22.1	25.3	29.5	24.3
2. Brazil	2.2	2.9	2.8	3.9	3.5	3.8	5.0	5.2	5.2	5.4
3. India	4.8	2.8	2.3	2.7	1.8	2.9	3.0	2.7	2.6	2.5
4. Korea			0.5	0.9	0.6	0.8	1.4	1.8	2.1	1.8
D. CPE										
1. Total	45.0	46.3	47.9	50.3	52.9	49.3	50.4	49.6	52.2	51.0
2. USSR	17.0	17.0	18.0	19.0	21.0	23.0	23.0	23.0	24.0	24.0
3. E. Europe (CMEA-6)	13.9	15.2	15.3	16.5	16.6	16.0	17.1	16.2	16.7	15.5
4. China	13.0	13.0	13.5	13.5	14.0	9.0	9.0	9.0	10.0	10.0
5. CMEA-7	30.9	32.2	33.3	35.5	37.6	39	40.1	39.2	40.7	39.5

(continued)

Table B-7 (continued)

	1980	1981	1982	1983	1984	1985	1986	1987	1988
A. World	221.5	209.9	200.5	205.6	217.1	213.0	217.3	227.2	
B. OECD									
1. Total	143.3	135.2	122.1	123.4	132.5	129.4	128.5	130.5	147.9
2. United States	44.3	40.2	33.0	34.3	37.8	37.1	32.7	35.6	48.3
3. Japan	30.9	30.5	28.7	30.4	33.3	31.6	31.5	32.6	32.4
4. EEC-9	49.9	47.0	44.1	43.6	45.9	44.9	47.9	47.4	50.6
5. United Kingdom	9.9	10.9	10.4	10.2	10.0	9.4	9.7	9.8	10.2
6. France	10.1	9.1	8.2	7.6	7.8	6.9	7.6	7.4	7.9
7. FRG	15.9	14.5	13.8	14.2	16.0	16.7	17.4	17.5	19.4
C. LDC									
1. Total	25.4	23.3	23.7	24.6	27.5	26.8	35.3	38.4	
2. Brazil	5.0	2.9	5.1	4.0	4.2	4.6	4.9	7.9	6.7
3. India	2.3	2.8	2.1	2.3	2.3	2.3	2.9	2.6	2.8
4. Korea	1.8	2.2	2.0	2.6	3.6	2.6	5.2	5.8	7.3
D. CPE									
1. Total	52.8	51.4	54.7	57.6	57.1	56.8	53.5	58.3	
2. USSR	25.0	26.0	27.0	29.5	30.0	30.0	26.0	29.0	
3. E. Europe (CMEA-6)	16.3	13.9	16.2	15.6	14.6	14.3	14.5	14.0	
4. China	10.0	10.0	10.0	11.0	11.0	11.0	11.5	13.5	
5. CMEA-7	41.3	39.9	43.2	45.1	44.6	44.3	40.5	43.0	

Note: Data for blank cells not available.

[1]Source: Metallgesellschaft Aktiengesellschaft, *Metallstatistic* (Frankfurt am Main: Metallgesellschaft AG, various issues).

[2]OECD, LDC, CPE, and CMEA definitions: see list of acronyms on page 270 of the statistical appendix.

[3]Tin consumption data for 1960 and 1961 are not available.

TABLE C-1. CRUDE STEEL, 1960–1987 305

Part C. Intensity of Metal Use

Table C-1. Crude Steel, 1960–1987[1,2,3]

	1960	1961	1962	1963	1964	1965	1966	1967
A. World	65.4289	65.7297	64.2895	66.1586	68.4521	68.3837	67.7963	68.5667
B. OECD								
1. Total	61.9191	60.6877	57.6610	60.1387	64.6952	64.4895	63.3149	63.1901
2. United States	65.4369	63.6827	61.2755	66.1919	72.5890	74.0422	72.1698	67.3124
3. Japan	78.5679	90.3746	74.2506	72.8508	73.9456	71.3594	79.4561	104.1976
4. EEC-9	60.0159	55.5740	54.2604	54.9916	58.4157	54.1441	52.5119	52.0271
5. United Kingdom	65.1254	53.3316	50.1095	54.0267	59.8113	58.1365	52.3414	51.4801
6. France	51.3066	49.6022	49.1785	48.8752	50.7407	45.2098	45.8261	45.8756
7. FRG	73.6682	66.1236	63.8985	61.0029	70.8278	63.2742	58.7319	54.8265
C. LDC								
1. Total	35.2189	36.4743	36.3443	35.5785	37.1897	37.0377	36.0886	35.8303
2. Brazil	46.7024	40.5576	40.9414	47.2547	45.5691	35.8605	50.0803	43.3749
3. India	60.1019	64.7423	75.9949	80.6508	76.1554	78.3873	73.3303	63.7481
4. Korea	12.4317	7.9865	23.2404	26.3832	15.1412	19.4597	31.1402	36.1632
D. CPE								
1. Total	96.6746	102.7556	107.1366	110.7661	104.1282	104.1257	105.2850	110.2981
2. USSR	103.1137	105.3479	109.6635	115.8096	109.0052	110.3206	110.6045	112.4987
3. E. Europe (CMEA-6)	83.6326	87.4957	89.3604	85.4174	88.2781	86.9757	87.9659	89.9662
4. China	78.4125	127.2229	142.2135	154.0122	109.3357	103.1375	110.8019	147.8100
5. CMEA-7	97.0705	99.8041	103.3478	106.0487	102.5628	103.1020	103.5717	105.5165

See notes at end of table C-1 on page 307.

(continued)

Table C-1 (continued)

	1968	1969	1970	1971	1972	1973	1974	1975	1976	1977
A. World	69.3758	71.1474	69.5430	65.7914	68.3978	70.9096	70.2792	63.3688	63.9511	61.3634
B. OECD										
1. Total	67.2109	67.1030	65.6606	58.7633	61.9688	64.7085	61.7800	51.3464	53.8369	49.5470
2. United States	70.3666	68.8895	63.4196	61.7121	63.2455	64.6937	62.8795	51.3556	54.1718	52.9687
3. Japan	90.9149	100.2117	103.8188	82.2434	90.5987	106.2815	93.4853	77.8729	74.8686	68.9110
4. EEC-9	61.9654	58.8947	58.2889	49.5382	53.2095	52.8820	49.8486	40.7617	46.8296	40.7192
5. United Kingdom	54.1045	55.6330	55.9518	44.8653	49.2194	49.5863	46.9224	41.3362	44.6603	37.8262
6. France	44.2554	51.3857	50.6553	43.9089	47.5348	46.8231	44.7747	34.5216	40.2173	32.4385
7. FRG	64.1641	68.4597	65.3942	55.4949	60.1617	57.9895	50.0571	44.0016	51.8699	45.1668
C. LDC										
1. Total	21.4641	37.1989	35.2655	39.2883	41.0914	43.6084	49.3210	47.6990	43.5083	47.2733
2. Brazil	49.1216	55.0756	55.7041	60.3340	56.2871	61.5368	75.4990	62.8855	52.3372	57.6585
3. India	56.0264	53.9174	54.6082	63.9761	77.1411	66.3180	68.8715	62.3869	57.5820	62.5553
4. Korea	35.4048	42.5653	45.1304	47.6268	45.7159	76.1781	79.7259	67.9344	78.9555	99.8646
D. CPE										
1. Total	111.1692	111.2462	108.7662	110.1228	112.3845	114.2483	116.3478	115.9880	115.0665	113.4583
2. USSR	110.9920	111.1000	108.5279	109.3115	112.7189	112.1434	114.7739	115.7220	115.4691	111.2809
3. E. Europe (CMEA-6)	90.7987	98.6167	97.5185	94.9993	95.0319	96.8016	99.3642	100.3882	101.9803	100.8367
4. China	171.8647	134.8722	124.8730	138.9512	140.3868	153.4990	151.4004	141.7520	126.4530	134.1681
5. CMEA-7	104.8155	107.3101	105.2844	105.0442	107.3359	107.5494	110.1336	111.0258	111.3802	108.1229

Table C-1 (continued)

TABLE C-1. CRUDE STEEL, 1960–1987   307

	1978	1979	1980	1981	1982	1983	1984	1985	1986	1987
A. World	62.5805	63.2444	59.6882	57.8498	52.9898	52.6179	54.2415	53.4830	51.8089	50.9715
B. OECD										
1. Total	49.1312	50.5963	45.6977	44.2006	37.3370	36.5421	39.4329	37.0448	34.8208	35.3755
2. United States	55.1515	52.0028	42.4040	46.2280	31.2636	33.9012	37.4234	34.3953	30.1696	31.2260
3. Japan	69.1426	77.0834	74.6010	64.6726	61.4448	56.2335	60.6960	57.2995	53.2998	55.3471
4. EEC-9	38.7655	41.4533	38.0766	34.5322	32.6763	31.1734	32.6168	31.2138	30.3830	30.4408
5. United Kingdom	36.3014	36.9620	26.1850	28.5462	26.9940	25.8733	25.9334	24.8434	23.9828	24.0167
6. France	31.4751	31.9458	30.7686	26.5273	25.6511	22.6640	22.6505	21.3298	20.5841	20.5725
7. FRG	43.2809	47.1113	42.4910	39.7920	34.4383	36.9297	36.9661	35.5499	34.3730	32.1693
C. LDC										
1. Total	49.6048	50.9701	52.1902	52.8408	50.7847	48.1967	48.8288	50.2668	46.8984	45.9702
2. Brazil	54.8991	55.2350	57.4746	49.3327	42.9870	35.8989	42.8332	44.6351	49.1245	48.1955
3. India	69.7533	81.9313	72.3714	82.3745	79.2998	64.8315	63.2242	65.5549	66.5394	68.2180
4. Korea	109.5516	110.4503	88.9800	112.0492	93.2549	97.2780	111.0231	111.3190	111.4329	135.0177
D. CPE										
1. Total	119.0006	117.4738	114.2027	109.2431	107.3277	109.1395	107.3951	109.8052	110.5780	104.0437
2. USSR	112.6687	110.4472	107.9182	106.3815	104.4049	104.9895	103.1877	99.8725	99.4279	96.0605
3. E. Europe (CMEA-6)	101.6638	100.1240	99.4265	93.1078	91.7030	88.6665	86.1055	82.4211	80.5574	78.8732
4. China	167.1124	165.2894	149.0257	130.1525	125.9320	139.1310	135.3635	151.5994	153.5616	145.5857
5. CMEA-7	109.3543	107.3350	105.3894	102.5054	100.7115	100.3216	98.3019	94.8742	94.0009	91.0868

[1]Intensity of use defined as tons of metal consumed per million $ GDP.
[2]OECD, LDC, CPE, and CMEA definitions: see list of acronyms on page 270 of the statistical appendix.
[3]Source: Calculations using data from parts A and B of this appendix.

Table C-2. Primary Aluminum, 1960–1987[1,2,3]

	1960	1961	1962	1963	1964	1965	1966	1967
A. World	0.8144	0.8428	0.8879	0.9353	0.9552	1.0054	1.0933	1.0762
B. OECD								
1. Total	0.8910	0.8996	0.9638	1.0245	1.0612	1.1006	1.2155	1.1528
2. United States	1.1204	1.2695	1.4031	1.5107	1.5543	1.6488	1.7922	1.6578
3. Japan	0.6078	0.6542	0.5894	0.7113	0.6983	0.7468	0.8905	1.0184
4. EEC-9	0.7773	0.6906	0.7005	0.7318	0.7762	0.7473	0.8239	0.7903
5. United Kingdom	1.0550	0.8081	0.8083	0.8653	0.9224	0.8872	0.9000	0.8620
6. France	0.7972	0.7147	0.7845	0.7666	0.7398	0.7038	0.8030	0.7560
7. FRG	0.7982	0.7206	0.7015	0.7117	0.8160	0.7755	0.8192	0.8154
C. LDC								
1. Total	0.2046	0.2712	0.3032	0.3055	0.3161	0.3594	0.4302	0.4541
2. Brazil	0.5481	0.5542	0.5898	0.6627	0.6185	0.6866	0.9211	0.9498
3. India	0.3133	0.3625	0.5750	0.6861	0.5815	0.7584	0.8961	1.1721
4. Korea			0.5993	0.2143	0.0122	0.2137	0.2419	0.3597
D. CPE								
1. Total	0.9351	1.0132	1.0048	1.0506	1.0177	1.1118	1.1104	1.2308
2. USSR	1.0259	1.0990	1.0879	1.1648	1.1132	1.2343	1.2624	1.3267
3. E. Europe (CMEA-6)	0.7255	0.7406	0.7878	0.8131	0.8403	0.9178	0.9050	1.0578
4. China	0.8023	1.0018	1.1393	1.0288	0.8835	0.8444	0.7209	1.0646
5. CMEA-7	0.9328	0.9877	0.9945	1.0519	1.0284	1.1365	1.1514	1.2434

See notes at end of table C-2 on page 310.

Table C-2 (continued)

TABLE C-2. PRIMARY ALUMINUM, 1960–1987 309

	1968	1969	1970	1971	1972	1973	1974	1975	1976	1977
A. World	1.1618	1.2001	1.1801	1.2159	1.2723	1.3873	1.3991	1.1298	1.3308	1.3129
B. OECD										
1. Total	1.2710	1.3263	1.2964	1.3338	1.4120	1.5844	1.5730	1.1653	1.4622	1.4232
2. United States	1.8375	1.8409	1.7377	1.8983	1.9643	2.1952	2.2371	1.4353	1.8851	1.8926
3. Japan	1.1314	1.3118	1.3540	1.3867	1.5996	1.9650	1.6081	1.4083	1.8477	1.5481
4. EEC-9	0.8641	0.9414	0.9590	0.8782	0.9397	1.0263	1.0602	0.8515	1.0469	1.0152
5. United Kingdom	0.9015	0.8868	0.9044	0.7095	0.8701	0.9671	0.9985	0.7911	0.8642	0.8040
6. France	0.7238	0.8462	0.9010	0.7806	0.7779	0.8343	0.8618	0.7155	0.8394	0.8827
7. FRG	0.9925	1.0963	1.0787	1.0678	1.0903	1.2280	1.2451	1.0233	1.3197	1.2243
C. LDC										
1. Total	0.4446	0.4438	0.4707	0.5204	0.4808	0.4851	0.6036	0.6009	0.6161	0.6561
2. Brazil	0.8799	0.8366	0.7638	0.8434	1.0126	1.0224	1.1036	1.2130	1.1079	1.1201
3. India	1.2236	1.0307	1.3754	1.6015	1.4450	1.1981	1.0037	1.1670	1.2332	1.2570
4. Korea	0.3711	0.4832	0.5394	0.5489	0.5638	0.9695	0.6368	0.8285	1.0651	1.3783
D. CPE										
1. Total	1.2769	1.3014	1.3010	1.3272	1.3849	1.3956	1.4410	1.4373	1.4827	1.5034
2. USSR	1.3217	1.3035	1.3094	1.3219	1.3434	1.2827	1.2933	1.2965	1.3238	1.3362
3. E. Europe (CMEA-6)	1.1308	1.2247	1.2500	1.3102	1.3781	1.4524	1.5411	1.4832	1.5116	1.5285
4. China	1.4020	1.4700	1.3405	1.3645	1.5959	1.8470	1.9759	2.0074	2.2667	2.2804
5. CMEA-7	1.2633	1.2796	1.2919	1.3184	1.3540	1.3335	1.3680	1.3537	1.3808	1.3943

(continued)

Table C-2 (continued)

	1978	1979	1980	1981	1982	1983	1984	1985	1986	1987
A. World	1.3342	1.3470	1.2696	1.1905	1.1616	1.2228	1.2210	1.2050	1.1864	1.2050
B. OECD										
1. Total	1.4367	1.4571	1.3492	1.2428	1.1930	1.2884	1.2857	1.2358	1.2164	1.2661
2. United States	1.8915	1.8584	1.6568	1.4951	1.3278	1.5203	1.4980	1.3993	1.3175	1.3935
3. Japan	1.7180	1.7785	1.5476	1.4275	1.4492	1.5449	1.4421	1.4197	1.4097	1.5014
4. EEC-9	1.0097	1.0637	1.0479	0.9526	0.9764	1.0209	1.0530	1.0132	1.0388	1.0290
5. United Kingdom	0.7478	0.7656	0.7677	0.6522	0.6134	0.5860	0.6554	0.5984	0.6503	0.6133
6. France	0.8495	0.9184	0.9172	0.8184	0.8627	0.9088	0.8470	0.8473	0.8389	0.8547
7. FRG	1.2382	1.3291	1.2730	1.2475	1.2322	1.3234	1.3693	1.3371	1.3404	1.3108
C. LDC										
1. Total	0.7247	0.7373	0.7490	0.7248	0.7655	0.8163	0.8760	0.9620	0.9487	0.9808
2. Brazil	1.1040	1.1467	1.1934	1.0702	1.1419	1.1322	1.1799	1.3696	1.4377	1.3852
3. India	1.2905	1.4038	1.4505	1.4637	1.2527	1.1572	1.5711	1.4067	1.3952	1.4315
4. Korea	1.7655	1.4661	1.0814	1.5453	1.3705	1.5267	1.5083	1.6215	1.9587	1.8627
D. CPE										
1. Total	1.5070	1.5056	1.4582	1.4251	1.4049	1.3524	1.2963	1.3027	1.2895	1.1980
2. USSR	1.3438	1.3583	1.3281	1.3117	1.3056	1.2351	1.1678	1.1596	1.1350	1.0595
3. E. Europe (CMEA-6)	1.5224	1.4874	1.4770	1.4096	1.3622	1.3395	1.3664	1.3300	1.3031	1.2133
4. China	2.2251	2.1565	1.9183	1.8617	1.7899	1.7458	1.5563	1.5398	1.5211	1.4914
5. CMEA-7	1.3976	1.3973	1.3724	1.3403	1.3220	1.2649	1.2246	1.2084	1.1834	1.1040

[1]Intensity of use defined as tons of metal consumed per million $ GDP.

[2]OECD, LDC, CPE, and CMEA definitions: see list of acronyms on page 270 of the statistical appendix.

[3]Source: Calculations using data from parts A and B of this appendix.

Table C-3. Refined Copper, 1960–1987[1,2,3]

TABLE C-3. REFINED COPPER, 1960–1987   311

	1960	1961	1962	1963	1964	1965	1966	1967
A. World	0.9296	0.9539	0.9302	0.9438	0.9568	0.9364	0.9277	0.8599
B. OECD								
1. Total	1.0368	1.0650	1.0048	1.0304	1.0744	1.0504	1.0522	0.9477
2. United States	0.8902	0.9555	0.9797	1.0263	1.0362	1.0661	1.1774	0.9564
3. Japan	1.2276	1.3145	0.9911	1.0492	1.2041	1.0702	1.0922	1.2633
4. EEC-9	1.2038	1.1729	1.0761	1.0703	1.1288	1.0749	0.9565	0.9084
5. United Kingdom	1.6548	1.5122	1.4901	1.5207	1.6389	1.6450	1.4694	1.2432
6. France	0.8875	0.8653	0.8114	0.7912	0.8657	0.8137	0.7841	0.6976
7. FRG	1.3163	1.3623	1.1631	1.1135	1.1865	1.0736	0.8958	0.9805
C. LDC								
1. Total	0.3797	0.3836	0.3933	0.3677	0.3742	0.3538	0.2659	0.2567
2. Brazil	0.4933	0.5482	0.5626	0.5435	0.5019	0.4085	0.4855	0.4993
3. India	0.7853	0.8217	0.9118	0.8698	0.6720	0.6634	0.3505	0.4184
4. Korea			0.0365	0.1205	0.1709	0.1213	0.1596	0.2382
D. CPE								
1. Total	0.9069	0.9300	1.0197	1.0306	0.9374	0.9314	0.9365	0.9617
2. USSR	1.0578	1.0480	1.0891	1.1021	0.9987	0.9953	0.9876	1.0029
3. E. Europe (CMEA-6)						0.7426	0.7484	0.7574
4. China	0.9806	1.5026	1.6084	1.4525	1.2473	1.0666	1.0624	1.2284
5. CMEA-7						0.9172	0.9133	0.9268

See notes at end of table C-3 on page 313.

(continued)

Table C-3 (continued)

	1968	1969	1970	1971	1972	1973	1974	1975	1976	1977
A. World	0.8582	0.8854	0.8619	0.8288	0.8598	0.8885	0.8268	0.7341	0.8046	0.8179
B. OECD										
1. Total	0.9433	0.9891	0.9683	0.9100	0.9413	0.9830	0.8949	0.7443	0.8423	0.8624
2. United States	0.8704	0.9690	0.9267	0.8863	0.9275	0.9605	0.8704	0.6151	0.7607	0.7919
3. Japan	1.2664	1.3115	1.2191	1.1484	1.2511	1.4651	1.0871	0.9952	1.2057	1.2289
4. EEC-9	0.9598	0.9717	0.9683	0.8950	0.9138	0.9073	0.8895	0.8136	0.8604	0.8845
5. United Kingdom	1.2516	1.2507	1.2390	1.1272	1.1396	1.0730	0.9951	0.9075	0.8897	0.9831
6. France	0.7223	0.7718	0.7209	0.7106	0.7620	0.7559	0.7437	0.6533	0.6256	0.5393
7. FRG	1.1204	1.1191	1.1233	0.9837	1.0116	1.0436	1.0434	0.9228	1.0296	1.0466
C. LDC										
1. Total	0.2922	0.3117	0.3022	0.3198	0.3414	0.3423	0.3665	0.3333	0.3746	0.3918
2. Brazil	0.6230	0.6274	0.6760	0.7781	0.8127	0.8108	0.9555	0.8683	0.9142	1.0169
3. India	0.3709	0.4574	0.4670	0.5062	0.4956	0.5075	0.3746	0.1791	0.3685	0.3545
4. Korea	0.2707	0.2493	0.2644	0.2809	0.2987	0.3596	0.5800	0.8056	0.9572	1.0622
D. CPE										
1. Total	0.9531	0.9332	0.9055	0.9282	0.9691	0.9815	0.9630	1.0226	1.0353	1.0331
2. USSR	0.9702	0.9675	0.9353	0.9334	0.9576	0.9534	0.9179	1.0011	0.9792	0.9794
3. E. Europe (CMEA-6)	0.7546	0.7645	0.7305	0.7807	0.8288	0.8630	0.8670	0.8920	0.9351	0.9443
4. China	1.4020	1.1025	1.0724	1.1695	1.2984	1.3478	1.3831	1.3687	1.5433	1.4756
5. CMEA-7	0.9043	0.9059	0.8750	0.8878	0.9184	0.9263	0.9025	0.9677	0.9658	0.9688

TABLE C-3. REFINED COPPER, 1960–1987   313

Table C-3 (continued)

	1978	1979	1980	1981	1982	1983	1984	1985	1986	1987
A. World	0.8287	0.8295	0.7792	0.7778	0.7325	0.7230	0.7533	0.7127	0.7205	0.7176
B. OECD										
1. Total	0.8790	0.8681	0.7955	0.7997	0.7354	0.7367	0.7799	0.7134	0.7297	0.7192
2. United States	0.8347	0.8017	0.6948	0.7450	0.6213	0.6533	0.7135	0.6227	0.6794	0.6560
3. Japan	1.2878	1.3117	1.0937	1.1402	1.0990	1.0424	1.1168	0.9611	0.9291	0.9382
4. EEC-9	0.8500	0.8468	0.8257	0.7746	0.7596	0.7386	0.7671	0.7344	0.7390	0.7322
5. United Kingdom	0.9323	0.9145	0.7675	0.6322	0.6681	0.6486	0.6260	0.5924	0.5676	0.5240
6. France	0.5086	0.5524	0.6615	0.6527	0.6077	0.5778	0.6016	0.5751	0.5678	0.5540
7. FRG	1.0142	0.9884	0.9133	0.9126	0.9002	0.8989	0.9414	0.8704	0.8683	0.8845
C. LDC										
1. Total	0.3993	0.4432	0.4652	0.4588	0.4579	0.4354	0.4867	0.5127	0.5290	0.5942
2. Brazil	0.8303	0.9870	0.9905	0.7320	0.9920	0.6209	0.7575	0.7324	0.8649	0.8331
3. India	0.4631	0.4498	0.4790	0.4404	0.4744	0.5084	0.4298	0.5370	0.4951	0.5050
4. Korea	1.2265	1.3262	1.3458	2.0853	1.9295	1.9377	2.2015	2.3086	2.6107	2.3205
D. CPE										
1. Total	1.0237	1.0368	1.0014	0.9865	0.9646	0.9222	0.8888	0.8736	0.8520	0.8145
2. USSR	0.9766	0.9905	0.9332	0.9309	0.9167	0.8679	0.8304	0.8180	0.7828	0.7593
3. E. Europe (CMEA-6)	0.9347	0.9682	0.9808	0.9537	0.9208	0.9218	0.9369	0.8669	0.8569	0.8474
4. China	1.3907	1.3385	1.2905	1.2300	1.1727	1.0700	0.9634	0.9349	0.9127	0.8762
5. CMEA-7	0.9640	0.9838	0.9474	0.9376	0.9179	0.8833	0.8609	0.8320	0.8041	0.7848

[1]Intensity of use defined as tons of metal consumed per million $ GDP.
[2]OECD, LDC, CPE, and CMEA definitions: see list of acronyms on page 270 of the statistical appendix.
[3]Source: Calculations using data from parts A and B of this appendix.

Table C-4.   Refined Lead, 1960–1987[1,2,3]

	1960	1961	1962	1963	1964	1965	1966	1967
A. World	0.5124	0.5073	0.5041	0.5076	0.5026	0.4812	0.4784	0.4596
B. OECD								
1. Total	0.5441	0.5260	0.5172	0.5136	0.5090	0.4892	0.4829	0.4557
2. United States	0.4701	0.4542	0.4631	0.4637	0.4463	0.4355	0.4488	0.4094
3. Japan	0.4022	0.4431	0.3876	0.3883	0.4322	0.3688	0.3348	0.3349
4. EEC-9	0.6603	0.6260	0.6075	0.5918	0.5846	0.5609	0.5419	0.5290
5. United Kingdom	0.8461	0.7884	0.7826	0.7726	0.7970	0.7897	0.7276	0.6679
6. France	0.6049	0.5708	0.5204	0.5377	0.5107	0.4095	0.4538	0.4222
7. FRG	0.6107	0.5728	0.5667	0.5544	0.5491	0.5463	0.5038	0.5075
C. LDC								
1. Total	0.2456	0.2946	0.2875	0.3397	0.2925	0.2812	0.2895	0.2877
2. Brazil	0.3056	0.3946	0.3092	0.4314	0.2578	0.2329	0.2926	0.2898
3. India	0.3108	0.3806	0.4225	0.4426	0.3884	0.3985	0.4716	0.3660
4. Korea			0.3654	0.3348	0.3663	0.1328	0.2677	0.1798
D. CPE								
1. Total	0.5715	0.5795	0.6020	0.6057	0.6272	0.5913	0.5911	0.5921
2. USSR	0.5195	0.4796	0.4919	0.5145	0.5129	0.4894	0.5077	0.4916
3. E. Europe (CMEA-6)	0.6082	0.6146	0.6963	0.6545	0.7454	0.7063	0.6982	0.7139
4. China	0.6240	1.0644	1.1393	1.0894	1.0394	0.8888	0.7589	0.8189
5. CMEA-7	0.5470	0.5215	0.5555	0.5595	0.5851	0.5565	0.5669	0.5605

See notes at end of table C-4 on page 316.

TABLE C-4. REFINED LEAD, 1960–1987   315

Table C-4 (continued)

	1968	1969	1970	1971	1972	1973	1974	1975	1976	1977
A. World	0.4808	0.4761	0.4627	0.4572	0.4513	0.4547	0.4398	0.4693	0.4880	0.4960
B. OECD										
1. Total	0.4785	0.4718	0.4641	0.4485	0.4429	0.4498	0.4233	0.4476	0.4858	0.4992
2. United States	0.4659	0.4527	0.4699	0.4552	0.4613	0.4728	0.4603	0.4935	0.5341	0.5642
3. Japan	0.3292	0.3051	0.3127	0.2989	0.3038	0.3259	0.2683	0.3136	0.3555	0.3640
4. EEC-9	0.5400	0.5418	0.5190	0.5074	0.4926	0.4819	0.4544	0.4583	0.4958	0.5037
5. United Kingdom	0.6425	0.6297	0.5856	0.6029	0.5934	0.5595	0.6561	0.6164	0.6189	0.6100
6. France	0.4422	0.4576	0.4197	0.3897	0.3945	0.3961	0.3912	0.3411	0.3887	0.3479
7. FRG	0.5304	0.5371	0.4975	0.4470	0.4117	0.4215	0.4620	0.4108	0.4145	0.4677
C. LDC										
1. Total	0.2870	0.2708	0.2572	0.2703	0.2500	0.2615	0.2770	0.3174	0.3040	0.3186
2. Brazil	0.1793	0.1862	0.1784	0.2098	0.4056	0.4005	0.2996	0.4207	0.4048	0.4441
3. India	0.3489	0.2714	0.3523	0.2738	0.3519	0.3348	0.3440	0.2642	0.3787	0.3618
4. Korea	0.3056	0.3068	0.2821	0.2906	0.3048	0.2930	0.2814	0.2364	0.2159	0.3271
D. CPE										
1. Total	0.6266	0.6448	0.6111	0.6276	0.6367	0.6233	0.6272	0.6638	0.6485	0.6373
2. USSR	0.4906	0.4875	0.4824	0.5022	0.5206	0.5200	0.5257	0.5744	0.5483	0.5466
3. E. Europe (CMEA-6)	0.7113	0.7397	0.7411	0.7432	0.7414	0.7265	0.7219	0.7370	0.7180	0.6863
4. China	1.3144	1.3597	0.9532	0.9468	0.9197	0.8486	0.8644	0.8440	0.9163	0.8943
5. CMEA-7	0.5581	0.5641	0.5586	0.5741	0.5878	0.5819	0.5848	0.6242	0.5998	0.5889

(continued)

Table C-4 (continued)

	1978	1979	1980	1981	1982	1983	1984	1985	1986	1987
A. World	0.4803	0.4754	0.4478	0.4303	0.4244	0.4193	0.4142	0.4019	0.3933	0.3870
B. OECD										
1. Total	0.4768	0.4624	0.4238	0.4050	0.3993	0.3912	0.3947	0.3722	0.3668	0.3617
2. United States	0.5337	0.4983	0.4070	0.4057	0.4101	0.4085	0.3841	0.3592	0.3557	0.3695
3. Japan	0.3653	0.3631	0.3706	0.3477	0.3130	0.3082	0.3189	0.3084	0.2969	0.2761
4. EEC-9	0.4838	0.4808	0.4602	0.4328	0.4275	0.4182	0.4317	0.4055	0.4032	0.3961
5. United Kingdom	0.6255	0.6109	0.5543	0.5045	0.5111	0.5307	0.5238	0.4690	0.4715	0.4597
6. France	0.3376	0.3258	0.3236	0.3201	0.2901	0.2905	0.3057	0.3007	0.2906	0.2881
7. FRG	0.4366	0.4497	0.4068	0.4049	0.4105	0.3882	0.4245	0.3983	0.4043	0.3809
C. LDC										
1. Total	0.2995	0.3357	0.3184	0.3009	0.2940	0.3224	0.3108	0.3327	0.3454	0.3557
2. Brazil	0.3729	0.4178	0.3551	0.2491	0.1637	0.2134	0.2550	0.2738	0.2973	0.2987
3. India	0.3456	0.3869	0.3350	0.3331	0.3849	0.3178	0.3142	0.3309	0.3623	0.2964
4. Korea	0.4572	0.5146	0.5287	0.5653	0.4446	0.6107	0.5387	0.7038	0.8788	1.0070
D. CPE										
1. Total	0.6462	0.6432	0.6445	0.6323	0.6235	0.5939	0.5642	0.5554	0.5187	0.4921
2. USSR	0.5581	0.5681	0.5743	0.5642	0.5625	0.5374	0.5125	0.5015	0.4576	0.4562
3. E. Europe (CMEA-6)	0.7081	0.6931	0.7091	0.7002	0.6962	0.6724	0.6572	0.6528	0.6196	0.5601
4. China	0.8344	0.7808	0.7324	0.7148	0.6635	0.6054	0.5311	0.4839	0.4563	0.4474
5. CMEA-7	0.6033	0.6058	0.6144	0.6039	0.6014	0.5760	0.5539	0.5448	0.5042	0.4862

[1]Intensity of use defined as tons of metal consumed per million $ GDP.
[2]OECD, LDC, CPE, and CMEA definitions: see list of acronyms on page 270 of the statistical appendix.
[3]Source: Calculations using data from parts A and B of this appendix.

TABLE C-5. ZINC, 1960–1987   317

Table C-5.   Zinc, 1960–1987[1,2,3]

	1960	1961	1962	1963	1964	1965	1966	1967
A. World	0.6022	0.6068	0.6056	0.6210	0.6307	0.6178	0.6125	0.5978
B. OECD								
1. Total	0.6301	0.6408	0.6420	0.6587	0.6865	0.6699	0.6587	0.6214
2. United States	0.5746	0.5940	0.6241	0.6430	0.6674	0.7059	0.7017	0.6003
3. Japan	0.6078	0.8259	0.7995	0.9079	0.9588	0.8249	0.8799	0.9471
4. EEC-9	0.7209	0.7042	0.6768	0.6544	0.6790	0.6387	0.6061	0.5836
5. United Kingdom	0.8148	0.7398	0.6976	0.7228	0.7559	0.7138	0.6760	0.6249
6. France	0.6450	0.6703	0.6186	0.5715	0.6042	0.5259	0.5306	0.5207
7. FRG	0.7566	0.7424	0.6761	0.6327	0.6777	0.6606	0.6058	0.5922
C. LDC								
1. Total	0.3955	0.3662	0.3558	0.3493	0.3492	0.3485	0.3559	0.3599
2. Brazil	0.5115	0.4925	0.6041	0.5520	0.4210	0.4205	0.5289	0.4713
3. India	0.7550	0.9050	0.9928	0.8975	0.6822	0.7424	0.6432	0.5915
4. Korea			0.1754	0.4754	0.2625	0.5312	0.2677	0.4132
D. CPE								
1. Total	0.6367	0.6428	0.6414	0.6738	0.6251	0.6176	0.6231	0.6775
2. USSR	0.6014	0.5521	0.5313	0.5879	0.5264	0.5466	0.5440	0.6131
3. E. Europe (CMEA-6)	0.6660	0.6440	0.7471	0.7466	0.7248	0.6889	0.6824	0.6977
4. China	0.6240	1.1270	1.2063	1.0894	1.0394	0.8888	0.9106	0.9827
5. CMEA-7	0.6215	0.5806	0.5984	0.6389	0.5880	0.5906	0.5870	0.6393

See notes at end of table C-5 on page 319.

(continued)

Table C-5 (continued)

	1968	1969	1970	1971	1972	1973	1974	1975	1976	1977
A. World	0.6179	0.6347	0.5960	0.5912	0.6202	0.6342	0.6004	0.4911	0.5442	0.5226
B. OECD										
1. Total	0.6439	0.6638	0.6068	0.5948	0.6326	0.6520	0.5985	0.4391	0.5175	0.4897
2. United States	0.6235	0.6218	0.5352	0.5496	0.5875	0.5897	0.5306	0.3473	0.4531	0.3940
3. Japan	0.9522	0.9751	0.9257	0.8951	0.9425	0.9934	0.8582	0.6581	0.7985	0.7815
4. EEC-9	0.6161	0.6450	0.5931	0.5656	0.5966	0.6200	0.5852	0.4277	0.4853	0.4809
5. United Kingdom	0.6516	0.6608	0.6216	0.5964	0.5911	0.6055	0.5377	0.4172	0.4721	0.4700
6. France	0.4989	0.5509	0.4800	0.4662	0.5158	0.5383	0.5496	0.3988	0.4517	0.4262
7. FRG	0.6653	0.6800	0.6373	0.6046	0.6216	0.6288	0.5682	0.4325	0.4502	0.4481
C. LDC										
1. Total	0.3840	0.3826	0.3844	0.3764	0.3982	0.3927	0.3923	0.3605	0.3762	0.3821
2. Brazil	0.4995	0.4980	0.4491	0.5160	0.4850	0.5177	0.5509	0.4610	0.4956	0.5087
3. India	0.7743	0.7279	0.8235	0.7592	0.8592	0.6285	0.6952	0.6019	0.6543	0.6499
4. Korea	0.3449	0.4065	0.3878	0.4488	0.4572	0.6153	0.6269	0.6334	0.7189	0.8509
D. CPE										
1. Total	0.6899	0.7163	0.7161	0.7399	0.7472	0.7602	0.7740	0.7692	0.7741	0.7549
2. USSR	0.6323	0.6676	0.6695	0.6917	0.7066	0.7280	0.7510	0.7385	0.7285	0.7174
3. E. Europe (CMEA-6)	0.6932	0.7110	0.7208	0.7247	0.7287	0.7277	0.7330	0.7691	0.7875	0.7585
4. China	1.0515	0.9922	0.8937	0.9468	0.9197	0.8985	0.8891	0.8212	0.8681	0.8272
5. CMEA-7	0.6509	0.6808	0.6846	0.7016	0.7133	0.7279	0.7456	0.7479	0.7464	0.7298

TABLE C-5. ZINC, 1960–1987   319

Table C-5 (continued)

	1978	1979	1980	1981	1982	1983	1984	1985	1986	1987
A. World	0.5482	0.5365	0.5139	0.4956	0.4825	0.5020	0.4987	0.4813	0.4774	0.4723
B. OECD										
1. Total	0.5101	0.4974	0.4626	0.4379	0.4113	0.4426	0.4375	0.4194	0.4221	0.4138
2. United States	0.4225	0.3915	0.3268	0.3378	0.2946	0.3362	0.3295	0.3074	0.3176	0.3233
3. Japan	0.7599	0.7678	0.7103	0.6356	0.6216	0.6606	0.6322	0.6092	0.5738	0.5320
4. EEC-9	0.5042	0.4976	0.4919	0.4499	0.4294	0.4554	0.4580	0.4383	0.4426	0.4367
5. United Kingdom	0.4602	0.4378	0.3401	0.3519	0.3346	0.3207	0.3228	0.3232	0.3040	0.3007
6. France	0.4492	0.4419	0.5037	0.4134	0.3936	0.4007	0.4111	0.3569	0.3688	0.3436
7. FRG	0.5084	0.5192	0.4955	0.4556	0.4541	0.4951	0.5052	0.4720	0.4875	0.4998
C. LDC										
1. Total	0.4489	0.4431	0.4303	0.4296	0.4455	0.4624	0.4728	0.4757	0.4691	0.4941
2. Brazil	0.5676	0.5334	0.5564	0.4654	0.3670	0.4368	0.4753	0.5206	0.5120	0.5685
3. India	0.6786	0.7698	0.5913	0.6333	0.7469	0.6620	0.6300	0.6145	0.6076	0.5730
4. Korea	0.9679	1.1303	1.0894	1.1709	1.3324	1.4402	1.4181	1.3965	1.5148	1.5992
D. CPE										
1. Total	0.7613	0.7532	0.7632	0.7526	0.7537	0.7307	0.7217	0.6880	0.6621	0.6382
2. USSR	0.7270	0.7283	0.7394	0.7334	0.7292	0.7010	0.6812	0.6268	0.5961	0.5945
3. E. Europe (CMEA-6)	0.7991	0.7790	0.8012	0.7595	0.7336	0.6973	0.7063	0.6853	0.6498	0.6522
4. China	0.7351	0.7064	0.6976	0.7314	0.8024	0.8166	0.8152	0.7699	0.7301	0.6711
5. CMEA-7	0.7487	0.7436	0.7578	0.7410	0.7305	0.6999	0.6884	0.6436	0.6116	0.6112

[1]Intensity of use defined as tons of metal consumed per million $ GDP.

[2]OECD, LDC, CPE, and CMEA definitions: see list of acronyms on page 270 of the statistical appendix.

[3]Source: Calculations using data from parts A and B of this appendix.

Table C-6.   Nickel, 1960–1987[1,2,3]

	1960	1961	1962	1963	1964	1965	1966	1967
A. World	0.0572	0.0602	0.0569	0.0573	0.0641	0.0652	0.0671	0.0654
B. OECD								
1. Total	0.0624	0.0610	0.0547	0.0574	0.0673	0.0702	0.0732	0.0713
2. United States	0.0713	0.0762	0.0723	0.0729	0.0817	0.0902	0.0931	0.0838
3. Japan	0.0711	0.0726	0.0514	0.0673	0.0853	0.0716	0.0822	0.1025
4. EEC-9	0.0591	0.0518	0.0449	0.0476	0.0581	0.0587	0.0611	0.0586
5. United Kingdom	0.0821	0.0758	0.0711	0.0752	0.0987	0.0934	0.0853	0.0737
6. France	0.0727	0.0547	0.0440	0.0499	0.0608	0.0595	0.0660	0.0738
7. FRG	0.0587	0.0534	0.0446	0.0458	0.0541	0.0615	0.0656	0.0606
C. LDC								
1. Total	0.0022	0.0055	0.0049	0.0063	0.0052	0.0066	0.0071	0.0083
2. Brazil					0.0110	0.0106	0.0115	0.0110
3. India							0.0107	0.0119
4. Korea								
D. CPE								
1. Total	0.0736	0.0928	0.0996	0.0938	0.0939	0.0879	0.0863	0.0837
2. USSR								
3. E. Europe (CMEA-6)								
4. China								
5. CMEA-7								

See notes at end of table C-6 on page 322.

TABLE C-6. NICKEL, 1960–1987 321

Table C-6 (continued)

	1968	1969	1970	1971	1972	1973	1974	1975	1976	1977
A. World	0.0643	0.0624	0.0682	0.0598	0.0628	0.0668	0.0708	0.0569	0.0628	0.0579
B. OECD										
1. Total	0.0699	0.0685	0.0781	0.0658	0.0697	0.0758	0.0820	0.0600	0.0680	0.0611
2. United States	0.0738	0.0679	0.0743	0.0644	0.0717	0.0788	0.0849	0.0584	0.0620	0.0552
3. Japan	0.1080	0.1214	0.1475	0.1291	0.1153	0.1385	0.1430	0.1002	0.1320	0.1061
4. EEC-9	0.0623	0.0592	0.0654	0.0539	0.0595	0.0597	0.0657	0.0513	0.0580	0.0563
5. United Kingdom	0.0768	0.0743	0.0839	0.0675	0.0639	0.0625	0.0671	0.0544	0.0593	0.0586
6. France	0.0757	0.0733	0.0787	0.0666	0.0611	0.0549	0.0727	0.0572	0.0571	0.0592
7. FRG	0.0652	0.0628	0.0649	0.0532	0.0644	0.0786	0.0874	0.0622	0.0780	0.0719
C. LDC										
1. Total	0.0084	0.0078	0.0084	0.0086	0.0036	0.0124	0.0106	0.0101	0.0123	0.0120
2. Brazil	0.0109	0.0090	0.0146	0.0122	0.0066	0.0343	0.0389	0.0218	0.0240	0.0251
3. India	0.0105	0.0117	0.0144	0.0207	0.0142	0.0121	0.0226	0.0242	0.0254	0.0375
4. Korea							0.0123	0.0115	0.0224	0.0184
D. CPE										
1. Total	0.0836	0.0805	0.0777	0.0772	0.0839	0.0778	0.0805	0.0844	0.0875	0.0861
2. USSR					0.0930	0.0867	0.0876	0.0944	0.0948	0.0949
3. E. Europe (CMEA-6)					0.0529	0.0511	0.0596	0.0619	0.0701	0.0671
4. China					0.1082	0.0899	0.0889	0.0821	0.0868	0.0805
5. CMEA-7					0.0808	0.0760	0.0792	0.0844	0.0873	0.0865

(continued)

Table C-6 (continued)

	1978	1979	1980	1981	1982	1983	1984	1985	1986	1987
A. World	0.0609	0.0631	0.0590	0.0542	0.0530	0.0556	0.0603	0.0584	0.0570	0.0583
B. OECD										
1. Total	0.0660	0.0692	0.0630	0.0558	0.0541	0.0573	0.0636	0.0604	0.0584	0.0618
2. United States	0.0623	0.0566	0.0529	0.0503	0.0462	0.0501	0.0474	0.0480	0.0452	0.0433
3. Japan	0.1027	0.1302	0.1169	0.0967	0.0958	0.1011	0.1180	0.1063	0.0965	0.1124
4. EEC-9	0.0608	0.0661	0.0572	0.0507	0.0501	0.0513	0.0612	0.0574	0.0574	0.0614
5. United Kingdom	0.0595	0.0642	0.0428	0.0423	0.0423	0.0393	0.0463	0.0424	0.0458	0.0529
6. France	0.0566	0.0600	0.0586	0.0510	0.0474	0.0481	0.0569	0.0467	0.0452	0.0546
7. FRG	0.0863	0.0952	0.0826	0.0757	0.0712	0.0768	0.0927	0.0881	0.0871	0.0897
C. LDC										
1. Total	0.0129	0.0144	0.0174	0.0182	0.0166	0.0184	0.0227	0.0225	0.0288	0.0287
2. Brazil	0.0298	0.0341	0.0451	0.0401	0.0288	0.0297	0.0412	0.0430	0.0455	0.0470
3. India	0.0377	0.0431	0.0434	0.0557	0.0627	0.0689	0.0796	0.0662	0.0720	0.0847
4. Korea	0.0133	0.0124	0.0481	0.0582	0.0395	0.0331	0.0363	0.0390	0.0657	0.0484
D. CPE										
1. Total	0.0845	0.0849	0.0823	0.0808	0.0815	0.0816	0.0806	0.0810	0.0763	0.0716
2. USSR	0.0936	0.0947	0.0933	0.0917	0.0958	0.0968	0.0973	0.0978	0.0879	0.0812
3. E. Europe (CMEA-6)	0.0664	0.0677	0.0648	0.0626	0.0581	0.0593	0.0585	0.0581	0.0671	0.0658
4. China	0.0755	0.0706	0.0628	0.0632	0.0586	0.0535	0.0494	0.0462	0.0385	0.0466
5. CMEA-7	0.0854	0.0865	0.0848	0.0832	0.0849	0.0861	0.0862	0.0864	0.0819	0.0768

Note: Data for blank cells not available.

[1] Intensity of use defined as tons of metal consumed per million $ GDP.

[2] OECD, LDC, CPE, and CMEA definitions: see list of acronyms on page 270 of the statistical appendix.

[3] Source: Calculations using data from parts A and B of this appendix.

TABLE C-7. TIN, 1962–1987   323

Table C-7.   Tin, 1962–1987[1,2,3]

	1962	1963	1964	1965	1966	1967	1968	1969
A. World	0.0355	0.0350	0.0337	0.0316	0.0308	0.0289	0.0283	0.0277
B. OECD								
1. Total	0.0381	0.0370	0.0360	0.0337	0.0326	0.0308	0.0300	0.0297
2. United States	0.0373	0.0362	0.0365	0.0344	0.0334	0.0313	0.0305	0.0292
3. Japan	0.0461	0.0480	0.0479	0.0426	0.0432	0.0433	0.0421	0.0423
4. EEC-9	0.0408	0.0389	0.0364	0.0337	0.0314	0.0303	0.0293	0.0301
5. United Kingdom	0.0646	0.0602	0.0554	0.0531	0.0496	0.0471	0.0453	0.0451
6. France	0.0380	0.0354	0.0332	0.0292	0.0283	0.0262	0.0234	0.0247
7. FRG	0.0304	0.0282	0.0290	0.0260	0.0236	0.0231	0.0226	0.0246
C. LDC								
1. Total	0.0243	0.0238	0.0225	0.0206	0.0195	0.0172	0.0154	0.0150
2. Brazil	0.0272	0.0298	0.0233	0.0240	0.0204	0.0244	0.0273	0.0239
3. India	0.0540	0.0498	0.0524	0.0502	0.0536	0.0495	0.0392	0.0404
4. Korea								
D. CPE								
1. Total	0.0335	0.0353	0.0330	0.0318	0.0321	0.0301	0.0312	0.0296
2. USSR	0.0222	0.0225	0.0209	0.0197	0.0193	0.0185	0.0180	0.0175
3. E. Europe (CMEA-6)		0.0301	0.0299	0.0315	0.0338	0.0304	0.0356	0.0333
4. China	0.1407	0.1574	0.1351	0.1155	0.1024	0.1065	0.1139	0.0955
5. CMEA-7		0.0249	0.0237	0.0234	0.0238	0.0222	0.0234	0.0223

See notes at end of table C-7 on page 325.

Table C-7 (continued)

	1970	1971	1972	1973	1974	1975	1976	1977
A. World	0.0267	0.0257	0.0251	0.0258	0.0243	0.0209	0.0220	0.0203
B. OECD								
1. Total	0.0287	0.0278	0.0272	0.0276	0.0260	0.0218	0.0235	0.0210
2. United States	0.0269	0.0255	0.0249	0.0256	0.0229	0.0192	0.0217	0.0189
3. Japan	0.0425	0.0433	0.0427	0.0473	0.0415	0.0338	0.0398	0.0324
4. EEC-9	0.0287	0.0272	0.0269	0.0266	0.0256	0.0217	0.0216	0.0206
5. United Kingdom	0.0416	0.0394	0.0382	0.0365	0.0334	0.0290	0.0296	0.0286
6. France	0.0229	0.0217	0.0215	0.0217	0.0210	0.0179	0.0179	0.0162
7. FRG	0.0243	0.0240	0.0239	0.0243	0.0224	0.0189	0.0217	0.0200
C. LDC								
1. Total	0.0154	0.0135	0.0124	0.0158	0.0130	0.0125	0.0130	0.0140
2. Brazil	0.0201	0.0237	0.0206	0.0252	0.0206	0.0213	0.0255	0.0251
3. India	0.0408	0.0232	0.0192	0.0218	0.0145	0.0213	0.0218	0.0181
4. Korea			0.0152	0.0240	0.0148	0.0184	0.0285	0.0331
D. CPE								
1. Total	0.0280	0.0275	0.0277	0.0272	0.0276	0.0250	0.0247	0.0235
2. USSR	0.0167	0.0161	0.0167	0.0165	0.0175	0.0189	0.0180	0.0175
3. E. Europe (CMEA-6)	0.0328	0.0339	0.0325	0.0335	0.0321	0.0297	0.0308	0.0284
4. China	0.0774	0.0724	0.0730	0.0674	0.0692	0.0411	0.0434	0.0402
5. CMEA-7	0.0215	0.0214	0.0215	0.0216	0.0219	0.0222	0.0219	0.0208

(continued)

Table C-7 (continued)

TABLE C-7. TIN, 1962–1987   325

	1978	1979	1980	1981	1982	1983	1984	1985	1986	1987
A. World	0.0202	0.0193	0.0184	0.0171	0.0163	0.0163	0.0165	0.0158	0.0155	0.0156
B. OECD										
1. Total	0.0203	0.0201	0.0184	0.0171	0.0155	0.0153	0.0157	0.0149	0.0144	0.0142
2. United States	0.0184	0.0183	0.0165	0.0145	0.0122	0.0124	0.0127	0.0121	0.0104	0.0109
3. Japan	0.0307	0.0308	0.0292	0.0277	0.0254	0.0261	0.0272	0.0247	0.0240	0.0238
4. EEC-9	0.0201	0.0188	0.0177	0.0167	0.0156	0.0153	0.0157	0.0150	0.0156	0.0151
5. United Kingdom	0.0258	0.0242	0.0186	0.0207	0.0195	0.0185	0.0177	0.0161	0.0162	0.0157
6. France	0.0158	0.0149	0.0154	0.0138	0.0122	0.0113	0.0114	0.0100	0.0108	0.0103
7. FRG	0.0196	0.0189	0.0194	0.0177	0.0170	0.0173	0.0190	0.0193	0.0196	0.0193
C. LDC										
1. Total	0.0158	0.0124	0.0126	0.0114	0.0114	0.0118	0.0129	0.0124	0.0152	0.0159
2. Brazil	0.0239	0.0233	0.0201	0.0119	0.0207	0.0167	0.0168	0.0172	0.0166	0.0254
3. India	0.0163	0.0166	0.0143	0.0164	0.0120	0.0122	0.0117	0.0109	0.0131	0.0114
4. Korea	0.0350	0.0280	0.0288	0.0328	0.0282	0.0331	0.0422	0.0290	0.0518	0.0520
D. CPE										
1. Total	0.0237	0.0228	0.0233	0.0223	0.0232	0.0235	0.0223	0.0214	0.0193	0.0199
2. USSR	0.0176	0.0175	0.0179	0.0183	0.0188	0.0197	0.0195	0.0188	0.0157	0.0171
3. E. Europe (CMEA-6)	0.0285	0.0262	0.0276	0.0238	0.0274	0.0260	0.0236	0.0223	0.0216	0.0202
4. China	0.0397	0.0372	0.0349	0.0332	0.0309	0.0310	0.0272	0.0242	0.0233	0.0252
5. CMEA-7	0.0209	0.0201	0.0208	0.0199	0.0213	0.0215	0.0207	0.0198	0.0174	0.0180

Note: Data for blank cells not available.

[1] Intensity of use defined as tons of metal consumed per million $ GDP.

[2] OECD, LDC, CPE, and CMEA definitions: see the list of acronyms on page 270 of the statistical appendix.

[3] Source: Calculations using data from parts A and B of this appendix.

Index

Aluminum. *See also specific countries and country groups*
actual versus forecast consumption in CMEA countries, 152
beverage containers, 28, 60, 61, 68, 224–228, 231–233
elasticity parameter values of, 119
intensity of use, 9–10, 28, 39, 42–45, 56, 60, 61, 64, 68, 79, 81–82, 85, 94, 104, 108–110, 121–123, 139, 141, 142, 144, 308–310
inventory behavior, 52
in passenger cars, 162, 166–167, 186–187, 194–197, 204–205
prices, 64, 101, 105, 209–215
regression results for consumption of, 151
secondary metal consumption, 22–23, 55, 56
shortfall in CMEA consumption, 124
stage of use, 14
world consumption trends, 1, 2, 6–7, 204–205, 287–289
Argentina
copper imports, 88
GDP-based intensity of metal use, 84–86
trade policies, 87

Austria, materials substitution and beverage container industry, 241
Automobiles. *See* Passenger cars

Belgium, materials substitution and beverage container industry, 241
Brazil
aluminum consumption, 92–95, 98, 100, 287–289
aluminum exports, 100
copper consumption, 83–86, 92–93, 95, 98–100, 101–102, 290–292
copper exports, 100
copper imports, 88, 101
determinants of metal consumption, 91–102
domestic metal production, 98, 101–102
GDI, 108, 275–277
GDP, 84–85, 94, 95, 271–274
intensity of metal use, 83–85, 93–100, 101, 110–111, 142–144, 305–325
investment program, 93–94, 98, 110–111
lead consumption, 92–93, 96, 98, 102, 293–295
macroeconomic policy and performance, 93–98, 99–100, 110–111

Learning Resources
Centre